HENGROVE SCHOOL BRISTOL 1954 - 1974 A CASE STUDY

From Tripartite to Bilateral and Comprehensive Education

Published by:
HENGROVE SCHOOL HISTORY
PROJECT TEAM

AFC TAXIS LTD

Published by Hengrove School History Project Team

Printed by: Manor Printing Services
The Abbey Business Park
Charfield Road
Kingswood
Wotton-under-Edge
Glos. GL12 8RL
www.manorprinting.co.uk

Cover Design Advisor: Phil Wait Design
Heritage Interpretation Design
info@philwaitdesign.com

ISBN 978-0-9926367

Contents

Foreword

J Stephen Davies

As the days passed, Ruth Lim, nee Cowley, noted that reminiscences of her days as a pupil at Hengrove School were endangered by loss of memory, records and breath. Therefore, with the help of her trusty lieutenant, Ann Sell, she set about collecting memorabilia of those days and inaugurated this Hengrove School History Project, with emphasis on the earlier most endangered times.

The school was established in the early fifties under Doctor Perry as a bilateral institution, ie: grammar and secondary modern. By the time of our first "blockbuster" – "Hastings" of 1966 – and under its second Head, Philip Waterhouse, it was a fully-fledged comprehensive, retaining only traces of its bilateral past. This comprehensive nature did not begin to die until the departure of the school's third permanent headmaster, Pat Bird, and the loss of the 6th Form in the late 1980's. (Note: all new year groups were, and are here still, counted are First Years).

An ancient Roman, Petronius Arbiter, some 2,000 years ago, wrote: "I was to learn later in life, that we tend to meet any new situation by re-organisation, and a wonderful method it can be for creating the illusion of progress while promoting confusion, inefficiency and demoralisation." But life demands change! As comprehensivisation grew from the tripartite system, so do we hope that the students and staff of today's Academy may flourish as once did the pupils and teachers of Hengrove Comprehensive School as remembered by Ruth and her team.

Foreword - Rt. Hon. Don Foster MP

This is a fantastic book. Anyone reading it will quickly discover that it is so much more than a dry historical overview of a single comprehensive school in Bristol. Its vivid description of the lives of staff and pupils, the educational developments, the social and sporting events, the passions and arguments within the staff room and even the changing way in which the media covered school activities make this a vibrant slice of life to be enjoyed by those with or without any connection with Hengrove School.

My own connection was limited to a very brief spell teaching there and working for one of its former head teachers, Philip Waterhouse (details of which can be found in Chapter 3). While I, and another contributor as a Foreword writer Dawn Primorolo MP, worked with Philip at the resources for Learning Development Unit, we constantly heard the tales of his earlier leadership and of the school itself. Philip loved Hengrove and his stories explained why. Not everyone had the opportunities to hear those stories but this book more than makes up for that loss.

Foreword - Rt Hon Dawn Primarolo MP

This is a wonderful book, which does more than simply collate the history of a school, but tells the story of life in a comprehensive school for students and teachers alike. It is a vivid social history which has been compiled thanks to the huge efforts of the authors. Thousands of Bristol South residents have attended Hengrove School – now Oasis Academy John Williams – and will have many happy memories of their school days. This book brings so many of these memories together, with the additional benefit of photographs and plenty of original source material.

The whole book will be of interest to anyone who went to Hengrove, or knows the school well. I was especially interested in the chapter on Mr Waterhouse, who I worked with many years ago. He was a Headteacher ahead of his time – certainly giving sixth formers so much control over their new facilities was exceptionally forward thinking. It is clear from the original material that he worked hard for everyone at Hengrove, encouraging and celebrating success. I know that Mr Waterhouse was involved in the very early stages of the book, only to sadly pass away before its publication. This book is a fitting legacy not only to him, but to everyone who has taught or learnt at Hengrove.

Foreword - Margaret Thorpe

It is a great privilege for me to write a foreword to this excellent history of Hengrove School, where my father, Dr. Perry, was the first headmaster from 1954 to 1964. This marked the culmination of a distinguished teaching career and followed two previous headships in Bristol. Comprehensive schools were very new in Britain in the early 1950s and I remember his excitement and pride at being appointed Head of one of the first two such schools in Bristol, Hengrove and Lockleaze. There was similar enthusiasm and dedication among the first pioneering cohort of staff.

My father's philosophy was to offer all children the same opportunities as those available at the best schools, and in this he succeeded. I attended concerts given by an impressive school orchestra, and there were wonderful productions of Twelfth Night and Anne Frank's Diary in those early years. Academic success followed, and when the first A level students gained places at universities and medical school, his pride in the school was boundless. But it was not just academic success he encouraged; every student was helped to develop his or her full potential. At my father's funeral in January 1992 the presence of three Hengrove pupils and a teacher, who had braved the Cotswold snow to attend, was a moving tribute to all he achieved.

We owe a great debt of gratitude to the dedicated team who have worked tirelessly to ensure that the life of the school is not forgotten, but recorded magnificently for posterity in this volume.

Margaret Thorpe, December 2012

Introduction

"Absence makes the heart grow fonder"

We know this to be true in respect of people – it can also be true in respect of buildings.

The Hengrove Secondary School buildings that had dominated the suburb of Hengrove since 1954 no longer exist. As the following pictures show, they were demolished in 2010/2011 and replaced by a new ultra-modern building housing the Oasis Academy John Williams, just behind Christ Church Parish Church.

The demolition alerted several former pupils to the urgent necessity of preserving the memory of the school. We had spent our formative years there, forged life-long friendships, and been mentored and encouraged by a highly professional and dedicated staff. Hengrove Secondary School had given us wonderful opportunities, both academic and extra-curricular: it had prepared us for the rest of our lives.

Out of the rubble rose the inspiration to tell the story of the school. Of course we have fond memories of the school building – but the essence and spirit of the school lies in the lives and memories of the pupils and staff.

Enquiries at the City Record Office revealed a paucity of archive material about Hengrove School (ref. 21131/sc/Heg). It was, therefore, imperative that an archive of photographs, memories, artefacts be collected – a huge and urgent task. We simply could not allow Hengrove School to sink without trace – neither physically nor metaphorically.

There is a great story to be told – not only for the former pupils and staff but also the existing community of the Hengrove area and their descendants, for local government councillors, administrators and educationalists past and present, both local and nationwide.

Hengrove School was (together with Lockleaze) the first purpose-built comprehensive school in Bristol. When it opened in 1954 there were only sixteen comprehensive schools in the whole country. It was a pioneer in a national educational debate which still rages today. It became a social and cultural hub in the Hengrove area – particularly in the 1960s and 1970s.

Former pupils Ann Sell and Ruth Lim contacted former headmaster Mr Waterhouse and former Deputy Head Miss Place and shared with them their vision to preserve the memory of the school. They met in January 2011 together with Mr David John, former staff member, and the Hengrove School History Project was launched.

We agreed that we would initially confine our research to the period 1954-1974, coinciding with the first two headships.

Methodology and Acknowledgements

The project was advertised in the local press and by placing posters in libraries, health centres, GP surgeries and supermarkets, and by word of mouth.

Ann Sell located fourteen files of archive material from Hengrove School Library which had been taken to the new Oasis Academy.

Local historian Anton Bantock had started a small similar project at Bedminster Down School before he retired from teaching there. He kindly showed us the material he had collected in response to questionnaires, and encouraged us greatly, for which we thank him.

Thus we designed a questionnaire for former pupils and staff. We are grateful to Counterslip Baptist Church which helped us by photocopying 50 posters and 150 questionnaires. These were either placed in public spaces with the posters, or sent directly by post or e-mail to responders.

Knowle West Media Centre were very helpful to us – grasping the vision. They helped us set up an e-mail address, let us use their photocopier, and loaned equipment to record interviews.

Former pupil Mark Wilson scanned hundreds of photographs and documents. Another former pupil, Mike Leigh, later joined the team and has helped in so many ways, drawing on his expertise as a local historian and former City Records Office staff member.

Norma Davies also joined the team. Her knowledge of the Hengrove neighbourhood and community, plus her memories of Hengrove School both as a parent, and the wife of a former staff member, have been invaluable.

Mr Waterhouse was very keen to write the chapter on the musical life of the school. This was sadly not to be, as he became too unwell, but he asked Stephen Davies, Former Head of Music, to write it in his place. We are very grateful for his contribution to the project.

By early 2012 we had collected a huge archive of photographs, reports, plans, and newspaper articles, together with replies from just under one hundred former pupils and thirty former staff. We had spent hundreds of hours and hundreds of pounds of our own money.

We desperately needed funding. Following a networking trail from KWMC we discovered the Hengrove and Stockwood Neighbourhood Well Being Fund. We attended their community forum, promoted our project and were greatly encouraged by Ariaf Hussein, Community Development Worker, and Gemma Dando. We applied for and were awarded a grant of £1,000 for the expenses involved in collecting and collating the Hengrove School archive and preparing the material for placing in the City Record Office.

Various individuals have generously donated money to help and encourage us. They are as follows:-

Mrs Clutterbuck, Mr C Drew, Mr and Mrs Hobbs, Mr D John, Mr J Stephen Davies and Mr Seymour – all former staff. The son of Mr W Fletcher, former Deputy Head, donated money, many photographs and other documents.

Dr Perry's daughter, Mrs M Thorpe, was tracked down to Shrewsbury. She is most enthusiastic and donated a whole album of photographs, various papers, and two books written by Dr Perry in his retirement. We are most grateful to her, also for her financial contribution to our expenses.

For additional acknowledgements see pages 391 and 392.

Chapter 1
Anticipation
The Historical and Educational Context

This chapter describes the development of the rural landscape of the Hengrove area and the decisions that were taken to provide schools for the growing population.

From Fields to Suburb

The Hengrove area, as we know it, was still part of Somerset until the 1930's. It was a completely rural/agricultural area.

The 1921 map below shows Hengrove House, the estate of which included Hengrove Farm. The farmhouse still stands in Hengrove Farm Lane, opposite Hengrove Parade shops. Hengrove House itself was located in Newquay Road where Eagle House Youth Club now stands, but it was demolished in the 1970's.

Hengrove Lane can be seen running from Hengrove Farm eastwards to join the main Bristol to Wells road, now the A37.

Back Lane is clearly marked, running from Hengrove Lane. On either side are Hengrove Cottages and Hengrove Nurseries. Back Lane was later renamed Petherton Road.

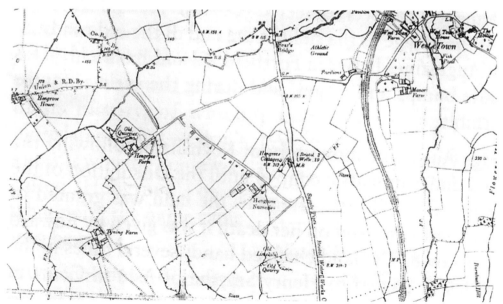

OS Map Somerset Sheet 6. 1921

In 1930 the Bristol City Boundary was extended to include the Hengrove area as we know it. Prior to this, the land on either side of the Wells Road from Knowle to Whitchurch Village was entirely rural. The Bristol Tram route ended at Red Lion Inn (now demolished) at the top of the Red Lion Hill in Knowle.

In the late 1920's and throughout the 1930's the Hengrove area was transformed into a built-up suburb of Bristol.

In 1927 the Knowle Stadium and Greyhound Track was built near the site of Hengrove Cottages between Back Lane (Petherton Road) and Wells Road.

Aerial view of Knowle Stadium c.1939

Bristol Airport was built in 1931, and John Hall's Paint Factory in 1933.

Christchurch (Hengrove) was built in 1934, and the Rectory in 1953. The Church Hall is to the right of the church and backs on to the school playing fields.

Petherton Road Infants School (below) was opened just before the outbreak of World War 2 when King George VI was newly on the throne (Coronation 1938). Miss Huet, previously at Fishponds College Infants School became Headmistress. The land at the rear of the school was still rented out for grazing.

Housing was built on the Wells Road, Petherton Road and Petherton Gardens, Dennor Park, New Fosseway Road, The Gilda Estate, Walsh Avenue and Airport Road – all privately built. The houses in Tarnock Avenue and Fortfield Road were built by the City Council.

As the population of the area increased, the need for a new Junior School became more and more urgent. Tyning Junior School (below) was not built until 1951 (temporary buildings 1949). Most of the children from Petherton Road Infants and Tyning Junior would enter Hengrove Secondary School at age eleven.

The Second World War and the Post War National Debate.

The years 1939-1945 were a time of national crisis as we were at war against Germany. Some Bristol schools were damaged by bombs, railings were requisitioned and 18,000 children were evacuated from Bristol. The Bristol Education Committee were concerned for the safety of school pupils. There were discussions about gas masks, air raid procedures, trenches and provision of toilets, water and lighting in air raid shelters.

A Coalition Government was formed under Churchill in 1940 and although the country was still at war, thoughts were turning to legislation for post war peacetime. There was much optimism, idealism and debate on a whole rash of proposed legislation affecting all areas of life – heralding the "Welfare State"[1].

The 1944 Education Act (Butler Act) replaced the Board of Education with a Ministry and guaranteed free secondary education for all up to the age of at least 14 years. What form this would take was open to interpretation. The Conservative Secretary of State for Education favoured a tripartite system – with children taking the 11+ exam in their final year of primary school and sent to secondary modern, secondary technical or grammar schools, depending on their perceived ability. In the event technical schools were never widely implemented – for 20 years there was a virtual bipartite system with fierce competition for available grammar school places (15% - 20% of total secondary places). Chuter Ede, former Parliamentary Secretary to the Board of Education wrote in The Times 14/4/44:

> *"I do not know where people get the idea of three types of school…I can find only one school for senior pupils and that is a secondary school. What you like to make of it will depend on the way you serve the precise needs of the individual in the country."*

Controversy surrounding the 11+ exam, together with increasing dissatisfaction with the secondary schools led to limited experiments with multilateral or comprehensive schools from the 1940's (e.g. West Yorkshire and Anglesey where the tripartite structure was not viable and in London, Coventry and Sheffield where existing schools had been destroyed in the war).

---

[1] 1942. Beveridge Plan report on National Insurance and Social Security.
1943. Ministry of Town and County Planning established.
1943. White paper on Educational Reconstruction.
1944. White paper proposes a National Health Service.
1944. Education Act (Butler Act)
1945. Family Allowance introduced.
1945. Labour Party wins General Election.
1946. Nationalisation of Bank of England, Civil aviation and coal.
1948. Nationalisation of Health Service.
1949/1950. Nationalisation of Gas and Steel Industries.

These multilateral/common/comprehensive schools were an alternative to the tripartite system and had already proven successful in Sweden, USA and USSR. Political and administrative support for the general introduction of comprehensive schools was strongest in London. The London County Council (LCC) Education Officer Graham Savage, influenced by the US High School system was a powerful advocate.

Back in Bristol

The Education Committee were studying the report of the Reconstruction Committee on Post-War Education and also the 1943 Government White Paper on Educational Reconstruction.

In 1944 the Education Committee discussed the acquisition of sites for new schools in Bristol. The 45 acres Bush Estate in Hengrove was earmarked for a secondary school base.

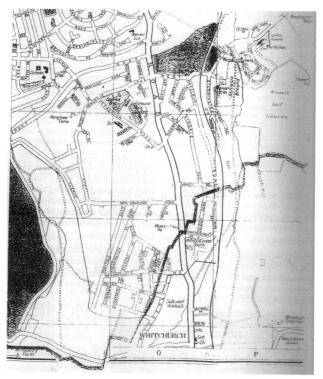

The 1950's map above shows the Bush Estate bounded by Petherton Gardens, Petherton Road, Wells Road, New Fosseway Road and Walsh Avenue. Petherton Road School can be seen, also the Knowle Stadium. Tyning School, built on Walsh Avenue near Leda Avenue in 1951 (temporary buildings 1949), is not shown.

This land was originally owned by the Bush Family who lived at Highcroft, 615 Wells Road, at the junction of Petherton Road and Wells Road (now a Veterinary Hospital - below).

The Bush Estate was surveyed in 1946, valued at £13,000 and purchased by the City Council in 1947. Below are copies of the legal documents.

Parliament and registered, under the Land Charges Act 1925, in the local registers kept by such local authority.

The full list of overriding interests to which registered land may be subject is contained in Section 70 the Land Registration Act 1925.

Fourteen acres were to be grassed to provide the "Bush Playing Fields" for use by various sports clubs. Twenty plus acres were to be leased out for cultivation until June 1948.

Peace Time Planning

With the return to peacetime in Europe in May 1945, Bristol could now plan ahead with optimism – a time of expansion in educational/health/housing provision and more, implementing the legislation of the 1940's for a Welfare State. A 1947 census on new housing estates in Bristol highlighted an urgent need of school accommodation for increasing numbers of children. There were discussions between the Ministry of Education, Bristol Education Committee and the Chief Education Officer from 1948 through 1949 into 1950 as to whether the new secondary school provision would be a continuation of the existing tripartite system or the alternative of bilateral or multilateral/comprehensive schools.

In July 1950 the Reconstruction Committee, unable to decide or agree between the two, submitted two alternative plans to the City Council. Either (1) A comprehensive/multilateral secondary school in one building providing 3 Grammar and 8 Secondary Modern streams or (2) separate buildings on the Hengrove site for the different types of school.

Concern was again expressed in October 1950 as to the urgent need for secondary school provision. The children from Tyning School could not go at age 11 years to existing schools as they were full and house building in the area combined with a rise in the birth rate was to lead to a 'bulge' of 11 year olds in 1953.

Hengrove School is born!

By November 1950, a decision had been reached and the City Architect submitted a plan for the first of three proposed secondary schools on the Hengrove (formerly Bush) site with a 4 form entry and providing 680 places. The school was to be named Hengrove Secondary School (See Appendix 1 for costings).

The building work started in September 1952. The school was scheduled to open in September 1954.

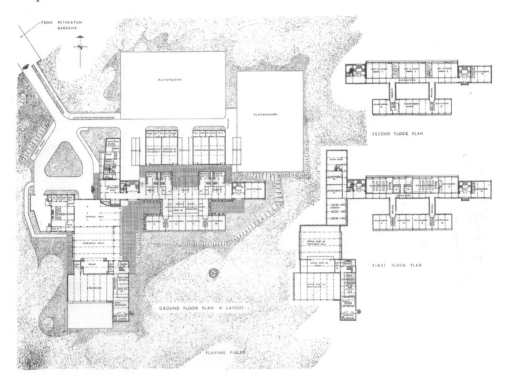

The pictures below show the main school entrance and car park at the end of Petherton Gardens and the Assembly Hall and Boys' Gym under construction.

By July 1953 the Bristol Secondary Education Committee realised that there would be a deficiency of grammar school places available for 1953-1957 based on the assumption of 20% of pupils transferring from primary schools. To remedy this shortage of places, it was agreed that one or more grammar streams would be provided in new secondary schools from 1954 – probably more a pragmatic decision rather than an ideological one.

Thus the new Hengrove School (and others in Bristol) would be a bilateral school when it opened in 1954. The inclusion of one or more grammar streams necessitated additional science laboratories. The plans were adapted and additional expenditure approved.

In February 1954 candidates for the Headship of Hengrove School were interviewed. Dr Reginald Perry was appointed (from a short list of nine) with effect from 1st September 1954.

By this time the school building was half completed, and at Committee level plans were already being discussed for Hengrove School Stage II in the School Building Programme for 1955-1956. Initially this was intended to be a separate building for girls only with a 4 form entry – with boys remaining in the original Stage I building, but this did not materialise.

A catchment area was discussed in February 1954 by the Secondary Education Committee. Only pupils living south of Airport Road would be admitted (unless exceptional circumstances prevailed). This would not apply to the grammar stream pupils – many would cross the city to attend. Also a long term policy was agreed to admit each year not more than three secondary modern streams and two grammar streams.

In its March 1954 meeting the same committee decided that in Hengrove School's first year, September 1954 – July 1955, there would only be 1st, 2nd and 3rd year pupils admitted – there would be no 4th form for that year. Also Dr Perry and the Chief Inspector of Schools were authorised to visit one or two comprehensive schools already up and running in other parts of the country.

A footpath approach to the new school from Walsh Avenue was considered (estimated cost £1,500) but was not to be approved until 1957 or 1958.

In May 1954 the Joint Staffing Sub Committee agreed the following new posts and allowances (for more about these staff members see Chapter 8)

- Mr R Green – Second Master
- Mr W Fletcher – French
- Mr Trivett – Mathematics
- Miss G A Martin – Senior Mistress
- Mr A Seymour – Geography

In July 1954 the members of the first Governing Body were named. The Education Committee would be represented by Alderman Chamberlain and Alderman Reade, the City Council by Alderman Raymond and Mrs Nutt and two 'others'; Mr Bill Graves (a local Councillor) and Mr Rogers.

The school caretaker Mr Brain (formerly at Connaught Road Primary School) was appointed and was housed temporarily at 130 New Fosseway Road until July 1955 when he moved to a house on site.

Hengrove School Opens!

In September 1954, Hengrove School opened its doors for the first intake of 350 pupils; 216 of which were first years. There were 2 grammar streams and 3 secondary modern streams. Hengrove School was thus the FIRST BILATERAL SECONDARY SCHOOL IN BRISTOL (jointly with Lockleaze). The pupils and staff were privileged to occupy a brand new purpose built building set in spacious playing fields. It was a bright new post war experiment that would attract visits from educationalists from near and far – even overseas.

11

Chapter 2
The Dr Perry Era 1954-1964
In the Beginning

On February 25th 1954 Dr Perry and eight other candidates were interviewed by the Joint Education Sub-Committee for two posts as Head Teacher of the brand new bilateral schools - Hengrove and Lockleaze.

Dr Perry was appointed Head of Hengrove School with effect from 1st September 1954. He had already served the Bristol Education Committee for 20 years, as Second Master at St George Grammar School, then as Head of Filton Secondary School. He was ideally suited for a bi-lateral school.

Hengrove Secondary School opened in September 1954 and with Lockleaze Secondary School was one of the first two bilateral schools in Bristol[1]. The first intake totalled 350 pupils – of which 216 were to enter the first year. There were 2 grammar streams and 3 secondary modern streams. The non-selected children were drawn from the thickly populated housing areas straddling the Wells Road from Airport Road to the City Boundary near Whitchurch. Some of the selected pupils were drawn from a wider area – some travelling from the north side of the city. Below is an aerial view of the school in 1954.

[1] Ashton Park and Bedminster Down Secondary (Bi-lateral) schools opened 1955. Brislington and Henbury Secondary Schools in 1956 (also Bilateral).

Mr Green was the Deputy/Second Master and Head of Science. He had formerly taught at St George Grammar School. The Senior Mistress was Miss A Martin. We have an early photo of the original staff – only 17 in number – contributed by Mr Fletcher's sons, taken in 1955 by Mr Fletcher. We can name some of the staff.

Standing L-R: ?, Mr Trivett, ?, Mr Seymour.
Middle row: ?, Mr Ricketts, Mr Foote, Miss Crowther, ?, ?.
Front row: Mr G. Hale, Mr Buckland, Dr Perry, Mr Green, Miss Martin, ?.

Valerie Elliot had vivid memories of her first day at the school in 1956 – they were printed in the 1959 school magazine when she was a 4th year student and are reproduced here.

CHAPTER ONE—In School

In welcoming our new first years we would draw their attention to some impressions gathered by old hands, in the hope that they may be of interest and encouragement.

MY FIRST DAY AT HENGROVE SCHOOL

I was greeted by a wide drive. To my left was a playground on which hundreds of children stood; some in groups chatting eagerly, others standing shyly on the tarmac, no doubt wishing they could be at home, or at their old school. To my right were the playing fields extending for acres into the far distance. And in front of me was a huge impressive building—the school. A wide flight of steps led to the main entrance—which I was sure we should never be allowed to use.

Slowly I made my way up the drive. I paused to read a notice painted upon the tarmac which said, " NO VEHICLES TO PROCEED BEYOND THIS POINT." Was I a vehicle? Of course not! I assured myself hastily.

As I reached the playground, a teacher appeared carrying a small handbell. We were told to line up, and to proceed in an orderly line to the assembly hall. And so we did. I had vague impressions of a wide corridor, and then a dining room separated from the Main Hall by a glass partition. We filed into the Hall, where the Headmaster, Dr. Perry—a tall impressive figure wearing a black gown—read our names and the forms to which we had been assigned. Appropriately our next visit was to the form room. There our form-master, Mr Cork, who confessed he was as new here as we, gave out exercise books and pens, while we all got to know each other.

A few minutes later we drank our milk, and then had break. We played touch on the playground until the bell rang, and then it was time for English. We were set an essay on " Hengrove School " but nobody knew what to write. And so to Maths and then dinner. Of the two, dinner was the more enjoyable; much different from our other school, where the menu was mostly soggy potatoes, fat and cabbage.

During the afternoon we stayed in the form room, getting to know our companions better. We were all very excited at the prospect of learning French and Science, but could just not get into the habit of calling Arithmetic "Maths."

At four o'clock we went home, tired, but very pleased with our first day at " Hengrove."

VALERIE ELLIOTT (4A3).

Some of the selected pupils travelled to school from their homes on the other side of the city. Miriam Pavey (now Woodey) and her older brother Eric remember:

"we had to travel right across the city on two buses, then cross the Wells Road, walk across the Greyhound Track/Knowle Stadium car park to Petherton Gardens."

This would have added at least one hour at the beginning and end of each day in all weathers! There were quite a few pupils who made the same arduous journey.

Hengrove School could be described as a "bilateral experiment". The teaching profession were interested to know how "the experiment" was working out. We have reproduced Dr Perry's article written for the Bristol Teachers Association Bulletin September 1955 (below).

6   BRISTOL TEACHERS' ASSOCIATION BULLETIN 1955

HENGROVE SCHOOL

By R. PERRY, M.A., B.Sc., Ph.D. (Headmaster)

Twelve months ago the eyes of all teachers were on the two new bilateral schools when they opened in September 1954. Today Dr. Perry, Headmaster of Hengrove Secondary School, gives us some impressions of what has been achieved in his school during this year.

Though Hengrove School has now been open for a little more than a year, it is still far too early to pass judgment on the bilateral experiment in Bristol.

Failure could be apparent in a few months, but success cannot be fully established until the school has been in existence for at least seven years, when the first children to complete the full course will pass out of the Sixth Form. In the meantime we gain experience, and already have gathered some useful information about the way children respond to the opportunities offered by the bilateral school. In other cities, or even in other schools in Bristol, different conclusions may be reached. I have only been asked to give my impressions of the first year at Hengrove.

I ought to say that I dislike the term "bilateral," which carries with it a suggestion of division — and a school with two sharply separated "sides" could hardly hope to be successful. "Of course, you will have a different uniform, or at least a different badge, for the grammar school children," said one teacher of my acquaintance, and I dare say there are parents who would like to see their little scholarship winners differentiated in this way. The consequences of such a policy will be obvious to all experienced teachers.

From the beginning at Hengrove, we have set out to build one school, not two, and to make all our children feel that they belong to the same community. "From each according to his ability; to each according to his needs," though now out of favour as a political slogan, has nothing wrong with it as an educational one, and might well be chosen as that of the new schools. We ask all our pupils to make a contribution to the success of the school, and the general response is good.

16

Most people will want to know how the "grammar" and "modern" children get on together. Although I use them in this article we try, in fact, not to use these terms in talking or thinking about our pupils; they are rather pointless in this school. Some classes are following a course that should lead to the General Certificate of Education and some are not, but the dividing line is not drawn by the selection tests conducted by the Local Education Authority. Even children in the lower streams know that it is possible that they may one day move into a General Certificate of Education course in some subjects, if they make the necessary progress, and I doubt therefore, if they are conscious of a sharp dividing line between two groups of children.

Since many of them have been together in their primary schools, and may even live next door to each other, the *move to the same secondary school does not seem a strange* one. Friendships made in earlier years tend to continue. Most children, however, choose their friends from among classmates, and the bilateral school will not change this characteristic of child behaviour, which is well known to teachers in all types of school. But there is a much greater "spread" than in the ordinary or modern school, and this is particularly noticeable in some school activities. In the school choir, and in the recorder groups, there are children from all streams mixing on easy terms; the Dramatic Society shows a cross-section not quite as wide; on the playing-field the intermixing is most marked. The school is divided into six houses, and house teams for cricket, football, hockey or netball are representative of all parts of the school. The Association Football XI includes boys from "grammar" and "modern" streams, and the captain, elected by his team-mates, is a boy who was not awarded a grammar school place.

I have been agreeably surprised by the way in which the children have settled down as one community. This is helped by the fact that, in the district, family circumstances do not differ too greatly. The unity of the school also owes much to the readiness of parents to provide their children with the school uniform. In 1954 we admitted 216 first-year children; of these over 200 wore uniform. This year we admitted 247, and there has been an even better response. This was achieved without pressure on parents, who have been very ready to co-operate in the "one school" policy. Visitors to the classrooms would find it hard to differentiate, at first sight, between, say, 1A and 1E.

It has been suggested that the "grammar school" child would suffer from a lowering of standards, social and academic, in the bilateral schools. No headmaster would shut his eyes to this danger, but we have seen little sign of it so far. If a bilateral school has capable teachers, experienced in the needs of the more gifted children, standards will be maintained. In practice the knowledge that others may catch them up tends to spur on those who have grammar school places. A normal General Certificate course has been offered to these children, and they are taught by men and women whose academic ability and qualifications are not, in my judgment, inferior to those of teachers in maintained grammar schools. The success of the General Certificate of Education courses in bilateral schools will depend upon our ability to attract and retain men and women of this quality.

What are the children who would normally have gone to modern schools gaining from the experiment? After consultation with the head teachers of their primary schools, and examination of the selection test results, we decided to start thirty-seven " border-line " children on a course parallel with that of the two "grammar school" forms. They were given the same books, the same equipment, and were taught by the same teachers. The results have been encouraging. There has been little sign of the sense of failure too often seen among children entering the modern school, since both parents and children realise that if a child has the necessary ability, failure in the 11+ examination will make no difference to the child's future. At the end of the first year it was clear that half the members of the " border-line " class had done as well as average members of the " grammar school " classes and most of the others well enough to justify a further trial. The implications of these findings, if borne out by further experience, are important.

Some of our critics have said that this is " letting children into the grammar school by the back door," a phrase which surely reveals a curious attitude towards children. Can we devise a better test of a child's ability to follow a General Certificate of Education course than a trial run of a year or two?

We owe it to our pupils to give them the opportunity to show what they can do, and in this instance the reward comes to those who are willing to work steadily over a long period. Apart from the " border-line " children, we have tried to organise the curriculum so that the door may be kept open as long as possible for those who develop late. In our second year we have been able to do this more effectively.

To some teachers it will seem that our object is to prepare the largest possible number of children for the General Certificate of Education examination. This would be a dangerous policy, and it is for this reason that I hope our bilateral schools will soon become comprehensive, so that pupils will have a genuine choice between several equally valuable courses. The bilateral school, offering only the alternative of a General Certificate course or a simple modern school course, would fail to meet the needs of a considerable proportion of its pupils. We all know that there are not merely two, or even three, kinds of children.

The needs of these children of average and below average intelligence call for the presence of teachers who have had good modern school experience. I hope Bristol teachers do not think there is no place, or only an inferior place, for the non-graduate in these schools. In making appointments, fitness for the work must be the deciding factor, and the keen and efficient non-graduate can make a most important contribution. For some work it is essential to have highly qualified graduates, but the non-graduate in a large bilateral school will find that he has greater scope and a variety of teaching which he would not get in a modern school, and that his contacts with the more able children will help to keep him on his toes, and to ward off that feeling of frustration which can be one of the occupational diseases of teaching. He need not fear that his graduate colleagues will hold him at arm's length. It is in the bilateral or comprehensive school, in fact, that we are most likely to achieve the ideal of " one profession."

18

the ideal of one profession.

> To those who fear that the size of these schools will be a serious disadvantage I can as yet offer no reassurances. Our total numbers during the first year were 350, and in the second year we have just passed the 600 mark. It will be another three years before numbers reach their maximum, but we are already making plans to lessen the difficulties which may then arise.
>
> I have tried not to draw too rosy a picture of our first year, but naturally I have emphasised the encouraging aspects. Not all children will respond to the opportunities offered them, and the bilateral school cannot turn a dull or average child into a clever one. No doubt some parents will be disappointed when this becomes clear; in the meantime we must guard against the danger that people may expect too much of us. We shall have many problems of organisation and of teaching for which solutions will have to be found, but I think that members of my staff, whose work has made possible this optimistic report, will agree that the outlook is full of promise.

Below is an early picture of the boys changing rooms (left) and south facing teaching block (right). The ground has not been grassed over yet (foreground) – probably 1954.

Probably late 1950's – view below of entire south facing side of the school – including the well-loved and original mature tree – does anyone remember what species of tree it was?

Lunch time in the Dining Room 1954-1955. Note Dr Perry on duty and Dinner lady Mrs Gitsham serving. She spent her entire career providing us with school dinners and retired in 1989. Her two sons attended the school.

The local press were also interested in the "bilateral experiment" – below is the February 29th 1956 article from the Western Daily Press and Bristol Mirror.

THE WESTERN DAILY PRESS AND BRISTOL MIRROR

WEDNESDAY, FEBRUARY 29, 1956

HENGROVE

A SCHOOL AND ITS PURPOSE

OPENED in September, 1954, Hengrove school is destined to become one of the first comprehensive schools to be developed by the Bristol Education Authority.

A comprehensive school takes in pupils, boys and girls, from junior schools, irrespective of their academic ability. Its task is to find out what those children are capable of doing and to provide them with the right sort of courses.

According to individual needs, the course will be an academic one leading to the General Certificate of Education; a commercial or technical one, at the end of which the children will qualify for a good certificate; a simple training, based on the "three Rs" and a fair amount of practical work.

RISING NUMBERS

The work at Hengrove school is developing from a start made with a couple of classes of children who had been awarded grammar school places, and four or five classes of boys and girls who had not. Now in its fourth term, Hengrove is still bi-lateral—that is to say, it accommodates both Secondary and grammar school pupils, but not, at present, technical pupils.

Today the numbers in the school have increased to 600 By September there will be 750 children in attendance, and ultimately 1,000 children, which will be in about three years' time. The next phase of building development is a new wing which will accommodate the boys and girls taking technical and commercial courses.

The first children to occupy the new wing will flow from the ranks of the present scholars at Hengrove, and start to specialise, as others will in commercial subjects, while the grammar school-place boys and girls profit from the opportunity to pursue their studies.

RESULTS THIS YEAR

Meanwhile, the basic work is continuing and will begin to show results by September — two years from the start of the school—when an assessment can be made of what the children are capable of doing in the upper school.

For the most part, the children live near the school. They wear the same type of school dress, and while they divide for different work in classes, they spend a lot of time together, beginning in the mornings with the assembly of the whole school for service.

Games, drama, art and music— the school has a string orchestra— provide a common meeting ground for secondary and grammar school pupils. So does the dining hall, the library and the gymnasium.

Before the children join the school, they are taken on a tour of it, in charge of the teachers of the junior schools they will be leaving. The parents of new entrants are also invited to see the school at work before their children go there.

Members of the staff at Hengrove School have had a wide experience of teaching in different types of schools.

Dr. R. Perry, the headmaster has served with the Bristol Education Authority for 20 years.

Before being appointed to Hengrove, as one of the first head teachers to have charge of a comprehensive school—ultimately in Bristol, Dr. Perry was headmaster of Filton Secondary School and before that, second master of St. George Grammar School.

Mr R. A. Green, the second master and senior science master, at Hengrove, is also a former member of the staff at St. George Grammar School.

2

3

4

5

The Pictures

1 Top—Hengrove School, Bristol, which will become one of the first comprehensive schools in the city. At present it is bi-lateral. It accommodates both secondary and grammar school pupils, but not technical pupils.

2 Top left—Rolling out the pastry. Children with grammar school places at Hengrove School being shown by Miss B. V. Bain, domestic science mistress, how to make a tasty pie.

3 Second left—Getting to grips with the problem. Girls of Hengrove School studying biology under the direction of Mrs K. I. Quinton, biology mistress.

4 Third left—In the science laboratory. Boys of Hengrove School intent on an experiment being demonstrated by Mr R. A. Green, second master and senior science master.

5 Bottom left—Facilities at Hengrove School include this well-equipped library which is used by the children as a study for class work and individual learning.

6 Top right—Making music. Hengrove School is proud of its string orchestra which Mr F. R. Bishop, music master, has built up. Pictured at practice are, left to right, Michael Summers, Sigurd Klavenieks and Ian Bridgeman.

7 Second right—"The eyes of it." A lesson in biology for pupils of Hengrove School, who are seen at work on a delicate dissecting operation.

8 Bottom right—Good shot. Girls of Hengrove School enjoy a game of basket ball. How a goal should be scored. The ball dropped safely through the net.

1

7

6

8

Work to start on Stage II building

The Bristol Education Committee had been discussing a Stage II extension to Hengrove School. Finally in September 1956 they accepted an adjusted tender from Messrs John Knox Ltd amounting to £111,852-12sh. We have a copy of the plan below. This second stage development would open in 1958 – known as "The New Wing."

LOCATION PLAN.   SCALE   1/2500

Visit of Minister of Education

On 26 October 1956 the Minister of Education visited Bristol to open a group of new schools – Hengrove School was one of them. We have a copy of the Official Commemorative Programme in the archive. We reproduce here the Order of Ceremony, Introduction, Members of the Education Committee, and the entry for Hengrove Secondary School.

CITY AND COUNTY OF BRISTOL

EDUCATION COMMITTEE

OFFICIAL

OPENING

OF SCHOOLS

FRIDAY, 26TH OCTOBER, 1956

OPENING OF TWENTY-ONE NEW PRIMARY AND SECONDARY SCHOOLS

at the Council House, College Green, Bristol
on 26th October, 1956

ORDER OF CEREMONY

THE LORD MAYOR will take the Chair at 5 p.m.

DEDICATORY PRAYER

Introduction of the MINISTER by the
CHAIRMAN of the EDUCATION COMMITTEE

OPENING of SCHOOLS by the
MINISTER OF EDUCATION
The Rt. Hon. Sir David Eccles, K.C.V.O., M.P.

Ashton Park Secondary School
Bank Leaze Primary Schools—Junior and Infants' Departments
Bedminster Down Secondary School
Brislington Secondary School
Broomhill Primary School—Infants' Department
Dunmail Primary School—Infants' Department
Four Acres Primary Schools—Junior and Infants' Departments
Hareclive Primary Schools—Junior and Infants' Departments
Henbury Secondary School
Henbury Court Primary Schools—Junior and Infants' Departments
Hengrove Secondary School
Highridge Infants' School
Horfield Church of England Primary School
Lockleaze Secondary School
Redhouse Primary School
Speedwell Secondary Schools
West Town Lane Primary School—Infants' Department

VOTE OF THANKS

INTRODUCTION

F OR the fourth time since the War ended, Bristol is honoured by a visit from the Minister of
Education to open a group of new schools. On the first two occasions the late Mr. George
Tomlinson came to the City, followed by Dame Florence Horsbrugh in 1954. At to-day's
ceremony we are pleased to welcome the present Minister, the Rt. Hon. Sir David Eccles,
K.C.V.O., M.P.

Bristol is proud of its achievement in the provision of new schools and during the last
ten years no less than 10,240 places have been provided in the 29 schools which have already
been opened officially. To-day a further 21 schools providing 8,810 places are to be declared
open. This brings the total since the War to 19,050 places in 50 new schools. The momentum
of the school building programme is being maintained as the City faces the continuing need to
provide new places, not only for the still mounting numbers of children, but because the expansion
of the City into new housing areas continues the flow of young families into districts not served
by existing schools. It is significant that the total school roll in the City, which at present stands
at 66,250, is the highest ever recorded and also exceeds by about 18,000 the number at the
beginning of the post-war period. This continuing pressure on school accommodation is reflected in the fact that Bristol has at this moment ten major projects in course of construction and
seven more on the drawing board.

There is a significant difference in the composition of the list of schools to be opened by
the Minister to-day compared with those dealt with by his predecessors. For the first time the list
shows a high proportion of secondary schools, no less than seven of the schools being opened,
and between them they provide about half the places in the 21 new schools. This change reflects
two aspects of the present situation—the increasing demands for new accommodation for the
rising numbers of children of secondary age, and the turning point in the battle for providing
schools for the younger children. It is now anticipated that the previous emphasis on new
primary schools will recede steadily and that the need for this type of accommodation will be
confined to meeting requirements in new housing areas until such time as national policy makes
it possible to undertake on a large scale the rebuilding and modernisation of many of the older
schools in the City. Before this can happen, however, it is clear that there will be a number of

years during which the major effort must be concentrated on secondary schools, both to meet the rising numbers of children and also to remedy the serious deficiencies of teaching accommodation in many of the existing buildings.

The majority of the schools now being opened have been designed by the City Architect's Department, but it is interesting to note that three have been undertaken by private architects. This course has been taken primarily to maintain the momentum of the programme, but it has been of value also in bringing new approaches to the problems of school building during a time when every possibility has had to be explored to maintain the rate of building by exploiting the variety of construction methods and materials now available. Throughout this period the major pre-occupation of everyone concerned in school building has been to produce sound buildings which meet all the educational demands during a period of increasing building costs and imposed cost limits. It has also been, however, a period of absorbing interest in connection with the design of new secondary schools. Bristol has now built 40 primary schools since the War and, it may be claimed, has a wealth of experience in the design of schools for younger children. In the secondary field, however, there has been in recent years opportunity for much original thought in the specification and design of the new schools. In practically every case it has been necessary to build initial instalments which will later become part of larger schools serving school communities of greater size than have been previously encountered. There has been a high degree of consultation between the City Architect's Department and the Education Committee and its officers which has led to the successful translation of the new educational requirements into challenging and functional designs.

The Education Committee would wish to take this opportunity to express appreciation to Architects, Consultants, Quantity Surveyors and Clerks of Works for their part in the design and supervision of the building projects. Their sincere thanks are also extended to the various firms of Contractors and Sub-contractors who have been engaged on these extensive programmes.

It is very appropriate that the Minister of Education should have accepted the invitation to open these schools as, in the field of school building, there is very close association between his Ministry and the Local Education Authority. The contacts between his officers and those of the Education Committee reveal close mutual understanding of the technical, administrative and educational problems, and the Committee wish to take this opportunity of expressing their appreciation to the Minister and his staff for their continued co-operation and assistance.

MEMBERS of the EDUCATION COMMITTEE

Chairman:
Alderman R. St. John Reade, O.B.E., M.A.

Vice-Chairman:
Alderman Mrs. F. M. Brown

Alderman F. G. W. Chamberlain
Alderman F. C. Williams, M.A.
Councillor T. P. Barrow
Councillor Mrs. Helen Bloom
Councillor J. K. Browne
Councillor E. W. Byrt
Councillor Mrs. E. R. L. Cave, O.B.E.
Councillor R. G. Cooke, M.A.
Councillor R. R. Cunningham
Councillor K. A. P. Dalby, D.S.O.
Councillor C. H. Langham
Councillor J. A. S. Llewellyn

Councillor T. H. Martin, M.B.E.
Councillor J. H. Mustoe
Councillor P. J. R. Nash
Councillor F. D. Parry, T.D.
Councillor A. G. Peglar
Councillor N. G. Reece
Councillor Miss E. St. John, M.A.
Councillor L. K. Stevenson
Councillor Mrs. D. F. E. Tambling
Councillor Mrs. F. M. Vickery, J.P.
Councillor The Rev. F. C. Vyvyan-Jones
Councillor D. J. Watkins

Co-opted Members:

Mr. P. C. Berrill
The Rev. R. F. Cartwright, M.A.
Mr. E. F. Davey
The Rev. R. E. Davies, M.A., B.D.
Mrs. B. Edwards
Mr. R. R. Fryer

The Rev. R. Norris
Mr. L. Parker
Mr. L. G. Selway
Mrs. A. K. Venning, M.B.E.
Mr. E. A. White, J.P.
Mr. A. F. Wilshire, B.SC.

Town Clerk and Clerk to the Local Education Authority:
Alexander Pickard, C.B.E.

Chief Education Officer:
G. H. Sylvester, M.A.

City Architect:
J. Nelson Meredith, F.R.I.B.A.

Principal Assistant Architect (Education):
K. J. Watson, A.I.A.A.

Deputy Section Head:
S. E. Tong, A.R.I.B.A.

HENGROVE SECONDARY

Headmaster — Dr. R. Perry, M.A., B.Sc.

THE Hengrove site of 44·95 acres was originally intended to accommodate three secondary schools of which the building now being opened was to be the first. It was designed as a four form-entry school for boys with temporary accommodation for girls to enable it to operate as a mixed school for the first few years. It has now been decided that there will in fact be only two six form-entry schools on the site, one for boys and one for girls, the present school being extended to provide the enlarged boys' school. These extensions are about to begin. At a later date the six form-entry girls' school will be built which will enable the re-organisation into two single sex schools to take place.

The school was opened in September, 1954, and with Lockleaze was one of the first two bilateral schools in Bristol. Its non-selected children are drawn from the thickly populated housing areas which straddle Wells Road from Airport Road to the City boundary.

From the entrance hall a wing containing the hall, gymnasium and dining room extends to the south and to the east the main teaching accommodation is planned on three floors. Four workshops are provided in pairs as separate single storey buildings and two of these are temporarily fitted as housecraft rooms. The building is based on a structural steel frame with brickwork and mineral faced grey/pink concrete units as cladding. The upper floors and the main roofs are made of precast concrete units and the hall and gymnasium roofs are formed of light-weight decking.

The school has been built on one of the Committee's large general playing fields and forms an attractive feature amid the surrounding housing development. Within the campus is the large Tyning Junior School, also of post-war construction, from which the majority of the children are drawn, and also the Petherton Road Infants' School.

Ex pupils have sent in a number of documents relating to the early years of the school. We have a 1957 example of the letter sent to prospective parents.

CITY AND COUNTY OF BRISTOL

Education Department,
The Council House,
College Green,
BRISTOL, 1.

G. H. SYLVESTER, M.A.
Chief Education Officer
To whom all communications
should be addressed

1st June, 1957.

Telephone 2-6031

Please quote SE. 16/ **7750**

Dear Sir or Madam,   re Ruth

TRANSFERS TO SECONDARY SCHOOLS, SEPTEMBER, 1957

I am now able to inform you that, as a result of detailed consideration during this school year, it has been decided that your child is suited for the type of education provided in a secondary grammar school or in an equivalent form in one of the Committee's new bilateral schools.

In the allocation of a place in a particular school, your wishes as expressed on the form completed by you earlier this year, have been given every possible consideration. The degree of choice which you can be given, however, depends on the position of your child in an order of merit based on the marks obtained in the written examinations. Children highest in the list are allocated to the school of their first choice, until the stage is reached where all the places at particular schools are filled. Other children who would have preferred these schools have then to be offered their second choice, and so on. Thus those children who, although qualifying for a grammar school type of education, are some way down the order of merit may be offered a place at schools which were quite low in the order of preference of their parents. At a certain stage, the only available places may be at schools not chosen by the parents, in which case the place offered will be at the most accessible school at which places are still available. In accordance with this system the Education Committee are able to offer your child a place as a day pupil at

Hengrove Secondary School

from the commencement of next term, subject to the conditions set out in the leaflet "Transfers to Secondary Schools." Unless I hear from you to the contrary by 21st June, it will be assumed that you wish your child to attend this school. Information about uniform, school rules, etc. will be given to you by the Head of the school, either by letter or at a parents' meeting. If you would like to visit the school in the meanwhile, you are invited to communicate with the Head, who will be pleased to make arrangements for you to do so.

Should vacancies arise later at schools higher in your order of choice they will be filled by the strict application of the arrangements detailed above, and I shall write to you if a place at such a school can be offered to your child. This is done automatically and special application is unnecessary. Parents are specially asked not to make requests for reconsideration of the school to which their children have been allocated. Such a request will not affect the system whereby each child is allocated to the school of his highest choice at which a place becomes available. No information can be given about examination marks and the relative positions of children.

In offering this place, the Education Committee ask parents to consider very carefully the question of keeping the child at school at least until the completion of the five-year course, i.e., until the end of the school year in which the 16th birthday is reached. You will be required to complete an agreement form undertaking to keep your child at school for this period, If, after careful consideration, it is not your intention to keep the child at school after 15 years of age, you are asked not to accept the place as, by so doing, you may be preventing some other child from having the opportunity of a full five-year secondary course at the school.

The Committee have reserved a few places for boys and girls in boarding schools, and if you desire to apply for one of these you should write to this office for form S.E.1. quoting the above reference. Only those children who, in the opinion of the Committee, are in real need of this type of education because of difficulties at home, will be considered. It is therefore advisable not to apply if your child can be educated suitably in a day school. School fees will be remitted, or charged in whole or in part in accordance with an income scale. I should like to point out, however, that for most boarding schools the cost of initial clothing which you would be expected to provide would be fairly high, and incidental expenses would also be your responsibility.

Yours faithfully,

G. H. SYLVESTER,

Chief Education Officer.

Parents were encouraged to buy their children books from the recommended list below:

<u>CHRISTMAS BOOK LIST 1957</u>

This Book List is again issued as a guide to those of you who are thinking of giving books as Christmas presents. It covers a wide variety of interests, and all the books listed are confidently recommended as being among the best of their kind.

N.B. In every case, books suitable for younger pupils are listed first and a space divides them from those more fitted for older boys and girls.

The School Librarian will be pleased to advise parents or children on the choice of suitable reading matter for pupils.

Books by all the well-known authors are published in Dent's Everyman Series (6/-); World's Classics (6/-); and Collin's Classics (5/-). These are all good editions, covering a wide range of authors, and could form the foundation of a very useful library.

In addition, the following are recommended:-

Alcott	Little Women	Blackie	5/-
Grahame	Wind in the Willows	Methuen	8/6
Kipling	Kim	Macmillan	10/6
Mayne	A Grass Rope	Oxford	10/6
Campbell	Horse of Air	Kegan Paul	12/6
Dickens	David Copperfield	Dent	6/-
Conrad	Four Tales	Oxford 6/-: Dent 6/-	
Eliot	The Mill on the Floss	Collins	5/6
Hilton	Lost Horizon	Macmillan 7/6: Pan 2/6	
Thompson	Lark Rise to Candleford	Oxford	8/6
Hardy	Under the Greenwood Tree	Macmillan	6/6
	Mayor of Casterbridge	"	6/6
Bennett	Old Wives' Tale	Dent	6/-
Collins	The Moonstone	Dent	6/-
Lawrence	Selections from Seven Pillars of Wisdom	Methuen	7/6

<u>Geography and Travel</u>

Lamb	Modern Adventure	Harrap	8/6
Grimble	A Pattern of Islands	Murray	6/-
Wymer	Great Explorers	Oxford	8/6
Trent	Exploring the Rocks	Phoenix	9/6
Fleming	Brazilian Adventure	(Cape	10/-
		(Penguin	3/6
Harrer	Seven Years in Tibet	Pan	2/6
Post	Venture to the Interior	Hogarth	10/6

<u>History and Biography</u>

Watson	Beyond the Sunset	Oxford	6/-
Redmayne	Transport by Land	Murray	10/6
Allen	The Story of the Village	Faber	12/6
Kamm	They Served the People	Bodley Head	9/6
Woolley	Digging Up the Past	Benn	10/6
Moore	Isaac Newton	Black	6/6

A Series of "Brief Lives" published by Collins at 7/- are excellent biographies, and the Batsford Junior Heretage at 6/6 have a variety of titles dealing with Churches, Castles, Dress, Transport, etc.

<u>Science and Mathematics</u>

Wallace	Boys' Book of Science and Invention - Evans 12/6		
Clarke	The Young Traveller in Space - Phoenix 8/6		
Boltz	Wireless for Beginners	Harrap	8/6
Smeltxer	Man and Number	Black	7/6
Barrow	Your World in Motion	Macmillan 8/6	
Farrell	Plastics	E.?.A. Press 8/6	
Taylor	The Young Chemist	Nelson	7/6

N.B. The 'Observer' series, published by Warne at 5/- form excellent pocket guides on a variety of subjects likely to appeal to the young scientist.

Pets and Hobbies

| Arstrop | Enjoying Pets | Dobson | 12/6 |
| Denham | Let's Keep a Pet | Nelson | 9/6 |

An excellent series on the care of pets is published by Cassell at 4/6.

Baron	Have You a Camera?	Muller	4/6
Rensaller	Your Book of Magic	Faber	5/6
Knock	The Railways of Britain	Batsford	6/-
Wiggin	Fishing for Beginners	Phoenix	8/6

Music and Art

Russell	A History of Music for Young People	Harrap	9/6
Davis	A Music Dictionary	Faber	12/6
Borland	Instruments of the Orchestra	Novello	5/6
Vale	How to Look at Old Buildings	Batsford	6/-

Languages

G. Seidman	Fritz and Liesl	U. London Press	1/9
Fabrizius	Der Schwarze Teufel	Murray	3/-
Thoma	Laus buben geschichten	Blackie	2/9
	Legacy of Rome	Oxford	18/-

Subscription to 'Ca Va!' or other magazines obtainable in School. Approximately 1/6 per term. This also applies to German Magazines.

| | Harrap's Concise French Dictionary | Harrap | 8/6 |
| | 'Mon Premier Dictionnaire' | Linklater | 7/6 |

Careers

| Heal | Book of Careers for Girls | Bodley Head | 10/6 |
| Watterson | Careers for Boys | Lock | 12/6 |

Career novels, giving a good insight into working conditions in a variety of occupations, are published by the Bodley Head Press at 7/6, and the Oxford Press at 8/6, among others.

Nursing and the Home

	Red Cross First Air Manual	Macmillan	4/6
Belilios	A Handbook of First Aid	Tindall Cox	7/6
Laskie	Cookery for Girls	E.U.P.	7/6
Nash	Cooking Craft	Pitman	12/6
Edinburgh	Book of Cookery Recipes	Nelson	6/-
Bull	Basic Needlework	Longman	8/6
Lund	The Art of Home Making	E.S.A. Press	8/6

If you feel that these books are not entirely suitable for your purposes, may we draw your attention to the Book Token System. This enables you to buy a token, to any value from 2/6 upwards, which can be exchanged by the recipient at any bookshop.

These Tokens, and the books listed above, may be obtained from:-

Messrs. Georges, Park Street
Stanley Roberts, The Triangle
Branches of W.H. Smith
Peter Dalwood, Colston Street

Messrs. Baker, The Mall
Lexicon Library, The Bush
H. Hockey, Blackboy Hill
Pied Piper, Park Street.

There was a strict uniform and homework code and an examination system. The following were issued to a prospective pupil about to enter the school in September 1957

HENGROVE SCHOOL
GIRLS

UNIFORM   School uniform may be obtained from Messrs. Baker Baker Ltd., College Green.   It is hoped that all parents will make it possible for their children to wear uniform.   The following is a complete list from which parents may select.

RAINCOAT   Dark green, double breasted detachable hood. Interlined shoulders, deep hem. From 88/6 (32") A better quality is also available.

BLAZER   Dark green, single breasted.   From 48/6 (6)

GYM TUNIC   School grey. V neck with tailored flared skirt and deep hem for lengthening.   From 49/11 (32")

BLOUSE   Cream long sleeves.   Poplin from 18/3 (6) Winter weight from 25/11 (7)

TIE   Dark green and silver 5/11 – 6/11

CARDIGAN   Dark green or school grey.   From 21/- (28")

BERET   Dark green 6/4

FELT HAT   Dark green 17/11

SCARF   Dark green and grey (12/11)

HAIR RIBBON   Dark green or white

SOCKS   White, grey or dark green

BADGES   Hat band 7/6,   Beret badge 3/-,   Blazer badge 5/9

SUMMER DRESS   Green stripe rayon.   White collar and buttons. From 30/6 (32").   Material 4/11½d per yard. The material can be obtained at school later in the year.

For P.E.   Dark green tailored shorts From 27/11 (24" waist) Sports blouse, Cellular " 14/11 (32") Dark green knickers   " 3/2 (12)

A scarf knitting pattern may be obtained from school.

Messrs. Baker allow a special discount of 5% on the first purchase of school uniform.

It is a rule of the School that JEWELLERY (other than a wrist watch) should NOT be worn.

ALL ARTICLES OF CLOTHING SHOULD BE CLEARLY MARKED WITH THE OWNER'S NAME.

GAMES   All pupils are expected to take part in games, physical education and swimming classes unless medically excused. If your daughter plays hockey a pair of canvas hockey boots will be useful.   Gym knickers and vests are available at the School, but parents may prefer to buy from Messrs. Baker.

HOMEWORK   A reasonable amount of homework will be set and parents are asked to see that this is done.   A satchel will be needed to carry books.

ABSENCE FROM SCHOOL   Please send a note giving the reason for absence when your daughter returns.   In the case of prolonged absence, a medical certificate should be sent to School.

Term begins Monday, 9th September 1957.

HENGROVE SCHOOL

The system of examinations in Forms 1,2,3,4, is now as follows:-

Autumn and Spring Terms: Tests are given at half-term, and the end of term. The result of these tests are given on the report as a percentage mark. In addition the effort made by the pupil is assessed by means of a letter:

A- working very hard.
B- good effort.
C- satisfactory.
D- little effort made.

Thus 25B means that the child is trying but gained only a low mark in the tests. Similarly 70C means that though the test results are good, the child could be making more effort.

Summer Term: Examinations at the end of term.

Below is the Headmaster's Letter from The Hengrove School Magazine Vol 2 July 1957 – the end of the school's third year.

HEADMASTER'S LETTER

At the end of this term Hengrove School will have completed its third year, and soon, with the opening of the New Wing, will enter on a further period of expansion. This will call for great effort on the part of staff and pupils, as new courses are developed. If the spirit of our early years is maintained, I have no doubt that we shall be able to take advantage of the opportunities that will be offered.

About ninety boys and girls entering the Fourth Year are now preparing for the General Certificate examination to be held in 1959, in a wide field of subjects. This examination will be the first great test of the school's work, and I hope that all will realise that they are now entering upon a critical period of their school career.

The Education Committee, in co-operation with the Union of Educational Institutions, has introduced a new Secondary Schools' Examination, which will be open to boys and girls who are not able to reach the standard of the General Certificate, but are willing to remain at school for an extra year. The new certificate will be well worth having, for it will be a guarantee that a good general standard of education has been reached, and will be most useful to boys and girls entering commerce and industry. A special class has been formed to prepare for this examination, and about thirty pupils have asked to be admitted to it. English Language will be a compulsory subject, and at least three other subjects must be offered. The examination will meet the needs of those who are following the new Technical and Commercial courses.

You will read in this magazine accounts of the successes of the past year. In the field of sport we have done very well, and the school teams are to be congratulated. Cups or shields for Basketball, Athletics and Life Saving have been won, and these represent particularly good achievements for so young a school. They reflect great credit upon pupils and staff.

There will be a number of staff changes at the end of term. Mr. Seymour leaves to become Headmaster of Sefton Park Secondary School, and Mrs. Roach to become Deputy Head of the new Monk's Park Secondary School. They have both been with us since the school opened, and have done much to help us lay foundations. Mr. Scarlett and Miss Hawken, who have given such valuable work in Physical Education, and Mrs. Taylor, are also leaving. We wish them happiness and success in their new schools. Mr. Foote, who was with us in our first year, returns from the Royal Air Force, and we shall have the help of many well-qualified and experienced new members of the staff.

There may be a short period of difficulty before the New Wing is fully completed, but we can look forward to the future with confidence.   R. PERRY.

Further Expansion

By 1958 the pupil numbers had reached 800 and were likely to reach 1,000 in the next year or two. The stage II extension opened in 1958 to accommodate the swelling numbers.

The ground floor housed the Girls' Gymnasium, Shower Room, General Store, Changing Rooms, Office for Miss Place, Staff Room, 4 classrooms, a Housecraft Room and a Geography Room. For the pupils taking Technical Subjects there was a Metalwork Room, a Woodwork Room, a Drawing Room and a Mechanics Lab.

The 1st floor housed a General Science Room, a Needlework Room, 3 more classrooms and the Girl's toilets.

The 2nd floor housed a General Craft Room, the Commercial Room (typing etc.), 3 more classrooms and the Music Room which had a door linking the new extension with the original building.

We have a photograph of the girls in the Commercial Class with their teacher Mrs Clutterbuck. They did not know then how useful their keyboard skills would become in the computer age!

Hengrove School's Fourth Birthday

The Headmaster's Letter in Vol 3 of the Hengrove School Magazine July 1958 reflects the excitement and new possibilities presented by the opening of the "New Wing" in 1958.

HEADMASTER'S LETTER

This issue of the magazine appears as we near the end of our fourth year. We knew when it began that it would be a difficult time for us, since our numbers rose to 800 before the New Wing was ready. However, we were soon able to provide accommodation in the school for all our pupils, and though harassed by the turmoil outside and the presence of many workmen in the 'old' building, we have survived and look forward to a year in which we shall be freed from all these distractions.

The constant roar of air-compressed drills has impressed upon us all the fact that this school is built upon rock, and we hope that the foundations of educational success have also been soundly laid. The magazine again records substantial achievement in many fields; our games and athletics have flourished, the school play was a great success, and work in the classroom progressed so well that we have been encouraged to enter our first candidates for the General Certificate of Education, rather earlier than we had intended.

As a famous Greek statesman said long ago, it is men, not walls, that make a city, and we all know that however good the buildings and equipment provided by the Education Committee may be, our future depends upon the ability and energies of the teaching staff and our boys and girls, and the co-operation of parents. In all these things we have been fortunate during the past four years, and it is our task now to encourage and develop the spirit of co-operation that so far has served us so well.

Next term we shall be able to inaugurate full Technical and Commercial courses, using the splendid facilities provided in the New Wing. We shall prepare boys and girls for the new U.E.I. Secondary Schools' Certificate, and here are fine opportunities for achievement. Over a hundred boys and girls are remaining at school for a fifth year, and we hope that many of these will remain to enter the Sixth Form in September 1959. No members of the present staff are leaving us this term, and we shall welcome twelve · additional teachers in September.

Apart from the Commercial and Technical accommodation, the New Wing will be the home of first and second year classes. Mr. F. J. Buckland will be master-in-charge of this Department, and these pupils will have their own morning assembly and will, we hope, develop a community life of their own within the school. This will be a good thing in so large an organisation and will help them to feel completely at home when they join us from their junior schools.

I am grateful to all who have given me such generous assistance during the past year, and have helped to make so much of my work a pleasure.

Pupil Jennifer Burgess wrote a humorous account of her impressions of the school in the December 1959 School Magazine.

More thoughts about the school and its staff, or, "Who the cap fits let him wear it!" . . .

From the outside Hengrove Academy looks like any ordinary school in the middle of a field; but brother, inside it's completely different from any other!

There are many classrooms, the numbers of which are not consecutive, but are arranged with wild abandon and vary from floor to floor. On the second floor (counting in continental fashion) exist three evil science labs: one full of the most terrifying instruments, another full of fascinating smells, and the other full of skulls and slow-worms in various degrees of decay. The bottom floor has quite ordinary classrooms, and has a corridor leading into the " New wing." Here the rooms have plywood desks and no clock, and remind one of army barracks, though maybe they are even worse.

The top floor, which is continuous over the old and new wings, holds many terrors for such as I. The first room is a mix-up of paintings, clay models, huge tables and ordinary chairs. The next is the Art room proper, where balmy daisies repose amongst paint brushes on the teacher's table. The wall is covered with ' expert ' paintings of bowls of waxen fruit and of pan-faced people with knock-knees and five little sausages on each hand. A shelf running along the side of the room has wet masterpieces scattered along it, more pots of brushes, and paint-soaked palettes.

The History room has enthralling pictures of ancient houses, and the Needlework room, a huge place, has machines of various parentage ranged along the side of the room. There are, too, awesome pictures hanging on the walls, of gigantic machines with huge needles. Next are the Geography and Music rooms; the first has heavy green curtains with what looks like ornamental patches of lace and which closer inspection reveals as holes. Here, also, are vast glaring maps of violent hues, and on a table in the corner stands a fading globe, battered and worn. The Music room has a brown piano, backless, and a matching man to play it.

An Assembly Hall, two gymnasiums, and a library are also to be found about the building. In the library stories of Henry

6

VIII revel under shelves headed 'Geography,' and stories of Sherlock Holmes under 'Musicians and Composers.' The gym. has windows on one side with wooden ribs resting against them. The cold wooden floors are most pleasant to warm bare feet, and the many splinters are calculated to make anyone happy. The one sane room is the Assembly Hall, with its imposing stage and red curtains.

But it is the people in it that really make a school. The students (us) are many and various, and have different ways of walking around. Some strut along with a look of angelic goodness, others bounce merrily around, bumping into, and slapping the backs of, everyone in sight—excepting those awesome figures in black mourning robes that sweep along the corridors. (These we call teachers).

These teachers vary considerably in size and manner: short, dark, Welsh masters haunt biology labs., bald Polish men haunt physics labs., and white-haired men with vibrant voices and spectacles haunt chemistry labs. Whilst in the library, tall stout grey-haired men, short red-faced men with receding hair, and thin black-haired men are wandering.

On the bottom floor in their cosy little dens are to be found the secretary tapping away on her typewriter, the senior mistress sitting in state, and the head of the school reposing in his chair. One might see wandering about jolly natured little English masters, or short, dark Geography mistresses; slim, elegant, auburn-haired language mistresses stalking around with plump Latin masters.

Hengrove is indeed a school of character and colour of a kind not found in any but a goony school such as ours; but we revel in it!

JENNIFER BURGESS (3A2)

Do you remember the school reports? We have a sample below.

HENGROVE SCHOOL
TERM REPORT

Summer _____ 1958

Name_____   Attendance_____ 126

Form __18___   126

	Exam.	Term		Initials
RELIGIOUS KNOWLEDGE	87	B	Thoughtful intelligent work	
ENGLISH	70	B+	A very sound year's work, showing progress in all branches of the subject.	LTC.
HISTORY	62	A-	Very good indeed.	JA.
GEOGRAPHY	65	B+	A good term's work	FCC.
FRENCH	90.	A.	An excellent result following a year of hard work & concentration.	
GERMAN or LATIN				
MATHEMATICS	83	B	V. Good	DBB
SCIENCE	84	A.	Ruth has maintained her standard well.	JB.
COOKERY				
NEEDLEWORK	49	C+	Usually good but exam results - practical and theory disappointing	P.J.
WOODWORK				
METALWORK				
WORKSHOP DRAWING				
ART		C+	Some pleasing work done.	MEC.
MUSIC	80	B-	Good progress. More violin practice necessary.	BC.
PHYSICAL EDUCATION			Very good. Ruth has worked hard	

SCHOOL ACTIVITIES Violin Group
Swimming Group
1st Year Rounders team.

FORM REPORT Ruth is to be congratulated on a good first year's work. She takes an active part in her school life and is developing into an attractive personality.
ME Crowther. Form-Master/Mistress

R. Perry Headmaster

41

Little did we appreciate how hard the teachers worked at the end of term with exams to mark and reports to write.

In 1957 a system of Prefects was introduced, with a Head Boy and Head Girl from 1958. The Prefects system was phased out in 1967.

The Prefect's Roll Book will be placed in the City Records Office. It contains the signatures of the Head Boy, Head Girl and Prefects, year by year.

In 1957 there was no Head Boy or Head Girl but the following were Prefects:

Girls: C. Ayers, P. Boyd, M. Dudbridge, Z. Gioria, S. Hall, S. Hedges, K. Partridge, J. Reed, A. Richards, P. Rosser, L. Sheppard, S. Werlock, A. Bennett, D. Orme

Boys: J. Bright, K. Drew, R. Long, J. Lugg, R. Seymour, D. Shore, M. Stephens, D. Summers, M. Taylor, P. Tremblett, R. Townsend, M. Woolaway, A. More and M. Parsons.

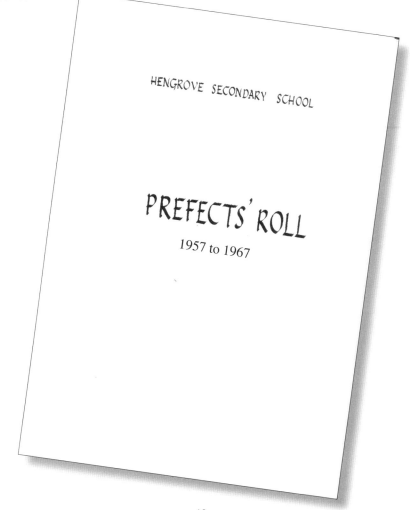

HENGROVE SECONDARY SCHOOL

PREFECTS' ROLL

1957 to 1967

In 1958 - 59 the first Head Boy and Head Girl appear in the roll.

1958 ~ 1959

HEAD BOY *David Summers.*

HEAD GIRL *Mary Dudbudge.*

1958 ~ 1959

Re-elected:

Cynthia Ayers.

Arlene Bennett.

Sally Hall.

Sally Hedges

Diane Orms.

Joan Reed.

Anne Richards

Pat Rosser

Lesley Sheppard.

Sandra Wherlock.

Kenneth Dew.

Tony Lugg.

M. Parsons

D. Shore.

P. Tamblett.

M Stephens

M. Taylor.

R Townsend

M. Woolaway.

Elected:

Christine Ball

Milly Cameron

Pat Eyre.

Elaine Jones

Lesley Long

Sophie Nussbaum.

Hazel Robinson.

Ian Bridgeman.

Colin Birt

Clive Bennett

John Gardiner.

Michael Major

Anthony Manchester

Christopher Rupps.

Michael Whitfield.

Unfortunately space does not allow the reproduction of all the names year by
year - you can inspect the Prefects Roll Book in the City Records Office.

End of the First Chapter in School's History

Dr Perry's Report from the December 1959 School Magazine makes interesting reading. We have a photo of the four boys outside Buckingham Palace when they received their Duke of Edinburgh's Gold Awards. (See Chapter 5).

HEADMASTER'S REPORT

At the end of the Summer Term, we came to the end of the first chapter in the School's history. More than a hundred boys and girls who entered in 1954 had completed a five-year course, and sat for either the General Certificate of Education or the Secondary Schools' Certificate. These examinations were a test of the work that had been done during our early years, and the results were awaited with keen interest, tinged in many cases with anxiety. It is good to be able to record they were very satisfactory. Almost all those whom we expected to obtain good certificates did so; some. who had not worked hard enough, also received their deserts. There were others who deserved greater success, but failed in some subjects by a very narrow margin; many of them will take the examination again this term.

Form 5B, which achieved 100% success in the Secondary Schools' Certificate Examination, deserves particular commendation; it may be safely said that we shall never do better than this! It appears that all our leavers have found employment, and many of them seem to have embarked upon promising careers.

Thirty-two boys and girls returned to school to enter the Sixth Form, and most have begun work for the Advanced Level of the General Certificate. This, no doubt, will surprise both the friends and the critics of the comprehensive school.

This magazine lists many of our activities of the past year, though it can hardly present a complete picture. I think the outstanding achievement is that of the four boys who have qualified for the Gold Award of the Duke of Edinburgh's Scheme. They will go to Buckingham Palace to receive their certificates from him on 3rd November.

All these things should be an inspiration to us. Our first pupils have set a fine example to those who follow, and I am sure that there are many of these who intend to do even better. Certainly much remains to be done, and we must not allow ourselves to become complacent.

R. PERRY.

We have a photo of the staff in the late 1950's. Although the faces are indistinct we can see that the staff numbers had grown considerably to around 41, in line with the increase in pupil numbers to 750-800.

In the same December 1959 magazine are pupils' accounts of a variety of school activities, events and news in brief. These reflect the dedication of the staff, their generosity with their time and the diversity of experiences offered to the pupils.

CHAPTER FIVE—School Activities, Events, and News in Brief

THE ENGLISH SOCIETY

The English Society has now reached the end of its second year. In the last term we have welcomed the fourth year to our meetings, and hope they will continue to come.

We have had various speakers, including members of staff. A few weeks ago Miss Crowther showed us paintings and talked about art. This proved especially interesting to those of us who no longer take art. Mr. Swift, who recently arrived back from Australia, told us of his travels and showed us a film of the country and the school where he had taught. He also brought back a tape-recording of a production of *Iolanthe* which the school did. We also learnt something of America from Miss Hicks who was teaching in our school from America last term. She told us about her home-town, Colorado Springs, and about the life of the school at which she teaches.

teaches.

Earlier in the term we had a visit from a member of one of Bristol's leading newspapers who told us something about the production of a daily newspaper Around the same time we showed the film " Great Expectations " in the Church Hall at Christchurch. Other children in the school were invited, and we hope that it will have encouraged them to join the society when they are old enough.

We have been to see all the productions which the Bristol Old Vic have put on this season. Of all the plays we have seen. I am sure most will agree that the translation of Edmond Rostand's *Cyrano de Bergerac* was the best. The lead in this production was played by Peter Wyngarde who was outstanding.

To end this year the society had hoped to visit Stratford, but as this would have interfered with our examinations, we have been to London to see the modern American musical *West Side Story*.

Finally, we should all like to thank Mr. Pyle who has done so much to make the society a success.

SALLY HEDGES (5A1).

SCHOOL PLAY

Just before Christmas the school put on three public performances of *Macbeth*. The production was well received, and credit for its success must go to its hard-working producer Mr. Sterry, as well as to the enthusiastic cast.

20

A VISIT TO BORDEAUX

A large group of children from many Bristol schools left Temple Meads on March 16th for Bordeaux. We reached our destination on the evening of the 17th, after a very long and tedious journey. Our French hosts were waiting for us at the station.

A few days later an excursion was arranged for us. We visited Libourne, St. Emilion, and some vineyards. Most of the day we spent looking around St. Emilion, a very old town. At another vineyard we sampled some wine.

Three days later the Easter holidays began. Easter is celebrated for a fortnight there, and the shops stayed open all the time. I was at Arachon for Easter, and think most of the English children went there as well. At the end of the fortnight we returned to Bordeaux, and school!

French schools begin at 8 a.m. and finish sometimes at 5, and other times at 3 or 4 p.m. Times are not so regular as at home.

Bordeaux is very old, and some of the streets are narrow and dirty. I visited the factory where *Sud-Ouest*, a French newspaper is printed. Towards the end of my stay I visited an old church in the city and went into the crypt. There were about a dozen bodies down there which had been buried about a hundred years, and which the earth had preserved; one of the bodies even had a whole set of teeth!

47

A few days before we returned home, another excursion was arranged for us. We visited some old chateaux in the district. It was very interesting, although the castles were in ruins.

On April 15th, we began the long journey home. On the way we stopped in Paris for a night and a day, and visited as many places as possible in the time. We did find time to go up the Eiffel Tower. We left Paris in the evening of April 16th and arrived at Southampton in the early hours of the next day.

ANN CARRUTHERS (4A3).

A TRIP TO STREET YOUTH HOSTEL

On Saturday, June 20th, at 9.30 a.m., a party from the Hengrove Outdoor Club met at the bus station to catch a bus to Street; we were off to spend the week-end at the Street Youth Hostel, near Wells. The outing, which consisted of 12 boys and 12 girls, was arranged and conducted by Mr. Swift and Miss Bevan. The journey took about $1\frac{1}{2}$ hours, and the rest of the morning was spent in the Street open-air swimming pool. At 3 p.m. we started the $1\frac{1}{2}$ mile hike to the hostel, and as we arrived there early, we had time to explore the nearby woods before the hostel opened at 5.

When we got inside we bought up two crates of lemonade! At 7.30 we had a good three-course dinner. We were in bed by 10.

Next day, after breakfast, and when we had completed our alloted chore, we hiked the three miles to Glastonbury Tor, and then climbed the tor. There, by the old tower, we ate our packed lunch in the company of a dog and several cows. After we had eaten we set off back for the Street swimming pool, stopping on the way for lemonade. We were dressed again by 4, and ready for the bus home.

As for the hostel, it was built like a Swiss chalet; the girls slept in the hostel building, but the boys slept in a sort of comfortable shed. We all ate together in a room which also served as a common-room. We all had an enjoyable time, and I should like to thank Mr. Swift and Miss Bevan for all of us for giving up their week-end on our behalf.

MICHAEL LEIGH (1C).

The full cast of Macbeth, 1959

YHA trip to St Briavels, 1950's

We have an account of the school camp at Exmouth – Orcombe Point Camp. This site was owned by Bristol Education Committee. Sleeping was in tents but there was a kitchen that provided meals. The camp site was right on the coast with its own beach.

SCHOOL CAMP AT EXMOUTH

Our School Camp was at Orcombe Point, Exmouth, this year. We set off in the Coach on the Saturday, and settled down to a steady drive. On the Somerset plain we saw cuttings which drain the area of Wells, Bridgwater and Glastonbury. Some two hours later the coach stopped at a café, so that we could stretch our legs. Just before we left, two more coaches pulled in, carrying children from Monks Park and Hotwells. These children we would meet later at camp, as they were also going to Orcombe Point.

As we left a few spots of rain began to fall. From then onwards the rain poured down all the way to Exmouth. We arrived at 10 a.m. Unfortunately we were unable to eat our packed lunch on the cliffs as we had hoped to do, because of the rain, so we ate it in the coach. After lunch the time came for us to climb the steps up to the camp. In the driving rain most of us were unable to see anything of the camp site.

The Warden in charge showed us our tents, and Mr. Miller told us who was in each tent. This done we all had to collect four blankets to make our beds. By 5.0 p.m. we were all settled in after changing into some of our old clothes. Everybody was looking forward to tea at 5.30 p.m. which was very welcome. The rest of the evening was ours, spent in playing games and examining the camp site. At 8.30 p.m. we had supper and soon time came for us to go bed at 9.45 p.m. This Saturday night was a great experience for those of us who had not been to camp before.

Sunday morning we were up long before reveille, officially at 7.30 a.m. We folded our blankets and cleared the camp area, then went to the wash houses to wash. After washing each morning it was time for breakfast, and then tent inspection. The neatest tent held the school pennant for the day. The weather was good and warm, and it was very pleasant walking along the cliff path on the way to Church.

22

In the afternoon we went with Mr. Thomas to Sandy Bay beach, and went swimming or played cricket. In the evening Group 3 went looking for firewood for cooking a high tea on Monday afternoon. The evening was changing and we thought a change of weather would come. By now we were making friends with girls and boys from Monks Park school. As we went to bed that night we heard two loud bangs which we would understand later in the week.

On Monday we woke up to hear rain beating on the tent. That morning we started on the weekly time-table consisting of nature rambles, campcraft, cooking, high tea, tent-erection, map-reading and first aid and sanitation. Our file work started, of which we had eight pages of questions to answer during the week. Gradually the weather improved, until in the evening, we were able to play football, cricket and rounders, and by bedtime we were tired.

Tuesday came, with a thrill, as we were hiking to Hayes Barton, twelve miles away from camp. We were to split up into two groups, Miss Pleass with the girls, Mr. Miller with the boys. At Hayes Barton there is the house in which Sir Walter Raleigh was born. At about 10.0 a.m. we started out. For the first boys and girls were together, then we split up, seeing each other later on. The weather kept on changing, with showers and then sunshine. On Bicton Common, nine or ten miles away from camp, the boys saw the Royal Marines in battle dress, practising. Whilst going over Bicton Common we came upon wild strawberries and we wished then that we had bought some cream at Hayes Barton. Some time later we arrived and met the girls.

After we had eaten our sandwiches we were taken for a conducted tour. We saw the bed Sir Walter Raleigh was born in, and other interesting articles. Time came for us to leave, and thanking the guide we took our leave. Off we started, walking again, but not for long as we were going to East Budleigh. All weary we staggered into East Budleigh, very thankful as the bus came in. After an enjoyable bus ride we arrived at Budleigh Salterton to stay for about an hour, shopping. The hour passed quickly and soon with all of us at the bus stop we clambered on to the bus. Very much later, back at camp after a thrilling and enjoyable day, we were lying on our beds when we were told that a Coastguard was coming to tell us all about the Coastguard Service, and we were to hear about the two bangs we heard on Sunday night.

All of us put on our blazers and waited the arrival of the Coastguard. He told us of the work of the coastguards and about the different rockets which are used as distress signals. It was very interesting. He told us about what happened on Sunday night. Some people were in a little dinghy when the engine broke down.

and they started drifting. Unfortunately they had no rockets but they found a piece of rag, oil and a match. The rag gave off a great flame, and luckily some people in Dawlish Warren saw the light and phoned the police. All the bangs which were heard were two rockets from the Coastguards telling the people that help was on the way. In all, said the Coastguard, twenty-seven phone calls were made to London, and a rescue plane stood by for two hours in case it was needed. During a rescue operation the Coastguards can call on the public, the Navy, the Air Force and the Army for any help they want. It was all very interesting and finished off a wonderful day.

By Wednesday our file work was half done, and the day passed quietly and nothing extraordinary happened, except that we saw a four-masted schooner on the horizon, and looking at it through binoculars; it was quite big. Most of all during the week we were looking forward to our coach tour trip over Dartmoor, via Wide-combe-on-the-Moor, Buckfast Abbey, Paignton, Dawlish Warren and Teignmouth, including Torquay. We were going on this trip the following day, Thursday.

Thursday morning was beautiful and the sea calm. We were to leave at 10.30 a.m. Soon we were singing in the coach, and our first stop was on Dartmoor. The coach stopped at the top of a hill, and the driver pointed to Haytor which we were to climb. At the top he said you could see seven counties. It was thrilling climbing it, and at the top we had a good view. Half an hour later we were off again to Widecombe-on-the-Moor. When we arrived it was about 12 o'clock. We visited the old Church and Almshouses, saw the wishing well and bought postcards showing Old Uncle Tom Cobley.

Next stop was at Buckfast Abbey, where the monks make their own wine and honey. Luckily the abbey was open and inside it was very beautiful. There was a splendid Altar, shining like gold, which many had not seen before. It was all very interesting to us, but soon we left. Our next stop was at Paignton where we could stay for one hour. Some children bought presents for their parents or went on the sands. Time seemed to pass very quickly, and by 5.0 p.m. we were leaving Paignton. The coach passed through Starcross, where we saw the tower which was built 100 years ago by some people who tried to run trains on air. Also we passed through the Earl of Devon's Estate, seeing some of his herd of five hundred deer. So ended another thrilling day. We arrived back at camp just in time for tea. After tea, as it was a fine evening, we played games; but about 7.30 p.m. it began to rain. The boys were able to play soft-ball in readiness for a match against Monks Park School on the Friday night.

After our work on Friday morning, we all went to the beach for a swim. Miss Pleass had to be helped into the water with the assistance of eight people. In the afternoon Group 2 went to town for shopping, and Groups 1 and 3 cooked a high tea. After tea the boys played Soft Ball against Monks Park, and the girls played them at rounders. As it was the last night we had a camp fire to end a very happy weetk. We sang all the songs we knew, and had a few solos. When bedtime came we were very reluctant to go.

On Saturday we left the camp site at 11.30 a.m. The girls again had packed sandwiches for us to eat on the beach, and some of us had our last swim. The coach arrived at 1.30 p.m. carrying more children for the next week. At 2.10 p.m. we started on our way back to Bristol. It was a comfortable trip, stopping again for refreshments. At 6.0 p.m. we arrived back at school to meet our parents on the steps of the front entrance. We all thanked Miss Pleass, Mr. Miller and Mr. Thomas for a very enjoyable camp at Exmouth.

STEPHEN MEAD (1st Year)
BARRY COBLEY (3rd Year)
PAM ISAAC (3rd Year).

R-L: Susan Munday, Linda Watts, Mrs Joy Edmands (P.E. Teacher), Dorrie Elberton and Ann Withers.

Also in the 1959 School Magazine were the following articles about the annual sports day, open day and end of term trip to Windsor.

ANNUAL SPORTS DAY

The annual sports day, held this year in July, was blessed with fine, sunny weather. Quite a few mums and dads were present, and everyone seemed to be having a good time. Adequate refreshments were organised by Mr. Hobbs, and many heated competitors (and bystanders) could be seen quenching their flaming cheeks in a half-pint of lemonade or a man-size choc-ice.

JUNIOR FORM VISIT TO WINDSOR

Almost all the children in the 1st and 2nd Years (about 370) had a most enjoyable visit to Windsor. Most of the arrangements were made by Mr. Wood, and everything, from the train journey to Bourne End, the trip to Windsor by boat, to the tour around Windsor Castle, went off smoothly. A lot depended, too, on the behaviour of the party, and this was exemplary. Fine, sunny weather set the seal on an excellent day.

OPEN DAY

An open day was held almost at the end of the Summer term, and much of the school activity was demonstrated to parents. Most of the staff stayed for the first session before tea, but as it turned out there were no more visitors than staff present. After tea, however, there was a very good gathering, and as all the afternoon's items were repeated in the evening programme, nothing was lost. Parents were glad to see the work their children were doing, and to speak to teachers about their child's progress.

25

Annual Sports Day 1950's

We have photos of a 1950s Sports Day taken by Mr Fletcher and donated by his sons. The competitors were divided into six Houses: - Athens, Argos, Corinth, Sparta, Thebes and Olympia and competed against each other for the highest score.

Most crucial – the refreshments team (below). In the background are the rear gardens of houses in New Fosseway Road.

The spectators – look at the old fashioned prams! Note that the Bush Training Centre has not been built yet.

And below, the finishing line and officials recording the times and results.

Sports Day was quite an organisational challenge for the staff and groundsmen. Below – marshalling the pupils/competitors and high jump.

Relay race on large track – note the loud speaker car.

There are more photos of sports in Chapter 5.

Junior Form Visit to Windsor - A Former Pupil writes

"I can remember the Junior Form visit to Windsor in 1959 clearly. Yes the weather was perfect and I particularly remember the beauty of the scenery as we went by boat from Bourne End to Windsor and the grand Windsor Castle. I remember we all sat inside St George's Chapel in the Castle Grounds – I think someone gave us a talk and then......I fainted and had to be carried out into the fresh air by friends and staff. I think I was delicate for the rest of the trip but remember having a picnic sitting on the grass and on reaching Bristol my friend took me home – she a pillion passenger on her Uncle's motorbike and me in the side car. Quite an eventful day!"

Amidst all the summer fun were the inevitable School Exams. Opposite are the GCE and UEI results for Summer 1959 extracted from the 1959 School Magazine. Perhaps your name is there?

G.C.E. RESULTS (O-LEVEL) *Summer 1959*

We extend to the following our congratulations, and hope to see many of these names among our first A-level results in two years' time.

KEY : Figures in brackets represent number of subjects passed.
5TH FORM ENTRIES.

Boys—P. Bale (5), A. Batchelor (4), C. Bennett (6), C. Birt (7), I. Bridgeman (5), S. Brown (2), C. Cogan (2), J. Gardner (4), F. Hayward (2), N. Hendy (1), J. Hughes (1), M. Hutton (4), B. Iles (1), P. Lovell (1), M. Major (5), A. Manchester (3), R. Mockridge (3), C. Rupprecht (3), B. Shore (2), D. Summers (6), P. Temblett (4), I. Weaver (2), S. Williams (2), M. Woolaway (6), J. Bartlett (2), D. Butcher (2), S. Clarke (2), R. Coxall (1), N. Hurford (3), A. Lugg (3), R. Metcalfe (3), M. Parker (3), A. Sage (2), N. Stephens (1), M. Taylor (3), J. Tovey (6), R. Townsend (5).

Girls—C. Ayers (4), P. Banbury (3), P. Boreman (2), S. Hall (6), G. Halls (2), S. Hedges (7), L. Long (5), J. Neale (2), D. Needs (3), S. Nussbaum (5), C. Paul (2), J. Reed (4), J. Richards (1), H. Robinson (5), P. Rosser (7), R. Brunt (3), M. Coggins (1), D. Davis (2), S. Delaney (5), M. Dudbridge (7), S. Farmer (3), P. Sharp (3), L. Sheppard (3), D. Spiller (2), J. Stinchcombe (5), J. Waddleton (3), A. Weston (6), M. Anderson (1), J. Gerrish (1), A. Haskins (4), A. Richards (3), P. Eyre (2), J. Shearman (4).

4TH FORM ENTRIES.
Some Fourth Form pupils took the G.C.E. examination in one or two selected subjects.

Boys—B. Cook (2), M. Crewe (1), T. Dark (3), R. Duckett (1), D. Harrison (2), R. Martin (1), E. Pavey (2), M. Summers (3), P. Trott (1), R. Davis (1).

Girls—C. Bacon (2), A. Battrick (1), S. Harvey (2), J. Mattfield (1), E. Burge (1), M. Chivers (2), J. Clutterbuck (1), M. Davis (1), V. Elliot (1), J. Fidler (1), M. Fisher (1), J. Fox (2), C. Gainard (1), S. Hurford (1), H. Smallcombe (1), C. Stone (1), J. Vale (3).

U.E.I. RESULTS

Boys—N. Clements (6), M. Cottle (5), R. Coxall (7), C. Godfrey (7), J. Goodman (4), D. Goverd (8), M. Parsons (5), B. Townsend (5), M. Whitfield (6).

Girls—C. Ball (8), A. Bennett (4), M. Etherton (8), L. Ibbotson (6), D. Orme (8), M. Payne (4), B. Sams (4), J. Sealey (7), S. Wherlock (6), W. Williams (8), H. Yeates (8).

58

These pupils would have been the first intake into Form 1 in 1954 – the pioneers. Some we know have already died – others we have been unable to contact.

We do not have copies of the 1960 School Magazine – nor for subsequent years – but below we have photos of the production of "Twelfth Night" November 1959 – you may recognise the actors.

The 1960's

Did you keep copies of the examination papers? One pupil did – she sent in her G.C.E English Language 'O' Level paper for Summer 1960 which she passed.

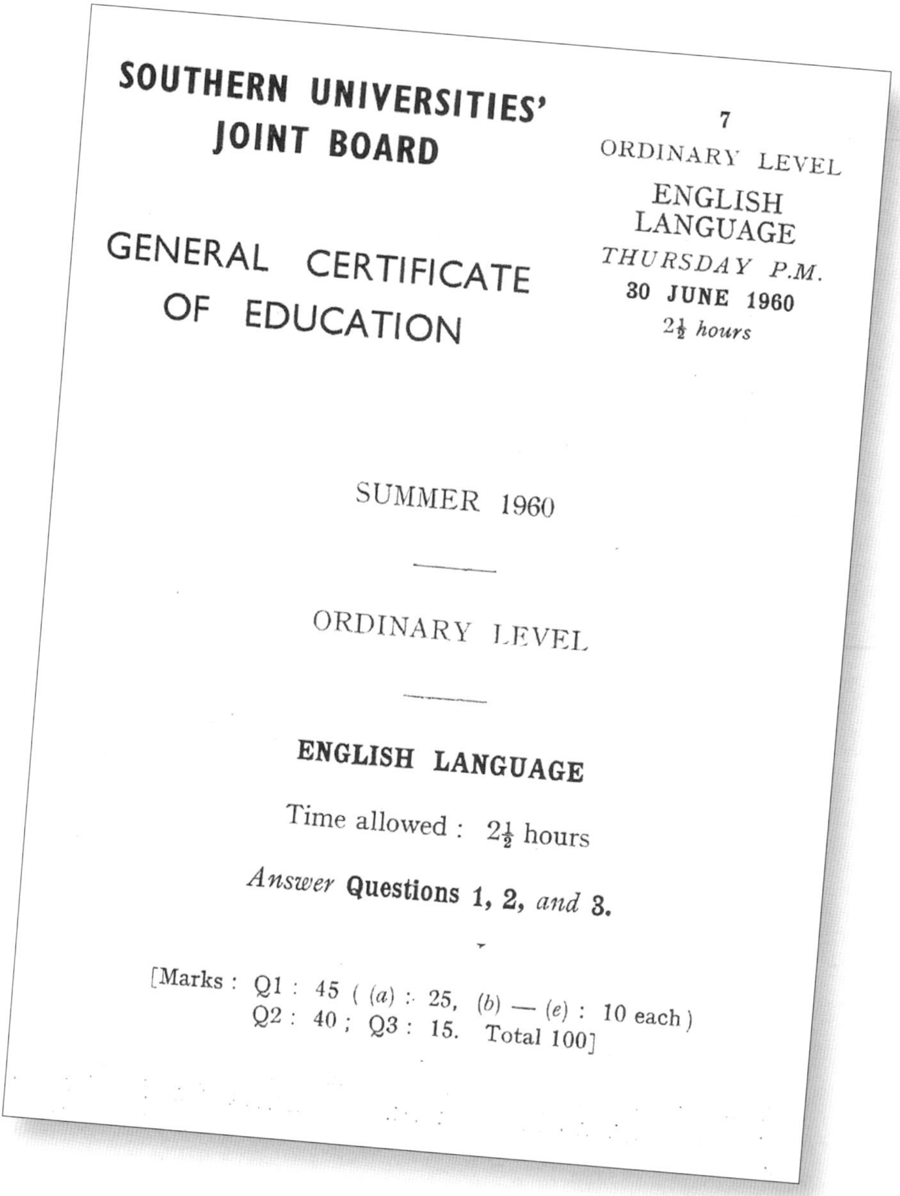

SOUTHERN UNIVERSITIES' JOINT BOARD

7
ORDINARY LEVEL
ENGLISH LANGUAGE
THURSDAY P.M.
30 JUNE 1960
$2\frac{1}{2}$ *hours*

GENERAL CERTIFICATE OF EDUCATION

SUMMER 1960

———

ORDINARY LEVEL

———

ENGLISH LANGUAGE

Time allowed : $2\frac{1}{2}$ hours

Answer **Questions 1, 2,** *and* **3.**

[Marks : Q1 : 45 ((*a*) : 25, (*b*) — (*e*) : 10 each)
Q2 : 40 ; Q3 : 15.   Total 100]

By 1960 the musical life of the school was flourishing. We have a programme of the April 1960 concert. The members of the orchestra named can be seen in the photos sent in by former pupils.

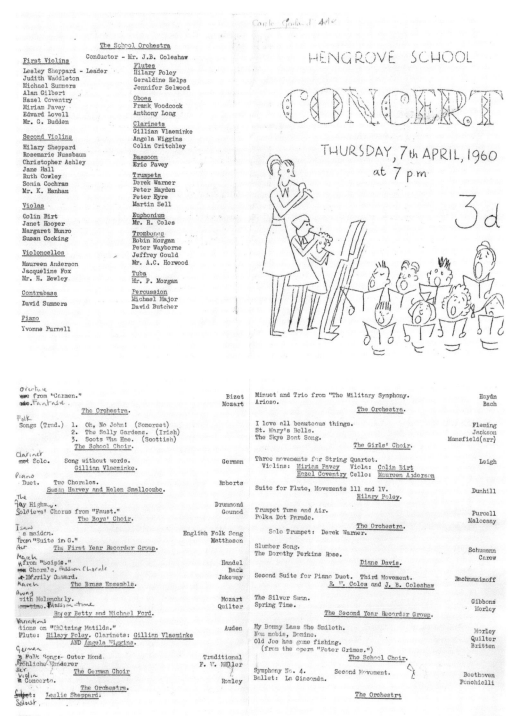

Carol Garland A/k

HENGROVE SCHOOL
CONCERT
THURSDAY, 7th APRIL, 1960
at 7 pm

3d

The School Orchestra

Conductor - Mr. J.B. Coleshaw

First Violins
Lesley Sheppard - Leader
Judith Waddleton
Michael Surmers
Alan Gilbert
Hazel Coventry
Miriam Pavey
Edward Lovell
Mr. G. Budden

Second Violins
Hilary Sheppard
Rosemarie Nussbaum
Christopher Ashley
Jane Hall
Ruth Cowley
Sonia Cochran
Mr. K. Hanham

Violas
Colin Birt
Janet Hooper
Margaret Munro
Susan Cocking

Violoncellos
Maureen Anderson
Jacqueline Fox
Mr. H. Bewley

Contrabass
David Summers

Piano
Yvonne Purnell

Flutes
Hilary Poley
Geraldine Helps
Jennifer Selwood

Oboes
Frank Woodcock
Anthony Long

Clarinets
Gillian Vlaeminke
Angela Wiggins
Colin Critchley

Bassoon
Eric Pavey

Trumpets
Derek Warner
Peter Hayden
Peter Eyre
Martin Sell

Euphonium
Mr. R. Coles

Trombones
Robin Morgan
Peter Wayborne
Jeffrey Gould
Mr. A.C. Horwood

Tuba
Mr. P. Morgan

Percussion
Michael Major
David Butcher

Overture
from "Carmen." ..... Bizet
Fantasie. ..... Mozart
    The Orchestra.

Folk
Songs (Trad.) 1. Oh, No John! (Somerset)
             2. The Sally Gardens. (Irish)
             3. Scots Whn Hae. (Scottish)
    The School Choir.

Clarinet
Solo. Song without words. ..... German
    Gillian Vlaeminke.

Piano
Duet. Two Chorales. ..... Roberts
    Susan Harvey and Helen Smallcombe.

The
Jay Highway. ..... Drummond
Soldiers' Chorus from "Faust." ..... Gounod
    The Boys' Choir.

I saw
a maiden. ..... English Folk Song
from "Suite in G." ..... Mattheson
Air The First Year Recorder Group.

March
from "Scipio." ..... Handel
Chorale. Passion Chorale. ..... Bach
Merrily Onward. ..... Jakeway
March The Brass Ensemble.

Away
with Melancholy. ..... Mozart
sometime. Blossom time ..... Quilter
    Roger Betty and Michael Ford.

Variations
tions on "Waltzing Matilda." ..... Auden
Flute: Hilary Poley. Clarinets: Gillian Vlaeminke
                    AND Angela Wiggins.

German
Folk Song:- Guter Mond. ..... Traditional
Fröhliche Wanderer ..... F. W. Möller
    The German Choir.

Violin
Concerto. ..... Rowley
    The Orchestra.
Soloist: Leslie Sheppard.

Minuet and Trio from "The Military Symphony." ..... Haydn
Arioso. ..... Bach
    The Orchestra.

I love all beauteous things. ..... Fleming
St. Mary's Bells. ..... Jackson
The Skye Boat Song. ..... Mansfield(arr)
    The Girls' Choir.

Three movements for String Quartet. ..... Leigh
Violins: Miriam Pavey Viola: Colin Birt
Hazel Coventry Cello: Maureen Anderson

Suite for Flute, Movements 111 and 1V. ..... Dunhill
    Hilary Poley.

Trumpet Tune and Air. ..... Purcell
Polka Dot Parade. ..... Malcosay
    The Orchestra.
Solo Trumpet: Derek Warner.

Slumber Song. ..... Schumann
The Dorothy Perkins Rose. ..... Carow
    Diane Davis.

Second Suite for Piano Duet. Third Movement. ..... Rachmaninoff
    R. W. Coles and J. B. Coleshaw.

The Silver Swan. ..... Gibbons
Spring Time. ..... Morley
    The Second Year Recorder Group.

My Bonny Lass She Smileth. ..... Morley
Non nobis, Domine. ..... Quilter
Old Joe has gone fishing. ..... Britten
    (from the opera "Peter Grimes.")
    The School Choir.

Symphony No. 4. Second Movement. ..... Beethoven
Ballet: La Gioconda. ..... Ponchielli
    The Orchestra

December 1960 was a busy time. The School Prizegiving was held on 2nd December 1960 – we have the programme but do not know where the majority of the pupils are today. Do you know where they are? We would be interested to know for the record in the Archive. The first three pupils to pass an 'A' Level G.C.E are recorded here.

HENGROVE SCHOOL, BRISTOL

—◦—

PRIZEGIVING

Friday, 2nd December, 1960

at 7.15 p.m.

—◦—

PROGRAMME

Chairman's Remarks:
Alderman P. W. RAYMOND, *Chairman of the Governors*

Headmaster's Report:
Dr. R. PERRY, M.A., B.Sc., Ph.D.

Presentation of Prizes by:
Mrs. W. A. WILKINS

Address by:
W. A. WILKINS, Esq., M.P.

Vote of Thanks:
SALLY HEDGES, *Head Girl*

SPECIAL AWARDS

Librarian Prize ...	...	...	Ian Gilham.
Sports Prize	...	...	David Summers.
Sports Prize	...	...	Anne Webb.
Prize for Perseverance	...	...	Mavis Barnett.
Prize for Perseverance	...	...	Pauline Stafford.
Orchestra Prize ...	...	...	Lesley Sheppard.
HEAD BOY'S PRIZE ...	...	...	David Summers.
HEAD GIRL'S PRIZE	...	...	Sally Hedges.

HOUSE AWARDS

House Cricket Cup	...	...	Argos.
House Hockey Cup	...	...	Sparta.
House Netball Cup	...	...	Argos.
House Athletics Cup	...	...	Thebes.
House Athletics Bowl	...	...	Thebes.

ADULT

HENGROVE SCHOOL

PRIZEGIVING

Friday, 2nd December, 1960.

7.15
in
School Hall

ADMISSION BY TICKET ONLY

PRIZE LIST

—◦—

SOUTHERN UNIVERSITIES' JOINT BOARD
GENERAL CERTIFICATE OF EDUCATION AT
ADVANCED LEVEL

Patricia Bambury—Art.
Hazel Robinson—English.
Jocelyn Shearman—Art.

GENERAL CERTIFICATE OF EDUCATION AT
ORDINARY LEVEL

D. Butcher, R. Clegg, P. Clough, B. Cook, R. Crago, M. Crewe, R. Culverhouse, T. Dark, R. Davis, R. Duckett, B. Dunn, J. Gardiner, I. Gilham, J. Gunter, D. Harrison, J. Hazell, C. Hinton, P. Kempson, R. Long, B. Mackenzie, R. Martin, R. Nation, J. Parker, E. Pavey, C. Senior, D. Shortman, T. Sims, M. Summers, P. Trott, R. Tugwell, D. Wade, N. Wallington, A. Watkins, C. West, D. Woodruff, M. Woolaway.

Maureen Anderson, Carol Bacon, Patricia Bambury, Mavis Barnett, Ann Battrick, Patricia Beacham, Lesley Bright, Enid Burge, Diane Burt, Ann Carruthers, Anne Chesterman, Margaret Chivers, Joan Clutterbuck, Mary Davis, Jennifer Dyer, Jacqueline Elbrow, Valerie Elliott, Jacqueline Fidler, Muriel Fisher, Jacqueline Fox, Carole Gainard, Claire Gallop, Janet Gibbs, Mary Haines, Susan Harvey, Susan Hurford, Pamela Kelly, Jane Mattfield, Angela Nash, Joyce Neale, Margaret Nicholas, Rose Marie Nussbaum, Sophie Nussbaum, Kathleen O'Toole, Judith Owen, Pat Phillips, Hazel Phippen, Hilary Poley, Dorothy Pollard, Ann Price, Valerie Price, Yvonne Purnell, Hazel Robinson, Josephine Roper, Merle Russell, Jane Seward, Lesley Sheppard, Victoria Skuse, Helen Smallcombe, Caroline Stone, Kathleen Tugwell, Jeanette Vale, Bernice Vicars, Christine Vicary, Gillian Vlaeminke, Ann Webb, Moya Webb, Pamela Webley, Elaine Wills.

UNION OF EDUCATIONAL INSTITUTIONS
SECONDARY SCHOOL CERTIFICATE

C. Allen, C. Cherry, K. Derham, M. Derrick, R. Harvey, A. James, B. McKenzie, J. Perrington, D. Pike, M. Rees, D. Rogers, P. Sheppard, D. Shortman, R. Tugwell, N. Weston, R. White.

Jennifer Bayton, Marlene Bealey, Christine Cooper, Myrna Endicott, Susan Granfield, Mary Haines, Hilary Ham, Valerie Hawkins, Pamela Kelly, Dawn Pippard, Victoria Skuse, Janet Spear, Pauline Stafford, Yvonne Turner, Moya Webb, Anita Williams, Rosemary Yeandle.

SUBJECT PRIZES

FORM VI

English	...	...	...	Hazel Robinson.*
Art	...	...	...	Patricia Bambury.
				Jocelyn Shearman.
Human Biology ...	...	...	Hazel Robinson.

FORM VA

English Language	...	...	...	R. Nation.
English Literature	...	...	...	Caroline Stone.
History	...	...	...	R. Long.
Geography	...	...	...	B. Cook.
Religious Knowledge	...	...	...	Janet Gibbs.
French	...	...	...	Helen Smallcombe.
German	...	...	...	T. Dark.
Latin	...	...	...	M. Summers.
Biology	...	...	...	Mavis Barnett.
Chemistry	...	...	...	T. Dark.
Physics	...	...	...	M. Summers.
Mathematics	...	...	...	B. Cook.
Art	...	...	...	Jane Seward.
Music	...	...	...	E. Pavey.
Woodwork	...	...	...	J. Parker.
Metalwork	...	...	...	R. Davis.
Domestic Subjects	...	...	...	Mavis Barnett.

FORM VB

English	...	...	...	Pamela Kelly.
Mathematics	...	...	...	R. White.
Commercial Subjects	...	...	Valerie Hawkins.
Woodwork	...	...	...	D. Rogers.
Science	...	...	...	P. Knight.

FORM PRIZES

Form Vb1	...		K. Derham	Yvonne Turner
Form Vb 2	...		R. Harvey	Susan Granfield
			P. Sheppard	Myrna Endicott
Form IVa1	...		I. Gilham	Gillian Vlaeminke
			R. Hardwell	Claire Gallop
Form IVa2	...		A. Gilbert	Marcyl Barton
			F. Woodcock	Jennifer Burgess
Form IVb1	...		R. Crawford	Diane Hart
			R. Mead	Lorraine Mead
Form IVb2	...		R. King	Diane Farrell
Form IVg	...		J. Miles	Diane Davies

63

One pupil remembers that every Christmas there was a special Post Box placed in the foyer for internal postage of Christmas cards.

We also have the programme from the 1960 Christmas Concert of Acting and Singing.

CAROL SINGING

Accompanied by the School Orchestra.
Leader: Miriam Pavey.   Conductor: J. B. Coleshaw.

-oOo-

39. Once in Royal David's City.
       (v. 4 Junior Choir   v. 5 Senior Choir)

36. O come, all ye Faithful.
       (v. 3 Senior Choir   v. 4 Junior Choir)

255. God rest you merry, gentlemen.
       (vv. 1, 2 and 3 Junior Choir   v. 7 All)

266. The First Nowell.
       (v. 4 Senior Choir)

257. In Dulci Jubilo.   The Senior Choir.

       Christians Awake!   The Junior Choir.

38. While shepherds watched their flocks.

       How far is it to Bethlehem? Senior Choir.

37. Hark! the herald angels sing.

45. As with gladness men of old.

The Wakefield Shepherds' Play

1st Shepherd	Derek Reaves
2nd Shepherd	Mark Wilson
3rd Shepherd	Robin Williams
Mak, the sheep stealer	Alan Robinson
Gill, Mak's wife	Judith Halliday
Angel	Mary Cadblin
Mary	Pat Callop
Joseph	Martyn Purnell

SCENE: The Moor near Wakefield and
              sometimes in Mak's house.

STAGE MANAGEMENT	Lis Pollit and Juliet Green
LIGHTING	Mr. Blackmore, Ronald Richards, Alan Hayward
COSTUMES	Mrs. Savage
MAKE UP	Mr. Bryant
MUSIC	Mr. Coleshaw

A MUMMERS' PLAY

This is an old, traditional play, performed by the
villagers for the local gentry.

LIST OF CHARACTERS

FATHER CHRISTMAS   J. R. ROBERTS

PAGE   A. PEARSON

TURKISH KNIGHT   H. CHASEY

ST. GEORGE   T. SHORT

DOCTOR   B. ROGERS

JERRY DOUT   A. HORWOOD

BEELZEBUB   R. ELLWAY

JACK FINNEY   D. BAGGS

and introducing by popular request . . .

D. RAGOW-BOLD
(by kind permission of his wife)

Freely adapted from a play by AVON
Produced by Knight and Day
Mr. Chasey's cigarettes by ABDULLAH
Mr. Baggs appears by permission of
SWINDON BOWLING CLUB.
Wigs by B.....D of MAYFAIR.

The following photos of the staff Mummers Play were supplied by Mr Roberts.

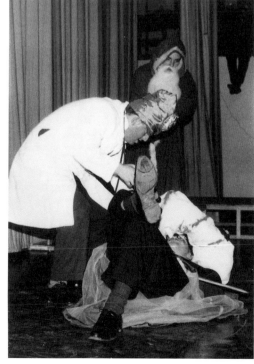

As pupils we did not see Dr Perry very often. He would appear on the stage at assemblies, a stately figure, wearing his academic gown. One pupil has described him as *"a remote god-like figure"*; we were rather in awe of him. When we were in the final year of school we would be invited to have lunch with him and a few other pupils in his study! We all found it a rather terrifying prospect but actually he was very kind to us and took an interest in our lives and future plans. One pupil still has her lunch invitation.

The Headmaster requests the

pleasure of the company of

...*h....Garland*.....

at lunch on Thursday

...*2...3...6.1*....

in his study.

R.S.V.P.

The local press carried an article on the 24 November 1961 School Prizegiving – reproduced below

Even at times of dispute, teachers always put their pupils first, Dr. R. Perry, headmaster of Hengrove School, said yesterday.

Speaking at the school's annual prize-giving last night, he said: "May I remind you that all through the dispute, the great majority of teachers continued to put the interests of their pupils first."

The word overtime did not exist in teachers' vocabulary.

"The man who produces a school play must be prepared to give perhaps 130 hours of his time during the autumn term."

The man or woman who takes children to camp must be on duty for 16 hours a day. The games staff and helpers give up Saturday mornings, their lunch hours and early evening.

No teacher, he said, could be compelled to do these things.

"Yet at Hengrove and at thousands of other schools, there are always men and women found to do these things, not for payment, but for the satisfaction they get from them."

The young teacher had the same spirit of service. "There is no danger of the old standards deteriorating."

Dr. Perry thanked parents who "do not send their sons and daughters to school wearing the more extreme teenage fashions."

This year, the school's first pupils had left for university and training college.

It was an important event as it showed pupils who had the necessary ability and would work could complete a full General Certificate course in a comprehensive school and pass on to institutes of higher education.

The results at "A" level, while not remarkable, were encouraging. Thirteen certificates were gained on 24 subject passes. At G.C.E. Ordinary level, 93 pupils passed.

Prizes were presented by Mr. Richard Ainley, Principal of the Old Vic Training School.

Prize-winners

Subject prizes—Patricia Rosser, Ann Richards, David Summers, Colin Birt (2), Sally Hedges (3), Duncan Neagle, Paul Stradling, Jennifer Burgess, Michael Thomas, Alan Ferrier, Gillian Vlaeminke (4), Hilary Poley, Frank Woodcock, Roger Hardwell (2), Jennifer Dyer, Elizabeth Payne, Pauline Dutton, Richard Mead, Lorraine Mead, Trevor Goverd, Roger Kempson, Richard Crawford.

Form prizes—Richard Crawford, Barry Gitsham, Stewart Massey, David Ford, Kenneth Sealey, Andrew Young, David Dowling, Dennis Babey, Paul Rupprecht, Roger Salter, Clive Davis, Margaret Hazzard, Susan Cocking, Ruth Cowley, Sheila Richards, Ann Spreadborough, Hazel Coventry, Lynne Brunyee, Janet Griffin, Jennifer Wyatt, Jennifer Kenna, Jacqueline Davis.

Special awards—Catherine Hewitt, Elizabeth Pollitt, Claire Gallop, David Summers, Jacqueline Fox, Diane Burt, Susan Tyrell.

Head boy's prize—David Summers; head girl's prize—Sally Hedges.

House awards—cricket, Sparta; hockey, Thebes; netball, Thebes; athletics cup Argos; athletics bowl, Olympia.

Duke of Edinburgh Award (gold standard)—N. Wallington, E. Pavey.

PUPILS ARE TOP PRIORITY SAYS HEAD

JACQUELINE FOX, head girl of Hengrove School, receives her award at the school prize-giving from Mr. R. Ainley, principal of the Old Vic Theatre School. Watching are (left to right) Dr. R. Perry (headmaster), Ald. F. G. W. Chamberlain (chairman the governors), Cllr. W. A. Bush and Miss G. A. Martin (senior mistress).

We have the Programme. Note that there were 13 students who passed 24 'A' Level G.C.E subjects between them. They had been in the first intake into the school in 1954. At 'O' Level there were 93 students who passed at least one subject and the UEI Secondary School Certificate had 21 student passes.

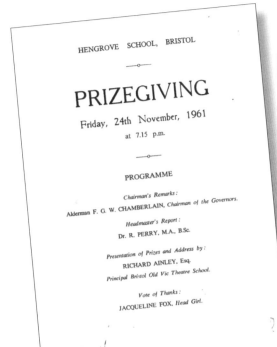

HENGROVE SCHOOL, BRISTOL

—o—

PRIZEGIVING

Friday, 24th November, 1961

at 7.15 p.m.

—o—

PROGRAMME

Chairman's Remarks:
Alderman F. G. W. CHAMBERLAIN, *Chairman of the Governors.*

Headmaster's Report:
Dr. R. PERRY, M.A., B.Sc.

Presentation of Prizes and Address by:
RICHARD AINLEY, Esq.
Principal Bristol Old Vic Theatre School.

Vote of Thanks:
JACQUELINE FOX, *Head Girl.*

SPECIAL AWARDS

Librarian Prize	Catherine Hewitt, Elizabeth Pollitt
Sports Prize	Claire Gallop
Sports Prize	David Summers
Orchestra Prize	Jacqueline Fox
Prize for Perseverance	Diane Burt
Prize for Perseverance	Susan Tyrell
HEAD BOY'S PRIZE	David Summers
HEAD GIRL'S PRIZE	Sally Hedges

HOUSE AWARDS

House Cricket Cup	Sparta
House Hockey Cup	Thebes
House Netball Cup	Thebes
House Athletics Cup	Argos
House Athletics Bowl	Olympia

DUKE OF EDINBURGH AWARD

Gold Standard: N. Wallington, E. Pavey.

PRIZE LIST
SOUTHERN UNIVERSITIES' JOINT BOARD
GENERAL CERTIFICATE OF EDUCATION AT ADVANCED LEVEL.

C. Bennett	Physics.
C. Birt	English Literature, French, German.
D. Butcher	English Literature, History.
M. Hutton	Geography.
D. Neagle	Geography, Mathematics.
D. Summers	English Literature, Geography, Music.
R. Townsend	Geography.
M. Woolaway	Biology, Chemistry.
Lesley Bright	English Literature.
Sally Hedges	Biology, Chemistry, Physics.
Ann Richards	English Literature, History.
Patricia Rosser	English Literature, French.
Jocelyn Shearman	English Literature.

GENERAL CERTIFICATE OF EDUCATION AT ORDINARY LEVEL.

R. Adams, C. Ash, G. Ayers, R. Chappell, R. Cheek, R. Clatworthy, R. Clegg, S. Cook, R. Crago, R. Crawford, R. Culverhouse, C. Davies, P. Ellis, A. Ferrier, D. Ford, A. Gilbert, I. Gilham, B. Gitsham, T. Goverd, M. Hales, R. Hardwell, C. Hinton, M. Jennings, R. Joliffe, R. Kempson, P. King, K. Ladd, D. Massey, S. Massey, R. Mead, C. Senior, P. Stradling, M. Thomas, N. Wallington, F. Woodcock, D. Woodruff.

Patricia Baker, Marcyl Barton, Sally Bennett, Jennifer Burgess, Diane Burt, Susan Cocking, Rosamund Coleman, Carol Coles, Ruth Cooper, Ruth Cowley, Ruth Dalling, Esmé Dayment, Margaret Dixon, Pauline Dutton, Jennifer Dyer, Claire Gallop, Carol Garland, Ann Goulstone, Janet Gray, Juliet Green, Kerstin Handley, Margaret Hazzard, Geraldine Helps, Janet Hooper, Arlene Hucker, Diane Jakeway, Patricia Long, Janice Mabey, Anne McNamara, Lorraine Mead, Jennifer Miller, Margaret Munro, Angela Nash, Rosemarie Nussbaum, Eileen O'Connell, Judith Owen, Andrea Paul, Hazel Phippen, Hilary Poley, Anne Price, Gabrielle Remnant, Sheila Richards, Joy Sanders, Janet Sawyer, Heather Scotland, Valerie Sellick, Jennifer Selwood, Hilary Sheppard, Rosemary Silk, Ann Spreadborough, Caroline Stone, Sally Summerhayes, Gladys Sweet, Gillian Vlaeminke, Angela Wiggins, Ruth Williams, Christine Withers.

UNION OF EDUCATIONAL INSTITUTIONS
SECONDARY SCHOOL CERTIFICATE.

R. Clatworthy, R. Crawford, C. Davies, R. Hardwell, R. Jay, R. Kempson, K. Ladd, M. Livingstone, R. Mead, P. Mellor, P. Nott, B. O'Connell, C. Priddle, P. Stradling

Ann Curry, Pauline Dutton, Margaret Hazzard, Lorraine Mead, Elizabeth Payne, Sally Summerhayes, Susan Tyrell.

SUBJECT PRIZES
Form VI.

English Literature	Patricia Rosser
History	Ann Richards
Geography	David Summers
French	Colin Birt
German	Colin Birt
Biology	Sally Hedges
Chemistry	Sally Hedges
Physics	Sally Hedges
Mathematics	Duncan Neagle
Music	David Summers

Form VA

English Language	Paul Stradling
English Literature	Jennifer Burgess
History	Michael Thomas
Geography	Alan Ferrier
French	Gillian Vlaeminke
German	Gillian Vlaeminke
Biology	Hilary Poley
Chemistry	Frank Woodcock
Mathematics	Roger Hardwell
Art	Gillian Vlaeminke
Music	Gillian Vlaeminke
Woodwork	Roger Hardwell
Domestics Subjects	Jennifer Dyer

Form VB

English	Elizabeth Payne
	Pauline Dutton
Mathematics	Richard Mead
Commercial Subjects	Lorraine Mead
Woodwork	Trevor Goverd
Science	Roger Kempson
Metalwork	Richard Crawford

FORM PRIZES

Form VA	Richard Crawford	Margaret Hazzard
Form IVA1	Barry Gitsham	Susan Cocking
	Stewart Massey	Ruth Cowley
Form IVA2	David Ford	Sheila Richards
	Kenneth Sealey	Ann Spreadborough
Form IVA3	Andrew Young	Hazel Coventry
	David Dowling	Lynne Brunyee
Form IVB1	Dennis Baber	Janet Griffin
	Paul Rupprecht	Jennifer Wyatt
Form IVB2	Roger Salter	Jennifer Kenna
Form IVG	Clive Davis	Jacqueline Davis

We have the handbill for the December 1961 production of "The Diary of Anne Frank", photos and the programme. It is thought that Juliet Green went on to realise her ambition to become a professional actress – can anyone confirm this?

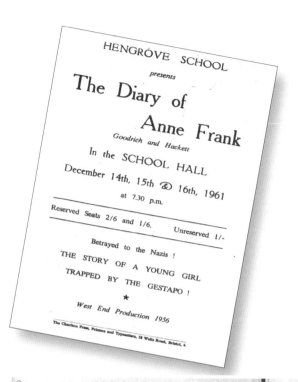

HENGROVE SCHOOL

presents

The Diary of Anne Frank

Goodrich and Hackett

In the SCHOOL HALL

December 14th, 15th & 16th, 1961

at 7.30 p.m.

Reserved Seats 2/6 and 1/6.   Unreserved 1/-

Betrayed to the Nazis !

THE STORY OF A YOUNG GIRL TRAPPED BY THE GESTAPO !

★

West End Production 1956

The Charlton Press, Printers and Typesetters, 28 Wells Road, Bristol, 4.

2

THE DIARY OF

dramatised by

Persons in the play

MR. OTTO FRANK	MICHAEL HARRISON
MIEP GIES	JUDY BRATBY
MRS. VAN DAAN	JENNIFER SELWOOD
MR. VAN DAAN	MICHAEL DYER
PETER VAN DAAN	BARRY GITSHAM
MRS. EDITH FRANK	CATHERINE HEWITT
MARGOT FRANK	SUZANNE ABBOTT
ANNE FRANK	JULIET GREEN
MR. KRALER	STEPHEN MEAD
MR. DUSSEL	DAVID WATKINS

Directed by Geoffrey Andrews

Associate Producers

ANGELA NASH and HILARY POLEY

Setting by Peter Bioletti

assisted by

ROSEMARY SELLICK and JILL VEVERS

3

ANNE FRANK

Goodrich and Hackett.

There will be ONE interval. Refreshments will be available in the Dining Hall.

The action of the play passes in the top floors of a WAREHOUSE in AMSTERDAM, HOLLAND.

The first scene shows Anne Frank's father re-visiting the hide-out where during the last war he, his family and friends spent 25 months, to escape almost certain death at the hands of the Gestapo. The words of Ann's Diary, which he finds in the attic, take us back to reveal a picture of their lives.

The SET was constructed in the School Workshops under the Direction of D. Whittock, and Executed by Ian Stoate, Michael Tate and John Ashford.

Help given by the Theatre Royal, King Street, is gratefully acknowledged.

MUSIC, taken from the Symphony No. 7 "Leningrad" by Shostakovich, suggested by J. D. Colesha.

SPECIAL EFFECTS devised by H. G. Roberts, Angela Nash and Hilary Poley.

MAKE-UP created by I. A. Bryant, and Executed by C. Hellings, A. Jones, J. Bennett, T. Short, Pat Ford, Shiela Richards, Liz. Pollitt, Margaret Munro, Janet Freeman, Lesley Perrott.

DECOR.
    Christine Purnell, Carolyn Poulton, Pat Frost.

STAGE DIRECTORS

Ivor A. Bryant and H. Gareth Roberts

ASSISTANT STAGE MANAGERS

Keith Scribbins, Christopher Kear, Alan Robinson, Colin Holt Phillip Troft, David Harrison, Roger Chappell, Andrea Bowery Nigel Wallington.

LIGHTING

Robert Wynne, Richard Culverhouse, Stuart Cook, Stewart Mass

AMPLIFICATION

A. B. Blackmore, Peter Sands, Terry Wilson, David Holliday, Geraldine Helps.

BUSINESS MANAGEMENT

J. Bunce and W. T. Cork

BOX OFFICE

Hazel Coventry, Lynne Brunyee, Jane Peters, Carol Cole, Judith Orme, Denise Truscott, Carol Harrhy, Barbara Selway, Valerie Phillips, Julia Nash, Geraldine Hooper, Lorna Rebou Caroline Thompson, Janet Griffen.

FRONT OF HOUSE

M. Adams, E. Arnold, D. Clarke, D. Dowling, R. Hearring, L. Rogers, J. Price, B. Spindler, A. Young.

CATERING

Organised by L. Wood and P. Gelling and assisted by John Golding, Robin Williams, Peter Bateman, Graham Batchel For the Cast, Tony Ball.

Previous Productions

A Midsummer Night's Dream 1957

Macbeth 1958

Twelfth Night 1959

Tobias and the Angel 1960

School Trips outside of Bristol or abroad were an annual highlight of the summer term or vacation. We have a photo of the 1961 trip to Blenheim Palace led by Mr Roberts, Mr E Bromwich and other staff. Mr Roberts recalls:

"A train was chartered to take the whole of the 1st and 2nd pupils to Blenheim Palace. One boy fell in the River Thames which is quite wide at that point. When asked what happened he said 'I didn't see it!'"

Former pupil Carol Garland remembers her trip to Paris led by Mr Bewley, Mr Buckland and others in April 1958 – here are her photos.

We also have a copy of the itinerary for the annual trip to Switzerland in Summer 1962. Some of our readers may have been on the trip.

Tuesday - 21st August 1962.

Meet at Temple Meads (under the clock)	10.40 a.m.
Arrive Paddington (London)	1.36 p.m.
Depart Victoria	approx. 3.00 p.m.
Depart Folkestone	" 6.00 p.m.
Depart Boulogne (France)	" 9.00 p.m.
Arrive Bale (Breakfast)	" 7.30 a.m.
Depart Bale (Switzerland)	" 9.25 a.m.
Arrive Interlaken	" 12.32 p.m.

Wednesday - 29th August 1962

Depart Interlaken	evening.
Depart Bale	late evening.
Depart Calais or Boulogne	during the morning.
Arrive Folkestone	about mid-day.
Arrive Victoria	about tea-time.
Depart Paddington	6.45 p.m.
Arrive Bristol (Thurs.Aug.30th)	9.04 p.m.

To help us to get to know each other

Mr.& Mrs.Bewley
Miss Bewley
Mr.& Mrs.Fletcher

Lorraine Anstey	(3A2)	Roger Bailey	(3B2)
Carol Baker	(2A1)	Keith Ckark	(2A2)
Jean Bevan	(2G1)	Anthony Contoy	(3B2)
Sheila Brain	(2B1)	Peter Edwards	(4B2)
Hazel Derrick	(2B1)	William Fletcher	
Denise Dwyer	(5B2)	Christopher Gibbs	(2G1)
Susan Dwyer	(2B2)	David Hoskins	(2A2)
Christine George	(2A2)	Malcolm Hathway	(2B1)
Angela Graves	(2B2)	John King	(3B2)
Gillian Guest	(2B2)	Lawson Page	(4B3)
Lynda Harris	(2G1)	Raymond Pike	(2B1)
Carol Harvey	(2B1)	Barry Russell	(2B2)
Barbara Hoyle	(2A2)	Michael Sennett	(4B3)
Hazel Johnson	(3A2)	Allen Spear	(4B3)
Geraldine Meikle	(2A1)	Thomas Thomas	(2B1)
Carolyn Paulton	(4B1)	Roger Thompson	(2A2)
Julia Price	(2B1)	Robin Williams	(3A1)
Brenda Rogers	(3A2)		
Susan Trevillion	(5B2)		
Trudy Watts	(2A1)		

We shall visit as many as possible of the following places:-

Bâle (or Basel) - an international railway junction on the River Rhine. We arrive at a French platform and make our way for breakfast to a Swiss platform. There is also a German station in another part of the town.

Murren - a mountain resort overlooking the Lauterbrunnen Valley.

Lake Thun - the lake nearest to our hotel.

Thun - the town at the other end of Lake Thun.

Spiez - a little town on Lake Thun.

Lake Brienz - the other lake.

Brienz - where the wood carving is done.(Notice the carved sign posts).

Harder - our nearest mountain.

Niesen - the pointed mountain! to the west.

Interlaken - a little town, situated on the River Aare, between Lakes Thun and Brienz.

The Jungfrau - the mountain that you see in the south. At sunset, the snow seems to turn pink. We shall visit it by the highest railway station in Europe.

Kleine Scheidegg - the little railway junction on the way to the Jungfrau.

Grindelwald - the glacier village on the way back from the Jungfrau.

Rothorn - the mountain on the northern shore of Lake Brienz.

Schynigge Platte - the mountain to the right, looking from the entrance of Hotel Krone.

Niederhorn - the mountain overlooking Lake Thun, opposite the Niesen. The summit is reached by very original means!

The Three Passes - this all day excursion will take us over the Grimsel, Furka and Susten Passes. One of the sights is the Rhone Glacier, the source of the River Rhone, which runs across Switzerland, through Lake Geneva, and then southward through France to the Mediterranean Sea. You will also see the entrance to the St.Gotthard Tunnel.

Trummelbach Falls - these falls are inside a mountain, a couple of miles beyond Lauterbrunnen.

We have received a number of items regarding the 1962 November Prizegiving. For the first time, three students passed GCE 'A' Levels at scholarship level – all scientists. Fifteen students took 'A' Levels and achieved 36 passes – some with Distinction. At 'O' Level there were 115 candidates achieving one or more passes. The Union of Educational Institutions (U.E.I) Secondary School Certificate boasted 35 pupil entries. For the first time the programme included an impressive list of University and Training College entrants – 18 in all. The programme is reproduced below.

HENGROVE SCHOOL, BRISTOL

—o—

PRIZEGIVING

Tuesday, 20th November, 1962

at 7.30 p.m.

—o—

PROGRAMME

Chairman's Remarks :
Alderman F. G. W. CHAMBERLAIN, *Chairman of the Governors.*

Headmaster's Report :
Dr. R. PERRY, M.A., B.Sc.

Presentation of Prizes and Certificates by :
THE SHERIFF'S LADY (Mrs. Stanley W. Evans).

Address by :
THE SHERIFF OF BRISTOL (Stanley W. Evans, Esq., O.B.E., J.P.)

Vote of Thanks by :
GILLIAN VLAEMINKE, *Head Girl.*

PRIZE LIST
SOUTHERN UNIVERSITIES' JOINT BOARD
GENERAL CERTIFICATE OF EDUCATION AT
SCHOLARSHIP LEVEL

Brian Cook	Physics.
Thomas Dark	Chemistry, Physics.
Michael Summers	Chemistry, Physics.

ADVANCED LEVEL

Brian Cook	Physics (Distinction) Pure Mathematics, Applied Mathematics (Distinction).
Thomas Dark	Chemistry, Physics, Pure and Applied Mathematics (Distinction).
David Harrison	English Literature.
Roger Martin	Chemistry, Physics, Pure and Applied Mathematics.
Eric Pavey	English Literature, Geography, Art.
Michael Summers	Chemistry, Physics, Pure and Applied Mathematics.
Philip Trott	History, Geography, German.
Nigel Wallington	Geography.
Martin Woolaway	Biology, Physics.
Jacqueline Fox	English Literature, History, French.
Susan Hurford	Domestic Subjects.
Jane Mattfield	Botany, Zoology, Chemistry.
Angela Nash	English Literature, History.
Caroline Stone	English Literature, History, French.
Jeanette Vale	Physics, Pure Mathematics.

ORDINARY LEVEL

M. Adams, R. Adams, E. Arnold, C. Ashley, R. Ashley, G. Ayers, G. Banwell, S. Barnes, A. Barratt, M. Brewer, R. Cheek, P. Chivers, J. Clark, P. Click, S. Cook, D. Corlett, C. Critchley, A. Davis, D. Dowling, M. Dyer, D. Ford, B. Gitsham, R. Green, M. Hales, I. Hampton, R. Harding, D. Hull, M. Jennings, R. Joliffe, C. Kear, P. King, C. Law, E. Lovell, K. Lovell, D. Lucas, D. Massey, S. Massey, B. Pearson, L. Rogers, P. Rupprecht, K. Scribbens, K. Sealey, C. Senior, D. Smith, D. Tayler, D. Warner, P. Wayborn, D. Whitnell, D. Woodruff, A. Young.

Patricia Baker, Maureen Battcock, Sally Bennett, Judith Bratby, Heather Brooks, Judith Brown, Ann Chamberlain, Barbara Christie, Susan Cocking, Rosamund Coleman, Carol Coles, Hazel Coventry, Ruth Cowley, Ruth Dalling, Esmé Dayment, Maureen Drewitt, Patricia Ford, Janet Freeman, Angela Gale, Ann Goulstone, Lesley Graham, Juliet Green, Jane Hall, Kerstin Handley, Geraldine Helps, Janet Hooper, Arlene Hucker, Dianne Jakeway, Patricia Kemp, Joy Legge, Christine Lewis, Bernette Limbrick, Marion Lock, Patricia Long, Janice Mabey, Patricia Massey, Margaret Munro, Julie Nash, Pamela Nicholls, Jane Nutt,. Eileen O'Connell, Judith Orme, Andrea Paul, Lesley Perrett, Elizabeth Pollitt, Sheila Richards, Carolyn Roberts, Patricia Rowe, Joy Sanders, Janet Sawyer, Barbara Selway, Jill Seward, Hilary Sheppard, Christine Snell, Ann Spreadborough, Janet Stewart, Gladys Sweet, Margaret Tanner, Marilyn Townsend, Denise Truscott, Susan Watts, Angela Wiggins, Pamela Williams, Ruth Williams, Jennifer Wise.

UNION OF EDUCATIONAL INSTITUTIONS
SECONDARY SCHOOL CERTIFICATE.

M. Adams, E. Arnold, F. Bright, D. Clark, A. Davis, D. Dowling, M. Dyer, D. Hull, J. Price, L. Rogers, D. Smith, A. Young, Lynne Brunyee, Hazel Coventry, Christine Crew, Denise Dwyer, Janet Griffin, Carole Harrhy, Catherine Hewitt, Geraldine Hooper, Maureen Husbands, Angela Jones, Elizabeth Lewis, Julia Nash, Judith Orme, Jane Peters, Elizabeth Pollitt, Jean Pye, Lorne Rebouse, Pamela Rogers, Barbara Selway, Caroline Thompson, Susan Trevillion, Denise Truscott, Jennifer Wyatt.

SUBJECT PRIZES
Form VI.

English Literature	Caroline Stone
History	Caroline Stone
Geography	Philip Trott
French	Caroline Stone
German	Philip Trott
Botany	Jane Mattfield
Zoology	Jane Mattfield
Chemistry	Thomas Dark
Physics	Brian Cook
Science	Michael Summers
Mathematics and Science	Roger Martin
Mathematics	Brian Cook, Thomas Dark.
	Michael Summers
Art	Eric Pavey
Domestic Subjects	Susan Hurford

Form Va

English Language	Pamela Williams
English Literature	Susan Cocking
History	Pamela Williams
Geography	Ruth Cowley
Latin	Susan Cocking
French	Philip King
German	Philip King
Religious Knowledge	Gladys Sweet
Biology	Rosamund Coleman
Chemistry	Stewart Massey
Physics	David Ford
Mathematics	David Ford
Art	Juliet Green
Music	Susan Cocking
Metalwork	Richard Cheek
Domestic Subjects	Janet Stewart

Form Vn

English	Pamela Rogers
Mathematics	Ronald Green
Commercial Subjects	Barbara Selway
Science	Susan Trevillion
Woodwork	David Dowling
Metalwork	Richard Waite

74

FORM PRIZES

Form VB1	Leslie Rogers	Barbara Selway
Form VB2	Paul Rupprecht	Maureen Husbands
Form IVA1	David Lucas	Susan Watts
	Geoffrey Wetton	Bridget Toole
Form IVA2	Keith Scribbens	Valerie Smith
	Alan Dawe	Carol Wride
Form IVA3	David Whitnell	Sheila Evans
	David Weston	Lesley Graham
Form IVB1	Walter Stimson	Rita Povey
	Peter Haydon	Christine Tungatt
Form IVB2	David Bennett	Elizabeth Hatch
	John Shore	Lynda Coombes
Form IVB3	Michael Sennett	Marian Smith
	David Butler	Jacqueline Sanford
Form IVB4	David James	Denise Domaille

SPECIAL AWARDS

Librarian Prize	Keith Scribbens
Sports Prize	Marcyl Barton
Sports Prize	Nigel Wallington
Orchestra Prize	Gillian Vlaeminke
Prize for Perseverance	David Dowling
Drama Prize	Juliet Green and Barry Gitsham
HEAD BOY'S PRIZE	Michael Summers
HEAD GIRL'S PRIZE	Jacqueline Fox

DUKE OF EDINBURGH AWARD

Gold Standard : John Miller.

HOUSE AWARDS

House Cricket Cup—Sparta	House Hockey Cup—Sparta
House Athletics Cup—Sparta	House Athletics Bowl—Argos
House Netball Cup—Thebes	

UNIVERSITY AND TRAINING COLLEGE ENTRANTS

1961   Sally Hedges—Royal Free Hospital, London University.
David Butcher—St. John's College, York.
Ann Richards—Avery Hill College, London.
Patricia Rosser—Goldsmiths' College, London.
David Summers—St. Luke's College, Exeter.
Robin Townsend—St. Luke's College, Exeter.

1962   Brian Cook—Leicester University.
Thomas Dark—Leicester University.
Jane Mattfield—Nottingham University.
Caroline Stone—Hull University.
Michael Summers—Birmingham University.
Jacqueline Fox—St. Katharine's College, Liverpool.
Susan Hurford—St. Osyth's College, Clacton-on-Sea.
Jocelyn Shearman—High Melton Hall, Doncaster.
Nigel Wallington—St. Luke's College, Exeter.
Roger Martin—Bristol College of Science and Technology.
Eric Pavey—Bristol College of Science and Technology.
Jeanette Vale—Bristol College of Science and Technology.

The Western Daily Press carried this article headed "11 – plus Must Go, Says Head." Dated 21/11/62 .

We have photos of the audience, both pupils and parents and an Invitation Card.

11 - plus must go, says head

Western Daily Press Reporter

Dr. Reginald Perry, head-master of Hengrove School, Bristol, is looking forward to the day when the 11-plus examination is banned.

He said at last night's prize-giving that he was not satisfied that the school was getting the best out of children who had failed the examination, although G.C.E. and U.E.I. examination results were good.

Boys and girls who failed the 11-plus started off with the discouragement of failure.

"Many of them have been wrongly labelled, and there are still teachers who—subconsciously perhaps—still attach importance to the label," said Dr. Perry.

"It will be a good day for the children when we can abolish this examination.

"Even then we shall be faced with the problems presented by children of good ability who have been late developing, or for some reason have remained uninterested in school work.

"There is, I am sure, a reservoir of talent here which we have only begun to tap."

A winning failure

Dr. Perry said one of the sixth-formers who had gained a university place had years ago failed the 11-plus.

Guest of honour was the Sheriff of Bristol, Mr. Stanley Evans. Mrs. Evans presented the following prizes:

SUBJECT PRIZES: Caroline Stone (3), Philip Trott (2), Jane Mattfield (2), Thomas Dark (2), Brian Cook (2), Michael Summers (2), Roger Martin, Eric Pavey, Susan Hurford.

Pamela Williams (2), Susan Cocking (3), Ruth Cowley, Philip King (2), Gladys Sweet, Rosamund Coleman, Stewart Massey, David Ford (2), Juliet Green, Richard Cheek, Janet Stewart.

Pamela Rogers, Ronald Green, Barbara Selway, Susan Trevilion, David Dowling, Richard Waite.

FORM PRIZES: Leslie Rogers, Barbara Selway; Paul Rupprecht, Maureen Husbands; David Lucas, Susan Watts, Geoffrey Wetton, Bridget Toole; Keith Scribbens, Valerie Smith, Alan Dawe, Carol Wride; David Whitnell, Sheila Evans, David Weston, Lesley Graham; Walter Stimson, Rita Povey, Peter Haydon, Christine Tungatt; David Bennet, Elizabeth Hatch, John Shore, Lynda Coombes; Michael Sennett, Marian Smith, David Butler, Jacqueline Sanford; David James, Denise Domaille.

SPECIAL AWARDS: Keith Scribbens, Marcyl Barton, Nigel Wallington, Gillian Vlaeminke, David Dowling, Juliet Green, Barry Gitsham, Michael Summers, Jacqueline Fox.

HENGROVE SCHOOL

PRIZEGIVING

TUESDAY, 20th NOVEMBER, 1962
at 7.30 p.m. in School Hall
Presentation of Prizes by the Sheriff's Lady
(Mrs. Stanley W. Evans)
Address by the Sheriff of Bristol
(Stanley W. Evans, Esq., O.B.E., J.P.)

Admission by Ticket only.

The Bristol Evening Post also covered the Prizegiving – headed "Good day when it is goodbye to 11-plus – Head Speaks of Wrong Labels"

'HEAD SPEAKS OF WRONG LABELS'

Good day when it is good-bye to 11-plus

A Bristol head-master said last night it would be a good day for the children when the 11 - plus examination could be abolished.

Dr. Reginald Perry, head of Hengrove School, Bristol, said boys and girls who failed the 11-plus "start off with the discouragement of failure."

Many of them had been wrongly labelled, and there are still teachers who — subconsciously perhaps—still attach importance to the label.

Even after the abolition of the 11-plus they would be faced with the problems presented by children of good ability who had been late developing, or for some reason had remained uninterested in school work.

THE SHERIFF'S WIFE, Mrs. Stanley Evans presenting the orchestra prize to Gill Vlaeminke, head girl of Hengrove School. Also in the picture are (left to right), Sheriff, Michael Thomas (head boy), Dr. R. Perry (headmaster), Ald. F. G. Chamberlain (chairman of the governors) and Miss G. A. Martin (deputy head)

NOT SATISFIED

Dr. Perry said at last night's prize-giving that he was not satisfied that the school were getting the best out of children who had failed the exam — although G.C.E. and U.E.I. exam results were good.

"There is, I am sure, a reservoir of talent here which we have only begun to tap."

Dr. Perry said that one of the sixth formers who had gained a university place had years ago failed the 11-plus.

The U.E.I. secondary schools' examination had proved its value in providing a goal for children of good average ability who were prepared to stay on at school for an extra year.

"I wish more parents would recognise the fact that it is better to have a good secondary school certificate than a poor G.C.E.," said Dr Perry.

cnt'd.

A-LEVEL PASSES

Fifteen advanced level candidates had gained 36 passes, 42 fifth-formers had averaged four ordinary level passes each, and 17 who had once failed the 11-plus averaged three ordinary passes each.

Guest of honour was the Sheriff of Bristol, Mr. Stanley Evans, and Mrs. Evans presented the prizes

SUBJECT PRIZES: Caroline Stone (5), Jane Maitfield (5), Philip Trott (2), Brian Cook (2), Thomas Dark (3), Roger Martin, Michael Summers (2), Eric Pavey, Susan Hurford, Pamela Williams (2), Susan Cocking (3), Ruth Cowley, Philip King (2), Gladys Sweet, Rosamund Coleman, Stewart Massey, David Ford (2), Juliet Green, Richard Cheek, Janet Stewart, Pamela Rogers, Ronald Green, Barbara Selway, Susan Trevillon, David Dowling, Richard Waite.

FORM PRIZES: Leslie Rogers, Barbara Selway; Paul Rupprecht, Maureen Husbands; David Lucas, Susan Watts, Geoffrey Weston, Bridget Toole; Keith Scribbens, Valerie Smith, Alan Dawe, Carol Wride; David Whitnell, Sheila Evans, David Weston, Lesley Graham, Walter Stimson, Rita Povey, Peter Haydon, Christine Tungatt, David Bennet, Elizabeth Hatch, John Shore, Lynda Coombes; Michael Bennett, Marian Smith, David Butler, Jacqueline Sanford; David James, Denis Domaille.

SPECIAL AWARDS: Keith Scribbens, Maryel Barton, Nigel Wallington, Gillian Vlaeminke, David Dowling, Juliet Green, Barry Gitsham, Michael Summers, Jacqueline Fox.

77

The End of the Dr Perry Era

We come now to 1963/1964 the final academic year of Dr Perry's Headship. He would retire in March 1964 after nine years and two terms at the helm of the school, from its inception as a post-war experiment in bilateral/comprehensive education.

Miss Martin would retire from her position as Deputy Head in December 1963 – one term ahead of Dr Perry. She would be replaced by Mr Fletcher as Deputy Head and Miss Place as Senior Mistress.

We have below a photograph of the staff, now 48 in number, with Dr Perry and Miss Martin, taken in December 1963 immediately before Miss Martin retired.

Below are all the girl Prefects with Miss Martin in December 1963. Their names can be found in the "Prefect Roll Register" which will be deposited in the City Records Office.

The next photograph, also taken in December 1963, shows all the Prefects with Dr Perry and Miss Martin.

Dr Perry's final Prize Giving was postponed from Winter 1963 to January 1964. We have the programme which includes GCE 'O' and 'A' Level results, and UEI results. This exam would be replaced by the Certificate of Secondary Education CSE in 1965.

HENGROVE SCHOOL, BRISTOL

—o—

PRIZEGIVING

Friday, 31st January, 1964

at 7.30 p.m.

—o—

PROGRAMME

Chairman's Remarks:
Alderman F. G. W. CHAMBERLAIN, Chairman of the Governors.

Headmaster's Report:
Dr. R. PERRY, M.A., B.Sc.

Presentation of Prizes and Certificates by:
Mrs. G. H. MOORE.

Address by:
G. H. MOORE, Esq., M.Sc., F.P.S., F.R.I.C.
(Principal of the Bristol College of Science and Technology).

Vote of Thanks by:
BARRY GITSHAM, Head Boy.

FORM PRIZES

Form VB1	Robert Coates	Geraldine Turner
Form VB2	David Bennett	Christine Harris
Form VB3	Raymond Norville	Jane Francis
Form IVA1	Geoffrey Ferris	Carole Curtis
Form IVA2	Ronald Pring	Ann Gough
Form IVB1	Alan Jennings	Diane Morgan
Form IVB2	George Garland	Erica Smith
Form IVB3	James Mawer	Christine Witts
Form IVG	Terry Edwards	Mary Price

SPECIAL AWARDS

Librarian Prize	David Corlett
Sports Prize	Martin Lock and Marcyl Barton
Orchestra Prize	Miriam Pavey
Prize for Perseverance	Christine Rudd
"Heather Dennis" Music Prizes	Jane Hollely and Edward Allen
HEAD BOY'S PRIZE	Michael Thomas
HEAD GIRL'S PRIZE	Gillian Vlaeminke

DUKE OF EDINBURGH AWARD

Gold Standard   Gillian Vlaeminke

HOUSE AWARDS

Cricket Cup—Sparta	Hockey Cup—Sparta
Athletics Cup—Olympia	Netball Cup—Argos
Athletics Bowl—Sparta	Rounders—Olympia

UNIVERSITY AND TRAINING COLLEGE ENTRANTS

Carol Bacon—Bedford College, London University.
Sophie Nussbaum—Kirby College, Liverpool.
Angela Nash—Furzedown College, London.
Michael Thomas—Chester College.
Michael Whitfield—Bristol College of Science and Technology.
David Woodruff—Bristol College of Science and Technology.
Martin Woolaway—Brighton College of Technology.

PRIZE LIST

SOUTHERN UNIVERSITIES' JOINT BOARD
GENERAL CERTIFICATE OF EDUCATION.

ADVANCED LEVEL

Ian Clarkson	History.
Michael Thomas	History.
Frank Woodcock	Chemistry.
David Woodruff	Chemistry, Pure and Applied Mathematics (Distinction).
Hilary Poley	English Literature.
Jennifer Selwood	English Literature.
Gillian Vlaeminke	German.

ORDINARY LEVEL

C. Ashley, S. Barnes, G. Batchelor, D. Bennett, L. Bennett, M. Bennett, R. Bignell, A. Bridges, G. Blunsum, D. Carter, R. Cheek, J. Clark, R. Coates, B. Cooper, C. Critchley, W. Davies, A. Dawe, P. Edwards, G. Ferris, J. Gill, J. Golding, J. Gould, A. Gregg, C. Hamlen, P. Haydon, A. Hayward, P. Holliday, B. Hughes, D. Humphries, J. Iles, R. Jolliffe, B. Jones, R. Kays, C. Kear, A. Keen, T. Keevil, M. Law, M. Leigh, M. Lock, R. Long, E. Lovell, K. Lovell, D. Lucas, S. Lyons, B. Manning, T. Martyn, R. Matthews, S. Mead, M. Nussbaum, R. Osborne, B. Pearson, R. Pond, R. Pring, R. Richards, A. Robinson, P. Sams, K. Scribbens, J. Shore, M. Silvester, J. Spiller, W. Stimson, D. Tayler, S. Warfield, D. Warner, M. Warren, P. Wayborn, D. Weston, G. Wetton, A. Whitfield, D. Whitnell, R. F. Williams, R. K. Williams, M. Wilson.

Suzanne Abbot, Dolsie Ames, Linda Ashman, Janet Ballinger, Linda Blannin, Heather Brooks, Judith Brown, Susan Butler, Freda Casbolt, Ann Chamberlain, Barbara Collins, Pauline Cooke, Patricia Cooper, Carole Curtis, Christine Day, Christine Ellison, Sheila Evans, Patricia Ford, Elaine Forster, Janet Freeman, Patricia Frost, Angela Gale, Ann Gough, Ann Goulstone, Lesley Graham, Jane Hall, Christine Harris, Jacqueline Harris, Linda Harvey, Jeannette Haskins, Elizabeth Hatch, Heather Hawkes, Jane Hedges, Susan Hobbs, Ruth Ibbotson, Hazel Johnson, Patricia Kemp, Joy Legge, Susan Leonard, Christine Lewis, Marion Lock, Patricia Massey, Judith McNamara, Susan Muller, Pamela Nicholls, Jane Nutt, Miriam Pavey, Lynette Pease, Lesley Perrott, Elizabeth Pollitt, Rita Povey, Rosemary Rendall, Sheila Richards, Carolyn Roberts, Patricia Rowe, Gillian Rowlands, Christine Rudd, Yvonne Sandford, Jacqueline Sanford, Pauline Selway, Jean Shaddick, Christine Snell, Josephine Stenner, Janet Stewart, Rosemarie Stone, Margaret Tanner, Alison Taylor, Bridget Toole, Ann Vevers, Margaret Vlaeminke, Susan Watts, Carol Wride.

UNION OF EDUCATIONAL INSTITUTIONS
SECONDARY SCHOOL GROUP CERTIFICATE.

D. Bennett, D. Butler, R. Coates, W. Davies, D. Fry, J. Gill, J. Gould, C. Hamlen, P. Haydon, R. Howlett, D. Humphries, A. Keen, S. Manning, R. Morgan, R. Norville, J. Peer, B. Purnell, R. Richards, M. Rogers, P. Rogers, J. Shore, A. Spear, M. Spear, W. Stimson, J. Stokes, S. Warfield, A. Whitfield.

Dolsie Ames, Susan Butler, Christine Day, Christine Ellison, Jane Francis, Patricia Frost, Christine Harris, Elizabeth Hatch, Carolyn Oxley, Susan Pike, Susan Pocock, Rita Povey, Christine Purnell, Christine Rudd, Yvonne Sandford, Jacqueline Sanford, Christine Tungatt, Geraldine Turner.

SUBJECT CERTIFICATE

M. Bennett, P. Bevan, G. Blunsum, C. Brown, D. Carter, J. Clark, D. Corlett, A. Dawe, P. Edwards, J. Gillman, D. Lay, M. Lock, S. Lyons, L. Page, S. Poole, C. Pullinger, M. Tate, B. Walsh, D. Watkins, D. Weston, I. Whiting.

Margaret Clark, Pauline Cooke, Lynda Coombs, Jeannette Haskins, Susan Hobbs, Ruth Ibbotson, Carolyn Poulton, Rosemary Seymour, Margaret Shattock, Marion Smith, Jill Thompson, Janet Tustin.

SUBJECT PRIZES

Form VI.

Mathematics	David Woodruff
History	Ian Clarkson
English Literature	Hilary Poley

Form VA.

English Language	Carolyn Roberts
English Literature	Keith Scribbens
History	Keith Scribbens
Geography	Barry Pearson
French	Robert Pond
German	Christine Snell
Religious Knowledge	Lesley Graham
Chemistry	Christopher Kear
Biology	Barry Pearson
Physics	Barry Pearson
Mathematics	Raymond Williams
Art	Michael Leigh
Music	Derek Warner
Domestic Subjects	Miriam Pavey
Metalwork	Alan Dawe

Form VB.

English	Rita Povey
Mathematics	Robert Coates
Commercial Subjects	Susan Butler
Science	Christine Ellison
Woodwork	Walter Stimson
Metalwork	Roy Richards

80

Dr Perry gave his final report at this event. He pays tribute to the dedication of the staff, praises the Duke of Edinburgh Award Scheme and reflects on the changes in education, health and parental attitudes since the 1930's. He commends the comprehensive school for leading the way in discovering the powers of the average pupil. We reproduce the full text below which makes for interesting reading at the end of the first era of the school's life.

HEADMASTER'S REPORT FOR 1962 - 63

PRIZEGIVING - 31st JANUARY 1964

Mr. Chairman, Principal Moore, Governors, Parents and Pupils,

It is nearly ten years since Hengrove School was founded, and I have much pleasure in giving you a report on our continuing efforts to establish here a framework of comprehensive education that will enable boys and girls of widely differing abilities to find satisfaction and happiness in their development.

I must first refer to the loss the school has suffered in the retirement of Miss G. A. Martin, who had been Senior Mistress and Deputy Head since 1954. During all this time she has been responsible for the welfare and discipline of the girls, and her long experience and understanding of this have made her service to the school quite invaluable. This is reflected in the regard which old pupils and parents have for her, and I need hardly say how grateful I am for all she did here. We are glad to have her here with us this evening. Mr. Fletcher has been appointed Deputy Head, and Miss Place has succeeded Miss Martin as Senior Mistress.

We had fewer pupils than usual sitting for the 'A' level of the G.C.E. examination, because our entry in 1956 was a small one, with a lower level of ability. Our 6th form is growing, and the next few years should bring good results. Seven 6th form pupils have been accepted for University or Training College next autumn.

Our results at 'O' level of the examination were reasonably satisfactory. Seventy-two pupils from the 'A' forms gained passes in 288 subjects, an average of 4 per pupil. As they included many who had not passed the 11+ examination, they did very well. Twenty-six other pupils from the 'B' forms also obtained General Certificates in one, two or three subjects, and you will perhaps be surprised to learn that these included pupils who had actually been in 'backward' classes when they entered the school, and now have added one or two G.C.E. subjects to their very good U.E.I. certificates.

During the past five years 135 children who failed the 11+ examination have secured General Certificates, and some have gone on to University and Training College. It is not always realised that very few of our 'selected' pupils passed the 11+ with high enough marks to gain admission to Grammar Schools. Practically all our 'O' and 'A' level results have been achieved by pupils who would never have been accepted by the Grammar Schools, and this is true of all our comprehensive schools.

Sixty-seven pupils obtained Secondary School Certificates of the U.E.I.; 43 of them have full 'group' certificates, and the average number of passes obtained was seven. Next year this examination will be replaced by the Certificate of Secondary Education which will have a wider acceptance. It is being planned and controlled by teachers, who know the needs and abilities of their pupils, and it is therefore to be welcomed. It will be far more suitable than the G.C.E. for many pupils of the kind who have taken that examination in the past. The General Certificate 'O' level examination syllabuses have too often been drawn up to meet the needs of the small proportion of boys and girls who will go on to University; they are often too academic and in some instances are out of date.

By way of relief from their work in the classroom, we have provided for our pupils a wide variety of activities. Youth Hostel visits at week-ends and during the holidays have been enjoyed by many boys and girls, and there were school camps at Wareham and Crowcombe, as well as week-end training camps. Parties from the school visited Belgium and Switzerland, and a group of boys had a walking holiday in the Austrian mountains.

For the second year, we planned an 'Expedition Day' in the summer term, and practically the whole school went off in coaches to places of interest in the West of England and Wales.

We have been fortunate at Hengrove in having men and women in charge of Physical Education who have a real understanding of what is meant by that term. They have always been concerned to promote the health and well-being of our boys and girls, by teaching and by personal example. Games here are played for enjoyment and the development of skills and not just for the sake of winning. Coaching is never limited to the school teams, but is given freely to all our pupils. Perhaps because this is our policy, we have played games with a good deal of success. Last year, Hengrove won the Bristol Schools Rugby Cups, for both juniors and seniors, and the senior cup team completed a remarkable four years period without a single defeat by boys of its own age. One boy played for the England Association Football team - our first international - and another figured in the International Rugby trials. The girls too provided several members of the County Netball teams, and several other representative honours were won.

On other occasions I have spoken of the importance that I attach to the Duke of Edinburgh's Award Scheme. It has, of course, received a good deal of publicity, but even now I don't think its value is fully realised. Its emphasis on Public Service, on sensible physical training and fitness, on the right use of spare time, and above all on the necessity for perseverance in all that one undertakes, make it a most useful school activity. The scheme looks for and develops those qualities that are found not only in clever boys and girls but in pupils of average or even poor academic ability. All can participate, and gain both self-respect and respect for the abilities of others. Its value to the Comprehensive school is obvious. Hengrove was one of the first schools to enter the scheme. To date the boys have obtained 9 Gold Awards (This is quite remarkable) 18 Silver and 81 Bronze Awards. The girls, who began a little later have 1 Gold, 18 Silver and 76 Bronze Awards, and I have no doubt that they will soon overtake the boys.

In a few weeks I shall leave Hengrove, after a long and satisfying career as a schoolmaster. Perhaps you will forgive me if, for a few minutes, I comment on some of the changes that I have seen.

First, the vastly improved health and physique of children. I remember well the days when too many children came from homes where the father was unemployed, or employed for inadequate wages; quite plainly many of them did not get enough to eat, nor were they properly clothed, and this showed in their general health and appearance. If anyone still thinks that working people waste the better wages they earn today, he should come into our schools and see a class of boys stripped down for a lesson in the gym. How different are these alert and well-built boys from those in the 1930 s.

Another great change has come over the attitude of parents
to education. Now that they can afford to keep their children at
school they are only too anxious to do so. They believe that the
courses provided in schools will be of real benefit to their children.
Two thirds of our boys and girls at Hengrove stay on to 16, and the
proportion is increasing. I believe that co-operation between
parents and teachers is stronger than it has ever been.

Thirdly, we now demand much higher standards of work from our
pupils and achieve them. If you don't believe this, compare the
present G.C.E. 'A' level syllabus with those of 4-5 years ago. There is more
to be understood and learnt, and higher marks have to be obtained
for a pass. This applies to other examinations too. Of course, we
are still criticised because some of our pupils are not up to standard,
especially by those who expect 15 or 16 year old leavers to be as
mature as young men and women of 21. But this criticism grows less.
Only in the last five years have we managed to recover from the
damage done to our schools during the war years, and the equally
difficult post-war period. When I look back at the 1940 s I wonder
how we survived as we did.

And lastly, perhaps the most important change of all. How much
more is now done for the pupil of about average ability. In all our
schools these children are achieving things, in and out of the classroom, that would have seemed quite impossible even ten years ago. Some
of the examination results I have quoted demonstrate this, but as I
said last year, there is still much that we can do to discover and
help those children who form the great untapped reservoir of talent,
the existence of which is denied only by those teachers who don't
know how to meet this challenge.

In the discovery of the powers of the average pupil, the
comprehensive school has done much to show the way. The rise of
these schools constitutes the last development to which I would refer.
Some people regret the controversy that rages around them, but growth
and progress are always the results of conflict. If all teachers were
satisfied with our edueational system, it would be a poor outlook for
Britain. It is now pretty clear that comprehensive education has
increased, is increasing and will continue to increase. 100 years
ago, at the time when there were fierce disputes about the reform of
Parliament, Sydney Smith, the wise and witty Canon of Bristol Cathedral,
told the story of a Mrs.Partington who, when the Atlantic overflowed
her doorstep at Weymouth, was seen heroically pushing the waves back
with a broom. The opponents of political change had just about as
much hope of success, he said. When I read the letters in my evening
newspaper, it is plain that the Mrs.Partingtons of our generation are
doing their best.

Now for the last time, I must thank all those who have made my
stay at Hengrove a pleasant one. We have had here a high proportion
of good and helpful teachers who have thought it well worth while to
make a success of comprehensive education. They have given me both
loyalty and friendship, which I value. I have good reason, too, to
be grateful to our cheerful and very efficient secretaries.

The Committee's inspectors and officials, who have their own
problems of administration, have always been sympathetic and friendly,

even when they could not give us what I asked for. Nor could any
Headmaster have had a better relationship with his Governors.

I must say a word of thanks to the Headmaster and Staff of
Tyning Junior School. Mr. Burman retires at the end of this
term. Our work here has been made easier by the good grounding
so many of our pupils have received in his school.

And finally, my thanks to the parents of Hengrove, who have
not only provided us with large numbers of pleasant and co-operative
pupils, but have been remarkably good-natured and sensible in their
relations with the school.

Farewell to Dr Perry

It was a long and fond farewell. On 21st March 1964 there was a Retirement
Dinner attended by Governors and Staff. The Evening Post carried an article
"The End of Term" on 24th March 1964. (See overleaf).

The Head Boy Barry Gitsham, Head Girl Ruth Cowley and two younger pupils
presented Dr Perry with a gift on behalf of the 1000 pupils in the Assembly Hall.

Dr Perry had interviewed candidates for his successor and knew he was passing
Hengrove School into the capable hands of Mr Philip Waterhouse.

He could do so knowing that he had been at the helm of a post-war educational
revolution which would greatly enhance the future life opportunities of his pupils.
Both staff and former pupils speak positively of "the Perry era" at Hengrove School.

—EVENING POST, TUESDAY, MARCH 24 1964

The end of term...

...AND TOMORROW THERE WILL BE A THOUSAND FAREWELLS FOR DR. PERRY

This week a number of Bristol teachers will be leaving their posts for the last time as they pass to a well deserved retirement.

One of the best known of them is **Dr. Reginald Perry**, headmaster of Hengrove School, for in addition to being a schoolmaster he is a frequent lecturer at the University and the Folk House on local history.

Now 60, Dr. Perry has previously been headmaster of two other Bristol schools—Speedwell and Filton Avenue Junior Mixed School. Earlier still he was second master at St. George Grammar School.

A married man with two grown-up daughters, he has no intention of sitting down and taking life too easily.

First he intends to take a holiday . . . a long holiday. This will take the form of a three months' tour on the Continent, mainly in the South of France. He hopes to indulge in one of his pet hobbies—photography.

Even busier

When he returns and settles down in Bristol he expects to be busier than ever, lecturing about the history of Bristol and Gloucestershire.

First, however, come the farewells at Hengrove. The first takes place tonight at a dinner attended by the governors and staff.

Tomorrow he will receive presentations from the school's 1,000 pupils and in the evening it will be the turn of the parents.

What with the normal end of term thrown in, quite a week to remember.

Dr. Perry.

A silver tea set and salver is presented to Dr. Reginald Perry (right), headmaster of Hengrove School, Bristol, at a farewell dinner to mark his retirement by Ald. F. G. W. Chamberlain, chairman of the governors. Mrs. Perry is in the centre.

Evening Post 24/3/1964

In the words of a former pupil, now himself a retired Secondary/Upper School Headmaster:

> "The staff held Dr Perry in the highest esteem and were motivated by his total belief in the comprehensive system of education."

Chapter 3
The Mr Waterhouse Era 1964-1974
Consolidation, Expansion and Innovation

A former pupil remembers her first encounter with Mr Waterhouse, the new Headmaster.

> *"We were Sixth Formers in our final Summer Term at Hengrove School. Dr Perry, the Headmaster throughout our seven years had just retired. The year was 1964 – the Summer Term. His successor Mr P. S. Waterhouse came to talk with us. He seemed quite young with an easy and approachable manner, twinkly eyes and a northern accent."*

He asked us an amazing question:

> *"If we were planning an exclusively Sixth Form Centre – what would we like to include? Carpets? Armchairs? Coffee and dining area? I was stunned! He was asking US?"*

This all seemed far removed from our experience of Sixth Form. Was it all revolutionary wishful thinking? You will see as you read this chapter that it became a reality.

In his own words we have some of Mr Waterhouse's memories of his early days at Hengrove. These were written especially for the Hengrove School History Project in 2011.

In 1964 I was happy in my first headship in Wolverhampton. However, when I saw the advertisement for the headship of Hengrove I was tempted. Both my wife and I were Bristol graduates and my first job had been a happy four years spent at Cotham Grammar School. I put in my application. Within a few weeks I was invited for interview.
On the big day I arrived mid-morning and was shown into the small Deputy Head's room along with five other candidates. We talked together, sharing our experiences.

The interviews took place in the Head's room which was next door. After a brief period I was invited in again and offered the job. I accepted. The governors then announced that a lunch had been prepared for them and the successful candidate. The school was already into its afternoon session and we walked along empty corridors to the Domestic Science Department. They were a friendly and relaxed group and the lunch seemed to go on for ever. At last I had to take my leave as I had a train to catch. I walked back along the long corridor which was deserted because the school had already gone home. I suddenly felt very uncertain and depressed. Why had I not been allowed to meet staff or look round the school? Were they hiding something? Ought I to have insisted before accepting the job? By the time I reached the entrance foyer I was feeling thoroughly depressed.

In the entrance hall a man was sitting. He rose as I appeared and came over to me. "My name's Bill Fletcher. I'm the Deputy Head. I just wanted to say two things to you. First, I want you to know that I applied for the headship and was not even offered an interview and I'm resentful about that, but I obviously don't blame you. Second, you will have 100% loyalty and cooperation from me, and I hope we shall make a great team."

I shook his hand warmly and we talked and laughed together for several minutes. Eventually I resumed my way towards my train. On the journey home I found that my uncertainty and depression had vanished. I knew that I had a great ally.

My first day at Hengrove was hectic in the extreme. There were so many people to meet, so much information to absorb, so many ideas to be considered, so many decisions to be made. At the end of the day I was thoroughly exhausted. Suddenly I was aware that the school had gone quiet; everybody had gone home. I sat at my desk staring into space and doubts and uncertainties crowded in on me. Had I met everybody I should have met? Had I said the right things? Had I done the right things? This job was surely too big. It was an impossible task.

Then there was a tap at the door. The door opened a little way and a head popped round. It was Olga Place. She said, "I'm going home now. I just wanted to say.............I enjoyed today!" I found myself smiling back at her and heard myself say "And so did I!" We both laughed and talked together for several minutes. In a few moments my confidence had been restored. I made my way home feeling much better. I spent a quiet evening at home and "......although impatient for the morning, I slept soundly and had no need of cheering dreams. Facts are better that dreams!"

Throughout my ten years at Hengrove Bill Fletcher and Olga Place were constant sources of support and encouragement; and countless teachers and pupils owe a great deal to them.

Mr Waterhouse's first annual Prizegiving soon came around in November 1964 towards the end of his second term.

We have the programme – the UEI passes are recorded for the final time as it was to be replaced in 1965 by the CSE (Certificate of Secondary Education) exam. We also have an excellent photo of the Head Boy and Head Girl, Mr Waterhouse and D W Humphries, Director of the Bristol University Department of Education.

HENGROVE SCHOOL, BRISTOL

PRIZEGIVING

THURSDAY, 26th NOVEMBER, 1964

at 7.30 p.m.

———o———

PROGRAMME

Chairman's Remarks :
CHAIRMAN OF THE GOVERNORS

Headmaster's Report :
P. S. WATERHOUSE, Esq., M.A.

Address and Presentation of Prizes and Certificates by :
D. W. HUMPHREYS, Esq., M.A.

Vote of Thanks by :
KEITH SCRIBBENS, *Head Boy.*

SECONDARY SCHOOL CERTIFICATE

Certificate Prize	Linda Watts
Certificate Prize	Robin Garland
Certificate Prize	Peter Neville
Science	Ann Withers
Mathematics	Barrie Withers
English Language	Jill King
French	Diane Morgan
Commercial Subjects	Patricia Soper

FORM PRIZES

Form IVA1	M. Gould	Ann Dodge
Form IVA2	R. Pike	Jessica Blair
Form IVB1	L. Garratt	Susan Dwyer
Form IVB2	C. Burgess	Patricia Hurley
Form IVs	R. Stokes	Heather Crouchen

SPECIAL AWARDS

Librarian Prize	Patricia Gallop
Sports Prize	Geoffrey Wetton and Marion Lock
Orchestra Prize	Christopher Ashley
5th Form Prize	Peter Neville and Ann Withers
(awarded by Dr. R. Perry, previous Headmaster)	
"Heather Dennis" Music Prizes	William Spear and Miriam Allen
HEAD BOY'S PRIZE	Barry Gitsham
HEAD GIRL'S PRIZE	Ruth Cowley

DUKE OF EDINBURGH AWARD

Gold Standard	Janet Freeman

HOUSE AWARDS

Athletics Cup—Argos	Netball Cup—Olympia
Athletics Bowl—Argos	Hockey Cup—Sparta

UNIVERSITY AND TRAINING COLLEGE ENTRANTS

Ruth Cowley	University of Cardiff
Diane Jakeway	City of Cardiff Training College
Angela Wiggins	City of Birmingham Training College
Sheila Richards	Dudley Training College
Patricia Baker	Avery Hill Training College, London
Janet Freeman	Bishop Otter College, Chichester
Marion Lock	City of Derby Training College
Stewart Massey	College of Advanced Technology, Loughborough
Stuart Cook	Northern Polytechnic College, London
Royston Joliffe	City of Nottingham Training College

Printed by The Charlton Press, 28 Wells Road, Bristol, 4. Tel. 76465.

PRIZE LIST

SOUTHERN UNIVERSITIES' JOINT BOARD
GENERAL CERTIFICATE OF EDUCATION

ADVANCED LEVEL

Roland Ashley	Engineering Drawing
Richard Cheek	Engineering Drawing (Distinction)
Stuart Cook	Physics, Pure Mathematics
Michael Dyer	Engineering Drawing
Michael Hales	Engineering Drawing
Royston Joliffe	Botany, Zoology
Stewart Massey	Chemistry, Physics.
Patricia Baker	Music
Ruth Cowley	Botany, Zoology, Chemistry
Juliet Green	English Literature
Andrea Paul	English Literature, Zoology
Sheila Richards	English Literature
Joy Sanders	Zoology
Angela Wiggins	English Literature, Music
Ruth Williams	English Literature, Zoology.

ORDINARY LEVEL

M. Arlett, T. Ashford, R. Bailey, S. Barnes, R. Barton, D. Bassett, G. Batchelor, D. Bennett, L. Bennett, J. Bessell, R. Biggs, R. Bignell, T. Burt, R. Coates, R. Coggins, S. Cook, A. Conroy, J. Coventry, W. Davies, B. Dawes, R. Dollin, P. Edwards, G. Ferris, G. Garland, M. Gould, A. Gregg, G. Griffiths, M. Hamilton, C. Hamlin, R. Harris, D. Haskins, P. Haydon, A. Hayward, R. Hedges, B. Iles, J. Iles, R. Kays, D. Kerby, J. Logan, R. Long, S. Manning, R. Mathews, S. Mead, R. Morgan, R. Osborne, R. Oxley, D. Pickard, R. Pring, R. Richards, A. Robinson, P. Sams, B. Shattock, J. Shore, M. Silvester, M. Spear, J. Spiller, C. Topley, B. Turner, W. Wells, R. Williams, M. Wilson.

Carol Baker, Linda Blannin, Barbara Collins, Carol Curtis, Ann Dodge, Madeline Evans, Janet Freeman, Susan Goodsir, Ann Gough, Ann Goulder, Ann Goulstone, Karen Hall, Jacqueline Harris, Linda Harvey, Dianne Jakeway, Susan James, Lynda Jordan, Jill King, Victoria Knight, Susan Leonard, Marion Lock, Geraldine Meikle, Diane Morgan, Margaret Nicholls, Brenda Parker, Lynette Pease, Geraldine Perchard, Rosemary Rendell, Jean Scully, Pauline Selway, Christine Snell, Patricia Soper, Madeline Southey, Rosemary Stone, Carol Thompson, Bridget Toole, Margaret Vlaeminke, Linda Watts, Trudy Watts, Ann Withers.

UNION OF EDUCATIONAL INSTITUTIONS
SECONDARY SCHOOL GROUP CERTIFICATE

R. Garland, M. Gillam, R. D. Harris, A. Jennings, D. J. Kerby, P. Malin, B. Manning, B. Mathews, P. Neville, B. Shattock, M. Spiers, B. Turner, B. Withers.

L. Aplin, B. Day, D. Etherton, S. Goodsir, J. King, D. Morgan, J. Pedelty, P. Soper, N. Summerhayes, L. Watts, A. Withers.

SUBJECT CERTIFICATE

M. Arlett, S. Allison, T. Ashford, R. Bailey, R. Barton, S. Banfield, G. Batchelor, P. Bateman, D. Beaves, J. Bessell, R. Bignell, T. Burt, A. Conroy, B. Davies, P. Edwards, M. Ford, G. Garland, C. Gitsham, J. Golding, K. Goldsworthy, G. Griffiths, R. Hellin, R. Hellier, M. Hobbs, B. Hughes, B. Iles, G. Jacobs, K. Kiely, R. Long, J. Mawer, R. Pring, K. Randall, D. Roman, R. Richards, R. Sharples, M. Silvester, M. Spear, J. Spiller, C. Topley, R. Williams, C. Williams, M. Wilson.

L. Anstey, M. Brown, J. Cox, M. Evans, S. Evans, C. Eyre, C. Hinton, S. James, H. Jayne, V. Knight, K. Lawrence, C. Nicholls, M. Nichols, J. Nye, B. Parker, L. Pease, G. Perchard, C. Thompson, V. Whale, C. Winter.

CERTIFICATE FOR COMMERCIAL SUBJECTS

L. Aplin, M. Brown, B. Day, D. Etherton, S. Evans, J. King, D. Morgan, C. Nicholls, J. Nye, J. Pedelty, E. Smith, P. Soper.

SUBJECT PRIZES

ADVANCED LEVEL

Engineering Drawing	Richard Cheek
Physics	Stuart Cook
Chemistry	Stuart Massey
Botany	Ruth Cowley

ORDINARY LEVEL

English Language	Stuart Cook
Art	Bridget Toole
Geography	W. Davies
Metalwork	Derek Pickard
French	Alan Hayward
Mathematics	Bruce Iles
Woodwork	John Kerby
Chemistry	Richard Mathews
Music	Christopher Topley
Human Biology	Carol Curtis
History	Rosemary Rendell
Biology	Pauline Selway
English Literature	Rosemary Stone

Speech Day 1964
Guest: Mr. D Humphries - Director of University Education Dept.,
Head Boy: Keith Scribbons - now a lecturer at Worcester University
HEADMASTER. MR. P. WATERHOUSE.

In his fairly lengthy speech he gave a resumé of the academic and extra-curricular life of the school during 1963-1964. He also made some very exciting and revolutionary predictions for the future – the school would grow bigger; further building extensions would be planned; Hengrove would become a 'flexible school'; and there would be challenges ahead. Read on to see the challenges unfold.

Prizegiving, 26th November 1964

Mr. Chairman, Mr. Humphreys, Governors, Parents and Pupils,

May I, firstly, extend my own welcome to Mr. Humphreys and to our guests and parents.

The year 1963 - 4 has brought some considerable change to Hengrove School because in December 1963 Miss G. A. Martin who had been Senior Mistress and Deputy Head since 1954 retired and in April 1964 Dr. R. Perry who was the school's first headmaster also retired. At the last Prizegiving Dr. Perry paid tribute to Miss Martin's services to the school and I know that the pupils, staff and parents would not wish me to let the opportunity pass of expressing their appreciation of Dr. Perry's own leadership during the first ten years of the school's history. He is often spoken of in the school and obviously remembered with great affection and respect and this says everything.

In the summer of 1964 fifteen pupils obtained successes in the Advanced level G.C.E. examinations, and as a result ten obtained places in institutions of Higher Education. 103 pupils obtained passes at the Ordinary level of G.C.E. and 86 obtained passes in the Secondary School Certificate of the Union of Educational Institutions. This latter examination was conducted in 1964 for the last time. In 1965 it is being replaced by the new Certificate of Secondary Education which will be a marked advance for this is a teacher-controlled examination and it will have a nation-wide currency. Parents should know that a Grade I pass in the new C.S.E. will be the equivalent standard of an Ordinary Level pass in G.C.E. and steps are already being taken to gain acceptance of this fact in the eyes of employers and professional bodies. I sincerely hope that parents of Hengrove pupils will quickly recognise the need to complete the fifth year and to enter for this examination. It is also wise to recognise that a good pass in C.S.E. is infinitely preferable to a fail in G.C.E. In the eyes of the outside world "failed G.C.E." is not a qualification.

It is heartening to see the numbers of our pupils who are staying on in the VIth form where it is now possible to follow courses to Advanced Level or Ordinary Level or a combination of both, or to follow practical courses with a bias towards Nursing or Secretarial work. At present we have 60 students in the VIth form and I am sure this will increase during the next few years as the pupils and their parents come to realise the wide range of opportunities available to them. It is particularly pleasing to see there a number of pupils who were not regarded as capable of academic success when they were eleven years of age !

Of the 208 pupils who left the school during 1963 - 4, 80 left from the fourth year, 93 from the fifth year and 35 from the sixth and seventh years. All received help and guidance from the careers master and the Youth Employment Officers. The range of employment is enormous and we applaud particularly those pupils who break new ground, one to the Royal Academy of Dramatic Art, one to the Atomic Energy Authority at Aldermaston, one to the Foreign Service, one to an integrated Nursing Course at Hammersmith Hospital, one to the new Fire Service Cadet Scheme and many others too numerous to mention. We hope that all our leavers will come back often to report on their progress.

It is pleasing to report that the Old Pupils' Association continues to flourish.

- 1 -

91

Outside the classroom life at Hengrove has been as vigorous as ever. Our pupils are particularly fortunate in the opportunities they get for organised outdoor pursuits. The staff organising Youth Hostelling acknowledge only the shortest close season in winter. The first week-end took place on the 1st February and others followed regularly until the longer tour organised in South Devon during the summer holiday. We aim to introduce and arouse enthusiasm for this type of activity so that our pupils will arrange their own tours long after they have left the school. Week-end camps were also organised in the summer and longer camps at Wareham and at Exmouth. During the holidays parties have visited the continent, Paris at Easter and Switzerland in the summer.

The school continues to participate actively in the Duke of Edinburgh's Award schemes. To date there have been eleven gold, 38 silver and 162 bronze awards. Over 160 pupils are currently registered. These figures are a wonderful tribute to the perseverance of the pupils and the helpful encouragement they are receiving from the staff.

The total effort of the school in representation games has been enormous. In the winter season four hockey teams and five Netball teams played regularly. Three girls obtained County Netball badges. Five rugby teams and five soccer teams were fielded and six of our boys represented Bristol. There were two basketball teams and three boys represented Bristol.

In the summer season there were four school cricket teams, three rounders teams, two girls' tennis teams and three athletic teams. Five pupils competed in Athletics at County level and one boy obtained his county colours at the All England Championships. In swimming both boys and girls continue to gain certificates for distance and for A.S.A. Survival awards and R.L.S.S. Safety awards. Two boys represented Bristol against Cardiff. Canoes have made their appearance in the school and I am sure we shall hear more of this activity in the future.

Music activities are continuing to flourish with senior and junior choirs, the School orchestra and the school brass band. The latter has been much in demand locally by various organisations. Our pupils have taken an active part in the Bristol Secondary Schools Music Festival.

Our Chess Club with a membership of 50 continues to play at a high standard and one pupil, for the second year in succession was runner-up in the National Youth Championships. The U.15 A team has won every league game for the past 2½ years.

The VIth form society is a new society which now arranges its own programmes of lectures and social activities. It has recently extended its range to give VIth form pupils an opportunity to engage in social service in the neighbourhood.

In the Spring term the Dramatic Society gave a most successful production of "A Man for All Seasons" and are at present hard at work rehearsing for "Twelfth Night" which is due to be performed at the end of this term. The Dancing Club provides a most popular diversion for a large number of pupils and some very pleasant social evenings have been organised.

Other clubs and societies which have operated during the year are an Art Club, a Woodwork Club and Swimming Clubs.

I must add that I think one of the school's notable achievements during the year has been the assimilation of a new headmaster. This is not always an easy task and I should like to express my appreciation of the great help I have received from pupils and staff alike. I must make particular mention of the energy and devotion of the Deputy Headmaster and the Senior Mistress who have carried so much responsibility during these last two terms. I hope my report has been a fair statement of what happened in 1963 - 4 and I hope I shall be forgiven any errors or omissions remembering that I only joined the school during the last term of the school year.

It is tempting to speculate about the future. Certainly we know that the school is to grow bigger in three years time. Certainly we know that from September next we shall become a true neighbourhood school. We are already thinking deeply about this new growth and this new responsibility. I hope that when our extensions are planned, we shall attempt to progress by applying architecturally some of the following assumptions :

a) that for part of their time in school some pupils will be out in the adult world on their own;
b) that pupils' time will be often arranged so that they will be able to carry through a particular job of work or pursue a particular interest with reasonable continuity - we shall not always fragment our day in 40 minute particles as at present;
c) that they will have a personal interest and concern in the actual running of the community and the actual care of the grounds and buildings;
d) that each will have some degree of choice in the work he or she does;
e) that there will not always be rigid demarcation lines between subjects or between the academic and the practical;
f) that private study under guidance and supervision will be part of the normal programme for all senior pupils; and for part of the time they will be working in groups larger or smaller than the traditional class of 30;
g) that clubs and societies will form an integral part of the school's programme;
h) that more use will be made of visiting speakers and discussion leaders;
i) that our school day will become altogether more flexible both in its total length and in the way in which it is divided up;
j) that not only will the pupils go out more into the community but the community will come more into the school.

Ideas of this kind present a challenge to the school. My impressions after only a short period of service here are that we have pupils of great potential both academically and socially, a loyal and hard-working staff, a friendly and energetic Board of Governors, parents who support the school, a Local Authority administration in which one can have complete faith. These are the ingredients of success and I find myself looking forward to the future with confidence and optimism.

We have below the list of Head Boy, Head Girl and Prefects for 1964-1965 together with a photo of two Girl Prefects, Ann Withers and Linda Watts, proudly wearing their badges.

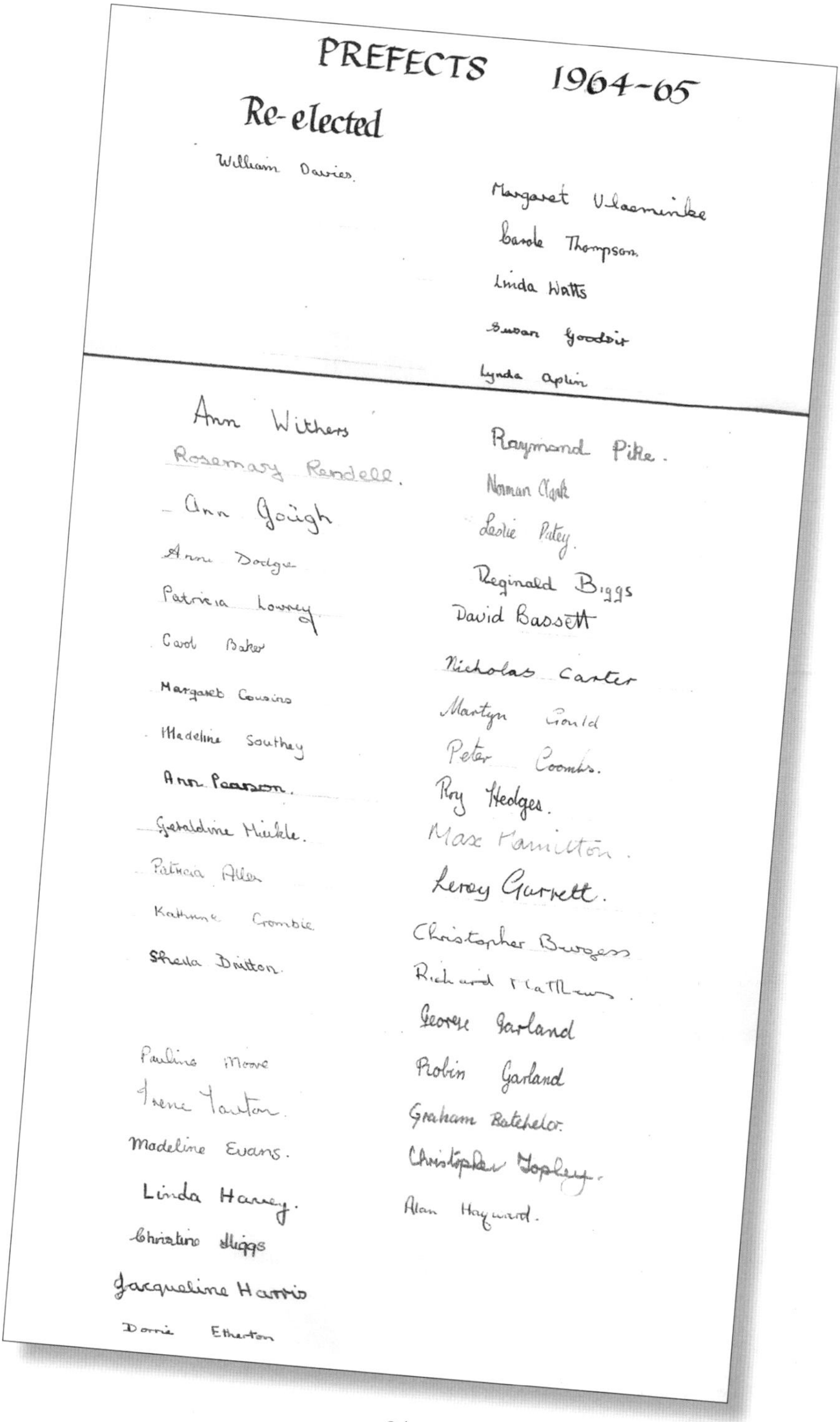

PREFECTS 1964-65

Re-elected

William Davies.

Margaret Vlaeminke
Carole Thompson.
Linda Watts
Susan Goodsir
Lynda Aplin

Ann Withers
Rosemary Rendell.
Ann Gough
Ann Dodge
Patricia Lowrey
Carol Baker
Margaret Cousins
Madeline Southey
Ann Pearson.
Geraldine Meikle.
Patricia Allen
Kathryn Crombie
Sheila Dutton.

Pauline Moore
Irene Tauton
Madeline Evans.
Linda Harvey.
Christine Higgs
Jacqueline Harris
Dorrie Etherton

Raymond Pike.
Norman Clark
Leslie Patey.
Reginald Biggs
David Bassett
Nicholas Carter
Martyn Gould
Peter Coombs.
Roy Hedges.
Max Hamilton.
Leroy Garnett.
Christopher Burgess
Richard Matthews.
George Garland
Robin Garland
Graham Batchelor.
Christopher Topley.
Alan Hayward.

1964 – 1965

HEAD BOY

Keith Scribbins.

HEAD GIRL

Ann Goulstone.

DEPUTY HEAD-BOYS

DEPUTY HEAD-GIRLS

Jan Shaddick

Ann Withers and Linda Watts

December 1965 was a busy time. The School Prizegiving took place on 3rd December 1965 – Mr Waterhouse's Second Prizegiving evening.

We have below the programme and the text of the Headmaster's Report for the year 1964-1965. Read on for details:

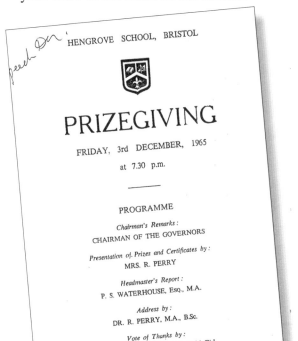

HENGROVE SCHOOL, BRISTOL

PRIZEGIVING

FRIDAY, 3rd DECEMBER, 1965

at 7.30 p.m.

———

PROGRAMME

Chairman's Remarks:
CHAIRMAN OF THE GOVERNORS

Presentation of Prizes and Certificates by:
MRS. R. PERRY

Headmaster's Report:
P. S. WATERHOUSE, ESQ., M.A.

Address by:
DR. R. PERRY, M.A., B.Sc.

Vote of Thanks by:
MARGARET VLAEMINKE, Head Girl.

PRIZE LIST

SOUTHERN UNIVERSITIES' JOINT BOARD
GENERAL CERTIFICATE OF EDUCATION

ADVANCED LEVEL

Christopher Ashley	English Literature, Geography
Stephen Barnes	Chemistry, Physics, Pure and Applied Mathematics
Barry Cooper	Chemistry, Physics
Colin Critchley	Botany, Zoology
Edward Lovell	Chemistry
Barry Pearson	Chemistry, Physics—Special Paper—(Merit) Pure and Applied Mathematics
Robert Pond	Physics, Pure and Applied Mathematics
Peter Sams	Chemistry, Physics, Pure and Applied Mathematics
Keith Scribbens	English Literature, History — Special Paper — (Distinction)
Derek Warner	Pure and Applied Mathematics
Geoffrey Wetton	Chemistry, Physics, Pure and Applied Mathematics
Ann Goulstone	Religious Instruction, English Literature
Jane Hedges	Religious Instruction, Art
Christine Snell	French, German
Bridget Toole	English Literature, History, Art
Susan Watts	English Literature, French

ORDINARY LEVEL

R. Allen, A. Bach, D. Bailey, D. Bassett, G. Batchelor, R. Biggs, R. Bignell, M. Brown, N. Carter, K. Clark, N. Clark, A. Conroy, P. Coombs, J. Coventry, W. Davies, B. Dawes, R. Dollin, E. Phillips, R. Elder, M. Ford, A. Forsey, F. Fox, G. Garland, R. Garland, C. Gitsham, J. Golding, M. Gould, B. Greenwood, A. Gregg, M. Hamilton, D. Huskins, A. Hayward, R. Hedges, N. Howarth, B. Hughes, J. Iles, R. Kays, D. Kerby, C. Lee, J. Logan, R. Long, H. Marsh, T. Norris, R. Osborne, R. Oxley, R. Parsons, L. Patey, A. Pearson, D. Pickard, R. Pike, R. Richards, S. Salisbury, J. Sampson, A. Shore, R. Thompson, C. Topley, W. Wells, M. Wilson, B. Withers, E. Woolley.

L. Aplin, C. Baker, J. Blair, C. Cooper, K. Crombie, A. Dodge, D. Etherton, M. Evans, M. Faithful, M. Filer, M. Gambling, A. Gough, K. Hall, J. Halliday, L. Harvey, C. Higgs, B. Hoyle, D. Jacobson, L. Jordan, P. Lowrey, G. Meikle, M. Patten, A. Pearson, J. Price, S. Room, C. Rudland, J. Scully, M. Southey, C. Thompson, S. Vaughan, M. Vlaeminke, L. Watts, T. Watts, S. Winter-Smith, A. Withers.

CERTIFICATE OF SECONDARY EDUCATION
Certificate Prizes

Leroy Garrett	Thomas Thomas
Stephen Mabey	Susan Dwyer
Richard Mundy	Carol Tipping
Robert Purnell	

FORM PRIZES

Form IVA1	Alan Shore	Mary Faithful
Form IVA2	Alan Curtis	Nina Biggs
Form IVB1	Richard Stone	Margaret Francis
Form IVB2	Philip Wait	Eleanor Brooks
Form IVx	Alan Wheeler	Pamela Payne

SPECIAL AWARDS

Sports Prize	William Davies and Margaret Vlaeminke
Orchestra Prize	Jean Shaddick
5th Form Prize (awarded by Dr. R. Perry)	Norman Clark and Julia Price
Heather Dennis Music Prize	Sharon Whyatt and Trevor Iles
Hinett Trophy (Junior Sportsman of the year)	Alan Pring

DUKE OF EDINBURGH AWARD

Gold Standard	Ann Goulstone

UNIVERSITY AND COLLEGE OF EDUCATION ENTRANTS

Keith Scribbens	Goldsmith's College, London University (B.Sc. Sociology)
Ann Goulstone	Whitelands College of Education
Colin Critchley	Regent Street Polytechnic (B.Sc. Hon. Zoology)
Raymond Elder	Culham College of Education
Jane Hedges	Brighton College of Arts and Crafts
Jean Shaddick	Wrexham College of Education
Bridget Toole	Brighton College of Arts and Crafts University Entrant 1966
Susan Watts	Queen Mary College, London University (B.A. Hon. French)
Barry Cooper	Rugby College of Technology. B.Sc. Engin.
Barry Pearson	S.W.E.B. Student Apprenticeship. Tenable at the proposed University of Bath. B.Sc. Elect Engin.
Robert Pond	The proposed City University, London. B.Sc. Hon. Physics.
Peter Sams	Bristol Siddeley Appprenticeship. B.Sc. Engin. Tenable at the proposed University of Bath
Geoffrey Wetton	Portsmouth College of Technology. B.Sc. Hon. Physics.
Stephen Barnes	University of Warwick. B.Sc. Molecular Science.

CERTIFICATE OF SECONDARY EDUCATION

B. Allen, R. Allen, A. Bach, D. Bailey, R. Bowyer, C. Burgess, C. Burt, K. Clark, P. Coombs, J. Crago, B. Dawes, T. Dix, R. Dollin, A. Durrington, J. Ferris, L. Garrett, C. Gibbs, W. Goss, J. Haines, J. Harding, R. Harris, D. Haskins, R. Hedges, G. James, R. Jones, J. Logan, S. Mabey, D. Manning, G Mills, R. Mundy, C. Mizon, T. Norris, R. Oxley, L. Patey, R. Pike, R. Purnell, S. Salisbury, J. Sampson, B. Selway, S. Shepherd, C. Silman, C. Smith, J. Stadden, A. Thomas, T. Thomas, R. Thompson, R. Williams, W. Wells, E. Wooley.

P. Allen, L. Aplin, S. Arnett, C. Brain, S. Britton, P. Brown, M. Clarke, C. Cooper, M. Cousins, K. Crombie, H. Derrick, S. Dwyer, D. Etherton, M. Evans, M. Filer, L. Frost, P. Gallop, J. Geater, A. Graves, G. Guest, K. Hall, L. Hall, P. Harris, B. Hoyle, D. Jacobson, A. Jones, M. Livingstone, J. Lovell, P. Lowrey. L. Mears, G. Meikle, P. Moore, J. Mulkern, G. Perchard, M. Poole, B. Richards, G. Stimpson, S. Room, C. Rudland, I. Tawton, C. Tipping, T. Watts, E. Wilson.

SUBJECT PRIZES

ADVANCED LEVEL

History	Keith Scribbens
Chemistry	Barry Pearson
Physics	Barry Pearson
English Literature	Bridget Toole
Mathematics	Barry Pearson

ORDINARY LEVEL

Human Biology	Linda Aplin
Music	Jessica Blair
Chemistry	Ann Dodge
	Reginald Biggs
Physics	Nicholas Carter
Metalwork	Keith Clark
History	Norman Clark
English Language	John Coventry
Geography	Robert Dollin
English Literature	Martin Gould
Mathematics	Derrick Kerby
Art	Leslie Patey
French	Christine Higgs
	Geraldine Meikle
Domestic Science	Lynda Jordan
Biology	Julia Price
Religious Instruction	Julia Price
German	Alan Hayward

96

HEADMASTER'S REPORT FOR THE YEAR 1964-65

PRIZEGIVING, 3RD DECEMBER, 1965

Mr. Chairman, Dr. & Mrs. Perry, Ladies & Gentlemen,

May I firstly extend my own welcome to Dr. and Mrs. Perry. It is a great pleasure to have them with us once again.

1964-5 has been a busy year for the school mainly because of innovations, some of which were initiated in the school, others from outside. The first new arrival was the new Certificate of Secondary Education. Staff were involved throughout the year in the work of subject panels, in preparation of syllabuses, in marking and moderating. Although all this work made considerable inroads into the teachers' time it is pleasing to report that our pupils did extremely well in the examination and that the C.S.E. has already acquired the hoped for recognition throughout the country. Our results in the G.C.E. examinations were also very pleasing. For many fifth year pupils good results at the Ordinary Level made a firm foundation on which to build Sixth form work. For our Sixth Form a set of really splendid results at Advanced Level opened the doors to Higher Education. Their names and achievements are recorded on your programme. *VI* *Keith Sandbourne* *Ann Goldstone* *1965 — a good vintage year.*

The second new event came in the Autumn Term when Staff and pupils co-operated in a mammoth Autumn Fair to raise money for the school fund. A grand profit of over £400 resulted and during the rest of the year we have been spending the money - we hope wisely - in support of our many extra-curricular activities. *Support — personal contr.*

This was quickly followed by an experimental Careers Convention. It was supported by over 30 organisations and parents and pupils from the third form upwards. We shall certainly repeat it. *Elaborate*

Community Service is not new to Hengrove. The Lower School continued to make its weekly collections for the Freedom from Hunger Campaign and each form in the school prepared Christmas parcels for delivery to elderly or invalid people. It was the VI Form that broke new ground. They provided the highlight of the Autumn Term by a brilliant piece of purposeful organisation. Co-operating with the N.S.P.C.C. they ran a party for 60 deprived children drawn from all over the city. They drew many gasps of admiration and found many lumps in throats that evening. They followed this up by regularly helping at a junior Youth Club at a neighbouring Primary School. *+ their own charity concert in the Spring Term.*

The Hengrove School Association came into being during the year. Composed of parents and friends of the school it aims to support the school in any way possible. It is currently planning to raise money to give a completely new look to the school library. *Vigorous + lively committee & great source of strength to the school in future*

Effort and time given to all these new ventures has not been given at the expense of carrying on the strong traditions of the school.

In the games field the school has done remarkably well. I refer not so much to the number of victories we have had (although these have been very great) but more to the number of teams we have been able to field in a very wide range of competition games and to the high standards of play and general behaviour achieved by our players. I must pay a very warm tribute to the devotion and skill of the staff who voluntarily accept responsibility for all this. The high standards they set form one of the school's strongest supports. *Rugby once*

97

Music and Drama have been well represented by a fine production of Twelfth Night and a Carol Concert in the Autumn Term and a most inspiring music concert in the Spring Term. *Mention Carol Concert*

Outdoor pursuits, always strong at Hengrove, continued to flourish. Youth Hostelling is almost all the year round; camping flourishes in the summer months and expeditions farther afield to Exmoor, the Lake District and Austria were all made during the summer holiday.

Clubs and Societies abound. We have Judo, Badminton, Basket Ball, Gym Clubs, Swimming Clubs, a Dance Club, Chess, Dancing, Natural History, Gardening, Cookery for Boys, Archery, a VI Form Society, Woodwork, Go-karts, as well as large groups of both boys and girls preparing themselves for the Duke of Edinburgh's award. The amount of staff time and effort involved in all these is considerable and I hope that both pupils and their parents are always mindful of this.

As I said at the beginning it has been a busy year. For me it has represented my first full year in the school and it has been a time of observation and thought about the future. We are now at the planning stage of our extensions which will be built in the year 1967-8. The school will then grow to its full size - an eight form entry school with a population of about 1300 pupils. We are already hoping that the extensions will largely consist of special accommodation for the older pupils where private study, tutorial and discussion work will be very well catered for and where our senior pupils can withdraw with some privacy and dignity. We are also hoping to see an "Arts Centre" with a distinctive character of its own, with provision for a wide range of Arts & Crafts, Drama and Music. *(2) A new library - great emphasis on P.S.* *(1) Sw. pool. 3 times the size. Support from H.S.A.*

The school is already a long way towards the ideal of a flexible school which I presented last year. During last year the staff had several discussions about our curriculum and organisation and some experiments have been initiated in the current year. We are combining with Brislington School in order to make a full programme of General Studies available to our VI formers. This is a most important antidote to the excessive specialisation which the normal programme of 3 'A' levels imposes. We are also carrying out in various parts of the school experiments in team teaching designed to give us greater flexibility. We are constantly finding ways of sending our senior pupils out into the adult world and bringing the adult world into the school.

The school has, I believe, a most interesting future ahead of it. But I think today is a special occasion when we can afford to look back. With its retired Headmaster as guest of honour, strong support from representatives of the Old Students Association, reports from Universities of some brilliant successes by our Old Pupils and a constant trickle into the school of ex-pupils from nearly every possible walk of life, all of whom expressing loyalty and affection, Hengrove is a comprehensive school which has grown up.

Mr Waterhouse added the following in his own handwriting but we have retyped it:

All our achievements are the product of co-operative endeavour by staff and pupils. I should like to pay a warm tribute to the loyalty, energy and good humour of the staff and I know they would wish to be associated with my thanks to the many local citizens who so generously give us help. It is surprising how many of them willingly give up their time to come to have talks and discussions with groups of our pupils as acting unpaid teachers.

I should like to mention particularly on this occasion our District Inspector, Mr Boxall, who goes into semi-retirement at the end of this term. It is pleasant to know that he will continue his association with the school for a short time.

Lastly, to the Governors of the school, may I say thank you for all the support given to the school; their meetings are always vigorous, lively and friendly, never dull.

Thirteen days later the school held the Christmas Concert 1965. We have a copy of the programme.

HENGROVE SCHOOL, BRISTOL

Christmas

Concert

Thursday, December 16th, 1965

7.30 p.m.

—o—

Admission by Programme 1/-

Massed Choirs:
God Rest You Merry, Gentlemen
Arr. M. Bailey

Senior Choir: Susanni Arr. Martin Shaw

*Carol: Hark! the Herald Angels Sing Mendelssohn
(A.M. No. 37)

2nd Year Choir:
(a) The Carol of the Drum K. Davis
(b) The Birds Arr. Martin Shaw

Brass Band

Senior Choir:
(a) The Stable Bare Words and Music by C. Toply
(b) The Garden of Jesus Geoffrey Shaw

Massed Choirs: Sans Day Carol Arr. Martin Shaw

*Carol: The First Nowell Traditional
(A.M. No. 266)

1st Year Choir:
(a) The Grassmere Carol Arthur Somervell
(b) A Child's Song at Christmas Pasefield

Brass Band

Massed Choirs: On This Day Arr. Gustav Holst

Massed Choirs: Gloria in Excelsis Deo Eri

2nd Year Boys: The Truth from Above Melo
Margaret V

*Carol: See Amid the Winter's Snow Sir J.
(A.M. No. 261)

Senior Choir: The Crown of Roses Tsel

Brass Band

2nd Year Choir: Mary's Boy Child Jester

*Carol: O Come, All Ye Faithful J.
(A.M. No. 36)

Massed Choirs:
(a) The Seven Joys of Mary Tr
(b) Merry Christmas Mar

The audience is invited to stand and sing the Carols m

Conductors: M. J. Bailey, Miss M. Donovan.
Accompanist: Miss E. Parsons.
Solo Flute: Margaret Vlaeminke.

Stimulated by our discussions in 2011 on the Hengrove School History Project, Mr Waterhouse kindly wrote another article which reveals his innovatory philosophy.

He identified 2 styles of headmastership reflecting new theories of management – 'benevolent dictatorship' and 'aspiring democrat' and rejected both. He wanted to manifest something more positive and creative. You can read more in his article "Some More Newcomers":

Some More Newcomers

During my early years at Hengrove I became convinced of the importance of welcoming and integrating newcomers, both pupils and staff. Perhaps I was influenced by my own experiences as a newcomer.

There were already in place comprehensive arrangements for the smooth transfer of pupils from their primary schools. But I wanted to go further and to let them spend their first day in the school simply getting to know the place and the people.
I was curious to find out how they were perceiving these innovations. So I decided to join a little group of girls at their lunch table on their first day at Hengrove.
I asked them how they were getting on. The girl on my immediate right quickly took over. She said her name was Christine and proceeded to recount all the events of the morning. They had met their new form teacher, the head and deputy head of the lower school and a few others. She rattled off what their respective responsibilities were. "But", she said,"We haven't seen the Head yet. I've no idea what he does!" Suddenly alarm bells were ringing in my head. I thought I had better come clean before things got embarrassing. "As a matter of fact, "I said, "I'm the Head." The faces of the girls fell; that is, all except Christine, who leaned forward, smiled and said, "Well, exactly what do you do?" The faces of the other girls were now registering crisis. Fortunately, my instinctive response was to burst out laughing and suddenly all confidence was restored. We spent the rest of the meal chatting together like old friends.
I was happy with this feedback. But Christine had touched a raw nerve. What exactly did I do? And what exactly should I be doing?

I was not happy with the implied management style at Hengrove. It seemed that the staff had been encouraged to make all their decisions and to solve all their problems themselves. Only a limited number of decisions or problems were passed to the Head. I discovered that the style had a name – 'Management by Exception'. I remember bitterly exclaiming on one occasion, " I handle only two kinds of problems: those that are impossible to solve, and those that are extremely unpleasant!" I was being forced into the role of a 'God of Wrath'!
I searched for better ways of working. Consulting my fellow Heads in the Bristol area, I recognised two styles: the benevolent dictator who worked very hard making all the decisions for the school; and the aspiring democrat who believed that every decision had to be made by one or other of a long list of committees. I rejected both; I wanted something that was more positive and creative.

The hint came from David Prowles, a newly appointed Head of English. Towards the end of his first year, he came to me and said, "I want you to tell me how I'm doing." "Fine!" I replied, "Delighted to have you on the staff." He shook his head. "No. I mean that I want a thorough appraisal of the work of my department and some guidance about the future." To cut a long story short we had that discussion. It was thorough and constructive, but neither of us hesitated to express disappointments or criticism. At the end I knew instantly that this was the way forward. I immediately invited all Heads of Department and all Heads of Year to prepare for the same kind of conversation. They were all quickly enthusiastic and improvements and developments soon became a normal part of all our lives. In particular, as soon as objectives had been agreed my own efforts were directed at providing the support and the members of the section would work really hard to achieve the targets they had set for themselves.
Today all this sounds obvious, but, at the time, it was a bit revolutionary. Word got around. I found myself on the circuit as a management guru – first a lecture to the Heads of Bristol schools; then a paper and presentation to the Schools Council (the national body for research and development); then a keynote lecture to the Department of Education's first course on School Management, then

several invitations to run courses on School Management; then an interview on the BBC's Education Programme; and ultimately a keynote lecture at an international conference held at Canberra University (this a few years after leaving Hengrove).

It was tempting to respond to all the offers but I hope I managed to keep my feet on the ground. I knew that the school had to come first.

I was concerned too about the induction of young teachers, those who arrived fresh from their training and in their probationary year. A simple solution presented itself. The Department of Home Economics laid on a once a week lunch for them They were in charge of the event and they were empowered to invite anyone to join them for lunch and discussion. It was an instant success; many senior staff who were invited expressed enthusiasm for the opportunity to explain themselves in a non-threatening situation.

Then I added a bonus. I invited one group of young teachers to present their own report on the school with particular attention to the induction and support for beginning teachers. The result was both illuminating and reassuring.

The Prefects, Head Boy and Girl for 1965-1966 are reproduced below – also the school was represented at the 17th Annual Concert by Secondary School Children at the Colston Hall in May 1966.

1965 – 1966

HEAD BOY
William Davies.

HEAD GIRL
Margaret Vlaeminke

DEPUTY HEAD BOY
Alan Hayward.

DEPUTY HEAD GIRL
Linda Harvey.

PREFECTS 1965–1966

Re-elected

A. Pearson.
A. Tredge
G. Michle.
C. Baker
P. Lowrey.
G. Higgs
K. Crombie
H. Southey

R Biggs
D. Bassett
R. Hedges.
Max Hamilton.
Norman Clark.
W. Conter.
L. Pettey.
M. Gould.

Elected

Lynda Jordan.
Jud. Halliday
Angela Graves.
Susan Dwyer
Susan Armet
Jane Mulkern.
Jennifer Nicholas
Margaret Tiler
Julia Price
Jannie Blair
Mary Hamburg.

D Bailey.
John Haines.
G J Mills.
Jeffery Harding
A. Bark
Stephen Sainsbury.
John Logan.
Bryan Davie.
Jack F Bacon.
William Goss.
David Hoskins.
Robin Harris.

102

SIXTEENTH ANNUAL

CONCERT
(2nd Series)

by

Secondary School Children

Friday, May 13th, 1966 at 7.0 p.m.

AT

COLSTON HALL

Entertainments Manager: F. K. COWLEY

MASSED CHOIR   MADRIGAL SINGERS
FOUR PART CHOIR   RECORDER PLAYERS
SCHOOLS' ORCHESTRA   BRASS BAND

Conductor: A. VAUGHAN DAVIES
Music Adviser to Bristol Education Committee

BRISTOL SCHOOLS' MUSIC SOCIETY

PROGRAMME · · SIXPENCE

ORCHESTRA

Homage March from the Sigurd Jorsalfar Suite	Grieg (1843–1907)
Finale from Symphony No. 5 in C Minor	Beethoven (1770–1827)
Alla Marcia from Karelia Suite	Sibelius (1865–1957)

FOUR-PART CHOIR

Benedicite .. .. Vaughan Williams

MASSED CHOIRS

The Old Hundredth Psalm Tune   Vaughan Williams
    "All People that on Earth do Dwell"   (1872–1958)

(arranged for the Coronation of her Majesty Queen Elizabeth II at Westminster Abbey on 2nd June, 1953)

The audience (seated) is invited to join in the singing of Verses 1, 2 and 5

Verse I
    All people that on earth do dwell,
    Sing to the Lord with cheerful voice;
    Him serve with fear, His praise forth tell.
    Come ye before Him, and rejoice.

Verse II
    The Lord, ye know, is God indeed,
    Without our aid He did us make
    We are his folk, He doth us feed,
    And for His sheep He doth us take.

Verse III
Verse IV }   Choirs only.
     (Orchestral interlude)

Verse V
    To Father, Son, and Holy Ghost,
    The God whom heaven and earth adore,
    From men and from the angel host
    Be praise and glory evermore. Amen.

SECONDARY SCHOOLS TAKING PART

MASSED CHOIR   *Associate Conductors: Miss N. Gee, Mr. M. Bailey.*

Ashton Park School	Speedwell Girls' School
Baptist Mills School	Speedwell Boys' School
Bishopston School	St. Bede's School
Connaught Boys' School	St. Bernadette School
Fishponds Mixed School	St. George Boys' School
Greenway School	St. George Girls' School
Hengrove School	St. Mary Redcliffe Boys' School
Lockleaze School	Southville Mixed School
Marksbury Secondary School	Temple Colston School
Monks Park School	Wick Road School
Pen Park School	Whitefield Boys' School
Portway Secondary School	Whitefield Girls' School

FOUR PART CHOIR   *Associate Conductor: Mr. B. M. Simms.*

Brislington School	Merrywood Grammar School for Boys
Central Commercial School	Monks Park School
Collegiate School	Pen Park School
Colston's Girls' School	Red Maids' School
Cotham Grammar School	Rose Green High School
Fairfield Grammar School	St. George School
Lockleaze School	St. Mary Redcliffe Boys' School

MADRIGAL SINGERS   *Associate Conductor: Miss M. Blacklock.*

Duncan House School	Redland High School
Merrywood Grammar School for Girls	Rose Green High School

BRASS BAND   *Associate Conductor: Mr. E. Davidge.*

Cotham Grammar School	Portway Boys' School
Fairfield Grammar School	Speedwell Boys' School
Greenway School	St. George School
Hengrove School	St. Mary Redcliffe Boys' School
Lockleaze School	Wick Road School
Merrywood Grammar School for Boys	Whitefield Boys' School
Monks Park School	

SCHOOLS' ORCHESTRA   *Associate Conductors: Messrs. Ayres, Budden, Morris, Alexander, Davis, Dunster and Miss H. Cope.*

Ashton Park School	Hengrove School
Bedminster Down School	La Retraite High School
Bishopston School	Lawrence Weston School
Brislington School	Lockleaze School
Bristol Grammar School	Merrywood Grammar School for Girls
Cathedral School	Merrywood Grammar School for Boys
Clifton College	Monks Park School
Clifton High School	Queen Elizabeth's Hospital
Colston's Girls' School	Redland High School
Cotham Grammar School	Rose Green High School
Duncan House School	Speedwell Girls' School
Fairfield Grammar School	St. Brendan's College
Greenway School	St. George School
Hartcliffe School	Withywood School
Henbury School	

RECORDER PLAYERS   *Associate Conductor: Miss D. J. Heath.*

Bedminster Down School	Merrywood Grammar School for Girls
Bishopston School	Monks Park School
Collegiate School	Portway Secondary School
Connaught Girls' School	Rose Green High School
Duncan House School	St. Bede's School
Greenway School	St. George Girls' School
Hengrove School	Speedwell Girls' School
Lockleaze School	Whitefield Girls' School
	Withywood School

Included in the orchestra (leader, MR. GEORGE BUDDEN), which accompanies the singing are students from Newton Park Training College, and principal players from the Schools' Orchestra.

Young, Humphrys & Lodge, Ltd., Bristol

In November 1966 the whole school was involved in the production of "Hastings: a Tapestry in Music". The script had been written by Harold Chasey – the Senior History Teacher – the music composed and conducted by Maurice Bailey – the Head of Music. It commemorated the 900th Anniversary of the Battle of Hastings in 1066. Mr Waterhouse spoke for many when he said in his speech at the Prizegiving in December 1966.

> *"Many visitors, experienced members of the teaching profession, shared my own conclusion that I had not experienced the like of this in any school before."*

The whole school decided it should be repeated in March 1967 (See Chapter 6).

Mr Waterhouse's Third Prizegiving Speech on 15 December 1966

The year had been one of stability and consolidation – pupil numbers rising to 900 – 950.

As you read the speech overleaf you can sense the rising excitement regarding the forthcoming Stage III extension. There would be a new VI Form Centre, an Arts Centre, a Swimming Pool, a new Library Suite and much more. Read on for details.

HEADMASTER'S REPORT FOR THE YEAR 1965/66

SPEECH DAY, 15TH DECEMBER, 1966

Mr. Chairman, Alderman and Mrs. Parish, Ladies and Gentlemen, Hengrove School has had its twelfth birthday this term and I hope my report will show that the school year 1965/66 has been one of progress in all aspects of school life.

It has been a year of stability and consolidation rather than of spectacular growth and development. Our numbers on roll have remained fairly constant between 900 and 950. We have been particularly fortunate in that during the year only four full-time teachers left the school and each one of these left for a promotion. Only one full-time teacher leaves at Christmas; Mr. J.T. Evans, the Head of our English Department, has been appointed Headmaster of Presteigne Grammar School in Radnorshire. The young teachers recruited in 1964 and 1965 are all still with us and they have proved, without exception, to be splendid additions to the strength of the school. Some change, of course, is always good and it is right that teachers should seek promotion but in these days a headmaster knows all too well that the quality of work, the discipline and the general morale of the school depend very markedly on a certain amount of continuity of effort from the teaching staff of the school. Hengrove has had this during the last year and I know that I am not alone in my impression that it shows very clearly indeed.

This short period of stability has given us the opportunity to make useful progress on several matters concerning our curriculum and our internal organisation. Perhaps no one of these is spectacular in itself but the building of high quality work, good discipline and a good tone generally are things which do not make newspaper headlines.

We co-operated with Brislington School to organise a joint scheme of Sixth Form General Studies. We are anxious that our Sixth Formers shall not become narrow-minded specialists, which some of them would certainly do if left entirely to the mercy of the 'A' level subject syllabuses. I know that the opinion is shared by Brislington School that the Sixth Formers have benefited both educationally and socially by this linking of the two schools.

We began to make experiments in providing subject courses for non-examination pupils in the Fourth year, with the intention that eventually these would be expanded to cater for the special needs of these pupils when the school leaving age is raised in 1970. Our organisation was on a team teaching basis and this means that pupils may work sometimes in very large groups, sometimes in very small groups according to the nature of the work they are doing. It has enabled us to accomplish much more than is possible in the rigid division into classes of 30. We have made similar experiments in the teaching of music in the lower school and this same type of organisation has made it possible for a larger number of children to learn a musical instrument in school time. This system of organisation gives us great flexibility and many more of the staff are keen to take part in such experiments as soon as conditions are right.

We have made a complete overhaul of our system of records and reports. We have aimed to make the maximum amount of information available to teachers and parents with as little clerical work as possible for the teaching staff. Parents will now receive six reports each school year and I hope that they will regard this greater frequency of reporting, with all the opportunities for consultation, as an indication of our determination to involve them as much as possible in the education of their children. The staff will benefit too by having all the information about a pupil's work and welfare in one place.

We have made great strides in building up our arrangements for the tutorial and pastoral care of individual pupils. We still have a long way to go but I have been very heartened by numerous examples of real care shown by form teachers and year tutors during the year. We shall be taking every opportunity of developing this essential decentralisation while, at the same time, guarding our lines of communication carefully in order to preserve a sense of unity and common purpose within the school.

A new power has risen in our midst! I refer to the Hengrove School Association, the birth of which I reported last year. Already the Association is a going concern but the signs are that the school is going to benefit a great deal in the near future from the interest and enthusiasm shown by this very lively organisation. I strongly urge parents who have not already done so to join the Association in order to be able to participate fully in the very worthwhile programme which has been planned for 1967. We have continued to organise our Parents' Meetings so that parents and subject teachers can consult each other; these have always been very well attended and staff and parents alike have come to feel that they are an essential part of each year's work.

Staff and pupils gave up an enormous amount of time and effort as usual in the summer term to external examinations. We had 58 candidates for G.C.E. 'O' Level and 108 for the Certificate of Secondary Education. The number of candidates at 'A' level was somewhat smaller this year but we are expecting to have one of our biggest entries in 1967. Already 18 Sixth Form students have applied for University and College places.

On the games field the school has maintained its traditions; not only do we cover a very wide range of team games, not only do we achieve considerable success in competition with other schools, but the high standards of play and general behaviour of our players are frequently the subject of favourable comment by outside observers. Credit for this must go to those teachers who give up so much time and effort for the benefit of the pupils.

Youth Hostelling, Camping and Continental travel are still on the menu and Hengrove pupils have this year set foot on Exmoor, the Lake District, the Isle of Man, the Isle of Wight, Brittany as well as numerous spots nearer home. A new venture this year was an adventure expedition to Lundy Island for fifth year boys after their external examinations. A most interesting exhibition of painting, photography and geological field studies resulted.

All our clubs and societies continue to flourish and I hope that pupils and parents do not forget the generosity of the staff who make all these things possible. A very stimulating evening of Music and Drama was provided by the pupils of the lower school in the Spring and I cannot resist the temptation to stray into 1966/67 to mention the recent splendid achievement of the whole school in the production of "Hastings: a tapestry in music". Many visitors, experienced members of the teaching profession, shared my own conclusions that I had not experienced the like of this in any school before. If it is humanly possible we will repeat "Hastings" in the near future. *March 9th. decision of the whole se.*

Community Service retains its prominence in the school. The Lower School continues to make its weekly collections for the Freedom from Hunger Campaign and at Christmas time each form in the school adopts an elderly or invalid person to visit with a Christmas parcel. The Sixth Form keep up their tradition of an annual Concert in aid of charity and co-operates with the N.S.P.C.C. to run a party for children recommended by that organisation. A good link has been made with Ilminster Avenue Primary School which runs its own club for younger children. This is mainly staffed by Hengrove Sixth Formers. It is not without significance that one of our regular Speech Day prizes is now a prize for Community Service and the donor is a former head boy of the school.

Discussions started during the Autumn Term (a year ago) about the extensions to the school which were planned for the financial year 1967/8. Three main considerations had to be borne in mind: (1) the need to provide adequately and appropriately for a much larger Sixth Form; (2) the need to overcome the excessive fragmentation of specialist accommodation from which the school suffers at present; (3) the need to plan for the ideas and methods of the future not of the past. The plans which have resulted from this thinking have involved considerable changes to the existing buildings as well as a substantial amount of new building. The general intention has been to collect together specialist rooms in order to provide areas each with a distinctive character of its own. Thus in our reorganised school we shall have:- (1) A Science area. This will be in the existing building and will involve the creation of new laboratories, one for Advanced Physics, one for Advanced Chemistry and one for Advanced Biology together with a new science lecture room; (2) A centre for the Sixth Form. This will be in the new buildings and will include small seminar rooms, a dining room, and a quiet room; (3) A centre for the fourth and fifth year pupils who are not preparing for external examinations. This will be in the new buildings and will include a lecture room, small and large work rooms and areas for Practical Science and Home Economics; (4) An Arts Centre. This will be in the new buildings and will comprise a pottery studio, a 3-dimensional studio, a general craft room and a painting studio all of which will surround an Arts courtyard. These will be associated with rooms for Needlecraft and a whole suite of Music Rooms together with a Drama Studio; (5) improved accommodation for Geography and Commerce and for Modern Languages (Language Laboratory) and Physical Education (Swimming Pool); (6) A completely new Library suite. I would like to tell you about this as a model of involvement and co-operation. In the summer of 1965 the parents on the committee of the Hengrove School Association asked me to suggest a project towards which they could devote their money raising efforts. I made several suggestions to them and their choice fell on improved library facilities in the school. At that time I simply had thoughts of extending the existing library, but emboldened by their enthusiasm I decided to press for a completely new library suite in our extensions. The idea was warmly welcomed at the Council House and I confess to being quite overjoyed that my figure of 3,600 ft. was accepted. Our library will be bigger than the school hall! And it should be! Miss Hickson, Inspector of Schools, became a staunch ally and together we visited libraries in some of the London Comprehensive Schools. Our architects spent hours with us talking about the lay-out and fittings and many other friends gave us valuable advice and criticism. We are still a long way from the finished product but I shall always remember that this was a library that ~~the parents asked for.~~ originated in the minds of our parents.

I must express a general word of appreciation about the way in which these extensions have been planned. The close consultation between the school, the local authority administration and the architects, Messrs. Burrough and Hannam, has been truly excellent. Many of the senior staff in the school have experienced the great personal satisfaction of seeing their ideas taken up sympathetically and used in the planning of our new accommodation.

Our extensions have been brought forward into the current building programme and we are therefore to have them available sooner than we had thought. Certainly by 1968 the Hengrove school buildings will be bigger and very much better than they are now. ~~Meanwhile~~ our period of stability and consolidation will come to an end. With rising numbers (8 forms will in future come in each year) we shall soon reach a total of about 1300 pupils. This presents a challenge to the staff and to me. Size is a great advantage to the pupils - it offers them more varied opportunities both in work and play. But it presents problems in organisation which must be overcome if the school is to be fully effective on behalf of each individual pupil. I have every confidence that the preparations we are making now will serve us well when Hengrove is fully grown. We have enormous advantages — a loyal and

Mr Waterhouse added in his own handwriting the paragraph typed below:

We have enormous advantages – a loyal and energetic staff, a lively and friendly group of governors, parents who are giving every-increasing support to the school, a Local Authority in which one can have complete faith and last and by no means least a body of pupils of great potential both academically and socially. It is difficult to see how we can fail.

We have below the programme for the December 1966 Prizegiving.

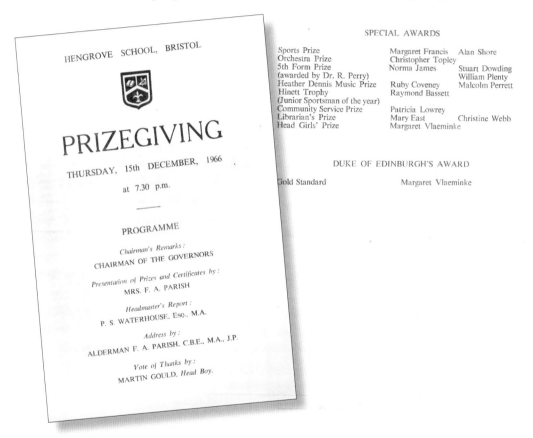

HENGROVE SCHOOL, BRISTOL

PRIZEGIVING

THURSDAY, 15th DECEMBER, 1966

at 7.30 p.m.

PROGRAMME

Chairman's Remarks :
CHAIRMAN OF THE GOVERNORS

Presentation of Prizes and Certificates by :
MRS. F. A. PARISH

Headmaster's Report :
P. S. WATERHOUSE. ESQ., M.A.

Address by :
ALDERMAN F. A. PARISH. C.B.E., M.A., J.P.

Vote of Thanks by :
MARTIN GOULD. Head Boy.

SPECIAL AWARDS

Sports Prize	Margaret Francis	Alan Shore
Orchestra Prize	Christopher Topley	
5th Form Prize	Norma James	Stuart Dowding
(awarded by Dr. R. Perry)		William Plenty
Heather Dennis Music Prize	Ruby Coveney	Malcolm Perrett
Hinett Trophy	Raymond Bassett	
(Junior Sportsman of the year)		
Community Service Prize	Patricia Lowrey	
Librarian's Prize	Mary East	Christine Webb
Head Girls' Prize	Margaret Vlaeminke	

DUKE OF EDINBURGH'S AWARD

Gold Standard   Margaret Vlaeminke

SOUTHERN UNIVERSITIES' JOINT BOARD

GENERAL CERTIFICATE OF EDUCATION

ADVANCED LEVEL

William Davies   Ronald Richards
Alan Gregg   Christopher Topley
Alan Hayward   Linda Harvey
Ronald Long   Jacqueline Harris

ORDINARY LEVEL

M. Allen, A. Bach, J. Bacon, D. Bailey, R. Brake, M. F. Brown, N. Carter, A. Curtis, W. Davies, B. Dawes, B. Dittmer, R. Dollin, J. Edwards, D. Evans, P. Farthing, A. Forsey, F. Fox, W. Giles, B. Greenwood, A. Gregg, J. Haines, J. Harris, R. Harris, D. Haskins, R. Hedges, N. Howarth, A. Hayward, R. Kays, C. Lee, J. Logan, G. Mills, A. Mundy, R. Parsons, A. Pearson, D. Rogers, S. Salisbury, R. Senior, R. Sherring, A. Shore, C. Topley, P. Vardakis, G. Wade, P. Walden, G. Withers, D. Bassett.

S. Armett, C. Baker, H. Biggs, J. Coles, K. Crombie, T. Dark, A. Dodge, P. Dunk, M. Faithful, M. Filer, M. Gambling, A. Gough, J. Halliday, J. Harris, L. Harvey, J. Hellier, C. Higgs, J. Hollister, I. Jeffries, L. Jenkins, J. Jones, J. Lewis, P. Lowrey, G. Meikle, J. Mulkern, A. Payne, L. Sharples, M. Southey, J. Stokes, G. Thomas, C. Thompson, J. Trebess, S. Vaughan, B. Vincent, M. Vlaeminke, C. Ashton.

CERTIFICATE OF SECONDARY EDUCATION

M. Allen, S. Biggs, R. Brake, M. F. Brown, M. Brown, B. Brunt, G. Baber, B. Chittock, P. Cleave, D. Colley, M. Coombe, A. Curtis, G. Dawe, B. Dittmer, S. Dowding, J. Edwards, D. Evans, M. Farley, P. Farthing, D. Filer, A. Forsey, F. Fox, W. Giles, R. Gough, J. Haas, J. Harris, M. Kemp, L. Kushner, M. Lawrence, S. Lock, J. Long, I. Mawer, G. Mills, B. Millett, J. Morrison, P. Moulder, A. Mundy, A. Nicholls, B. Nicholls, W. Owen, P. Parry, E. Page, R. Pearce, R. Pearn, B. Perrett, D. Roberts, D. Rogers, R. Senior, A. Shore, I. Silman, M. Stabb, S. Sumeghy, R. Stone, J. Tawton, P. Taylor, P. Thomas, T. Thomas, J. Turner, G. Wade, P. Waite, M. Watton, P. Watts, P. Walden, D. Warfield.

S. Armett, C. Ashton, A. Bane, E. Bessell, L. Bingham, E. Brooks, G. Burnett, E. Curry, S. Day, J. Davies, P. Dunk, D. Fancy, M. Francis, M. Gill, D. Groves, R. Hawkins, J. Hellier, J. Hollister, M. Jackson, N. James, I. Jeffries, L. Jenkins, D. Jones, A. Mall, S. Mizon, J. Mulkern, A. Payne, S. Price, A. Pye, C. Salisbury, L. Sharples, C. Spiers, J. Stokes, S. Summers, J. Trebess, S. Vaughan, P. Vickery, B. Vincent, R. Weekes, P. Whyatt.

SUBJECT PRIZES

ADVANCED LEVEL

Geography	W. Davies
	A. Gregg
French	A. Hayward
Botany	R. Richards
Zoology	R. Richards
	J. Harris
Music	C. Topley

ORDINARY LEVEL

Religious Instruction	M. Filer
English	M. Faithful
History	P. Walden
Geography	Glenda Thomas
French	Robin Harris
Human Biology	Patricia Lowrey
Chemistry	Nikolos Howarth
Physics	Nikolos Howarth
Mathematics	David Haskins
Additional Mathematics	Ann Dodge
	Roy Hedges
Geom. & M/c Drawing	Robert Dollin
Art	David Haskins
Music	Margaret Vlaeminke
Cookery	Judith Coles
Needlework	Ann Payne
Metalwork	John Harris

CERTIFICATE OF SECONDARY EDUCATION

Certificate Prizes

Malcolm Farley	Philip Wait
Dennis Colley	Christine Salisbury
Ian Mawer	Malcolm Lawrence

FORM PRIZES

Form IVA1	Hilary Arnold
Form IVA2	Janet Nial, Terence Long
Form IVB1	Mary East, Loxley Sutherland
Form IVB2	Adrian Morgan
Form IVG	Jacqueline Lewis

Towards the end of Summer Term in July 1967 the school invited parents and friends to the annual Concert of Music featuring Massed Choirs, Junior Choir, Brass Band, Madrigal Group, Recorder Group, Orchestra and even the staff. These concerts were the product of many hours of preparation and rehearsal.

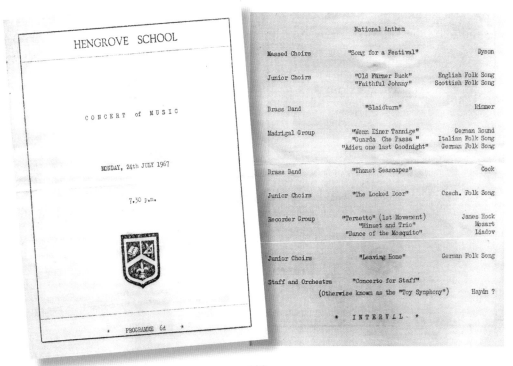

HENGROVE SCHOOL

CONCERT of MUSIC

MONDAY, 24th JULY 1967

7.30 p.m.

PROGRAMME 6d

National Anthem

Massed Choirs	"Song for a Festival"	Dyson
Junior Choirs	"Old Farmer Buck"	English Folk Song
	"Faithful Johnny"	Scottish Folk Song
Brass Band	"Slaidburn"	Rimmer
Madrigal Group	"Wenn Einer Tannige"	German Round
	"Guarda Che Passa "	Italian Folk Song
	"Adieu one last Goodnight"	German Folk Song
Brass Band	"Thanet Seascapes"	Cook
Junior Choirs	"The Locked Door"	Czech. Folk Song
Recorder Group	"Terzetto" (1st Movement)	James Hook
	"Minuet and Trio"	Mozart
	"Dance of the Mosquito"	Liadov
Junior Choirs	"Leaving Home"	German Folk Song
Staff and Orchestra	"Concerto for Staff"	
	(Otherwise known as the "Toy Symphony")	Haydn ?

* INTERVAL *

Orchestra	"Overture for a Festive Occasion"	Bailey
Choir	"Pick a Bale of Cotton"	arr. Gardner
Orchestra	"March" from "Scipio" "Elizabethan Serenade"	Handel Binge
From "Hastings"	"Requiem" "Hymn of Triumph"	
Orchestra	"Slow Music for a Ballet" "Breton Fiddle Tune"	Handel
Choir	"See the Gipsies"	Kodály
Vocal Duet	"Swansea Town" (Soloists : M. Perrett and W.Plenty)	Ratcliffe
Choir and Orchestra	"Homage to Sul" (See programme note)	Bailey
Orchestra	"Slow Minuet" "Farandole"	Lully Bizet
From "Hastings"	"Now we must Defend our Soil" "Finale"	

Mr Waterhouse's Fourth Speech Day – December 11th 1967

In April 1967 building had commenced on the stage III extension (see plans overleaf!) The staffing had become more heavily weighted at the younger end of the age scale. The habit of individual study (a skill for life) was being encouraged and there was a move away from the idea of 30 pupils in one classroom with one teacher…

Read on for more on these important changes.

110

Speech Day - 15th December, 1967.

Mr. Chairman, Mr. & Mrs. Thompson, Ladies and Gentlemen, I have great pleasure in presenting my report for the school year 1966/67, and of welcoming on this occasion, as our chief guests, Mr. Thompson, the chief education officer, and Mrs. Thompson. It is particularly appropriate that Mr. Thompson should be our chief speaker this evening because it is he, more than any other individual, who has been responsible for the enormous amount of administrative work in connection with the extensions to the school which are now in progress.

Our numbers have remained fairly constant during the year between 900 and 1000. Parents will remember that last year I remarked on the fact that only four teachers left the school during the whole of the school year, and commented that a short period of stability like that was of enormous value in building up our curriculum and internal organisation. I warned, however, that lulls often come before storms and during the year under review we have lost a greater number of staff, but two of them went to headships, one to a lectureship at a college of education, one emigrated to the new world, four others got promotion and two left to produced babies, which I think could be rated as a fair measure of achievement. It means now, of course, that our staffing is more heavily weighted at the younger end, and far from regretting this I welcome it because I am so enormously impressed by the quality of the young people entering the profession today. Our newcomers have already established themselves well and are making lively and interesting contributions to the work of the school. While on the subject of the staff, I should like to announce that Mr. Baird, the head of the school's Art Department, has been awarded a Schoolmaster's Travelling Fellowship by the Goldsmith's Company of London; this will enable him to spend a five month period next summer travelling in southern and eastern Europe and in Turkey, and we are all hoping that his studies of Florentine and Byzantine Art will enable him to enrich the work of his department here in school. This is a great honour which Mr. Baird has won for himself and we are pleased to bask in some reflected glory. Mr. Prowles, who has been our head of English since his appointment last January, has produced a most stimulating book for school use which has recently been published by Messrs. Collins. I know that it is already arousing considerable interest and I am sure that it will be very highly thought of when it arrives in the schools. Incidentally, Mr. Prowles has also found time since his arrival to accomplish an engagement to Miss Jones of the Geography staff!

The current fashion in education is for curriculum change. In the last few years there has been an enormous amount written on this subject and anyone who is not changing his curriculum is regarded as somewhat suspect. Here at Hengrove we are trying to move forward without being guilty of unseemly haste and without putting at risk some of the good things which already exist in the school. We have devised a course of Personal and Community Living for 4th and 5th year pupils and hope, eventually, to offer this syllabus in the C.S.E. examination. We are trying to include in it so many of those things that people say we ought to be teaching in school, like proper management of money, a better understanding of the mass media and advertising, a knowledge of social welfare arrangements in the country, and so on. Our Science teaching in the lower school is undergoing some changes in response to the stimulus from the workers of the Nuffield Foundation. We have not actually joined in the pilot experiment which is being conducted in Bristol, but we are very much tuned in to what is going on there and hope to make our own distinctive contributions. Our Modern Language department for some time now has been co-operating with the Nuffield Foundation Foreign Language Teaching Materials project at York University. Most of our children start their new languages by audio-visual methods now and we expect to have a language laboratory in about 12 months time. These are some examples of the quiet progress we are making here. We are not seeking to hit the headlines by chasing gimmicks or every new fashion that comes to our notice. I find myself thinking of the seed which fell on stony ground which shot up rather quickly but could not survive when the sun rose because it had no depth of earth. I hope our seed is falling into good soil where it will bear fruit a hundredfold, or sixtyfold, or thirtyfold.

Our Summer term, as usual, was very much taken up with examinations and it is a source of anxiety to me to realise how much the future of our pupils hinges on a few marks in 'A' level and 'O' level examinations. Nevertheless, we can be delighted with the success of our Upper Sixth. Over twenty of them went on to full-time higher education, following degree or other advanced courses in the universities, colleges of technology, colleges of education, Art and Drama. In view of the fact that there has been some publicity about the quantity and quality of the information available to sixth formers in schools about higher education, I should like to give parents a very firm assurance that we take a great deal of care to ensure that we have all information about courses of higher education properly housed and classified in the school Library and available to all our pupils, and that no sixth former who is qualified ever fails to get a place through lack of information. I know that many efforts have been made to supplement the work done by schools in this respect, but I am pleased to say that Hengrove pupils do not really need it, although they are, of course, fully at liberty to seek advice wherever they choose to do so. We have recently extended our services to include careers information. I felt for some time that the proper place for careers information is in the Library and we now have a complete Careers Library based on the classification recommended by the Central Youth Employment Executive, which is available at all times to all pupils. I am hoping, in the very near future, to open the Careers Library in the evenings for parents.

In the activities organised outside school hours the school has had a truly remarkable year. I am quite sure that the musical achievements have received widespread publicity through the extraordinarily interesting concert on the theme of the 'Battle of Hastings', but what I would like parents to know most of all is that three weeks after the mammoth effort of 'Hastings' the school Brass Band and Choirs put on a really delightful carol concert, and at the end of the school year in the summer all our performers combined in a general concert, in which the standard of singing and playing was of a very high order indeed. At one time or another we had over eighty pupils playing Chess in the school and the quality of play was extremely high. The school won the Bristol Boys' Senior championship and the Junior championship as well as the individual championship in both sections. We had success too at the South-west Regional championships and Roy Hedges of the Sixth form came second in the National championships of the Federation of Boys' Clubs. Out of school games also had a particularly successful year. The school were winners of the under 19 seven-a-side Rugby Tournament and also winners of the Woodcock Shield, the under 15 Soccer Tournament. The latter game was played at the City ground and was an extremely exciting game very well supported by pupils of the school. The school gave special recognition to the two teams by presenting each individual with a small medallion, the Hengrove School Assoc-iation very generously making a donation towards this. Several of our pupils have represented the city in games, athletics and swimming. While it is always pleasing to report successes there is always the additional pleasure of knowing the high standards which are demanded and obtained from both boys and girls in dress, attendance and behaviour. Youth Hostelling continues to flourish. Altogether there were fourteen weekends and two longer expeditions. At a time when the Duke of Edinburgh Award seems to be generally on the decline, I am happy to report that the scheme here continues to attract both boys and girls, but particularly girls, and the school is getting quite near to its 400th award since the scheme started. Many other school clubs and societies continue to flourish; there are camps, theatre parties, dances, sports day, careers conventions, an adventure camp at the Outward Bound school, Aberdovey, parties organised for other children not those in the school, brass band festivals, as well as the regular meetings of clubs and societies. We can still boast an Archery club and a boys' Cookery club in addition to many others more commonly found.

Building started on the site in April and we hope that our extensions may be ready in about twelve months time. Once again, I should like to express my appreciation of the way in which there has been the closest consultation with the staff of the school. I know that the staff feel themselves very much involved and I hope that the buildings will be better and more appropriate as a result. The extensions will consist of new areas for the upper school pupils, including a Sixth Form centre, an area for more informal work by 4th and 5th year pupils and a new Library. An Arts centre will also be included containing new Art and Craft studios together with additional accommodation for Needlecraft, and a whole floor devoted to Music and Drama.

Throughout the year I have been very conscious of the enormous amount of support that the school gets from the local community. The Hengrove School Association is growing in strength all the time. I often feel that the quality of their achievements deserves a better support from parents than they get now. Now that the Association has been in existence two years I feel I would like to pay a very warm tribute to the Secretary, Mr. J. Nial, and his Committee for the loyal and vigorous help they give the school on so many different occasions. There are many other willing helpers who come into school to talk to pupils about their own work or experiences; I find myself most impressed by their generosity and their enthusiasm. The Hengrove School Association, of course, is at present dedicated to the task of supporting the new Library, they hope to raise £1000 by their own efforts and I hope that parents will continue to support this so that this target can be reached by next year. I do not doubt for a moment that they will succeed. Already the suggestion has come from the Committee that we should go further afield for support for this venture and I am hoping that this may prove possible. Certainly as I see the way that the work of the school is developing I am completely convinced that we were right to ask for a library of these dimensions. More and more, we are putting the emphasis on pupils learning rather than on teachers teaching. The vast majority of our pupils will still have learning responsibilities after they leave school and often they will be on their own. It is very important that they should acquire early on the habit of individual study and the ability to make full use of the resources of a well-stocked library. We are moving away from the idea of thirty children in one box-like classroom with one teacher; we are thinking more of pupils working on individual assignments consulting with their teachers only as and when necessary. We already see examples of this in the Sixth form and also in the primary schools, somehow the middle of the secondary schools seems to have been left out so far. I think in future, at any given time, more than 10% of our school population will be working individually, either in specially designed study rooms or in the Library. I can see that the day is not too far in the future when 20 to 30% will seem a more reasonable proportion. Slowly but surely our Library is expanding to fulfil this future role. I hope that we shall get the support we need because it is going to be costly as well as hard work. We have enormous advantages in the school. The whole community is lively, friendly and energetic and, while we know that the next twelve months will produce a certain amount of turmoil as we begin taking over our new accommodation and accept modifications in the existing buildings, I know that the future is exciting for us and I envy our pupils their skill in planning their arrival on this planet at this particular point in history.

12th December, 1967.

We also have the programme for the 1967 Prizegiving; an article from the Evening Post 16th December 1967 and the final list of Prefects for 1966-1967. After this the Prefect system was phased out.

HENGROVE SCHOOL, BRISTOL

PRIZEGIVING

FRIDAY, 15th DECEMBER, 1967

at 7.30 p.m.

PROGRAMME

Chairman's Remarks :
CHAIRMAN OF THE GOVERNORS

Headmaster's Report :
P. S. WATERHOUSE, ESQ., M.A.

Presentation of Prizes and Certificates by :
MRS. H. S. THOMPSON

Address by :
H. S. THOMPSON, ESQ., M.B.E., B.Sc.
Chief Education Officer

Vote of Thanks by :
MARY FAITHFUL, Head Girl
ALAN CURTIS, Head Boy

Physics	C. Thomas
Mathematics	H. Arnold
Additional Mathematics	B. Greenwood
Geom. & M/c Drawing	R. Parsons
Art	H. Arnold
Music	M. Allen
Cookery	M. East
Needlework	M. East
Metalwork	A. Long

CERTIFICATE OF SECONDARY EDUCATION
Certificate Prizes

L. Sutherland	J. Cruxon
M. Harmer	L. Tilley
R. Lewis	D. Marsh

FORM PRIZES

IVA1	P. Sams	S. Whyatt
IVA2	N. Knowles	J. Johnson
IVB1	M. Smith	L. Honeyfield
IVB2	B. Noad	P. Moulder
IVG	R. Osborne	

SPECIAL AWARDS

Sports Prize	Lynda Jordan	Dylan Evans
Orchestra Prize	Edward Allen	
Librarian's Prize	Mary East	Christine Webb
5th Form Prize	Linda Tilley	David Holley
(awarded by Dr. R. Perry)		
Heather Dennis Music Prize	Stephen Rudall	
Hinett Trophy	Ronald Dix	
(Junior Sportsman of the year)		
Community Service Prize	Janet Nial	
Most Helpful Pupil	Rosemary Davies	
(awarded by Hengrove Old Pupils)		
Head Girls' Prize	Christine Higgs	
Head Boys' Prize	Martyn Gould	

DUKE OF EDINBURGH'S AWARD

Gold Standard	Patricia Lowrey

The Charlton Press, Printers and Typesetters, 28 Wells Road, Bristol, 4. Tel. 76465.

PRIZE LIST

SOUTHERN UNIVERSITIES' JOINT BOARD
GENERAL CERTIFICATE OF EDUCATION
ADVANCED LEVEL

J. Bacon	Engineering Drawing
D. Bassett	Physics, Pure and Applied Mathematics
G. Batchelor	Pure and Applied Mathematics
R. Biggs	Chemistry Physics
N. Carter	Pure & Applied Mathematics, Engineering Drawing
R. Dollin	Geography
M. Gould	English Literature and History
A. Gregg	Geography
Maxwell Hamilton	Chemistry, Physics, Pure and Applied Mathematics
David Haskins	Geography, Art
Alan Hayward	French, German
Kenneth Hedges	Pure and Applied Mathematics
Raymond Kays	Pure and Applied Mathematics
John Logan	Physics, Pure and Applied Mathematics
Lesley Patey	Art
Panayiotis Vardakis	English Literature
Jessica Blair	English Literature, Music
Ann Dodge	Physics, Pure and Applied Mathematics
Margaret Filer	English Literature, History
Mary Gambling	Religious Knowledge
Christine Higgs	Music
Lynda Jordan	English Literature, History
Jennifer Nicholls	Botany, Zoology
Julia Price	Religious Knowledge, English Literature, History
Madeline Southey	Botany, Zoology

ORDINARY LEVEL

E. Allen, C. Bacon, R. Baker, G. Batchelor, N. Bennett, P. Bird, R. Biggs, M. Brierley, P. Butler, M. Carter, N. Carter, N. Clark, P. Cleave, M. Cole, C. Collins, B. Colliver, M. Coombes, A. Curtis, C. Davis, B. Dittmer, D. Dinham, R. Dollin, J. Edwards, C. Ellis, P. Farthing, A. Forsey, F. Fox, M. Gould, K. Graydon, B. Greenwood, D. Harris, J. Haskins, A. Hayward, A. Hedges, R. Hopkins, N. Howarth, C. Hunt, C. Lee, R. Kays, J. Logan, A. Long, R. Long, T. Long, V. Mall, B. Mathews, W. Owen, E. Page, R. Parsons, L. Patey, P. Sams, R. Senior, A. Shore, W. Spear, M. Stabb, P. Tayler, C. Thomas, P. Vardakis, P. Walden.

M. Allen, H. Arnold, K. Burnett, J. Coles, J. Cole, M. Davis, P. Dunk, S. Dutton, M. East, J. Ellis, M. Folley, A. Gazzard, J. Goldsmith, D. Gwyther, J. Harris, J. Halliday, J. Hellier, D. Humphries, N. James, I.

Jeffries, L. Jenkins, P. Jones, P. Lowrey, J. Nial, J. Nicholls, A. Payne, J. Rorke, C. Salisbury, E. Selwood, C. Slade, P. Souch, J. Stokes, L. Tilley, S. Turner, V. Tyler, S. Vaughan, R. White, P. Whyatt, M. Williams, S. Woodland, E. Yea, C. A. Young, C. E. Young.

CERTIFICATE OF SECONDARY EDUCATION

E. Allen, K. Ashley, R. Baker, P. Barrow, J. Barton, N. Bennett, P. Bird, M. Brierley, P. Burlinson, D. Bussell, P. Butler, P. Caple, M. Carter, R. Chiddy, M. Churchill, P. Clark, N. Clarke, C. Collins, B. Colliver, M. L. Cooke, M. R. Cook, J. Cowley, J. Cruxon, C. Davis, S. Davies, D. Dinham, M. Edwards, C. Ellis, J. Francomb, P. Gibbs, D. Goodland, R. Gough, S. J. Gould, K. Graydon, J. Griffin, M. Harmer, D. Harris, D. Hartigan, R. Hellin, J. D. Hinam, M. P. Hinam, D. Holley, D. J. Hopkins, R. Hopkins, A. D. Hunt, C. J. Hunt, B. Iles, D. James, R. King, L. Kushner, R. Lewis, A. Long, T. Long, V. Mall, D. H. Marsh, P. J. Marsh, C Mitchell, N. Moore, J. Mullane, W. Owen, E. Page, B. Quick, K. Richards, M. Robertson, N. Roper, D. Smith, W. Spear, K. Summers, L. Sutherland, B. Taylor, P. Walden, P. Watkins, R. Wolfenden.

K. Burnett, J. Carter, J. Cole, M. Colewell, R. Davis, S. Dutton, M. East, J. Egerton, M. Ellis, M. Etherton, M. Folley, L. Gamlin, M. Gibson, J. Goldsmith, D. Gwyther, J. Harris, N. James, P. Jones, A. Mawditt, J. Morgan, J. Nial, E. Selwood, P. Souch, L. Thomas, L. Tilley, J. Tottle, S. Turner, V. Tyler, L. Wakeley, C. Webb, R. White, M. Williams, S. Woodland, E. Yea, C. A. Young, A. Yerbury.

SUBJECT PRIZES
ADVANCED LEVEL

English Literature	M. Filer
Geography	A. Gregg
French	A. Hayward
Pure & Applied Mathematics	M. Hamilton
Engineering Drawing	N. Carter
Music	J. Blair
	C. Higgs
History	M. Gould

ORDINARY LEVEL

Religious Instruction	E. Yea
English	H. Arnold
History	H. Arnold
Geography	H. Arnold
German	J. Rorke
French	J. Rorke
Human Biology	S. Vaughan
Biology	S. Woodland
Chemistry	C. Thomas

114

HEAD NOT WORRIED BY STAFF LEAVING

In the last year nine teachers have left Bristol's Hengrove School, the headmaster told parents at last night's speech day.

But he isn't worried. Seven were promoted and two expected babies.

"Far from regretting this, I welcome it," said Mr. P. Waterhouse.

"Our staff is now more heavily weighted on the younger end and this is not a bad thing at all."

Mr. Waterhouse talked of the current fashions in education and said the school was keeping up with the trends.

But he said they were not trying to hit the headlines with gimmicks.

SUCCESSFUL

One subject that has been introduced into the school's curriculum is personal and community living. He said he hoped this would be introduced on the C.S.E. syllabus.

This year had been successful parents heard, and Mr. Waterhouse said it was a good point to note that 20 G.C.E. A level students were now at further education centres.

Guest speaker was Chief Education Officer, Mr. H. S. Thompson, and his wife presented the prizes.

Form prizes. — P. Sams, N. Bowles M. Smith, B. Noad, R. Osborne, S. Whyatt, J. Johnson, Honeyfield P. Moulder.

Special awards.—L. Jordan, S. Allen, M. East, L. Tilley, S. Studall, R. Dix J Nial, R. Davies, . Higgs M Gould, D. Evans, C. Webb D Holley.

Duke of Edinburgh Award gold standard): Patricia Lowrey.

1966 — 1967

HEAD BOY
Martyn Gould

HEAD GIRL
Christine Higgs

DEPUTY HEAD BOY
Alan Hayward.

DEPUTY HEAD GIRL
Patricia Lowrey

PREFECTS 1966-1967
Re-elected

Christine Salisbury
Susan Stokes
Norma James
Mary Faulkner
Ann Payne
Glenda Thomas
Judith Coles
Stephanie Summers
Rosemarie Weeks
Linda Jenkins
Bonica Vincent
Irene Jefferies
Jan Hellier
Petrina Whyatt

Marion Davis
Pamela Dunk
Stephanie Vaughan
Richard J. Searcy.

Peter Cleave
John Edwards.
Laurence Breshner
William Owen
Philip Fashing
Alan Curtis
Richard J. Searcy.
Philip J. Walton
Barry Dittmer
Christopher M. Lee.
Andrew K. Pearson.
A. S. Forsey.
Michael O. Coombs.

The year 1968 was an extremely eventful one.

In April 1968 The Lord Mayor, Alderman The Reverend Vyvyan Jones and wife visited the school and toured the classrooms whilst work was in progress. Also visiting were the Bristol City Councillors who had spent many hours in Education Committee meetings discussing the school; Cllr Graves who lived locally, Cllr Gervas Walker, Mrs Gwen Barrow and Cllr/Alderman Chamberlain and his wife.

On November 1968 Mr Waterhouse's 5th Prizegiving was held for which we have the Programme but sadly we have no copy of Mr Waterhouse's speech. We also have more plans of the school's extensions.

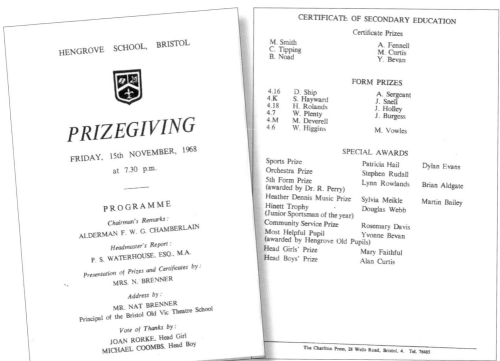

HENGROVE SCHOOL, BRISTOL

PRIZEGIVING

FRIDAY, 15th NOVEMBER, 1968

at 7.30 p.m.

PROGRAMME

Chairman's Remarks:
ALDERMAN F. W. G. CHAMBERLAIN

Headmaster's Report:
P. S. WATERHOUSE, ESQ., M.A.

Presentation of Prizes and Certificates by:
MRS. N. BRENNER

Address by:
MR. NAT BRENNER
Principal of the Bristol Old Vic Theatre School

Vote of Thanks by:
JOAN RORKE, Head Girl
MICHAEL COOMBS, Head Boy

CERTIFICATE OF SECONDARY EDUCATION

Certificate Prizes

M. Smith	A. Fennell
C. Tipping	M. Curtis
B. Noad	Y. Bevan

FORM PRIZES

4.16	D. Ship	A. Sergeant
4.K	S. Hayward	J. Snell
4.18	H. Rolands	J. Holley
4.7	W. Plenty	J. Burgess
4.M	M. Deverell	
4.6	W. Higgins	M. Vowles

SPECIAL AWARDS

Sports Prize	Patricia Hail	Dylan Evans
Orchestra Prize	Stephen Rudall	
5th Form Prize (awarded by Dr. R. Perry)	Lynn Rowlands	Brian Aldgate
Heather Dennis Music Prize	Sylvia Meikle	Martin Bailey
Hinett Trophy (Junior Sportsman of the year)	Douglas Webb	
Community Service Prize	Rosemary Davis	
Most Helpful Pupil (awarded by Hengrove Old Pupils)	Yvonne Bevan	
Head Girls' Prize	Mary Faithful	
Head Boys' Prize	Alan Curtis	

The Charlton Press, 28 Wells Road, Bristol, 4. Tel. 76465

PRIZE LIST

SOUTHERN UNIVERSITIES' JOINT BOARD
GENERAL CERTIFICATE OF EDUCATION
ADVANCED LEVEL

B. Dawes	Physics, Pure and Applied Mathematics
D. Evans	English Literature
A. Forsey	Physics
B. Greenwood	Physics, Pure and Applied Mathematics
D. Haskins	Geography, Art
N. Howarth	Biology, Chemistry
C. Lee	Geography
A. Pearson	Pure and Applied Mathematics
A. Shore	Engineering Drawing
M. Faithful	Religious Knowledge, English Literature
J. Halliday	English Literature, History
S. Vaughan	History, Geography
B. Vincent	English Literature

ORDINARY LEVEL

C. Bacon, P. Barrow, M. Brierley, R. Chasey, P. Clark, M. Cole, M. Coombs, A. Curtis, S. Davies, R. Davies, C. Davis, S. Dollin, A. Ellis, L. Fry, S. Gould, K. Graydon, J. Griffin, D. Hall, K. Hall, D. Harris, G. Harris, J. Haskins, A. Hedges, A. Hills, D. Holley, R. Hopkins, C. Howarth, N. Hunt, T. Iles, C. Jones, R. King, N. Knowles, R. Lewis, R. Lewis, T. Long, D. Marsh, A. Mathews, N. Moore, A. Morgan, B. Noad, P. Sams, P. Spindler, K. Summers, L. Sutherland, P. Tayler, C. Thomas, P. Walden, J. Whitehead, G. Williams, S. Wootten.

V. Barnaby, Y. Bevan, L. Bowkett, H. Cotton, H. Cox, R. Davis, S. Donahue, P. Dunk, M. East, B. Eisentrager, J. Ellis, K. Fletcher, M. Folley, M. Gibson, J. Goldsmith, F. Griffey, H. Guy, J. Hellier, C. Holley, P. Hough, D. Humphries, S. Hyde. L. Ivy, L. Jenkins, S. Jones, B. Lillington, A. Mawditt, P. Moulder, L. Mugridge, J. Nial, A. Payne, A. Plenty, P. Price, L. Rowlands, M. Scully, C. Slade, P. Stokes, L. Tilley, S. Whyatt, S. Wilkins, R. Williams, S. A. Woodlands.

CERTIFICATE OF SECONDARY EDUCATION

B. Aldgate, L. Arlett, K. Arscott, C. Bacon, C. Brain, R. Black, P. Blundell, M. Brierley, J. Bruce, D. Burt, R. Chasey, M. Coates, R. Davies, S. Davies, P. Dodge, S. Dollin, A. Ellis, P. Ford, L. Fry, S. Gould, K. Graydon, J. Griffin, R. Hain, A. Hall, D. Hall, K. Hall, G. Harris, J. Haskins, L. Harris, A. Hills, G. Holbrook, S. Hopkins, C. Howarth, N. Hunt, T. Iles, S. James, C. Jones, N. Knowles, P. Lewis, R. Lewis, W. Lewis, I. Mall, A. Mason, D. Marsh, M. Mead, J. Mitchell, A. Morgan,

D. Morgan, B. Noad, M. Norris, I. Payne, G. Pike, D. Roberts, N. Roper, J. Shore, G. Simpson, M. Smith, R. Smith, D. Spear, K. Summers, P. Tayler, T. Thomas, C. Tipping, R. Wallis, J. Whitehead, G. Whitelock, G. Williams, S. Wootten.

A. Bach, V. Barnaby, L. Bennett, Y. Bevan, L. Bowkett, L. Boucher, H. Burke, J. Canning, J. Chapman, H. Cotton, H. Cox, M. Curtis, R. Davis, J. Day, A. Dowling, S. Dunn, M. East, B. Eisentrager, J. Ellis, A. Fennell, K. Fletcher, A. Gazzard, M. Gibson, S. Grey, H. Guy, P. Hall, J. Hill, L. Hill, L. Honeyfield, C. Holley, L. Ivy, J. Johnson, P. Jones, S. Jones, D. Kirwin, B. Lillington, P. Moulder, L. Mugridge, V. Paisey, R. Paul, C. Phillips, M. Phippen, A. Plenty, P. Price, L. Rowlands, M. Scully, P. Stokes, J. Swift, L. Tilley, J. Whiting, S. Wilkins, R. Williams, S. Wood, C. A. Young, C. Young.

SUBJECT PRIZES

ADVANCED LEVEL

English Literature	M. Faithful
Geography	C. Lee
Biology	N. Howarth
Physics	B. Dawes
Pure & Applied Mathematics	B. Dawes
Engineering Drawing	B. Greenwood
	B. Dawes

ORDINARY LEVEL

Religious Knowledge	D. Hall
	S. Whyatt
English Language	A. Mathews
English Literature	P. Hough
History	S. Hyde
Geography	V. Barnaby
French	J. Ellis
Human Biology	J. Goldsmith
Biology	C. Slade
	V. Barnaby
Chemistry	J. Haskins
Physics	J. Haskins
Mathematics	P. Sams
Geom. & M/c Drawing	J. Haskins
Art	P. Hough
Music	R. Chasey
Needlework	S. Donahue
Woodwork	A. Ellis
Metalwork	B. Noad
Cookery	H. Cotton
Commerce	D. Holley

117

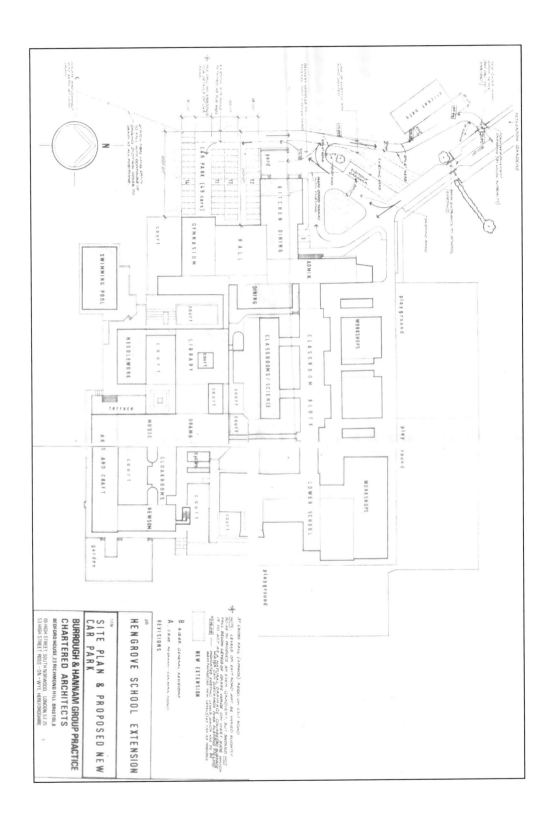

HENGROVE SCHOOL EXTENSION

CAR PARK

SITE PLAN & PROPOSED NEW

BURROUGH & HANNAM GROUP PRACTICE
CHARTERED ARCHITECTS

BEDFORD HOUSE, 23 RICHMOND HILL, BRISTOL 8
65 HIGH STREET SOUTH NORWOOD   LONDON S.E.25
53 HIGH STREET ROSS - ON - WYE, HEREFORDSHIRE

REVISIONS

A 28.8.68 GENERAL - CAR PARK ADDED
B 8.12.68 GENERAL REVISIONS

NEW EXTENSION

The New Extensions Open 1969

In January 1969 the new Sixth Form Centre opened – to be run largely by the pupils. This is the realisation of the dream hinted at 5 years earlier. David Harrison, himself a former pupil, wrote an article in the Bristol Evening Post on 16 January 1969.

The headmaster, Mr. P. S. Waterhouse.

Hilary Arnold (17) said: "It's wonderful. It gives us more freedom to develop as a sixth form and be creative in our own environment."

Peter Barrow (18) added: "This is a marvellous chance to let us act like people who have left school. We almost run ourselves now."

And Martin Brierley (17) said: "It gives us a real incentive to work. I think the idea will work very well and that the sixth formers will have the self discipline to work on their own."

THREE TUTORS

Mr. P. S. Waterhouse, the headmaster, said the sixth formers should be "almost absolutely self-propelled" under the three tutors responsible for them. At the opening cermony he told the sixth formers: "You now have a place which can become the creative part of the school, a place where ideas ought to emerge.

"You have the resources and facilities and, I hope, the energies, to cope with these ideas."

The centre includes an assembly hall, dining room, common room, reading room and study, as well as five small seminar or lecture rooms.

Moving in for the first day after the opening of the new sixth form centre at Hengrove School today.

The Sixth will help to run their new centre

by David Harrison

A sixth form centre opened at Hengrove School today and 72 youngsters moved in, welcoming the chance to run it largely themselves.

The Architects Journal published the following article entitled "Extensions to Hengrove School, Bristol". (see below)

EXTENSIONS TO HENGROVE SCHOOL, BRISTOL

**Architects—
Burrough & Hannam,
Group Practice, Bristol.**

These latest extensions to the school actually comprise stage 3 of the complete school buildings, although at the time of both stages 1 and 2, no further extensions were envisaged. The original 4 form-entry accommodation had been increased to 6 form-entry some years previously and this had necessarily resulted in a certain fragmentation of the specialist accommodation within the school. In order to rectify the situation, the architect's brief for stage 3 clearly proposed collecting together certain types of specialist accommodation into new areas or centres within the new extensions. The three main areas thus to be created were for the Arts; for Newsom children of the fourth and fifth years; and for the Sixth form including a new School Library. In addition, a swimming pool was to be provided and certain modifications carried out to some parts of the accommodation in the existing school.

One fact which emerges as having played a large part in contributing to the success of the new buildings, which the school certainly considers them, must undoubtedly have been both the good understanding which was created at a very early stage of the project between the architect and the headmaster of the school and also the active participation by the headmaster and his staff in the detailed planning of the several specialist areas within the new extensions. In particular here, mention should be made of the Arts Centre and the new Library whose detailed layouts were the result of extensive research into and study

tours encompassing the most up to date examples of their kind both at home and abroad.

The Arts Centre consists of four linked teaching spaces at ground level grouped around two sides of a rectangular courtyard which can be used as either an outdoor working or exhibition area. The teaching spaces, which are for Pottery, 3-Dimensional Work, General Craft and Painting are separated from each other, or rather more defined in relationship to each other by small stores, folding screens or a small study/reference area. On the first floor of the Arts Centre is situated the music department, consisting of two classrooms and then instrument stores and practice rooms. Adjacent to these rooms is a Drama Studio where theatrical experience can be gained.

The Library, considered the focal point of the new extensions from the educational point of view and therefore situated in a central position, is square in plan with a small central court, but here again we find several linked spaces, including a small careers library, a sixth form area, listening booths, a librarian's office and an associated classroom, as well as the main reading and book-stack areas.

In the planning brief the new Library was thought of very much in the overall context of the Sixth Form area and it does, in fact, form the first floor of this block. The informal layout of the accommodation for the sixth formers demonstrates very noticeably the freedom of expression and movement allowed to them at the present time, which of

course is considered vital in preparing them for the transition to university life after they leave school. A large central foyer, partly lit by rooflights from the Library court above, looks out onto a small intimate courtyard on one side and gives access to rooms for quiet study, group discussions or teaching. With an adjoining common room, this central foyer forms a multipurpose space which, in conjunction with a small servery, serviced by trolleys from the main kitchen, can be used for dining when required during the day and for social events organised by the students themselves during the evenings.

The area for Newson children is called the 'Clubhouse' and follows closely the recommendations made in the Newsom Report of 1963 (Half our Future) for providing suitable teaching areas for those children who are not necessarily going to pursue an academic course after leaving school. This accommodation is planned within a 3 storey block and includes seminar rooms, a lecture room, a practical science laboratory and a small self-contained flat. It was also hoped to provide a greenhouse in conjunction with the practical science laboratory but, unfortunately, owing to cost economics this had to be omitted.

The strongly differentiated areas required by the brief assisted the architect considerably in arriving at the design solution which was considered the most appropriate for the site. The existing school buildings were very large and defiant in scale, completely surrounded by large areas of wind-swept playgrounds or playing fields. Nowhere was a shrub or area of paving to be seen. In complete contrast to this, the new extensions have been kept comparatively small and informal in scale and consist of blocks of either 1, 2 or 3 storeys built around internal courtyards and forming enclosed areas with the covered walkways or the existing school buildings. Variations in treatment and detailing give each external space or court its own particular interest or character and, in particular, the aim has been to provide as stimulating an environment outside as inside the buildings so that the school children can just find simple enjoyment in using these spaces, whether they be alone or in groups.

The various blocks of the new extensions, together with the many open spaces created within and around them, could well have resulted in a fussy and untidy appearance of the scheme as a whole, especially in relation to the existing school. However, the restrained and simple detailing of the buildings externally, in juxtaposition with the paved areas make them an ideal foil and backcloth for the bustle of activity which takes place around and within them several times a day. The basic external cladding material for every part of the new extensions is a light grey coloured GRP cladding panel, which has a 1in. thickness of expanded polyurethane foam insulation integrally bonded to the back of it. At the time the building was completed, this was the first extensive use of the material as a cladding medium in this part of the country. The

14

121

architect had been at great pains to produce as maintenance free a building as possible, and one of the attributes of GRP is, of course, that it requires basically no maintenance. The material is weathering very satisfactorily and, due to a slight change of colour in some panels, the otherwise flat surfaces of the buildings are attaining a certain texture in their appearance.

The only other materials used throughout the scheme are a red facing brick, matching that of the existing school, for the three staircase towers and for the 6in. plinth up to floor level, and then timber and glass for the windows and doors. This same red facing brick is used for all the walls within the external works layout, whilst the blue black engineering brick used externally for paving the circulation areas is also continued through into the ground floor areas of the buildings themselves. This is part of the means by which the often harsh

demarcation between inside building and outside space has been softened, thus showing that both inside and outside are complimentary to each other in creating the built environment, wether it be in a school as we have here, or even at a much larger scale, in a city. If the architect has succeeded in making the users of the new extensions at Hengrove School aware of this fact, then one of his main objectives, apart of course from fulfilling his client's brief, will have been achieved.

When walking around the new extension, the visitor is struck by the general tidyness of the buildings and the courtyards and by the creative way in which both are being used. This allied to the fact that in the two years since completion, almost no damage has been done to anything, gives the impression that the children respect their new buildings and in return are having their school lives made more interesting by them.

The £200,000 new extensions, including the new Library, were officially opened by the Rt Hon Lord Mayor Councillor Mrs Mercia E. Castle, O.B.E., J.P. on 2nd May 1969.

BRISTOL EDUCATION COMMITTEE

The school Governors, Headmaster and Staff of Hengrove School
request the pleasure of the company of

at the school on 2nd May, 1969, when the new extensions
of the school, including the new library, will be opened by

The Right Hon. the Lord Mayor of Bristol
Councillor Mrs. Mercia E. Castle, O.B.E., J.P.

R.S.V.P. to the Headmaster,
Hengrove School, Petherton Gardens, Bristol, BS14 9BU.

2.45 p.m. for 3 p.m.

Everyone, pupils, teachers, parents and governors alike were excited by the new facilities – especially the large library. Mr Waterhouse described it as *"more of a Resources Centre."* In addition to 5000-6000 volumes of books it offered audio visual teaching material, newspapers, journals and language laboratories. It was four times the size of the original 1954 library – 4500 sq. feet and represented a vision of the future of education.

We have a good number of archive items which need no further explanation – read on.

BRISTOL EDUCATION COMMITTEE

HENGROVE SCHOOL
PETHERTON GARDENS
BRISTOL
BS14 9BU.

May we interest you in this exciting new venture at Hengrove School and enlist your support.

Industry, Commerce and professional organisations have always generously supported the cause of education, especially where there has been innovation. This new Library at Hengrove, in order to realise its full potential, needs resources beyond the normal provision from public funds. The parents and the school itself have already made great efforts; additional support would now be very greatly appreciated and used most effectively.

May we urge you to associate yourself with this innovation. One of the following suggestions might appeal to you : —

—a gift of books or materials in which you have particular interests ;

—a gift of money to buy books or materials on a subject of your choosing ;

—a gift of money for some equipment now being developed in the new technology of communication.

All gifts would be acknowledged permanently in an appropriate form—in a presentation book in the library listing all individuals and organisations which have made donations, on book plates or shelf labels, or on equipment.

The Headmaster would be very pleased to show you or your representative the new library which is ready and in process of being furnished or, alternatively, to visit you in order to explain more fully the school's objectives with respect to this new library.

We believe this is a fine project and we hope that you will want to associate yourself with it.

Yours sincerely,

HGW Chamberlain
CHAIRMAN OF GOVERNORS.

HEADMASTER.

John Thal   HON SECRETARY, HENGROVE SCHOOL
ASSOCIATION.

A NEW LIBRARY

AT

HENGROVE SCHOOL

The library will differ from existing school libraries in three important ways:—

— It is very large, big enough to provide individual study facilities for 10% of the present students of the school;

— It will make available **all** the means of acquiring information and ideas—books, magazines, newspapers, pamphlets, pictures, maps, slides, records, tapes, film, programmed learning;

— It is designed to change radically the organisation of students' time in school. Each individual will, early on in his or her school career, acquire the skills of independent study—the most valuable asset a young person can take with him into his career or into Higher Education.

Already the support for this venture has been generous:—

— The Bristol Education Committee and their advisers have backed the scheme and provided a fine building of great potential;

— The parents, staff and pupils of the school have jointly raised £2,000 to provide books and materials to add to the school's existing stocks;

— Many individual friends of the school have made private donations.

The areas of the library include a periodical and newspaper library, a careers library with an adjoining interviewing room, an area equipped for the use of audio-aids, a main stock area, a display area, a private study area, a sixth form library, a library of projects materials, a patio for summer use.

Hengrove School is a mixed comprehensive school which is growing rapidly and with a few years will have the responsibility for the education of some 1,500 young people up to the age of nineteen years from the Knowle, Hengrove, Whitchurch and Stockwood areas. The new library could well set a pattern for future developments elsewhere.

The enormous significance of this venture to the school, the neighbourhood and the City and to the progress of education generally has encouraged the school to seek support beyond its own immediate sphere.

Printed by C. J. Mason & Sons Ltd., Cater Road, Bishopsworth, Bristol, BS13 7TP.

A NEW LIBRARY AT HENGROVE SCHOOL

This is not only an event of great significance in the life of the school but it also represents a vision of the future of education.

The Lord Mayor of Bristol, Councillor Mrs. Mercia Castle, has graciously consented to perform the opening ceremony of this new library on April, 17th, 1969.

The Careers section of the Library is a very large and carefully organised collection of literature produced by institutions of Higher Education, the professions, industry and commerce. The photograph shows part of the temporary Careers Library at present in use.

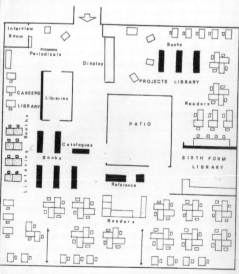

The Layout of the New Library.

125

HENGROVE SCHOOL

THIS BOOK RECORDS THE NAMES OF THOSE
WHO MADE THIS LIBRARY POSSIBLE   APRIL 1969

The Right Hon. the Lord Mayor of Bristol

Councillor Mrs Mercia E. Castle, O.B.E., J.P.

who   opened the new library on

May 2nd, 1969.

THE SCHOOL GOVERNORS

Chairman: Alderman F. G. W. Chamberlain.

Vice Chairman: Councillor Mrs G. Barrow.

Reverend. W. F. Bacon

Mrs. A. M. Comer.

Mr. L. Clutsom.

Mr. P. H. Drewett.

Mr. S. Dunn.

Mrs. L. E. Graves.

Councillor W. Graves.

Mr. W. Pinnell.

Mrs. G. V. Sprackling.

Mr. W. Storey.

Alderman F. C. Vyvyan Jones

126

No.	NAME		NAME

OFFICERS OF THE LOCAL AUTHORITY

Mr H. Thompson	Chief Education Officer
Mr L. Williams	Deputy Education Officer
Mr L. H. Derbyshire	Inspector of Schools
Miss W. M. Hickson	Inspector of Schools
Mr D. J. Dalloway	Technical Asst (Building)
Mr A. Forster	Technical Asst (Furniture)
Mr A. Toogood	Technical Asst (Cleaning)
Mr H. J. Tozer	Assistant (Furniture)

TEACHING STAFF

Mr P. S. Waterhouse	Headmaster
Mr W. Fletcher	Deputy Headmaster
Miss O. Place	Senior Mistress
Mrs S. Allan	
Mrs J. Avery	
Mr K. Bond	
Mrs J. Barrett	
Mr H. Bewley	
Mr F. Buckland	
Miss J. Bunce	
Mr H. Chasey	

NAME	DATE	NAME	DATE	NAME
Mr D. Chivers		Mr P. Haydon		Miss J. Percival
Miss S. Collins		Mrs R. Holland		Mr D. C. Prowles
Mr W. Cork		Mr E. R. Hollely		Mrs S. Prowles
Miss M. Counsell		Mr F. J. Haynes		Miss C. Robbins
Mr J. S. Davies		Mrs M. Hope		Mr B. Rogers
Miss R. Davies		Mr D. Jackman		Mr L. J. Slatter
Miss K. Denne		Mr D. John		Mr A. Sisman
Mr K. Goldthorpe		Mrs M. Lane		Mrs A. Stephens
Miss J. Griffiths		Mrs M. Moon		Miss J. Stewart
Mr R. Grant		Mr A. Nussbaum		Mr O. R. Swift
Mr G. Hale		Mr M. O'Callaghan		Mr E. Whitnell
Mr F. Hanham		Miss B. C. Oliver		Mr L. Wood

DATE | NAME | DATE | NAME

PART-TIME TEACHING STAFF

Mrs V. Atkinson
Mrs M. Clutterbuck
Mr C. Drew
Miss P. Greenslade
Miss E. Harries
Mrs J. Haydon
Mrs M. K. Powell
Mrs M. A. Polkey

ANCILLARY STAFF

Clerical Assistants

Mrs S. Burt
Mrs M. Dennis
Mrs B. Lambert

Library Assistant

Mrs B. Townsend

Laboratory Technicians

Mrs S. Hillard
Mrs S. Lenny
Mr H. Ricketts

HENGROVE SCHOOL ASSOCIATION

Committee Members.

Mr J. Nial.
Mrs J. Nial.
Mr P. Hill.
Mr D. Brine.
Mr R. Hutton.
Mrs Neal.
Mrs Bassett.
Mrs Sweet.
Mrs Macey.

FORMER COMMITTEE MEMBERS.

Mr C. Greenwood.
Mr Richards.
Mr R. Humphreys.
Mr Mitchell.
Mrs Rowlands.
Mr Mulkern.
Mrs Thomas.
Mrs Paul.

NAME	NAME

INDUSTRY AND COMMERCE.

John Hall & Sons (Bristol & London Ltd)	The Hamlyn Group.
Harveys Bristol Ltd.	Methuen Educational Ltd.
Co-operative Retail Society.	W.D. & H.O. Wills.
Marks & Spencers Ltd.	Keith Pople Ltd.
Hubert H.P. Trist & Co, Ltd.	The Cornmarket Press Ltd.
Boots The Chemist.	Ginn & Co Ltd Publishers
James Galt Publishers.	Modern Educational Aids Ltd.
Bodley Head Publishers.	A. & C. Black Ltd.
Broughtons of Bristol.	George's.
Stillit Books Ltd.	Cassell & Co. Ltd. Publishers.
E. Arnold (Publishers) Ltd.	

DATE	NAME	ADDRESS

PARENTS.

	NAME	ADDRESS
	Mrs Teale	7. Gilda Square, West. 4.
	Mrs T. Ray.	112, Minehead Road 4
	Mr & Mrs Meikle.	49. Long Eaton Drive. 4.
	Mrs Cook.	55. Wharncliffe Gdns 4.
	Mr Goodrich	89. Tarnock Avenue. 4.
	Mr Mr H. Watkins	64. Hill Avenue. 3.
	Mrs Lawrence.	5, Drayton Close. 4.

In the following pages are views of the new Stage III Extensions – they are of a white/grey colour on the left of the picture below. In contrast the Stage I buildings are pinkish in exterior finish (far right) and Stage II buildings are red brick (centre).

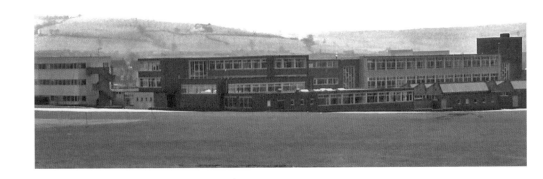

The Evening Post carried a very interesting article on 12 December 1969 entitled "Just Dawning: a New Era of Adventure", written by Max Barnes. He had visited the school 14 years earlier and was very impressed by the *"continuing adventure in education still unfolding in the school."* He describes well the wonderful facilities on offer. The article is reproduced below.

HENGROVE School stands on the threshold of the most exciting chapter in its story.

Because of a £200,000 extension scheme completed earlier this year, it is now geared to the new era of advanced teaching techniques.

Hengrove School has more than 1,000 pupils and is still growing steadily. A school on this scale could quite easily become a sprawling, impersonal place defeated by its sheer size.

Thanks to being allowed to have a hand in planning its own extensions, Hengrove now has a layout that is an open invitation to fluid movement. A school that has the tools to encourage individual research and work and uses them to the fullest extent.

Fourteen years ago when I last visited this school, I called it an adventure in education. When I went back a few days I found the adventure was still continuing.

But in a school that had grown not only in size but in stature. A school that has now acquired a sixth form of 80 boys and girls whose poise and self assurance is typified by head girl Sharon Whyatt and head boy Christopher Bacon.

Envied

My tour of the school started in the head's study. This is what Mr. Philip Waterhouse, the head, told me: "The education authority involved the staff of the school in the planning of the new additions.

"As a result we have got an accumulation of things which fit exactly our needs and look ahead to our future needs."

We set off on a visit of some of the new features which must make Hengrove one of the envied schools of Bristol. First its magnificent new library.

"Perhaps more a resources centre than a library," explained the head as he showed me round the remarkable resources of a school library with a difference.

For this is a library where you can absorb knowledge in a hundred and one fascinating ways. You can borrow a tape from the librarian on an endless range of subjects, then sit at a study booth and plug it in to your head phones.

Freedom

You can take your pick of the mass of information which this school has gleaned from many parts of the world. You can watch an educational film in colour.

Consult the information packed careers' section or browse among shelves that will eventually hold between five and six thousand volumes.

Many of the youngsters I found in this resources centre were here as individuals studying on their own. Like the sixth formers working in the space set apart for group studies. Like the rest of the new centre, it was attractively furnished with a light airy atmosphere.

For those who like statistics, the school library once covered a thousand square feet. Now it occupies four thousand square feet.

Headmaster Philip Waterhouse

Next call was on the new sixth form centre where 80 sixth formers enjoy a degree of freedom that would have been unthinkable not many years ago.

But who have also accepted the self-disciplines and responsibilities that go with this new way of school life.

The sixth formers elect seven committees from their own ranks to run this centre. Although there are three tutors, the centre is very much the sixth formers' own show.

Of course there are still problems to iron out. One of them, I was told by Christopher Bacon, was the feeling that they were perhaps a little isolated from the rest of the school.

Patio

As I joined them at their coffee break round their own coffee bar I was put at my ease by my young hosts. Boys and girls who were learning to run their own lives.

Along corridors and across charming patio gardenlets I followed the head to the new culture and arts centre.

A harmonious range of rooms in which I found a first-year class being initiated into the mysteries of the potter's wheel and next door an art class putting the finishing touches to paintings depicting the effect of looking at the sun and then shutting their eyes.

This is another fascinating department of life at Hengrove. One range of rooms is devoted to music. Next door in the drama studio a lissome class of

girls were intent on free style movements.

It was no coincidence that the music and drama suites were so close together, explained Mr. Waterhouse. One was complementary to the other.

We took in the new school swim pool where a first year class of boys had already mastered a businesslike crawl. This indoor pool has eliminated the long journey to Jubilee Baths.

There is so much to see at this school. But my own personal memory will be of a small, hand picked class who are collected from different parts of Bristol and arrive here in their own mini bus. All of them wear deaf aids.

Hengrove, in the midst of a challenging expansion programme, accepts responsibility for the well being and training of these youngsters who cannot hear properly.

It gives them patient personal tuition. Works out an individual time table for them. Goes to great pains to see they are integrated into the life of the school.

Max Barnes

Just dawning: a new era of adventure

EVENING POST, FRIDAY, DECEMBER 12 1969

131

The 1970's

In this new decade the school settled into the amazing new facilities. We have fewer archive items for 1970 – they include the Prizegiving programme from which can be gleaned many interesting details about student performance in exams and a wider variety of prizes. We unfortunately do not have a copy of the Headmaster's speech.

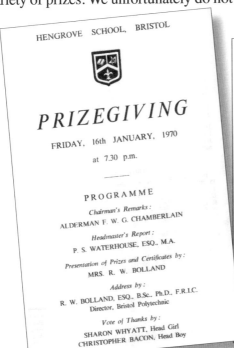

HENGROVE SCHOOL, BRISTOL

PRIZEGIVING

FRIDAY, 16th JANUARY, 1970

at 7.30 p.m.

PROGRAMME

Chairman's Remarks:
ALDERMAN F. W. G. CHAMBERLAIN

Headmaster's Report:
P. S. WATERHOUSE, ESQ., M.A.

Presentation of Prizes and Certificates by:
MRS. R. W. BOLLAND

Address by:
R. W. BOLLAND, ESQ., B.Sc., Ph.D., F.R.I.C.
Director, Bristol Polytechnic

Vote of Thanks by:
SHARON WHYATT, Head Girl
CHRISTOPHER BACON, Head Boy

PRIZE LIST

SOUTHERN UNIVERSITIES' JOINT BOARD
GENERAL CERTIFICATE OF EDUCATION
ADVANCED LEVEL

Martin Brierley	Engineering Drawing, Art
Michael Coombs	Biology
David Harris	Biology
David Holley	History, Art
Richard Senior	English Literature
Christopher Thomas	Chemistry, P. and A. Mathematics
Philip Walden	English Literature
Hilary Arnold	English Literature, History, Art
Linda Jenkins	Biology
Joan Rorke	French, German
Sallyanne Woodland	Biology

ORDINARY LEVEL

B. Aldgate, P. Avery, K. Baber, C. Bacon, P. Barrow, R. Bassett, D. Blackmore, S. Church, B. Colliver, S. Dollin, R. Elliot, P. Ferris, P. Greenwood, R. Hain, J. Haskins, S. Hayward, A. Hedges, G. Holbrook, D. Holley, L. Hughes, T. Iles, E. Jennings, N. Knowles, P. M. Lewis, R. Lewis, J. Linsdell, R. Lowrey, M. Moghadass, B. Noad, D. Peggram, A. Pring, H. Rowlands, D. Ship, M. P. Smith, J. Stokes, K. Summers, C. Thomas, C. Tipping, S. Vaughan, S. Webb, R. Walus.

V. Barnaby, Y. Bevan, J. Boundy, Y. Bouyer, L. Bowkett, H. Clamp, K. Connor, R. Coveney, G. Davey, S. Dunn, S. Edwards, S. Gazzard, M. Gibson, S. Grey, H. Guy, P. Hall, J. Holley, T. Lye, J. Matraves, P. Morris, A. Payne, A. Rowlands, P. Sage, M. Scully, A. Sergent, C. Slade, J. Smallcombe, E. Smithers, J. Snell, G. Soper, R. Tavener, M. Taylor, J. Wakeley, M. Watts, C. Whiting, P. Windows.

CERTIFICATE OF SECONDARY EDUCATION

P. Avery, K. Baber, B. Banfield, P. Barnes, R. Barrow, J. Bennett, D. Blackmore, C. Buckle, M. Carey, S. Church, C. Clarke, N. Cook, R. Davies, E. Davis, M. Deverell, M. Duckett, R. Elliot, A. England, J. Fairman, K. Fenwick, P. Ferris, A. Ford, A. Fricker, L. Fry, P. Greenwood, L. Harris, J. Harvey, M. Higgins, S. Hayward, G. Holbrook, L. Hughes, E. Jennings, N. Knowles, M. Lewis, P. M. Lewis, R. Lewis, R. Lowrey, D. Merchant, R. Meredith, A. Mildon, J. Mizon, D. Moore,

D. Morgan, M. Mullins, D. Nash, D. O'Connor, B. Patey, D. Pearce, C. Peggram, D. Peggram, S. Perchard, M. Perrett, W. Plenty, A. Pring, H. Rowlands, D. Ship, C. Showering, R. Silvester, M. O. Smith, M. P. Smith, R. Smith, J. Stokes, C. Tipping, D. Tipping, C. Travis, S. Vaughan, M. Wakefield, S. Webb, P. Weekes, J. Whitehead, P. Yea.

C. Alexander, K. Ball, H. Barnes, J. Boundy, Y. Bouyer, J. Burgess, L. Bowkett, D. Carpenter, E. Chapman, H. Clamp, G. Codrington, K. Connor, W. Cornock, R. Coveney, G. Davey, J. Davies, G. Davies, J. Day, P. Douglas, A. Dowling, S. Edward, B. Eisentrager, J. Farr, S. Gazzard, S. Grey, H. Guy, Y. Harding, P. Hedges, C. Hill, J. Holley, D. Kiely, B. Lillington, J. Logsdail, T. Lye, B. Marks, J. Matraves, C. Mitchell, J. Monkton, P. Morris, A. Owen, R. Pegler, A. Plenty, M. Read, L. Rowlands, J. Sage, P. Sage, M. Sanders, A. Sergent, J. Smallcombe, E. Smithers, J. Snell, G. Soper, A. Stones, C. Tape, R. Tavener, M. Taylor, M. Vowles, J. Wakeley, M. Watts, C. Whiting.

SUBJECT PRIZES
ADVANCED LEVEL

English Literature	H. Arnold
History	H. Arnold
Biology	S. A. Woodland
Art	D. Holley

ORDINARY LEVEL

Chemistry	D. Ship
Religious Education	H. Clamp
English Language	P. Sage
	C. Whiting
English Literature	H. Clamp
History	J. Snell
Geology	M. Scully
Mathematics	J. Snell
Geom. & M/c Drawing	B. Noad
Cookery	H. Clamp
Biology	T. Lye

CERTIFICATE OF SECONDARY EDUCATION
Certificate Prizes

S. Edwards	E. Chapman
M. Sanders	R. Tavener
B. Banfield	E. Davies

SPECIAL AWARDS

5th Form Prize (awarded by Dr. R. Perry)	Lynn Rowlands	D. Holley
Community Service Prize	Mary Read	
Most Helpful Pupil (awarded by Hengrove Old Pupils)	Cynthia Prescott	
Hinett Trophy (Junior Sportsman of the year)	S. Shepstone	
Head Girls' Prize	Joan Rorke	
Head Boys' Prize	Michael Coombs	

132

At Christmastime 1970 the school performed "Bethlehem" at Broadmead Baptist Church. The music was composed by Stephen Davies (Director of Music) with words by Head of History Mr Harold Chasey. It had previously been performed for three nights running at the school (see Chapter 6 for more detail, we have included a CD of excerpts with this book).

The Headmaster's Speech at the 1971 Prizegiving is missing from the Archive but we have the Programme.

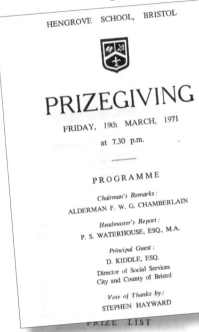

HENGROVE SCHOOL, BRISTOL

PRIZEGIVING

FRIDAY, 19th MARCH, 1971

at 7.30 p.m.

PROGRAMME

Chairman's Remarks :
ALDERMAN F. W. G. CHAMBERLAIN

Headmaster's Report :
P. S. WATERHOUSE, ESQ., M.A.

Principal Guest :
D. KIDDLE, ESQ.
Director of Social Services
City and County of Bristol

Vote of Thanks by :
STEPHEN HAYWARD

CERTIFICATE OF SECONDARY EDUCATION

Certificate Prizes

S. Amott	L. Bussell
N. Avery	J. Weeks
S. Hunt	J. Tubey
R. Baker	A. Hazell

SPECIAL AWARDS

5th Form Prize (awarded by Dr. R. Perry)	Sally Pearce	Royston Baker
Community Service Prize	Jacqueline Snell	
Most Helpful Pupil (awarded by Hengrove Old Pupils)	Helen Griffey	
Hinett Trophy (Junior Sportsman of the year)	Thomas O'Reilly	
Head Girls' Prize	Sharon Whyatt	
Head Boys' Prize	Christopher Bacon	

PRIZE LIST

SOUTHERN UNIVERSITIES' JOINT BOARD
GENERAL CERTIFICATE OF EDUCATION

ADVANCED LEVEL

Christopher Bacon	Chemistry, Physics, P. & A. Maths.
Brian Colliver	Zoology
David Harris	Biology
Jonathan Haskins	Physics, P. & A. Maths.
Anthony Hedges	Physics, P. & A. Maths.
David Holley	Religious Knowledge, Economics
Trevor Iles	English Lit., Geology, Music
Paul Sams	Chemistry, Physics, P. & A. Maths.
Christopher Thomas	Physics, Pure Maths., Applied Maths.
James Whitehead	Art
Vivien Barnaby	Biology, Chemistry
June Ellis	Biology, Chemistry, P. & A. Maths.
Brenda Eisentrager	Geology
Francine Griffy	English Literature
Penelope Hough	English Literature, Art
Susan Hyde	English Literature, History, Art
Aileen Plenty	English Literature
Christine Slade	Biology, Chemistry, P. & A. Maths.
Marion Scully	English Literature, Geology
Sharon Whyatt	Religious Knowledge, English Lit., History

ORDINARY LEVEL

P. Avery, D. Bagshaw, B. Banfield, P. Barnes, P. Barrow, R. Bassett, D. Brown, S. Church, C. Coles, P. Cook, J. Davies, P. Duckett, R. Elliott, C. Erskine, J. Fairman, K. Fenwick, P. Ferris, P. Fudge, P. Gentle, D. Goodman, S. Griffin, P. Greenwood, L. Harris, L. Hughes, S. Hunt, A. Kybert, G. Lane, J. Lindsell, N. Lockett, R. Lowrey, T. Mathews, A. Mildon, R. Mills, S. Nicholls, B. Patey, D. Phippen, S. Price, D. Purnell, A. Robb, H. Rowlands, S. Rudall, B. Sage, M. Sage, P. Stephens, K. Summers, S. Webb, R. Walden.

C. Alexander, K. Bagshaw, J. Ballard, T. Beake, Y. Bouyer, L. Brown, C. Burlinson, L. Bussell, D. Carpenter, K. Connor, R. Coveney, B. Crow, J. Davies, J. DeCoensel, S. Edwards, M. Gingell, F. Harper, A. Hazell, J. Hills, J. Holley, M. Hopkins, E. Jones, A. Little, J. Logsdail, J. Matraves, K. Mitchell, G. Neville, E. Owen, S. Pearce, C. Pennington, L. Rowlands, J. Savage, M. Scanlon, B. Shattock, J. Smallcombe, G. Soper, A. Stones, S. Richards, R. Tavener, R. Webb, E. Weekes, G. Winn.

CERTIFICATE OF SECONDARY EDUCATION

S. Amott, H. Avery, R. Baker, B. Banfield, D. Bagshaw, P. Barnes, H. Buckle, S. Church, D. Clarke, C. Coles, P. Cook, C. Cooper, G. Cox, P. Cox, P. Darts, M. Davies, J. Davies, M. Day, R. Dix, P. Duckett, P. Edwards, J. Emery, C. Erskine, J. Fairman, K. Fenwick, S. Frost, P. Fudge, P. Gentle, I. Giles, D. Goodman, S. Griffin, S. Hayward, W. Higgins, K. Holbrook, D. Holmes, P. Humphries, M. Hunt, S. Hunt, A. Kybert, N. Lockett, T. Mathews, A. Mildon, R. Miles, R. Mills, J. Mulkern, S. Nicholas, R. Nurse, R. Parker, G. Partridge, B. Patey, D. Payne, S. Pearce, M. Perry, D. Phippen, L. Pincott, S. Price, R. Puddy, D. Purnell, A. Robb, S. Rudall, J. Sage, R. Selwood, M. Smith, R. Smith, R. Stagg, P. Stephens, S. Webb, M. Wilmott, R. Woodburn, M. Wotton.

C. Alexander, S. Bacon, K. Bagshaw, T. Beake, L. Brown, C. Bull, C. Burlinson, L. Bussell, Y. Bouyer, D. Carpenter, K. Connor, R. Coveney, B. Crow, P. Curtis, J. Davies, J. DeCoensel, P. Edwards, B. Filer, M. Flay, M. Gange, L. Gibbs, M. Gingell, M. Greening, J. Greenwood, H. Griffey, A. Hazell, J. Hills, J. Holley, E. Jones, K. Jones, B. Kays, A. Little, J. Logsdail, C. Mitchell, A. Moss, G. Neville, E. Owen, S. Pearce, C. Pennington, M. Read, S. Richards, J. Savage, B. Shattock, R. Tavener, G. Townley, G. Tubey, R. Webb, E. Weeks, J. Weeks, G. Winn.

SUBJECT PRIZES

ADVANCED LEVEL

English Literature	S. Whyatt	S. Hyde
Economics	D. Holley	
Biology	V. Barnaby	J. Ellis
Chemistry	P. Sams	
Physics	P. Sams	J. Haskins
P. & A. Maths.	P. Sams	
Art	S. Hyde	
Religious Knowledge	S. Whyatt	

ORDINARY LEVEL

Religious Knowledge	L. Rowlands	
English Language	J. Ballard	
English Literature	M. Gingell	
History	M. Gingell	
German	K. Mitchell	
Human Biology	R. Coveney	
Biology	D. Brown	
Geology	J. Smallcombe	
Chemistry	D. Brown	
Physics	S. Price	A. Robb
Mathematics	D. Brown	
Geom. & M/c Drawing	C. Erskine	
Music	S. Nicholas	P. Stephens
Cookery	B. Crow	

Below is the Hengrove School Newsletter May 1971, written by Mr Fletcher the Deputy Head, which makes interesting reading.

NEWSLETTER

26th May 1971

Dear Parents,

The calendar tells me that we finish on Friday for the Spring Bank Holiday week. A surprising revelation. Let us hope that the weather remains/will be fine for us all.

I have been very disturbed to learn recently of several instances of bad driving in the immediate vicinity of the school - mainly excessive speed at times when children are going to or from school. We applaud the action of members of the public who report incidents to us at school or to Mr. Bailey, our friendly neighbourhood policeman. Be assured that we are always more concerned to prevent accidents than to invoke the law. A whole class of children is killed on the roads every school day.

Whilst on the subject -- or almost - may I suggest that you parents deposit your children at the top of the Gardens ? Apart from giving our younger brethren some much-needed exercise ('fit not fat' as Jack de Manio says) this would reduce the flow of traffic immediately and substantially. Save petrol too. You may re-address any complaints they may make to me. I shall listen.

More successes to report. Our first-year girls won the 'Minor Girls' Shield awarded to the team gaining the highest number of points in the Bristol Schools' Athletics Championships. Eula Clemmings, Bernadette O'Reilly, Alison Creedy and Brenda Rogers were responsible for this fine win. Our second and third year girls were runners up for the field events cup. Five girls will represent Hengrove at the Gloucestershire Championship on 12th June: Joanna Field, Sue Gazzard, Cherie Damsell, Anne Uphill and Angela Cohen will carry our best wishes with them. Miss Collins wishes to advertise the Fencing Club for 5th and 6ths on Wednesday evenings 7.30 - 9.00 pm. Done.

Can anyone use a seemingly endless supply of polythene containers of one-gallon capacity c/w screw cap ? They are ideal as water carriers for campers, for instance, and are available from me either free or - you've guessed it - in return for a small contribution to the School Fund.

A number of staff are leaving us at the end of term. I am always mildly surprised that people can contemplate leaving Hengrove, but they do, they do.

Miss Oliver is taking a year's secondment to the University of Bath to pursue her professional studies. Mrs. Griffiths has resigned, ready to accompany her husband wherever hydraulics engineering may take him. Similarly Mrs. Avery has set about clearing decks for a possible move with her doctor husband. Mrs. Salkeld likewise : her husband is taking an appointment in child welfare in South Wales. Mr. Slatter and Mr. Scobie have both volunteered for arduous toil in junior schools. Miss Stewart becomes Senior Mistress in a Middle School. And so on. Miss Galloway, Miss Hetherington, Mrs. Allan and Mrs. Goldthorpe will also be saying farewell in order to concentrate on various personal projects. They will all take with them our thanks and very best wishes for success in their several occupations. I shall be giving news of new staff in the next issue.

We shall take the Merit Holiday - won for us by the efforts of last year's senior pupils - on 9th July, by which time we fervently hope that this year's candidates will have revised thoroughly and all pupils will have wrought mightily to support the request for another one next year.

Before all that, however, we shall all meet again at the same time, same place on Monday 7th June.

Best wishes to you all,

W. FLETCHER
Deputy Head

134

BRISTOL SCHOOLS' MUSIC SOCIETY
COLSTON HALL
(Entertainments Manager: F. R. Cowley)

Friday, June 11th, 1971 at 7.30 p.m.

NOYES FLUDDE

Programme 5p.

In June 1971 The Bristol Schools Music Society performed 'Noyes Fludde' – The Chester Miracle Play set to music by renowned composer Benjamin Britten – at the Colston Hall. The set was designed by Hengrove School staff member Mr Christopher Drew. Under his direction the pupils of Hengrove built the set and acted as stage crew. The lighting and effects were also designed by Hengrove pupils – directed by Mr H Mullen. The Art Studios of Hengrove School designed the programme cover – (graphics: N Avery)

The children in the Choir and taking the part of Animals come from the following schools :—

Avonmouth C.E.	Elmlea	Henleaze	St. John's C.E.
Bank Leaze	Hannah More	Our Lady of the Rosary	Stoke Bishop
Bishop Road	Henbury Court	St. Mary Redcliffe	Westbury C.E.
Christ Church C.E.	Horfield C.E.	St. Teresa's	Weston Park
Doncaster Road	Hotwells	St. George	

The Raven — K. Harris (Westbury-on-Trym C.E. School)
The Dove — Dominique Alamichel (Westbury-on-Trym C.E. School)

The percussion parts are played by children from :—

Henbury Court School with Miss Doddrell
Stoke Bishop School with Mr. Comer
Westbury C.E. School with Mrs Jenkins

The recorder players come from :—

Avonmouth C.E.	Hannah More	Henleaze	St. John's
Bishop Road	Henbury Court	Our Lady of the Rosary	Stoke Bishop
Christ Church C.E.	Horfield C.E.	St. Mary Redcliffe	Westbury C.E.
Doncaster Road	Hotwells	St. George	Weston Park
Elmlea			

The Gossips' Children come from :—

Elmlea, St. John's and Westbury C.E. Schools

The following schools are represented in the Junior Schools' Orchestra :—

Ashton Gate	Elmlea	Horfield C.E.	Stoke Bishop
Bedminster Down	Filton Avenue	Oldbury Court	Tyning
Bishop Road	Four Acres	Romney Avenue	Waycroft
Bridge Farm	Henbury Court	Sea Mills	Westbury Park
Christchurch	Henleaze	Sefton Park	Weston Park
Dunmail	Holymead	Southville Jun.	

The masks have been made at school by the children under the general direction of Mr. Graeme Alexander (Schools Art Adviser).

The set has been designed by Mr. Christopher Drew of Hengrove School and built by pupils of the School under his direction. The Hengrove pupils also act as stage crew.

Lighting and effects have been designed by pupils of Hengrove School under the direction of Mr. H. Mullen.

Programme Cover Design from the Art Studios Hengrove School (Graphics : N. Avery).

Ceramic Ark and Animals from the Pottery Studios Bedminster Down School.

A very enterprising and compassionate group of Hengrove School pupils were photographed by the Evening Post in November 1971. They were presenting Peter Post with the proceeds of their Garden Fete to be passed to Sheiling School near Thornbury.

We also have a typed account of their fundraising efforts 1970-1971, and subsequent visit to the Sheiling School – written in December 1971.

Romayne Broome, Lisa Grant, Wendy Thomas, Nicole Harvey, Anne Baker, Anita Hill and Adrienne Selwood are Hengrove School young people always thinking about and helping others. Their recent garden fete was at 80, Hengrove Lane, and the £15.50 profit was handed to Peter Post for passing to Sheiling Schools to help the handicapped.

BRISTOL EDUCATION COMMITTEE

Headmaster :
P. S. WATERHOUSE, M.A.
—
Tel.: Whitchurch 6077.

HENGROVE SCHOOL,
PETHERTON GARDENS,
BRISTOL, BS14 9BU.

In 1970 we held a garden fete and made £7. We sent it to the Sheiling School in Thornbury which is a school for handicapped children. Then at Christmas we went carol singing and held a Christmas raffle and made £3.50 altogether. We also sent this to the Sheiling School through Peter Post. Then in 1971 we held a garden fete and this time made £15.50. Altogether it is £26. This time we were sent a letter inviting us to a Harvest Meal. We accepted and went to this school and after a lovely meal we were shown round the school. We found that the children were very friendly and happy. I wrote to Peter Post telling him of our enjoyable time.

About three weeks ago we received a letter telling us about the 1971 award scheme. It was to be held on the annual Pillar Box Firework Display on November 1st. We went and received a cup and a medal from the deputy Lord Mayor.

And now the school has a holiday on 14th December!

signed...Alison Broome,........
...Julia Smith..........
...Susan Johnson.....
...Romayne Broome.
...Jayne Gaffit...

In December 1971 a new school magazine was launched – entitled To't – produced mainly by V and VI Formers but anyone could contribute. Below is the cover page and copy of the first page. The entire magazine is held in the archive if you wish to read all the articles.

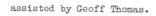

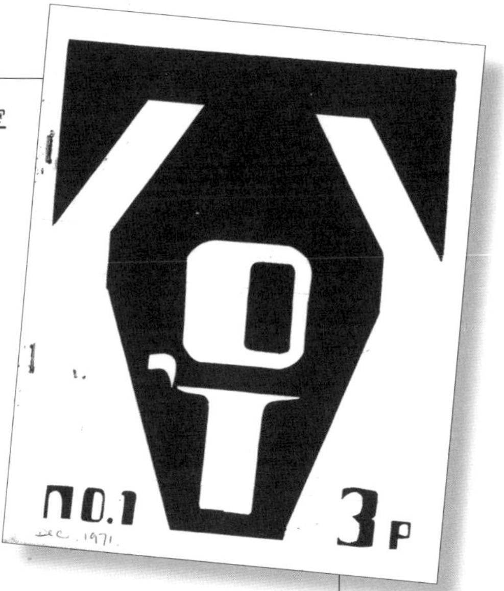

EDITORIAL STAFF

Feature Articles.   Jean Chiddy
                           Kate Mitchell
                           Sandra Woolley

Spot Reports.   Judith Wood
                           Jill Winn
                           Trudy Whitchurch

Poetry and Short   Richard Walden
      Stories.   Marian Scanlan
                           Linda Elliston

Illustrations and   Penny Smith
      Publicity.   Nigel Greenslade

Sales Manager.   Paul Wakely.

          assisted by Geoff Thomas.

———

POETRY contributed by students and staff of Hengrove School.

———

SPOT REPORTS contributed by Sandra Bartlett, Alison Broderick,
      Linda Bussell, Christopher Drew, Dave Goodman, Nigel
      Greenslade, Helen Griffey, Sylvia Meikle, Kate Mitchell,
      Howard Mullen, Sandra Richards, P.S.Waterhouse.

———

ACKNOWLEDGEMENTS to Mr.Drew for putting his own time and the
      facilities of the Art Department at our disposal.

———

THE TITLE: TO'T.   Words meaning TO THE POINT and spoken by the
      Servant in "Troilus and Cressida" (Act III, scene 1) by
      William Shakespeare.

———

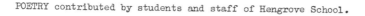

There is a paucity of archive material for 1972 – but the March 16th 1972 Evening Post carried an article about the Bristol 23rd Anniversary School exchange with Bordeaux and features a photo of pupils.

Bristol pupils fly off to Bordeaux

Bristol's 25th anniversary schools' exchange with Bordeaux got under way today.

And with the Hanover exchange on at the same time, it gave Bristol Airport one of its busiest days yet.

A Cambrian Viscount plane which took off to the waves of a hundred parents was the first of eight such flights to and from Bordeaux which will carry 470 youngsters in each direction between now and August.

The local schoolchildren will spend a month in Bordeaux with their opposite numbers and by the end of the summer a total of 950 Bristol and district schoolchildren will have been to Bordeaux and the same number of French youngsters will have been entertained here.

GERMAN

The Hanover exchange means the swapping of 120 children during the current first leg of the year's exchanges but by the autumn 220 English and 220 German schoolchildren will have shared each others' homes.

Masterminding today's exercise, as ever, was Mr. John Stewart, retired headmaster of Fairfield Grammar School, who initiated the first exchange with Bordeaux in 1947.

Typical of the youngsters off to France today — Rodney Chappell (14), of Hengrove School and Andrew Cowley (14), of St. George School, both with their fishing rods. "I'm going to do some spinning." said Rodney. "I'm going with a chap whose says the fishing is good and I'm keen to try it."

GIFTS

Gillian Rees (14), of Greenway High School, Worle, Weston-super-Mare, was taking a gift of Wedgewood and some chocolates for her French hosts.

Captain of the aircraft Richard Glading from Rhoose, Glamorgan, said: "It's funny that the youngsters going from here are always a more jolly crowd than the French we bring in return. My children never had this opportunity living in Wales and the organisers this side have something to be proud of."

Standing on a chair to get a better shot with his cine camera was parent Mr. Roy Steed, of Piling, seeing off his son Andrew (14), of Patchway High School. There too was Andrew's sister Frances who was on one of the Hanover exchanges in 1965. "I always found my exchange to be well

worth while and correspond with Hanover," said Fances. "This is Andrew's first exchange and I really envy him."

Mrs. Valerie Stuart, of Monsdale Drive, Henbury, waving off her daughter Tracey (15), said: "She's really been looking forward to this and she's determined to use her French in her career."

Mr. Tom Jones an agent handling the charter arrangements said: "This thing today is part of the very fabric of Bristol. You find this not only in the family ties with France that are growing up but in the commercial links."

Glenda Nicholas (left), of Hengrove, and Sue Sherwood, of Stockwood, share a final phone call to friends before leaving o n the first flight.

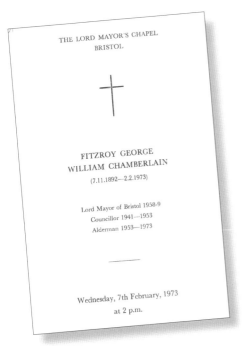

THE LORD MAYOR'S CHAPEL
BRISTOL

✝

FITZROY GEORGE
WILLIAM CHAMBERLAIN
(7.11.1892—2.2.1973)

Lord Mayor of Bristol 1958-9
Councillor 1941—1953
Alderman 1953—1973

———

Wednesday, 7th February, 1973
at 2 p.m.

Despite the lack of archive material for 1972 we know that for a whole year rehearsals were taking place for the forthcoming March 1973 production of "The Venturers" involving students of all ages and staff.

The End of The Mr Waterhouse Era

We come now to the Academic Year 1973/1974 which was eventful indeed and was Mr Waterhouse's last year at Hengrove.

The School was represented at the funeral of Ald. F G W Chamberlain on 7th February 1973. He had served Hengrove School as a Governor, Chairman of the Governors and a staunch supporter of the school since it opened in 1954.

The Bristol 600 Celebrations in 1973 marked the granting of a Charter by King Edward III to the City of Bristol giving it County status – a time of civic pride and a 600th Anniversary.

Hengrove School responded to this historic landmark celebration by staging a production of music and words " The Venturers" at the Colston Hall in March 1973. It had been a year in the making; the music written by Mr Stephen Davies and lyrics by Mr Harold Chasey with involvement right through the school (see more in chapter 6 – there are excerpts on the CD which accompanies this book).

Mr Waterhouse remembers:

"It was a great triumph. Tears were reported in the audience when Winston Campbell, a West Indian 13 year old sang with wonderful tone his solo. 'Why do you treat me so?' There were more tears when the choir sang a song for the 1940 blitz which ended on a long note at the exact pitch of the all-clear siren."

HENGROVE SCHOOL

HEADMASTER   P S WATERHOUSE M A

presents

the venturers

by HAROLD CHASEY and STEPHEN DAVIES

programme

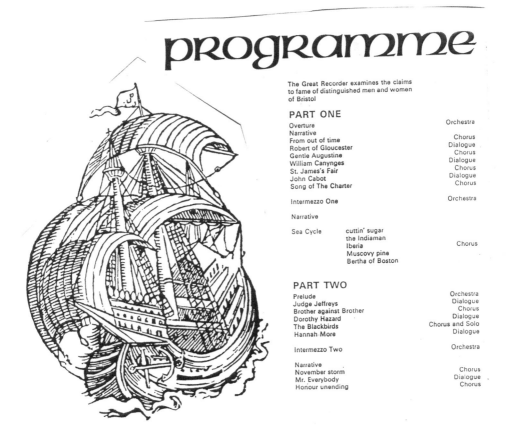

The Great Recorder examines the claims to fame of distinguished men and women of Bristol

PART ONE

Overture	Orchestra
Narrative	
From out of time	Chorus
Robert of Gloucester	Dialogue
Gentle Augustine	Chorus
William Canynges	Dialogue
St. James's Fair	Chorus
John Cabot	Dialogue
Song of The Charter	Chorus
Intermezzo One	Orchestra
Narrative	
Sea Cycle cuttin' sugar	
the Indiaman	
Iberia	Chorus
Muscovy pine	
Bertha of Boston	

PART TWO

Prelude	Orchestra
Judge Jeffreys	Dialogue
Brother against Brother	Chorus
Dorothy Hazard	Dialogue
The Blackbirds	Chorus and Solo
Hannah More	Dialogue
Intermezzo Two	Orchestra
Narrative	
November storm	Chorus
Mr. Everybody	Dialogue
Honour unending	Chorus

Hengrove School was represented at the 1973 Bristol 600 Needlecraft Contest. An article "The Way to Look Good." and photos from the local press are shown opposite.

140

The way to look good . . .

My immediate reaction to that pink linen safari suit was to wonder if its owner would like to flog it.

I've seen and admired a lot of the dressmaking that goes on in Bristol schools, but this was the first time I'd coveted an outfit made by a 15-year-old.

The fact that one person likes an item in a fashion show doesn't mean that everyone will agree that it's the best. So I was delighted when the expert judges thought it was good, too.

And awarded first prize (an automatic sewing machine) in the fashion section of the Bristol 600 Schools Needlecraft competition to Jane Furlong, student at St. Mary Redcliffe and Temple School.

They should be pleased with her, because a knitting machine was awarded to the school attended by the first prizewinner.

Jane is studying for O-levels and hopes to be a secretary. But following in mother's footsteps she makes most of her own clothes, and would very much like to work in a fashion design house.

She agreed with second prize winner Gill Forster (16) and third prizewinner, Sue Malin (16), both of Hengrove School, that the way to look good is to make your own clothes.

You could achieve quality of workmanship and fabric that most of the things in the boutiques didn't measure up to, they said. It's cheaper, too.

Gill had made a summer evening dress with the sheered bodice in red and white printed cotton, and the flounced skirt in the same print but with black motifs on white.

And Sue Malin had pro-duced a real show-stopper, she designed herself — a pair of patchwork pants (she'd done the patchwork herself too) with a sheered top.

Elizabeth Pell (17) from Brislington School came fourth with a battleblouse suit for which she had made both a skirt and pants, and Christine Row-cliffe (15) of St. Mary Redcliffe and Temple was fifth with her cotton dress involving two fabrics, one with a green and black print, the other a black and white spot.

The contest was run by Bristol Education Department and the Modern Sewing Machine Co. of Kingswood, to celebrate Bristol 600 and girls from 17 local secondary schools took part.

The 20 finalists in the fashion parade had been selected at earlier judging sessions from a mass of entries. And Robin Thomas, Head of the Fashion School at Bristol Polytechnic and his judging team picked out 12 which they felt could all have been winners.

They decided to award Highly Commended certificates to the seven runners up.

While the girls had made their clothes in class, they had all had complete freedom to choose styles and fabrics. And very happy everyone was with their selection, whether they had come up with trouser suits, summery dresses, party dresses, or a glamorous quilted housecoat.

Esther White, of Brislington School, who made this one, had even gone to the trouble of using up the scraps of fabric to make mules and hot water bottle cover. And was among the highly commendeds.

The Bristol 600 needle-craft competition gave Bristol schoolchildren an opportunity today to show their skills in dressmaking, embroidery and dressing period dolls. Picture shows Sue Malin (16), of Hengrove School, modelling her self-made outfit of knitted top and patchwork trousers beside one of the fabric paintings outside the Council House, where this afternoon's fashion parade preceded the prize-giving by the Lord Mayor, Ald. Wally Jenkins. (More pictures Page 3).

1373-1973

141

Two long serving members of staff Mr Buckland and Mr Cork retired in academic year 1973/1974. We have an excellent photo of 74 members of staff on the steps of the main school entrance. You should recognise some of them – where is Mr Jackman? Perhaps he was the photographer.

Farewell to Mr Waterhouse

We come now to Mr Waterhouse's departure from the school. Unlike his predecessor, he was still young (50's) and was not retiring but striking out into pastures new. He was interested in how pupils learned best and worked to encourage them to learn more independently. In his time at Hengrove he had overseen the move away from 30 pupils sitting in a box-like classroom with one teacher, to "self-supported learning", making full use of the wonderful Library/ Resources Centre. The Evening Post carried an article "Head Leads a Classroom Revolution" in December 1973.

Head leads a classroom revolution

MR. PHILIP Waterhouse, headmaster of Hengrove School, has been chosen to lead a revolutionary system of teaching which Bristol has agreed to pioneer.

He will be leaving Hengrove — where he has been for the past 10 years — at the end of the present term to become director of the Co-operative for Resource-based Learning.

The new venture started from a research project set up by the Nuffield Foundation to find out how schools could make the best use of teachers' skills and of new methods and equipment.

Mr. Waterhouse said of his departure: "It will not be easy because I have had 10 very happy years here and shall miss the warmth and vitality of this busy, friendly school. But my new job will be exciting and it could make a big difference to the quality of the work done in our schools."

The researchers made some pretty strong criticism of traditional classroom teaching and urged a shift towards ways of learning that are "not so utterly dependent on the teacher."

Mr. Waterhouse explains: "Their vision was of a classroom where each pupil would normally work on his own or with a fellow pupil using specially prepared materials for learning.

These would be unlike ordinary text-books; they would be loose-leaf sheets and small booklets written as guides to learning."

One of the great advantages of organising for individual work was that slow and average pupils could proceed at their own pace while the rapid learners and good readers could move on quickly.

Bristol Education Committee are the first education body to support such a venture financially and a "generous" grant is being provided by the Department of Education, who have also commissioned Bristol University to monitor the progress of the enterprise, which should be fully operational in a year's time.

143

Mr Waterhouse left Hengrove in December 1973. The pupils presented him with a handsome set of wine glasses and an LP of Mahlers Symphony No 8.

We have a very humorous two verse poem/carol (to be sung to the tune of the Christmas Carol 'Hark the Herald Angels Sing') and entitled "Hark the Hengrove Angels Sing" It was donated in rough handwritten form from Mr Waterhouse's personal archive papers and we do not know who wrote it – possibly a member of staff. It was probably sung to him at one of his leaving functions. It alludes to his interest in School Management styles, his hobbies of oboe playing and his future role as 'Resources King' in The Centre for Resource Based Learning – see Chapter 8.

1)   Hark the Hengrove angels sing
        Bye to our Resources King
        Bird in school the bell to ring
        Philip's going to do his thing
        Joyful all ye children rise
        Tears are falling from Doug's eyes   (Jackman)
        With the angelic staff proclaim
        Philip gone to make his name
        Hark the Hengrove angels sing
        Bye to our Resources King

2)   Hail the North-born annual guide
        Hail the oboe blowing wild
        Progress sure he'll always ask
        Guided by his own key task
        Mild he lays his school days by
        Now to all he'll give the lie
        With enlightened management
        From our path his steps are went
        Hark the Hengrove angels sing
        Bye to our Resources King

Another parting gift was a wonderful album of photos of pupils at work and of the new school extensions taken by Mr Jackman (Head of Geography). They form part of Mr Waterhouse's personal archive but he kindly gave permission for us to reproduce them.

HENGROVE SCHOOL
1964-1974

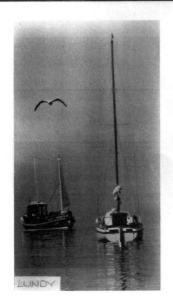

LUNDY

149

Headmasters Past, Present and Future.

In the photograph below, Dr Perry would have been 70 plus and the new Headmaster Mr Patrick Bird (left), a relatively young man. His would be the third Headship Era of the school which is beyond the remit of this book.

You can read more of Mr Waterhouse's future achievements in Chapter 8.

As the title of this chapter suggests, Mr Waterhouse had overseen a period of tremendous expansion and innovation. He is fondly remembered and maintained links with colleagues and former pupils right up until his death in 2012.

Chapter 4
Class Groups

The earliest class group photos were taken on the steps at the Main Entrance of the original 1954 building. The "New Wing" was opened in 1958 and after this date most group photos were taken on the Entrance Steps – many taken by Mr Hellier.

There are many photos without labels. We have not attempted to identify all individuals. This is where our readers will shine. Have you found yourself and your friends?

The captions will be printed below each corresponding picture.

A very early photo probably between 1954 and 1957 Mr Fletcher on the left –
Dr Perry on the right.

Another early picture with Mr Buckland.

Probably between 1954 and 1957. Back row right is Miss Crowther.
Not sure how the dog got into the picture!

Class 1A in Summer 1955. Not sure who the teacher is.

After September 1958 photos of Class Groups were taken on the steps of the Main Entrance to the "new" stage II wing.

The photo above is undated. The teacher is Mr Morgan.

Teacher Mr Cork – undated and no other information.

Form 1H in 1957/1958. We have the names in the archives. Teacher Mr Bromwich.

Form 4A taken in July 1959 supplied by former pupil Jackie Cooke nee Elbrow.

Back row L-R: Teacher Mr Pylle, Tom Dark, Michael Crewe, David Harrison, Roger Martin, Clive Senior, Brian Cook, Eric Pavey, John Gunter.
Middle Row L-R: Jackie Elbrow, Ann Webb, Muriel Fisher, Enid Burge, Jackie Fox, Anne Chesterman, Mary Davis.
Front Row L-R: Jane Mattfield, Bernice Vicars, Susan Harvey, Carole Bacon, Joan Clutterbuck, Jeanette Vale

Form 1F in 1957/1958. Do you recognise the teacher?

This could be Form 1L with Mrs Blackley – date uncertain but probably 1959 or early 1960's.

Form 1B undated – teacher is Mrs Field.

Form 1E with Mr Hellier in 1959/1960.

We have no date or details for the photo above – do you know?

The teacher is Mr Bromwich – regrettably no other details.

Form 1E – we have no date – do you know the name of the teacher?

Form 2E with Mr Hobbs, probably 1959.

Also taken in Summer 1959 is the small group of friends – on the spacious playing fields. The pupil on the extreme right emigrated to South Africa in later life.

Class 2A in Summer 1959 – who is the teacher?

Class 2B in Summer 1959 with Miss Bevan.

Class 2C – undated but probably 1959 who was the teacher?

Mrs Cameron's Class 1A in 1959 Summer.

We think this is Form 1F with Mrs Anglin (undated)

We have no details about this photo – do you remember the teacher's name?

Form 1J undated

The teacher was Miss Jackman. Form ? undated

Form 1G. Undated – teacher was Miss Newson?

Mr Foote with Form 1G – undated.

Form 1A in 1959 or 1960 teacher Mr Roberts

Form 1D with Mr Wood circa 1960

Form 1C Mr Blackmore 1959?

Form 3B 1961 Mrs Wilkinson was the teacher.

Mr Horwood with we think Form 1B. Undated but possibly Summer Term 1958 or 1959.

Mr Horwood again with a different Form 1B, probably 1959/1960. Winter Uniform

Possibly Class 1F – undated probably early 1960's. Teacher Miss Shaw?

Possibly Class 1F – teacher Mr Bryant – early 1960's ?

Form 1D undated

Mr Horwood Class 2A possibly 1961.

Mr Jackman – no details possibly late 1960's or early 1970's

Early 1960's – no details

Undated, but probably early 1960's – do you recognise anyone?

Mid 1960's, teacher Mr James.

Undated – which class was this?

1966-1967 Head Girl and 6 pupils.

Standing: J Nicholls and J Blair; Seated: L-R. K Crombie, A. Dodge, C. Higgs (Head Girl), Pat Lowrey (Deputy Head Girl), M. Southey.

Mr Jackman – possibly a Geography trip with 4th or 5th year pupils 1961 or 1962.

July 1962, Fifth formers including P. Long, P. Cook, A. Paul, J. Sawyer and A. Spreadborough.

Class 4s Hengrove School
From left: Allan Marsh,
Alan Knapp, Vernon Hall,
Robert Stokes, Ian Gillet,
Derek Marsh. (Seated)
Robert Parsons, David Leech,
Alan Cross 1964

Class 4S 1964.

Chapter 5
Girls' and Boys' Sports and other Extra-Curricular Activities

The sports facilities at Hengrove School were excellent from day one. The school building was set in 44 acres of playing fields with a view of Dundry ridge. There was a brand new fully equipped gym, showers and changing rooms. Initially these were shared by boys and girls.

The stage two extension completed in 1958 provided a second gym to be used exclusively by the girls – there was a shower room (walkthrough), large changing room, sick/first aid room with bed and an office for the Games and P.E. teachers.

The School Colours Badge was awarded to girls and boys for achievement in sport. It was worn proudly on the School Blazer.

School Colours

Won for Achievement in Sport
Rugby
Basketball
Athletics

In the initial years the pupils were divided into Houses which competed against each other for supremacy – especially at the Summer Sports Day. The Games teachers were of high calibre; experienced and dedicated. They gave many hours of their own time outside of school hours for Saturday morning fixtures against other schools, lunch time and after school practices. Their efforts were supplemented by some non-sports specialist staff who volunteered to help.

The achievements of the pupils at sport are referred to in the Headmaster's Reports in Chapters 2 and 3; also there are some photos of Sports Days in Chapter 2. This chapter has more archive photographs and additional material from School Magazines.

1957 Girls' Sports

This is the first detailed record we have of Girls Sports extracted from the Hengrove School Magazine Vol.2 July 1957.

THE SCHOOL NETBALL TEAMS

The netball season started with a tournament held at the Red Maids' School where we reached the third round to be narrowly beaten by Rose Green School. After this official opening to the season both netball teams attended many practices after school to bring our game up to the standard of that played by our opponents. We played the netball matches mostly on Saturday mornings against other bi-lateral schools and secondary schools in the Hengrove area, winning many of our matches. Our successful season was brought to a close when the first netball seven won the tournament at Brislington School, the second team coming a close second.

First VII: Played 15; Won 9; Lost 6; Drawn 0; Cancelled 2.

Second Years: Played 13; Won 6; Lost 6; Drawn 1; Cancelled 2.

Senior Netball Players: C. Pugh, L. Shepherd, P. Rosser, C. Thatcher, D. Davies, S. Hedges, M. Coggins, D. Neals, D. Bowell, T. Marquick, D. Britton.

Junior Netball Players: D. Pippard, A. Gosling, V. Hawkins, D. Pollard, T. Gibb, A. Williams, S. Matthews, V. Price, S. Wilkins.

PAT ROSSER (3A)

HOCKEY

In this season's hockey features the third year and second year teams have done extremely well. The third year team have won or drawn every match played and the second year team has lost only one game.

Although our teams have practised and played so enthusiastically we were unable to defeat the staff in the annual school versus staff match and the final score was 7—0.

LESLEY LONG (Form 3A)

First XI: Played 11; Won 9; Lost 0; Drew 2; Cancelled 3.

Second Years: Played 6; Won 4; Lost 1; Drew 1; Cancelled 3.

First XI: S. Hedges, T. Richards, P. Bambury, T. Richards, L. Long, D. Davies, D. Needs, M. Coggins, P. Eyres, C. Handley, E. Jones. Reserves: S. Delaney, T. Gerrish.

Second Years: H. Smallcombe, D. Pippard, P. Webley, V. Hawkins, F. Webb, T. Phelps, L. Bright, K. Tugwell, K. Gingwell, C. Bacon, D. Pollard. Reserves: T. Elbrow, T. Gibbs.

SCHOOL ROUNDERS TEAMS

The girls of both teams have worked hard to reach a good standard. This term we have not had many matches but the schools we have played we have beaten.

Soon there is to be a tournament in which Hengrove will be entering and I am sure both teams will do well.

ROUNDERS

3rd Year Team: D. Davies, G. Thacker, P. Rosser, L. Long, S. Hedges, G. Handley, P. Eyres, E. Jones, M. Coggins.

2nd Year Team: D. Pollard, V. Hawkins, D. Pippard, A. Webb, C. Bacon, T. Phelps, A. Gosling, S. Wilkins, K. Gingell, J. Gibbs.

1st Year Team: Y. Purnell, C. Garland, A. Price, G. Ford, V. Bryant, J. Poole, J. Owen, J. Williams, C. Withers, M. Barton, M. Harris.   CHRISTINE THACKER (4A)

ATHLETICS

So far Hengrove School has competed in two athletic meetings this season. The first was the South Bristol Inter-School Sports where we did exceptionally well. The second was the all Bristol School Sports, where again things could hardly have been better. We had three firsts, one second and a fourth in the track events, and one first and two seconds in the field events. Hengrove girls capped the afternoon by gaining the cup given to the school bearing the highest aggregate marks, in the middle girls section. We have been highly successful and it is hoped that we will go on to further honours at Gloucester on the eighth of June.

Results from Bristol School sports: M. Dudbridge, 150yds, 1st; M. Coggins, Hurdles, 1st; D. Davies, Hurdles, 2nd. Relay Team, 1st place. Junior High Jump, K. Gingell, 1st. Javeline, D. Needs. 2nd. Discus, T. Gerrish, 1st.

Gloucestershire: M. Dudbridge, 150yds., 1st; M. Coggins, Hurdles, 2nd; Relay Team, 1st place. (New record established).

GIRLS' LIFE SAVING

The following girls have passed life saving examinations in the year 1956-57.

Bronze Medallion: Julie Townsend, 4A; Valerie Dansell, 4A; Janet Martin, 4B; Mary Curtis, 4A.

Intermediate and Elementary Certificates: Anita Williams, 2D; Jacqueline Howick, 2D; Patsy Lean, 1D; Gillian Pearce, 1D; Susan Taylor, 1E; Diana Hooper, 2F; Julie Townsend, 4A; Mary Curtis, 4A; Sandra Warlock, 3E; Sheila Bloomfield, 2E; Valerie Damsell, 4A; Janet Martin, 4B; Cherry Horseman, 1B; Diana Haskens, 1F; Mary Haines; Anne Webb, 2A; Karen Gingell, 2; Roma Domaille, 2D; Kathleen Tugwell, 2C; Barbara Standen, 2F.

Unigrip Certificate: Kathleen Tugwell, 2C; Susan Taylor, 1E; Roma Domaille, 2D; Jacqueline Howick, 2D; Anita Williams, 2D; Anne Webb, 2A; Karen Gingell, 2; Patsy Lean, 1D.

West Area Swimming Gala Results.   Girls:

Placed in heats: Roma Domaille, Junior Front Crawl; Karen Gingell, Junior Breast Stroke; Anita Williams, Junior Breast Stroke; Judith Poole, Junior Breast Stroke; Karen Gingell, Junior Back Crawl; Roma Domaille, Junior Back Crawl.

1st in Finals: Junior Team Race. Intermediate Medley Race. Ann Webb, Junior Front Crawl, Junior Back Crawl, Open Individual Medley Race.

2nd in Finals: Junior Medley Team Race.

Other Results: Karen Gingell, 4th Junior Breast Stroke; Judith Poole, 5th Junior Breast Stroke.

HOUSE REPORTS

ATHENS HOUSE

Miss Place; Miss Pleass; Mr. Whitnell; Mr. Jones; Mr. Pyle; Mr. Buckland.

Our record during the past year in sports has been one of continual search for suitable players. In Soccer we have been only moderately successful and our season was not as good as we should like. In spite of this, two of our players, R. Hinton, who was our Soccer captain, and N. Clements have both done good work in the School team.

Our cricket team was not successful in the inter-House contests but we have a number of likely players in the Junior School and we hope to do better in the future.

In the Hockey and Netball Tournament our teams played well, although they were unsuccessful and the future will perhaps bring victory.

We offer our congratulations to Mary Dudbridge who brought honour to herself and to the House by winning the 150 yards race in the Bristol Schools' Athletic Sports.

R. HINTON (4A), L. ADAMS (4A)

ARGOS HOUSE

Miss Green; Mr. Bishop; Mr. Hobbs; Mr. Swift.

We have again had a good year in sport. Our Netball team was successful in winning the School Netball Cup and our Soccer and Hockey teams played very well especially during the later fixtures.

Our House has been well represented in the School teams. Several of our members have played in the School Soccer, Hockey and Basketball teams and have brought credit to themselves and to the House.

In the School production of *Midsummer Night's Dream,* which has been unfortunately delayed, we have several members who are taking important parts and we hope the play will be as successful as Argos House play was last year.

With the help of our House teachers we hope to produce even better results in the coming sports and other activities.

L. SHEPPARD (3A), M. WOOLAWAY (3A)

SPARTA HOUSE

Miss Bain; Mr. Scarlett; Mr. Fletcher.

In spite of the fact that we have been unsuccessful in our inter-House contests this year we have had every reason to be proud of our representation in School teams.

Our defeat by Olympia in the first round of the Cricket Tournament was a very close one but we hope to do better this year.

M. Stephens is Captain of the School Cricket and M. Cridge was in School Soccer and Basketball and also ran in the School Cross Country team with moderate success.

Our Hockey team was second in the House Hockey tournament, losing to Argos and Thebes and being winners in their other games. The Netball team, although unsuccessful, gave a good account of itself. R. OSBORNE (4A), JUNE GAY (4B)

OLYMPIA HOUSE

Mrs. Roach, Mr. Hale, Mr. Hollely, Mr. Bewley.

This has been a good year for our House. For the first time Olympia was the winner of the Soccer Competition, dropping only one point in five games. A very creditable result indeed.

We have strong representation in the School Soccer XI. R. Hammond, M. Harding, and J. Hughes have all played during the year for the School first team.

In the Junior teams L. Lanning, J. Robinson and A. Kent have played, and B. Isles and B. Griffin have played for the School Rugby team. We wish all these members continued success.

In the Cricket contest we reached the semi-final but were unfortunately defeated by Thebes.

R. Hammond has captained the School Basketball Team during the season.

The winning of the Hockey Cup by the House Team was a noteworthy achievement and we were proud when the Headmaster presented the cup to our Captain, Lesley Long.

This fine win was followed by our victory in the House Reading Contest and as a result there is now a book in the Library presented by Olympia to the School.

R. HAMMOND (4A), SALLY HEDGES (3A)

CORINTH HOUSE

Miss Thomas Miss Hawken, Mr. Corke, Mr. Seymour, Mr. Barley.

We have had a fairly good year although our position in the House Soccer Contest was a lowly one.

We were very pleased to see our team reach the finals of The Cricket Contest where they were unfortunately beaten by Thebes.

Both the Senior and Junior Cross Country teams distinguished themselves, winning their events in good style. A. Lugg, R. Long and M. Randall were chosen to represent the School in the Senior Cross Country race and C. Miller ran in the Junior race.

We have strong representation on the School Prefects List, M. Hewitt, C. Brooks, J. Lifton, R. Lillington and M. Randall all being Prefects.

Our Hockey Team, captained by Diane Needs, was moderately successful as was the Netball Team led by Joyce Neil.

Pat Bambury is in the School Hockey Team and has played strongly in many games.

Altogether, in spite of poor success in the House contests, we can be pleased with our progress but we must all make an effort to do better next year.   R. LILLINGTON (4A), M. HEWITT (4A)

THEBES

Miss Pleass and Mr. Nussbaum joined the House and were welcomed by the members last September.

In the girls' games we lost in the Netball final against Argos, 4—5; in Hockey, led by Janet Marquick, we won one and drew two games. Despite this, however, Hockey was not up to the usual Thebes standard. Next term we hope to have a big improvement with a larger fourth-year representation.

The boys were also second in football. We defeated Argos, Corinth and Athens and drew with Olympia. Michael Parsons was captain of the School Basket-ball team, though he has now left. David Summers also plays for the school in basket-ball, and he deserves our congratulations too for being a member of the Bristol Boys' Soccer team.

It was not our turn in Cross Country to do well, only finishing fourth with 367 points.

Altogether it has been a fairly satisfactory year, though there is not the interest in House activities which there could be.

IAN JOHNSTONE (4A), GILLIAN MILLS (4A)

GIRLS' EVENTS

FIRST YEAR
100 Yds.—12.8 secs. 1, J. Dyer; 2, M. Baxton; 3, C. Gallop.
Obstacle.—1, B. Gibbs; 2, C. Garland; 3, C. Coates.
Potato.—1, J. Webb; 2, J. Gray; 3, Y. Parnell.
High Jump.—3ft. 11in. 1, C. Gallop and J. Williams; 3, G. Vlaeminke.
Long Jump.—12ft. 3in. 1, M. Hazzard and M. Barton.
Relay.—1 min. 4 secs. 1, Corinth; 2, Argos; 3, Sparta.

SECOND YEAR
100 Yds.—12 secs. 1, V. Hawkins; 2, C. Bacon; 3, D. Pippard.
Hurdles.—1, V. Hawkins; 2, D. Pippard; 3, C. Bacon.
Obstacle.—1, H. Ham; 2, J. Wintle; 3, S. Broadley.
Potato.—1, H. Ham; 2, R. Wall; 3, J. Wintle.
High Jump.—4ft. 3in. 1, D. Pippard; 2, P. Weeks; 3, K. Gingell.
Long Jump.—13ft. 3in. 1, C. Vicary; 2, V. Hawkins; 3, S. Matthews.
Junior Relay Race.—58.8 secs. 1, Argos; 2, Thebes; 3, Olympia; 4, Athens;
   5, Corinth; 6, Sparta.

THIRD AND FOURTH YEAR
100 Yds.—12 secs. 1, M. Coggins; 2, M. Dudbridge; 3, E. Jones.
Hurdles.—11 secs. 1, M. Coggins; 2, P. Rossor; 3, D. Needs.
Obstacle.—1, D. Needs; 2, J. Sealey; 3, P. Eyres.
150 Yds.—20 secs. 1, M. Dudbridge; 2, P. Rosser; 3, E. Jones.
Potato.—1, K. Partridge; 2, J. Parsons; 3, B. Sarus.
High Jump.—4ft. 1in. 1, M. Dudbridge; 2, L. Sheppard; 3, A. Haskins.
Long Jump.—15ft. 6in. 1, P. Rosser; 2, E. Jones; 3, J. Stinchcombe.
Javelin.—47ft. 1, D. Needs; 2, D. Dawes; 3, L. Long.
Discus.—56ft. 10in. 1, S. Hedges; 2, P. Bambur; 3, J. Gerrish.
Relay.—1, Corinth; 2, Argus; 3, Athens; 4, Sparta; 5, Olympia; 6, Thebes.

SPORTS DAY

The Annual Sports were held on Wednesday, June 26th. We were pleased to welcome to them a large number of friends, including Mr. J. Milne, Chief Organiser of Physical Education.

The Sports Cup was presented to the captains of the winning House, Thebes, by Councillor Graves, who is Vice-Chairman of the School Governors.

Below a photo of Sports Day in the 1960's – Miss Place and Mr Miller.

1958 Girls' Sports

Below is the Games Report from the 1958 School Magazine and a photo of the First Year Rounders Team.

GAMES REPORT
NETBALL
TEAMS :

First VII: L. Shepherd, S. Hall, D. Davies, P. Rosser (Capt.), D. Needs, M. Coggins, S. Hedges.

Second VII: P. Eyre, S. Farmer, J. Gerrish, E. Jones (Capt.), M. Dudbridge, J. Stinchcombe, P. Boreman.

3rd Year VII: V. Hawkins, S. Wilkins, V. Price, A. Williams, J. Gibbs, D. Pippard (Capt.), D. Pollard.

2nd Year VII: C. Garland, J. Selwood, M. Barton, G. Helps, G. Vlaeminke, M. Allen, Y. Purnell (Capt.).

1st Year VII: L. Buimyee, J. Wise, E. O'Connell, R. Cowley (Capt.), P. Baker, P. Folkes, P. Williams.

All the Netball teams have enjoyed quite a successful season, but the 1st VII did particularly well by winning both School Tournaments held at Hengrove.

The standard of play has improved this year and next season we hope to send a team to the County Tournament.

HOCKEY

First XI: S. Hedges, J. Richards, P. Bambry, A. Richards, D. Davies, L. Long (Capt.), S. Delaney, C. Handley, P. Eyres, M. Coggins, E. Jones.

3rd Year XI: C. Bailey, D. Pippard, J. Gibbs, J. Phelps, C. Bacon, V. Hawkins, L. Bright, J. Roper, K. Gingell, A. Webb (Capt.), J. Elbrow.

2nd Year XI: C. Garland, J. Gray, P. Long, H. Poley, M. Barton, G. Helps, C. Coles, H. Phippen, Y. Purnell, J. Dyer, G. Vlaeminte (Capt.).

The weather caused quite a few matches to be cancelled this season. It also prevented the teams getting extra practice. However, despite these setbacks, the teams did quite well, and we hope for kinder weather conditions next term.

ROUNDERS

First IX: D. Davies, D. Needs, P. Rosser, J. Gerrish, L. Long, L. Shepherd, M. Coggins, P. Eyres, E. Jones. Reserves: C. Handley, J. Waddleton.

2nd Year IX: J. Gray, C. Garland, G. Helps, D. Satterley, G. Vlaeminte, J. Dyer, H. Poley, T. Purnell (Capt.), V. Bryant. Reserve: J. Reed.

3rd Year IX: D. Pollard, V. Hawkins, D. Pippard, A. Webb, J. Gibbs, C. Bacon, L. Bright, V. Price, S. Wilkins.

1st Year IX: D. Jakeway, L. Brumyu, J. Freeman, P. Williams, C. Coles, R. Cowley, M. Munro, J. Wise, P. Folkes. Reserves: D. Bavin, B. Broomfield, P. Baker.

Although we are rather near the beginning of the Rounders Term we have made a very pleasing start. We hope to continue on this level throughout the season.

ATHLETICS

Both boys and girls have taken part in the Bristol Schools' Athletic Sports this year. Both teams did very well but the girls were a little more successful and managed to win the " Hilda Wills Cup " for track events in the Minor and Junior Groups.

Five girls had been selected to represent Bristol in the Gloucestershire Championships on June 7th, at Cheltenham:— M. Coggins (Intermediate Hurdles); V. Hawkins (Junior Hurdles); C. Gallop, J. Dyer (100 yds. Minor); M. Barton (Minor Long Jump).

RESULTS OF THE BRISTOL SCHOOLS' ATHLETIC SPORTS

Minor 100 *yds.:* C. Gallop 1st; J. Dyer 2nd.

Minor Long Jump: M. Barton 1st.

Minor Relay Team: C. Gallop, J. Dyer, P. Williams, P. Folkes. 1st Place.

Junior Hurdles: V. Hawkins 1st.

Junior Relay Team: V. Hawkins, C. Bacon, M. Barton, A. Nash. 2nd Place.

Junior Javelin: D. Needs 1st.

Junior Discus: J. Gerrish 2nd; C. Garland 3rd.

Intermediate Hurdles: M. Coggins 1st.

Intermediate 100 *yds.:* J. Stinchcombe 3rd.

Intermediate 150 *yds.:* L. Shepherd 4th; M. Dudbridge 2nd; P. Rosser 4th.

Intermediate High Jump: M. Dudbridge 2nd; L. Shepherd 3rd.

Discus: P. Bambry 2nd.

Intermediate Relay Team: M. Coggins, M. Dudbridge, P. Rosser, J. Stinchcombe. 1st Place.

32

HOUSE NOTES
OLYMPIA
Mr. Hale; Mr. Bewley, Mr. Hollely; Mrs. Andrews; Mrs. Cameron.

BOYS.

Olympia has had a fairly good year although we did not win any championship during the season.

Our Soccer team was trying hard to win the Championship for the second year in succession, but despite the fact that everyone in the team made a great effort we were defeated in the first round.

Our Cross Country team was more successful. In a hard-fought race we were able to reach second place and thus gain credit for the House.

We have every reason to look forward with quiet confidence to further successes. M. THATCHER (4B)

GIRLS.

We were very sorry when Mrs. Roach, our House Mistress had to leave us, but we were glad to welcome two new members of staff to our House, Mrs. Cameron and Mrs. Andrews.

In the games field we did not achieve any outstanding successes.

Our Hockey Team, however, reached the finals and the players are to be congratulated on putting up a fine show.

In the House Reading Festival our Reading team was awarded third place.

These results give us every reason to be confident during the coming year. CHERE HANDLEY (4B)

SPARTA
Mr. Fletcher; Mr. Sterry; Miss Bain; Mr. Hanham; Mr. Wood.

BOYS. *Football*

The House Soccer team was unable to bring off any outstanding success during the year. After entering the House Competition in the second round against Argos, we were defeated, after a hard-fought game by 2—0. Stephens, our House Football Captain has also captained the School Soccer team during the absence of Summers, on several occasions.

Cross Country

Although our final placing in the House Cross Country event was only fifth, our team ran well. Hutton ran very well indeed and succeeded in spite of heavy opposition, in arriving home with the first few runners. P. COOK (4B), A. FRY (4B).

GIRLS.

On the whole the House was reasonably successful during the year.

Under the captainship of Dawn Pippard our Netball Team was placed second with 13 points.

We tied in the Hockey Tournament with Argos for first place, so the Cup was shared. Margaret Coggins, our Captain is also a member of the School Team.

In the House Reading Festival, our team was placed fifth and although this was a fairly low placing our team gave a good account of themselves.

DORELLE FOLKES (4B), MOLLY ETHERTON (4B).

ATHENS

Mr. Buckland; Mr. Pyle; Mr. Jones; Miss Place; Miss Pleass.

BOYS.

During the year the House has gained some ground and we can look back with pleasure on a number of achievements.

In Rugby Football we were successful in gaining wins in all out games.

In Soccer we had the honour of being runners-up in the House Competition. Unfortunately we were defeated by Argos 3—0 in the final, but our team can claim credit for a good performance.

Three members of our House team have made useful contributions to the School Soccer teams and no less than six of our Rugby players have represented the School. while two of our Cross Country runners were chosen to represent the School in the Inter-Schools Event.

M. COTTLE (4B), N. CLEMENTS (4B).

GIRLS.

It has been a somewhat disappointing year in games.

We were only able to reach fourth place in the Netball Tournament and our Hockey team was defeated in the Knock-out Competition.

Our Reading team reached fourth place in the School Reading Festival.

We have several very keen players in our House teams, but more support is needed from other members and then we may look forward with confidence to better results.

ARLENE BENNETT (4B), CHRISTINE BALL (4B).

CORINTH

Mr. Jackman; Mr. Cork; Mr. Blackmore and Miss Thomas.

BOYS.

This year we have no outstanding successes to report in the field of sport but several of our members have made useful contributions in the School Games Teams. Three members of our Soccer Team have played for the School and three representatives of the House appeared for the School in the Inter-Schools Cross Country event.

Unfortunately our Soccer Team was eliminated from the House competition quite early on but our Cross Country teams distinguished themselves in the School event which the Seniors won.

GIRLS.

We were sorry to say 'Goodbye' to Mr. Seymour and Miss Hawken during the year, although in each case we were able to offer congratulations. Mr. Seymour left to become headmaster of another school and Miss Hawken to be in charge of Physical Education in a Devon school.

We welcome Mr. Blackmore and Mr. Jackman, who have joined Corinth House.

The Netball and Hockey teams have had an enjoyable year. We reached fourth place in the Netball Tournament and some promising players are developing.

Our leading team reached a good position in the House Reading Festival and in all, Corinth House can look forward with confidence to the next year. CELIA EYERS (4B).

THEBES
Mr. Trivett; Mr. D. Bromwich; Mr. E. Bromwich, Mr. Nussbaum; Miss Crowther.

BOYS.

Football
Our Soccer team was not as successful this year as they were last year. In the House Competition they were beaten quite early on, by Athens, but since Athens reached the final round we can claim to have put up a fairly good performance.

Cross Country
Here too we were disappointed. Our teams ran well but they did not succeed in getting a place.

In general the year has brought no outstanding achievements but we look forward to better results next year.
A. SALTER (4B), J. ROBINSON (4B).

GIRLS.

Although we have had very little success in House competitions this year our teams have maintained effort very well.

We lost in both Netball and Hockey contests by a narrow margin. Argos defeated us in the Hockey Knock-out Competition by 1—0.

Our House Netball Captain, Pat Rosser has played for the School team this year.

We can congratulate our House Reading team which was awarded second place in the House Reading Festival. This was a very well-deserved achievement.
JUNE SEALEY (4B), MARION PAYNE (4B).

ARGOS

Mr. Hobbs; Mr. Wright; Mr. Macartney; Miss Green.

BOYS.

Football

During the year a Soccer Knock-out Competition was staged. Argos House, which fielded a young team under the captaincy of Webb, won their rounds and so carried off the Cup after defeating Olympia 1—0 and Sparta 2—0. This was the first time in the history of the House that we have won this cup and we hope for continued success in future competitions.

Rugby

In the Seven-a-Side Tournament we were unfortunately defeated in the first round but we hope to do better next time.

Cross Country Event

Our Junior Team was successful in winning this event after a very good race indeed. This early success promises well for the future.

M. WHITFIELD (4B).

GIRLS.

The House has had a very successful year.

The Netball Team, under the able direction of the captain, Lesley Sheppard, was successful in winning the Netball Cup.

The Hockey Team divided the honours with Sparta in the Hockey Tournament and the Cup is to be held jointly by the two Houses. Ann Richards our Hockey Captain also plays in the School Hockey Team.

To complete our list of successes, we also reached the first place in the House Reading Festival.

Altogether we have every reason to be proud of our results and we are looking forward to Sports Day to bring additional honours

Argos and Athens Houses jointly produced a 20 page House Magazine No. 1 – price 6d in December 1958. An original copy is available in the City Record Office with the Hengrove Secondary School archive material. It contains the Headmaster's letter, crosswords and other articles contributed by pupils including details of sports teams and results of matches. If you were at the school between 1954 and 1958 your name might be in the magazine!

1959 Girls' Sports

The 1959 School Magazine had less space dedicated to coverage of sports; but we do have the Girls' Athletic results 1959 and a sample of a Certificate awarded to a participant in the Relay Race (opposite).

SCHOOL SPORTS

During the year the school has engaged competitively in many games including hockey, swimming, netball, basketball, soccer, rugby, and cricket. All the school teams, both senior and junior, have had a very successful year. Hengrove is now a power to be reckoned with in Bristol school sport. Next year it is hoped that competitive archery will be added to the school's activity.

GIRLS' ATHLETIC RESULTS, 1959

Bristol Schools' Athletic Sports, June 6th, 1959 :

Intermediate Section.
100 yds. Mary Dudbridge, 1st Place.
80 yds. Hurdles Margaret Coggins, 2nd Place.
High Jump Mary Dudbridge, 1st Place.
High Jump Ann Haskins, 2nd Place.

Junior Section
75 yds. Hurdles Valerie Hawkins, 1st Place.
Discus Carol Garland, 1st Place.

Gloucestershire County Sports, June 13th, 1959 :
80 yds. Hurdles Margaret Coggins, 2nd Place.
75 yds. Hurdles Valerie Hawkins, 1st Place.
Discus Carol Garland, 3rd Place.

South West Regional Sports, June 28th, 1959 :
80 yds. Hurdles Margaret Coggins, 2nd Place.
75 yds. Hurdles Valerie Hawkins, 1st Place.

All England Schools' Athletic Sports, July 1959 :
75 yds. Hurdles Valerie Hawkins, 1st Place.

Swimming :
Anne Webb.
Junior Gloucestershire Back Stroke, 1st Place.
Senior Gloucestershire Back Stroke, 2nd Place.
Junior Western Counties Back Stroke, 3rd Place.
Senior Western Counties Back Stroke, 3rd Place.
Senior Bristol Schools' Back Stroke, 1st Place.
Senior S. Wales and S. West Schools Federation Back Stroke, 1st Place.
Picked to represent Div. 5 (S. Wales and S. West) for 100 yds.
Back Stroke at Hornchurch, Essex, on 30th and 31st October.

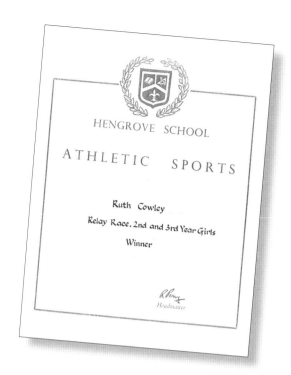

Mr Richardson provided a photo of the 1959 Staff vs Pupils rounders match (below).

Staff v. Pupils Rounders 1959
The staff cheated a little by hitting the ball to where the boys were sitting, they hid it until we had run round.
Back. Bob Miller, Denys Richardson, Middle. Kath Bevan, Olga Plaice, ? Geof Hale, ? Ann Please. Front. George Foote. PAM SHAW

1960 Girls' Sports

Former pupil Carol Garland participated in the Hengrove Athletic Sports in June 1960 and provided the programme below.

PROGRAMME

PROGRAMME

EVENT.

vent

1. High Jump Boys 3rd & 4th yrs. (Record 5')
   (A) Alpin ( ) (O) Mellor (1)
   (Sp) Chappell(2) (Th) Davis A. ( )

2. Long Jump Girls 3rd year (Record 14' 6")
   (A) B. Christie (2) (O) J. Orme ( )
   (Sp) R. Cowley (1) (Th) B. Broomfield ( )

3. Throwing the Javelin Girls 4th 5th & 6th yrs (record 76')
   (A) G. Vlaeminke ( ) (O) D. Davis ( )
   (Sp) C. Withers (2) (Th) G. Helps ( )

4. Throwing the Discus Boys 3rd & 4th yrs. (Record 114' 2")
   (A) ( ) (O) Brewer ( )
   (Sp) Adams ( ) (Th) Butler (2)
   Mathews

4a. Throwing the Discus Boys 5th & 6th yrs.(Record 112' 8")
   (A) Woolaway ( ) (O) Davis (2)
   (Sp) Gardner (1) (Th) Wallington ( )

5. Putting the Shot Boys 3rd & 4th yrs. (Record 38' 8")
   (A) Woolaway ( ) (O) Neagle (1)
   (Sp) Terris ( ) (Th) Mathews ( )

5a. Putting the Shot Boys 5th & 6th yrs. (Record 38' 8")
   (A) Dyer 3= (2) (O) Duckett ( )
   Yearman (Th) Summers D ( )

6. 100 yds. Girls 4th 5th & 6th yrs. (Record 12.2secs)
   (A) L. Sheppard ( ) (O) H. Sheppard ( )
   (Sp) C. Bacon ( ) (Th) J. Dyer ( )

7. 100 yds. Boys 5th & 6th yrs. (Record 10.8secs.)
   (A) Manning ( ) (O) D. Pike ( )
   (Sp)E. Pavey ( ) (Th) M. Summer ( )

8. 100yds. Girls 3rd year (Record 12.6secs.)
   (A) B. Christie ( ) (O) J. Wise ( )
   (Sp) R. Cowley ( ) (Th) M. Townsend ( )

9. 100yds. Boys 3rd & 4th yrs. (Record 11.8secs)
   (A) Ferrier ( ) (O) R. Waite ( )
   (Sp) J. Chappell ( ) (Th) A. Davis ( )

10. 100yds. Girls 2nd year (Record 13secs.)
    (A) J. Prior ( ) (O) S. Butler ( )
    (Sp) M. Pevey ( ) (Th) S. Abbobb ( )

11. 100yds. Boys 2nd year Record 11.9secs.)
    (A) Brumpton ( ) (O) Chapman ( )
    (Sp) Sennett ( ) (Th) Edwards ( )

12. 100yds. Girls 1st year (Record 13.1secs)
    (A) M. Vlaeminke ( ) (O) A. Goulder ( )
    (Sp) S. Wring ( ) (Th) G. Perchard ( )

13. 100yds. Boys 1st year. (Record 12.9secs.)
    (A) Randall ( ) (O) Batchelor ( )
    (Sp) Grippiths ( ) (Th) Hall ( )

14. High Jump Girls 3rd year (Record 4' 4")
    (A) B. Christie ( ) (O) J. Wise ( )
    (Sp) A. Paul (1) (Th) C. Crew (2)

15. Long Jump Boys 3rd & 4th yrs. (Record 16' 6½")
    (A) Ferrier ( ) (O) Ladd ( )
    (Sp) Clegg (1) (Th) Ash (2)

16. Throwing the Discus Girls 3rd year (Record 76')
    (A) J. Miller ( ) (O) J. Wise (1½)
    (Sp) R.Cowley ( ) (Th) P. Williams (1½)

17. 150 yds. Boys 1st year
    (A) Edwards ( ) (O) Batchelor ( )
    (Sp) B. Turner ( ) (Th) A. Robinson ( )

18. 150 yds. Girls 4th 5th & 6th yrs. (Record 17.9secs.)
    (A) E. Jones ( ) (O) ( ) C. Gallup
    (Sp) M. Barton ( ) (Th) A. Webb ( )

19. 150 yds. Girls 3rd year
    (A) B. Christie ( ) (O) P. Baker ( )
    (Sp) R. Cowley ( ) (Th) P. Williams ( )

20. 440 yds. Boys Open. (Record 56.4secs.)
    (A) Woolaway ( ) (O) Batchelor ( )
    (Sp) Senior ( ) (Th) D. Summers ( )

21. Hop Step and Jump Boys 3rd & 4th yrs. (Record 40')
    (A) Long ( ) (O) Ladd ( )
    (Sp) Clegg (1) (Th) Gillham (2)

21a. Hop Step and Jump Boys 5th & 6th yrs. (Record 40')
    (A) Manning ( ) (O) Ladd ( )
    (Sp) Senior (2) (Th) M. Summers( )

22. Obstacle Race Girls 1st year
    (A) C. Eyre ( ) (O) J. Hunt ( )
    (Sp) S. Wring ( ) (Th) S. Sennett ( )

23. Obstacle Race Boys 1st year
    (A) Ottenshaw ( ) (O) Ferris ( )
    (Sp) Sharples ( ) (Th) Gitsham ( )

24. Obstacle Race Girls 2nd year
    (A) S. Muller ( ) (O) B. Collins ( )
    (Sp) J. Dant ( ) (Th) C. Lewis ( )

25. Obstacle Race Boys 2nd year
    (A) Bevan ( ) (O) S. Ferris ( )
    (Sp) Nussbaum ( ) (Th) Wilkins ( )

3q 70 yds. Hurdles Girls 4th 5th & 6th yrs. (Record 10.5secs)
(A) V.Hawkins (.) (O) C. Gallop ( )
(Sp) J. Selwood ( ) (Th) P. Mosser ( )

40 80 yds. Hurdles Boys 3rd & 4th yrs.
(A) Gilbert ( ) (O) Jennings ( )
(Sp) A.N. Other ( ) (Th) Davis ( )

41 One Mile Boys Open
(A) Harvey ( ) (O) Davis ( )
(Sp) S. King ( ) (Th) Bennett

42. 4 X 110 yds. Girls 1st year Relay
1. 2.
3. 4. Argos

43. 4 X110 yds. Boys 1st year Relay
1. 2.
3. 4.

44. 4 X 110 yds. Girls 2nd year Relay
1. 2.
3. 4.

45. 4 X 110 yds. Boys 2nd year Relay
1. 2.
3. 4.

46. 4 X 110 yds. Girls 3rd year Relay
1. 2. Argos
3. 4.

47. 4 X 110 yds. Boys 3rd year Relay
1. 2.
3. 4.

48. 4 X 110 yds. Girls 4th 5th & 6th. yrs. Relay
1. Argos 2.
3. 4.

49. 4 X 110 yds. Boys 5th & 6th yrs. Relay
1. 2. argos
3. 4.

EVENT

26. High Jump Boys 5th & 6th yrs. (Record 5' 2")
(A) Knight (2) (O) Perrington (1)
(Sp) Hutton ( ) (Th) M. Summers ( )

27. Long Jump Girls 4th 5th & 6th yrs. (Record 15' 4")
(A) V. Hawkins ( ) (O) C. Gallop (2)
(Sp) M. Barton ( ) (Th) A. Williams (1)

28. 220 yds. Boys 2nd year
(A) Hockey ( ) (O) Ashley ( )
(Sp) J. Whiting ( ) (Th) J. Attwood ( )

29. 220 yds. Boys 3rd & 4th yrs. (Record 24.4secs)
(A) Jay ( ) (O) R. Waite ( )
(Sp) R. Walker ( ) (Th) King ( )

30. 220 yds. Boys 5th & 6th yrs. (Record 24.4secs)
(A) Denham ( ) (O) D. Pike ( )
(Sp) E. Pavey ( ) (Th) D. Summers ( )

31. Javelin Boys 3rd & 4th yrs. (Record 106' 3")
(1) Long ( ) (O) Selway ( )
(Sp) Senior ( ) (Th) Wallington (2)

31a. Javelin Boys 5th & 6th yrs. (Record 123' 7½")
(A) Townsend ( ) (O) Neagle ( )
(Sp) (Th)

32 Throwing the Discus Girls 4th 5th & 6th yrs. (Record 63')
(A) C. Garland ( ) (O) S. Hedges ( )
(Sp) M. Dixon ( ) (Th) R. Cooper (2)

33. High Jump Girls 4th 5th & 6th yrs. (Record 4' 3")
(A) L. Sheppard ( ) (O) C. Gallop ( )
(Sp) C. Bacon (1) (Th) P. Long (2)

34. Long Jump Boys 5th & 6th yrs. (Record 17' 2")
(A) Manning ( ) (A) Crewe (2)
(Sp) Nation (1) (Th) M. Summers ( )

35. 110 yds. Hurdles. Boys
(A) Woolaway ( ) (O) Neagle ( )
(Sp) Senior ( ) (Th) D. Summers ( )

36. 880 yds. Boys Open (Record 20mins. 20.4secs.)
(A) Hazel ( ) (O) Ladd ( )
(Sp) Sharples ( ) (Th) Thomas ( )

37. 70 yds. Girls Hurdles 2nd year (Record 12secs.)
(A) J. Prior ( ) (O) S. Brain ( )
(Sp) S. Watts ( ) (Th) G. Ball ( )

38. 70 yds. Girls Hurdles 3rd year (Record 11secs.)
(A) H. Coventry ( ) (O) P. Baker ( )
(Sp) J. Britton ( ) (Th) P. Williams ( )

Another former pupil, Carolyn Roberts (now Gill) remembers vividly a trip to a Saturday morning hockey match versus Penn Park School.

"We huddled together under the clock on the centre that cold winter Saturday morning scanning the green buses as they passed by. Those Burberries were never very warm, especially when we tied the belts tight and pulled them up as far as we can get away with when Miss Plaice wasn't on the prowl. Still it was the Sixties and we were the next fashion icons. Shame about the thick woollen bottle green shorts that rubbed the inside of your legs raw - still never mind, we would show them how to play!

Having studied the timetable we had managed to work out which bus would get us to Pen Park - it might as well be Outer Mongolia (hands up if you know where that actually is - I still don't after all these years) as we had never been further than the Downs on our own before. The double decker bus pulls in 'Come on girls, upstairs - hey watch that hocky stick'. How many of us are there, eight or nine? Good here come the other two now at least we've got a team! The bus trundles off through suburbs that to us are only names on the route map that's stuck to the glass panel behind the driver's head, until someone says they think this is where we get off. We grab our gym bags (no trendy backpacks for us, although one girl has got a Slazenger holdall that belonged to her dad, the lucky thing!) and pile down the stairs.

There is no sign of the school but someone has the bright idea of asking a postman who is on his early morning rounds and at last we see the school gates. We find the changing rooms and there is a communal sharp intake of breath because their team are huge! Even our goalie who is only just 5' 5" and the rest of us are either willowy (a la Jean Shrimpton) or titchy (more like Lulu). Still the honour of the school is at stake so here goes. We smile politely through chattering teeth as we make our way through the swirling fog onto the pitch.

I still don't know how, but that season we managed to win most of our matches. Maybe it was because we were such little squirts were just faster than the opposition, anyway we relished the victory and the talk on the bus on the way home was how Chris had won the first bully-off and how Les tackled that 6 footer, then Sue crossed to Sheila who passed to Babs and that great shot from Miriam was first goal to us. The two Jills and Ann did well at the back and Jennifer defended her goal like a Trojan.

Time to get off, bye girls, see you all on Monday - don't forget the school dance next week. But that's another story!"

We have a photo of the 1961 Hockey XI below.

Back Row. J Wise, M Munro, M Vlaeminke, M Locke, Miss Place, H Poley, J Stewart, J Freeman.
Front Row: G. Helps (deceased 2005), E O'Connell, D Jakeway, R Cowley, Pat Baker.

Below we have photos of Girls' Hockey and Netball Teams 1962.

Almost all the former pupils we have contacted – boys and girls – remember Miss Place. She was the Games and P.E. mistress. After Miss Martin the 1st Senior Mistress retired in 1963, she became Senior Mistress. She was very strict about school uniform- but was respected and well liked. She was inspirational, very professional and dedicated – always enthusiastic – even in very frosty weather on the hockey pitch!

In addition to her timetabled teaching she dedicated many extra hours to coaching in lunch times, after school and on Saturday mornings when we played against other schools.

Further she organised the Duke of Edinburgh Award Scheme for girls, involving a great deal of extra work. (See later in this chapter).

Miss Place was very involved in netball at a National level and eventually became an Honorary Life Member of the English Schools Netball Association. (see Chapter Eight).

There was a tradition of staff vs pupils matches involving Boys' Rugby Teams and Girls' Rounders and Hockey Teams.

Staff vs Pupils Hockey match 1962

Pat Eyre, a pupil, wrote a poem about the Annual Hockey Match in 1958.

THE " BATTLE "

(Annual Hockey Match)

Ten minutes before the ' line ' was crowded
Supporters cheered for school and staff.
Although for us the skies were clouded
At the start of the match of cunning and wrath.
When the whistle was blown and the ' bully ' made
The ' battle ' started and the ball was cleared.
The school had forgotten about being afraid
And the staff team was good (just as we feared).
Soon our chance came, and with a beautiful ' dribble ',
A forward brought it close to the goal.
She shot, but as so, their goalie—Dibble
Cleared with precision and skill.
Mr. Miller with a smile, did a four minute mile
On the wing, as I thought at the time.
Then, with a flick on his stick and a shot so quick
He made goal number one, ' mighty fine '.
The tussle continued as we went in for the kill,
But although we lost, it gave us a thrill.
Mr. Hale made us fail, as Miss Jones rapped my bones
And Miss Shaw finally took it with undoubted skill.
Another attack, with their forwards like gnus
Made the score 2—0 to the staff.
Later we shot the ball right through
But the ref said ' Sorry it's off '.
We were off side; but with backs like shrapnel
They scored again to make three
But with solid support from their inner-Whitnell,
Their tricks worked magnificently.
When the whistle went we were feeling quite bent
With the score to the staff 4—0.
With bruises and aches, but keenness awake
We'll win next year with more skill.

PAT EYRE (4A2).

195

1969 – 1974 Girls' Sports

The photos below were taken in the Girl's Gymnasium in the 1970's.

Below, the 2nd Year Dance Club.

Below, the 1970's Girls' Netball Teams

Hockey Teams in the 1970's (below)

We have in the archive the following list of important dates in girls' games from 1969. The list reflects the variety of activities and achievements.

Sat Oct 11 '69 - *Jill Cooper, Jenny Weeks and Kay Connor played for Bristol Netball team and continued to do so for the rest of the season.*

Sat Nov 22 '69 – *4th year hockey won the Bristol Schools hockey tournament.*

March 14 1970 – *At Hengrove the second All England Schools Netball tournament took place.*

Summer term '70 – *Susan Gazzard, Christine Slade, Wendy Cridge, Joanna Field, Ann Mills, Deborah Smithers and Cherie Damsell represented Bristol in athletics.*

Summer '70 – *Cherie Damsell with Wendy Cridge represented Gloucester.*

Summer '70 - *Cherie Damsell went to the National Competitions and succeeded in taking the 10th position in England.*

Autumn '70 – *Cherie Damsell, Carol Partridge, Julie Pearson, Katy Conner and Jill Cooper played netball all season for Bristol.*

Autumn '70 – *3rd year Netball won the Bristol Schools Tournament, so qualifying for the South West Tournament.*

Jan. 1971 - *3rd year Netball Team played at the South West Tournament, winning two matches and losing the other two.*

Summer Term '71 – *The 1st year girls' athletics team won the Bristol shield.*

Summer Term '71 – *Anne Uphill, Joanna Field, Angela Cohen, Susan Gazzard and Cherie Damsell represented Bristol in athletics.*

Summer Term '71 – *Alison Townley was given a Bristol Schools Swimming Trial.*

Summer Term '71 – *Anne Uphill and Susan Gazzard went to the Gloucester Championships. Cherie Damsell went to the National Athletic Championships and came 15th.*

Autumn Term '71 – *Julie Pearson was selected to attend an Outward Bound Course.*

Autumn Term '71 – *The 4th year Netball came 2nd in the Bristol Schools Tournament, so qualifying for the South West Tournament.*

Autumn Term '71 – Julie Pearson, Sonia Gillard, Jennifer White and Carol Partridge played County Netball all season.

Spring Term 1972 – 1st year girls cross - country team won the Bristol Schools shield.

Spring Term '72 – Claire Winter, Karen Miles, Julie Hill and Rachel Morgen members of the Bristol Cross-country winning team.

Easter '72 – Joanna Field went to the Outward Bound Course.

Summer Term '72 – Anne Uphill, Jane Stinchcombe, Bernadette O'Reilly, Susan Derrick and Carrie Lochran represented Bristol in athletics.

Summer Term '72 – Bernadette O'Reilly was selected for S.W. and National Championships. Anne Uphill went to S.W. Championships and was Gloucester reserve for National Championships.

Summer Term '72 – Junior Athletic Team won the Bristol Schools Athletic Cup. 1st year Athletic Team came 2nd in Bristol Schools Athletic Championships.

Summer Term '72 – The National Athletic Championships were held in Washington, County Durham. Bernadette O'Reilly came 2nd in her heat, and 6th in the semi-final.

Autumn Term '72 – Deborah Bishop was selected for the Outward Bound Course. 16 girls went on a netball tour to Woking, Surrey for a weekend. 4th year netball team came 2nd in Bristol Schools Tournament and qualified for the S.W. Tournament. Bernadette O'Reilly was selected for Potential International Training.

Below we present a further selection of Team photos and archive material.

U.15 X1 Hockey
V Jones, E Owen, J Tubey, S Pearce, C Burlinson, A Mass, G Winn, P Smith,
J Elws, A Dinham, P Coombs, C Kays, J Woods, C Eisentrager

2nd U.15 X1 Hockey
Below: S Nash, T Stevenson, C Sennington, L Chivers, K Walton, J Bracy, V
Andrews, J Hodge, A Smith, S Mckenzie.

Kathryn Mary Scully (nee Mitchell) was a student at Hengrove School 1965-1971.

Kathryn (Kate) was a fine gymnast and represented the school at Regional Level until she sustained a nasty fall from the vaulting horse and damaged her spine. She also played netball for the school.

Kate achieved Bronze, Silver and Gold Awards in the Duke of Edinburgh Award Scheme. She joined Avon Golds and continued to organise and give her time freely in making the Award available to many young people over the years. She attended many Award ceremonies at St. James Palace, often being presented to the Duke in recognition of her services to the scheme.

In 2009/10 she was awarded an M.B.E. for her services to Youth Work and the Duke of Edinburgh Awards Scheme. Sadly she was unable to attend Buckingham Palace to receive her medal from the Queen as cancer was beginning to take its toll. She was presented to Princess Anne in 2010 at Dorothy House Hospice in Winsley, near Bath, when she was able to wear her medal.

The first two of the photographs include Kathryn. These were sent in by her husband.

1st U15 XI Hockey
C Burlinson, J Weeks, A Mass, K Mitchell, T Beake, L Bussel, S Pearce,
W Chambers.

3rd Year Netball Team date uncertain G King, L Lasier, Miss Collins,
G Cooper, W Cridge, S Collins, J Field, G Levich, b Dodge, S Bartlett,
P Kenna.

1st Year 2nd Netball Team (not dated). J Harrison, L Redrup, R Merchant, S Sherwood, J Rose, V Harrison, J Mansfield, S Lacey.

2nd Year Netball Team (note dated). Miss Collins, S McAllister, P Jones, A Preston, J Edworthy, G Rapier, G Narlon, S Manfield, C Goodman.

1st X1 Hockey. Eileen Owen, Kay Conner, Lin Bussell, Sally Pearce, Tina Beake, Hazel Poole, Pauline Coombs, Pam Hunt, Sandra Woolley, Alison Thorne.

Gymnastics Club 1970-1971 Debra Haines, Elaine Weaver, Janet Sutherland, Elaine Gillard, Julie Fortune, Sharon Cole, Elizabeth Watts, Alison Townley, Jenny King, Carrie Laughtan, Debra Lyons, Linda Rose, Gill Pearson, Angela Quinn, Tania Homes.

U.13 Netball Team V11 J Fortune, J Sutherland, L Holwell, A Parker, B Flying, C Laughran, E Weaver, J Caines, D Lyons.

U.14 Netball Team V11 S Horely, C Damsell, J Pearson, S Gillard, C Partridge, J Whittle, S Williams – This was the team to qualify for the South West of England Tournament.

JUNIOR

Hengrove girls in top ten . . .

The under-15 netball team from Hengrove School are among the top 10 in England at their age level.

The school has been buzzing this week with the exploits of the team — Sonia Gillard, Caroline Bird, Elaine Weaver, Debra Haines, Julie Cains, Debra Lyons and Janet Sutherland — in the National Schools' Netball Tournament finals in Nottingham.

Hengrove, representing the West of England, were at Nottingham with 15 other finalists from all over England.

They came second in their section to qualify for the last eight and were eventually placed sixth — the highest ever position achieved by a Bristol area school.

The title was won by a Coventry school, who were in a class of their own. They beat Hengrove 14—2, for example

from Devon, in the final of the West of England tournament.

And four girls, captain Sonia, Elaine, Julie and Debra Haines, have played for the Bristol county junior team.

Unbeaten

Next season they are upping the age limit to Under-16, so we hope to get to the finals again," Hengrove P.E. mistress Sue Collins told me.

Hengrove are unbeaten in their local fixtures this season. They qualified to represent the West at Nottingham with a 6—3 win over Audley Park

The Under 15 Netball team was featured in the Evening Post 7th April 1973 (left)

Below is an extract from Hengrove School Newsletter 26th May 1971 – paragraph four – written by Mr Fletcher, celebrating more success in sports events

"More successes to report. Our first year girls won the 'minor girls' shield awarded to the team gaining the highest number of points in the Bristol Schools' Athletics Championships. Eula Clemmings, Bernadette O'Reilly, Alison Creedy and Brenda Rogers were responsible for this fine win. Our second and third year girls were runners up for the field events cup. Five girls will represent Hengrove at the Gloucestershire Championships on 12th June: Joanna Field, Sue Gazzard, Cherie Damsell, Anne Uphill and Angela Cohen will carry our best wishes with them. Miss Collins wishes to advertise the Fencing Club for 5th and 6ths on Wednesday evenings 7:30 – 9:00pm."

Duke of Edinburgh Award Scheme - Girls

This scheme was introduced nationally in 1957 for girls (1956 for boys). This means that Hengrove School was again a pioneer.

A former pupil writes:

"My memories of the expedition for Bronze level Duke of Edinburgh's Award are vivid. Three of us went by bus to somewhere in Gloucestershire and had to find a certain field where we had to cook our lunch using camping equipment. We had great difficulty opening a can of baked beans and ate them cold!

One of the girls was very sick on the bus home. She vomited all over my duffle coat!! It took a long time to get rid of the smell! – Memorable!

For the Silver expedition, Cherry Helps, Hilary Poley, Diane Jakeway and myself cycled to St Briavels Youth Hostel in October half term. It was raining and cold and we were soaking wet on reaching the Bristol side of the Aust Ferry (no Severn Bridge yet). The Wye Valley was beautiful but the hill from the River Wye up to the Castle housing the Youth Hostel at St Briavels was very steep and we struggled to push our bikes and luggage up to the top. We were relieved to collapse and rest at the Youth Hostel but after a hot drink we were asked to peel buckets full of potatoes for the evening meal! We certainly deserved our Silver Awards!"

There are references made in the Prizegiving Day programmes and Headmaster's Reports in Chapter 2 and 3 to the number of Awards gained. In the year 1962/3 the Girls achieved 1 Gold, 18 Silver and 76 Bronze Awards. By 1963/4 the Awards achieved by both Girls and Boys combined rose to 11 Gold, 38 Silver and 162 Bronze with a futher 160 in process.

By 1966/7 Boys and Girls combined were approaching the 400th Award.

We have copies of the certificates for Gold and Silver Awards and from her personal archive, an invitation to Buckingham Palace received by Miss Place (to accompany the recipient).

AWARDED BY
H.R.H The DUKE of EDINBURGH
To
Gillian Frances Vlaeminke
on attaining
THE GOLD STANDARD
of the
DUKE of EDINBURGH'S AWARD
26th November 1963

THE DUKE OF
EDINBURGH'S AWARD

Ruth Cowley

has passed

THE SILVER STANDARD

of

The Duke of Edinburgh's Award

February 1962

Miss O. Place

Hengrove School

Petherton Gardens

Bristol 4.

*The Equerry-in-Waiting to The Duke of Edinburgh
is desired by His Royal Highness to invite*

Miss O. Place

to attend a Reception for those who have reached the
Gold Standard in His Royal Highness's Award Scheme
at Buckingham Palace
on Tuesday, 26th November, 1963, at 4 p.m.

*Dress: Lounge Suit
or Uniform,
Afternoon Dress.*

Other Activities

Another activity available was Safety and Life-Saving First-Aid competitions. We have a letter and newspaper article dated 20 July 1973 showing that Hengrove School was placed second and naming the students involved.

CITY AND COUNTY OF BRISTOL

DEPARTMENT OF HEALTH

R C WOFINDEN
MD FRCP DPH DPA
Medical Officer of Health

GPO BOX No 201   TOWER HILL   BRISTOL BS99 7BQ

Tel (0272)21010 ext   279

P. S. Waterhouse, Esq.,
Headmaster,
Hengrove School,
Petherton Gardens,
BRISTOL
BS14 9BT

Your ref

Our ref   LDE/CLJ

20th July, 1973

Dear Mr. Waterhouse,

<u>Safety and Life-Saving First-Aid Competition</u>

Congratulations to your school being placed second in the above competition last Saturday.

Stuart Crossman and Paul Raymond gave a good performance, and I enclose two photographs for your school records. Photographs have also been sent to the boys at their home addresses.

Yours sincerely,

L. D. Ewles

L. D. Ewles (Miss)
Assistant Health Education Officer

Safety first

Winners of Bristol secondary schools' safety and life-saving first-aid contest, held at St. Mary Redcliffe and Temple School. Keith Brown and John Cox, the winning team from Brislington School, are holding the Ethel Boyce Memorial Rose Bowl, awarded by Bristol Home Safety Council. Other teams pictured, from left, are Fairfield School (Jasna Molnar and Wendy Richards), runner-up; Hengrove School (Stuart Crossman and Paul Raymond), second; and Withywood School (Joy Purnell and Karen Fogarty), third.

Summer Camps

Summer camps were very popular at Wareham and Exmouth (Carey Camp and Orcombe Point). Mr Richardson has memories of these. He writes:

Carey Camp, Wareham Dorset

"A summer holiday camp lasting a week that was organised by Bob Swift every year. He persuaded teaching staff (sometimes with their wives) to help him. The camp site had a permanent kitchen and dining area. Sleeping was in tents. The site owned by Bristol Education Committee was on the edge of the heath. Trips were taken to Swanage and Lulworth Cove. There was plenty of wildlife especially mosquitoes and a queue would form every evening for a dab of calamine lotion!"

There are also some photos of Orcombe Point in Chapter 2, supplied by a former student.

Boys' Sports

And

Other Extra-Curricular Activities

1954-1959

We have some very early photographs taken in 1954-1957 and extracts from the Hengrove School Magazine Vol 2 July 1957.

Taken during Evening Post Interview with D.Perry (then Headmaster) re. Comprehensiuue Education. 1956.

Bob Miller, Head of P.E. during Open Evening.

CRICKET 1957

In good cricket weather, three teams have been fielded this term. So far we have been successful against St. George (twice), Lockleaze (twice), Bedminster, but have lost to Brislington, Sefton Park.

TEAMS:

Under 15 XI: Stephens (capt.), Harding, Parker, Townsend, Lugg, Summers Woolaway, Manchester, Hammond, Randall, Lillington.

Under 13½ XI: Crockford (capt.), Senior, Knowles, Wallington, Sage, Hughes, Webb, J. Miller, Derrick, Tugwell, West, Cook, Watkins. (1956, Parker, Townsend.)

First Year XI: Gilbert (capt.), Mellor, R., Mellor, P., Ferrier, Long, Thomas, Dunsford, Goverd, Coombes, Smith, Jennings, Nott.

Stephens, Lugg and Knowles were selected for special coaching by the Schools' Cricket Association. Stephens was selected for a Bristol Boys' XI.

ROYAL LIFE SAVING SUCCESSES

The following gained *Elementary and Intermediate Certificates* together with Free Passes to the Baths:

J. Gunter, 2A; P. Temblett, 3B; R. Jones, 4A; E. Pavey, 2B; M. Preece, 2F; R. Crockford, 2D; C. Senior, 2A; S. Rogers, 2C; R. Tugwell, 2A; J. Knapper, 4A; J. Lillington, 4A.

Unigrip Certificates were gained by:

R. Whitchuch, 3GI; I. Johnston, 4A; J. Haines, 2E; M. Chester, 4A; C. Miller, 2E; J. Miller, 2E; R. Grinham, I; M. Francis, 4A.

Bronze Medallions (and Free Passes):

D. Summers, 3A; J. Johnston, 4A; A. Tiley, 4B; M. Randall, 4B; D. Goverd, 3P; I. Weaver, 3B; R. Hinton, 4A; R. Jones, 4A; M. Chester, 4A.

Bristol Schools' R.L.S.S. Trophy (Boys): This award has been won by the School for the greatest number of R.L.S.S. Awards per pupil.

BASKET-BALL
SCHOOL TEAM:

M. Parsons (capt.)	4A	D. Summers	3A
M. Randall	4B	M. Hutton	3B
R. Hammond	4A	A. Lugg	3A
R. Hinton	4A	R. Lillington	(Scorer)

The School Basket-Ball Team won the Bristol Schools' Basket-Ball Trophy which is awarded annually to the League Champions.

RUGBY

Further progress was made during the 1956-57 season. There are now many boys who are very enthusiastic about the game. We were able to form teams from the 1st, 2nd and 3rd years. Matches were played by these teams against several of the bilateral schools and some grammar and modern schools which field similar sides.

TEAMS:

1st Year XV: Burchill, Takle, Newman, Thomas, Chappell, Ellis, Robinson, Ferrier (capt.), Ash, Fairclough, Trenear, Livingston, Mead, Iles, Russe, Rich, Cobley, Richards.

2nd Year XV: Pavey (capt), Duckett, Watkins, Davies, Crago, Cherry, White, Dunne, Evans, Crochford, Wallington, Hall, Pike, Naish, Derrick, Davis, Brain.

3rd Year XV: Hazell (capt.), Hayward, Williams, Jones, Cogan, Batchelor, Harkess, Coxall, Quick, Griffin, Sage, Wilmot, Seymour, Iles, Blizzard, Bale, Bridgman, Gardiner, Manchester.

SOCCER

A full programme of games was carried out by the three Soccer teams, and some very interesting games were played against the grammar, bi-lateral and modern schools. Congratulations are offered to Summers (3A) who was selected five times for the Bristol Schools' Senior XI and to Lugg (3B) who was reserve for the Intermediate XI.

1st YEAR SOCCER

A special mention should be made of this team which has made a very good start in School matches, winning eight out of twelve matches played with one drawn game.

Team: B. Dunsford, R. Clegg (1A), J. Coombs, A. Long, A. Gilbert (1B), C. Loman, A. Kent, T. Goverd, M. Adams, R. Jay (1C), K. Millard, D. Robinson (1D), N. Jennings (1E).

TEAMS:

2nd Year XI: Long, Dark, Sage, Lugg, Hughes (capt.), Crewe, Webb, Summers, Lanning, Miller, Ball, Knowles, Tugwell.

3rd and 4th Year XI: Lillington, Plucknett, Parsons, Randall, Parker, Harding, Stephens, Tremblett, Sprague, Jones, Hinton (capt.), Hammond, Robinson, Summers, Cridge, Francis, Klavenicks.

An extract from the 1958 School Magazine Vol. 3 is reproduced below:

SCHOOL GAMES

RUGBY FOOTBALL

Three school teams were fielded during the season and all the matches were hard fought with narrow margin results.

A " Sevens " tournament was played for the first time and will now be a regular feature.

The game has an enthusiastic following in the School and the standard of play steadily improves. We look forward to the coming season when we will field an over 15's XV for the first time. It will be interesting to see how the amendments to the Laws will affect the game.

These are the principal amendments to the Laws:

1. *Knock-on.* If the ball is unintentionally knocked on in the act of catching it direct from a kick, and is recovered before it touches the ground, play is allowed to continue.

2. *Scrummage.* (a) All players must bind with at least one arm and hand around the body of' another player of the same team.

3. *Tackle.* It is not necessary to play the ball with the foot after a tackle.

4. *Penalty Kick.* (a) A scrummage may be taken in place of a penalty kick.

(b) The ball may be kicked in *any* direction.

5. *Place Kick.* The *kicker* may place the ball.

TEAMS:

1st Year XV: Hull, Massey, Chapple, Harding, Salter, Hampton, Stephens, Butler, Bessell, Backwell, Walker, Jennings (Capt.), King, Matthews, Davis, A., Ferris, Dyer.

Intermediate XV: Dunne (Capt.), Cherry, Parker, J., Brain, Davis, R., Davies (3B), Pavey, Pike, Iles, Fry, Ferrier, Robinson, Derrick, Hazel J., Crewe, Nation, White, Russe, Jay, Senior.

Under 15's XV: Hazell, Watkins, Townsend, Crockford, Lugg, Sage, Wallington, Iles, Batchelor, Bartlett, Wilmott, Bridgeman, Taylor, Clements, Jones, Quick, Seymour, Bright.

ASSOCIATION FOOTBALL

Congratulations are extended to D. Summers who was again chosen for the Bristol Schools' Senior XI which has been so successful this year.

The School fixture list was again comprehensive in its scope, there being matches played against all types of School. Weather adversely affected some matches adversely affected some matches, several were cancelled, but on the whole it has been an enjoyable season.

1st Year XI: This young team shows every promise of making a sound team. There were times when it lacked co-ordination, but towards the end of the season the boys combined better.

Team: Chapple, Stephens, Skiyins, Chivers, Harding, Young, White, Matthews, Hampton, Backwell, Ferris, Massey, Eyre, Hull (Capt.), Dyer.

Intermediate XI: The team had a very satisfactory season, winning a good proportion of their matches and generally maintaining a very fair standard. Towards the end of the season some excellent matches were played combining well both in attack and defence. This team holds good prospects for next year.

Team: Long (Capt.), Dunsford, Sage, O'Connor, Wilson, Tingwell, Edwards, Adams, Clegg, Miller, J., Jay, Gilbert, Senior, Tarr.

Under 15's XI: The team has been moderately successful, and although beaten frequently has never been outplayed, and often the football played has been superior to that of the victors.

Team: Hughes, Iles, Woolaway, Parker, Summers, M., Stevens, Crewe, Webb, Hutton, Lanning, Summers, D., Robinson, Ball, Dark, Crockford, Laskey, Harding.

BASKET BALL

Team: Lugg, Hutton, Dark, Crewe, Summers, D., Griffin, Summers, M., Woolaway, Crockford.

The Basketball team enjoyed another successful season, being beaten only once in the League Championship, and winning the Milne Knockout Cup Competition.

Summers, D., brought further honour to the School by again being selected for the Bristol Boys' Basket Ball team.

SALTER SHIELD

The Salter Shield presented to the winners of the invitation 4 x 100 yds. First Year Relay Team was again won by Hengrove in a record time.

Team: Gilbert, Ferrier, Iles, Jay, Long.

ROYAL LIFE SAVING SUCCESSES

Interest in this worthwhile pursuit is growing in the School and it should be recorded that Bronze Crosses have, for the first time, been won by pupils from this School.

BOYS: *Bronze Crosses:* Weaver, Goverd, D., Summers, D.

Bronze Medallions: Temblett, Gunter, Miller, J., Miller, C., Tugwell, Wade, Rogers.

Elementary and Intermediate: Ellis, Marten, Robinson, Lee, Harvey.

Free passes to the swimming baths are also awarded to all who pass these examinations.

CRICKET

Under 15's XI: Stevens, Townsend, Lugg, Webb, Summers, D., Crockford, Ruprecht, Clements, Woolaway, Parker, Wallington, Hughes, Knowles, Manchester, West, Perrington.

Under 13½'s XI: Senior (Capt.), Ingwell, Sage, Mellor, P., Mellor, R., Robinson, Parker, J., Lang, Williams, Dunsford, Derrick, Nott, Gilbert, Miller, T.

The under 15's XI is of a good all round standard and improving with every match.

The under 13½'s XI have played exceptionally well so far this season, having won every match at the time of going to press.

1st Year XI: This team has not had many fixtures but the boys are very keen and enjoy the games.

Team: Hull (Capt.), White, Menaugh, Massey, Matthews, Stevens, Salway, Skujins, Yeatman, Dyer, Davis, Bonwell, Harding, Cheek, Hampton.

Knowles has been selected again for special coaching by the Schools' Cricket Association and has been included in the final fifteen selected for the Bristol Boys' Team.

CROSS COUNTRY TEAMS

Following the Inter-House Cross Country Race, a Senior and a Junior team was selected to represent the School in the Inter-Schools' Invitation Race. The teams trained diligently, resulting in improved positions in the final placing.

Junior Team: Iles, Thomas, Newman, Lang, Jay, Massey, Chapple, Pinkham, Takle.

Senior Team: Long, Lugg, Harvey, Edwards, Miller, C., Gunter, Clements, Crockford, Quick.

P.E. Staff 1959

George Foote, Denys Richardson. There were three P.E. Staff but with the help of other staff we could put out five teams on a Saturday with two teachers with each team!

School Rugby Team 1958

Back Row

R Salter ? Stephens P Mathews R Waite D Reece D Massey D Hull R Butler B Walker ? White

Mr. Hale

Front Row

C Davies F Chappel M Jennings P Eyers M Dyer

219

Below we have an extract from the Hengrove School Magazine Vol 4 December 1959 followed by more photographs.

 BOYS' SPORTS RESULTS

HOUSE GAMES COMPETITION.

> *Junior Basket Ball*—Winners: Thebes.
> *Senior Basket Ball*—Winners Thebes.
> *Rugby 7-aside Tournament*—Winners: Athers.
> *Junior Soccer Competition*—Winners: Thebes.
> *Senior Soccer Competition*—Winners: Argos.
> *Cross-Country Competition*—Junior Winners: Sparta; individual champion, Massey.
> Senior Winners—Argos; individual champion, Harvey.
> House Champion of Cross Country by Aggregate: Athers.
> *Soccer 6-aside Competition*—Winners: Thebes.
> *Soccer 6-aside League*—Champions: Sparta.
> *House Cricket Competition*—Winners: Sparta.

SPORTS RECORDS

Soccer :

1st Year ...	...	P. 13	W. 9	D. 3	L. 1.
Intermediate XI	...	P. 11	W. 7	D. 0	L. 4.
Under 15 XI ...	...	P. 9	W. 4	D. 1	L. 4.
Under 16 XI ...	...	P. 8	W. 4	D. 0	L. 4.

Rugby :

Tabulated results are not to hand, but a reasonable amount of success was achieved by the Under 13 XV, the Under 15 XV, and the Under 16 XV.

7-aside Tournament—Winners: Athers.

Cricket :

The addition of a slip cradle and new nets resulted in a general all-round improvement in the standard of play in all four teams.

There were several very exciting matches and many commendable personal achievements.

Stephens, M. (Under 16's XI) and Tugwell, R. (Under 15's XI) are to be congratulated on representing their respective Bristol Boys' Teams.

esults :

1st Year XI ...	...	P. 6	W. 3	D. 0	L. 3.
Under 13½ XI ...	...	P. 8	W. 5	D. 1	L 2.
Under 15 XI ...	...	P. 6	W. 3	D. 0	L. 3.
Under 16 XI ...	...	P. 5	W. 4	D. 1	L. 0.

Swimming Awards :

Boys—Bronze Cross : C. Hole, D. Pennington, J. Gunter.
Bronze Medallion : C. Hole, D. Perrington, P. Ellis, C. Miller,
J. Miller, D. Rogers.
Elementary and Intermediate Certificates : Davies, Barnes,
Critchley, Cooper, Van Gorph, Jay, Perrington, Leigh.
In addition there were 46 4-length Certificates gained and 17
half-mile Certificates.

Basket Ball :

Junior Knock-out—Winners : Thebes.
Senior Knock-out—Winners : Thebes.

School Honours :

Archery—Shortman (Gloucester Junior Champion).
Basket Ball—Crewe, M. Summers (Bristol Boys' Under 15's).
Soccer—M. Summers (Bristol Boys' Under 15's).
Long, Jay, Hughes, Jennings (Bristol Boys' Finalists 1959).
Athletics—Hutton (H. S. J.) (Bristol Rep. in S.W. Champion-
ship) D. Summers, Lugg, Hughes (Bristol Schools'
Finalists).
Swimming—Critchley (Butterfly—1st in Bristol Schools' Finals)
Rugby—Fry, Russé, Iles, Robinson, Gilbert (Finalists).
Cricket—Tugwell (Bristol Schools' Under 15's XI).
M. Stephens (Bristol Schools Over 16's XI).

School Rugby Team 1959

Back Row								
Clive Davis	Barry Walker	Dudley Reece	Gerald Sage	Roger Salter	?	Richard Selway	Richard Waite	Teacher right - John Teacher far right Mr. Mor
Front Row								
?	?	Peter Eyers	?	Frank Chappel	Stuart Ferris	Martin Jennings		

Football Team 1958-59

Boys' Sports 1960's

Former pupil John Gill has sent in memories of his involvement with tennis, cross-country, rugby and swimming in the early 1960's. They reflect his passion for sports and the opportunities available at the school.

" I represented Hengrove School at tennis with Geoff Whetton, the half mile and cross country with Mike Harrison, swimming with Colin Critchley and rugby (Bristol boys) with Pete Wilkins.

We went to the Memorial Ground for training after school – John and Pete and 2 boys from Connaught Road School. We were in the minority – all the other boys were from independent schools. Also School Rugby XV with Peter Wilkins, Ian Whiting, Michael Sennet, Lawson Page, Bob Pond, Michael Lee (Leigh?). Chris Keir, Michael Bennett (Chopper), Steven Barnes, Barry Pearson and others.

In our 4th year our team beat teams from the 3rd and 5th years and a team of teachers and VI Formers. We only narrowly lost the final of Bristol Schools Tournament to Withywood School after a return match, having drawn at the Memorial Ground to a packed crowd.

The youngsters from the year below went on to win the Bristol Schools cup the following 2 years.'

School Basketball Team 1960

Robert Harding	Phill King	Roger Salter	Gerald Sage	Peter Eyers	Mr. Miller

Rugby Team 1960

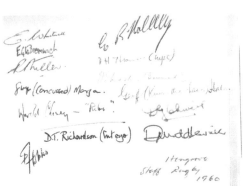

Hengrove Staff XVv. School 1st.XV

1960

The staff actually won! The comments in brackets refer to injuries suffered – mine was caused by one of my own team!

Back Row: Gwyn Morgan, Ted Hobbs, Derek Chivers, John Nash, Ted Whitnell, Harold Chasey, Ray Middlewick, Elton Bromwich, Pupil, Rid holliday, Geof Hale (Ref.)

Front Row: Ray Roberts, Denys Richardson, Bob Miller, Dave Thomas (Capt.) Pupil.

I believe the score was 11 - 9

Football Team 1963

Rugby Team 1962

First Year Rugby 1961

Early 1960 – Mr Whitnell and Rugby Team

D.Chaplin, R.Keys, -. Bateman, J. Golding, G.Batchelor   1960
A.Sheppard, T. Burt, T.Tainton, A.Gregg, C.Gitsham.

Unbeaten Rugby XV from 1962 - 1964

Ted Whitnell   Bob Mill (Head of P.E.)

Standing. R.Long. Silvester. T.Tainton. P.Sheppard. B.Turner
        (contd) - Alison. B.Matthews. P.Sage.

Sitting. R.Kays. T.Burt. T.Iles. G.Batchelor. C.Gitsham. A.Hobbs.
                                        - Griffiths.

Winners of Bristol Schools U.15. Rugby Competition.
Winners of Bristol Schools U.15 'sevens' Rugby Competition.

4th Year Cricket XI Team 1961

Sixth Form Cricket XI 1964

Third or Fourth Year Cricket Team 1962

Mixed 4th and 5th Year Cricket Team 1960

Hengrove 1st Year Cricket Team 1960 with Mr Roberts (left) and Mr Richardson (right).

Staff v School Cricket Team 1962.

Staff v School Cricket Team 1962. Note the toilet block, Petherton Road houses behind and Christchurch church hall on the right.

Tennis Team – undated

Cricket Team - undated

In 1967 Hengrove School was very proud to win the Bristol School's Woodcock Shield. Below is an extract from the Bristol Evening Post 1967.

Hengrove win the shield in extra time

HENGROVE 4. HART.
CLIFFE 3.

Hengrove came from behind at Ashton Gate last night to gain an extra-time victory when making their first appearance in Bristol Schools' Woodcock Shield final.

Hartcliffe got two goals in the opening 10 minutes. Robin Fry set the ball rolling with a header from Smith's centre and Sheedy added a second.

With Cashley powerful at centre-half, Hengrove came back strongly. Tony Green narrowed the gap with a free kick and a first time shot from left winger Taylor brought the equaliser just before half-time.

*   *   *

During the second half, Cashley spun a header against the cross bar for Hengrove and Smith was just off target for Hartcliffe.

The game went into extra time and Hartcliffe soon pulled ahead when Smith headed past Kevin Legg

Hengrove rallied and Martin Wilkins raced in from the right-wing to equalise. The decider came from centre forward Ring.

The Woodcock Shield was also won by the U15 Football team in 1973.

Available in the archive are typed accounts of matches against other schools with names and results for 1966 for:

Football 2nd year XI and Under 13 _ XI

Rugby 4th yr. XV; 3rd yr. XV; 2nd yr. XV; 1st yr. XV and senior XV

Also there are Team Sheets and Mr Chiver's Planning Book for 4th yr. XV and 2nd yr. XI 1966, which mentions Cashley who became a professional footballer for Bristol Rovers. Matches were mostly played on Saturdays with practices in lunch hours. Mr Richardson remembers that although there were three full time games staff, with the voluntary help of other members of staff they could put out five teams on a Saturday with two teachers with each team.

The Senior Boys Hockey Team was featured in an Evening Post article April 7th 1973 - reproduced here.

...and boys set for title

The netball girls are not the only ones at Hengrove School who are doing great things on the sports front.

The school's senior boys' hockey team, in only their third season, are set to take the Bristol Comprehensive Schools' League title for the second year running.

And they also recently won through to the final of the Bristol Schools under-18 tournament before being beaten by Colston's.

Two members of the school team, centre-forward and top scorer John Bryant and skipper Martin Pearce, have won places in the B.A.C. Hockey Club 1st XI and have also been playing for the Bristol Schools' under-19 side, as have winger David Crook and centre-half Ian Massey.

Hengrove are unbeaten in the league, including a 6—0 win over Withywood in which David Crook did all the scoring.

Other regular members of the side include kft half Nicholas Auger, fifth form pair Griffin (left-wing) Andrew Smith.

233

Duke of Edinburgh Award Scheme - Boys

Dr Perry's daughter writes:

"Hengrove was one of the first schools to take part in the Duke of Edinburgh's Award Scheme. In 1956 a pilot scheme was set up for boys. My father felt very honoured to be invited to Buckingham Palace to meet the Duke as the first awards were made."

Several boys received their Gold Awards from the Duke of Edinburgh at Buckingham Palace in October 1959. They were P. Temblett, D. Goverd, A. Sage and J. Gardiner (below)

The staff gave up time to run this - Miss Place, Mr Miller, Mr Richardson, Ray Roberts, Bob Swift and others. Mr Hale coached pupils in archery after school.

We have early photos of the boys Duke of Edinburgh Award activities – gymnastics, camping and visits to the Fire Service (overleaf).

G.Batchelor (floor) T.Dark (ball) N.Warrington, Byron Sage (Hands
D of E Fitness Tests - Gold Award.

A.Gunter (skipping) others not known (D of E Silver)

.Sage (handstand. ?   J.Knowles (jump) D of E Silver.

<u>Duke of Edinburgh's Award</u>

**Light weight camping –
John Nash, Ray Roberts, Bob Miller**

Jeffrey Knowles (Radio Officer in Merchant Navy.

On right, Nigel Wallington who went on to train at St.Lukes, Exeter.

Silver Award –Fire Station

Silver Fire Service Training

Bronze Award Hike – Goblin Coombe

Bronze Award Hike – Goblin Coombe with Mr Hobbs

We have extracted the following statistics from the archive regarding awards achieved by the boys.

1959 - 4 Gold
1961 - 2 Gold
1962 - 1 Gold
1962-63 - Total of 9 Gold, 18 Silver, 81 Bronze
1963-64 - Total of 11 Gold, 38 Silver, 162 Bronze, with 160 pupils registered
1966-67 - Approaching a cumulative total of almost 400 Awards.

Chess Club

In 1959 the Chess Club had a membership of 40 and met most lunch hours during the autumn and spring terms. It was run by Mr Wood.

David Bagshaw was a very keen and able member of the club – he was unable to play active sports due to a medical condition. His mother has provided the following photographs of David and others.

In 1966, Mr Wood organised a chess match against Russian sailors whose ship had docked in Bristol! What an experience!

Hengrove School vs Russian Sailors 1966

240

Some pupils participated in the Bristol District Chess League Under 13 Division Team Championship 1966 or 1967. The Evening Post featured the following picture of the team.

Back row: Colin? , Danny Holmes, David Bagshaw
Front Row: ? ,   Bernard Durston,   ?

Chapter 6
Music
(Contributed by Stephen Davies)

INTRODUCTION

In academic circles Music is usually regarded as a minority subject. Yet, largely through its performance component, it may appear to dominate the work of a whole school and may thus level the playing field between newer and older establishments. If our treatment seems to favour Music, it is less a reflection of our regard and more due to the nature of the subject.

Two later sections of this chapter illustrate this nature. The long list of instrumental performers numbers many who contributed in non-musical fields but are especially remembered only as names in concert programmes. The "Venturers" group photographs provide a rare pictorial record of a flourishing school population.

From early times many names and events were lost before the school became alive to the needs of the archivist. Nevertheless, we know that in these formative years under the headship of Doctor Perry, Music Master J B Coleshaw established a prosperous orchestral and choral tradition.

THE BLOCKBUSTERS

From the late sixties, music at Hengrove enjoyed three benefits. (1) Hengrove became the founding centre of the South-East Bristol Saturday Morning Music School (2) Like many other schools, it was well served by the LEA's peripatetic instrumental staff (3) The school revelled in the blockbuster tradition inspired by the words of Head of History Harold Chasey and powerfully supported by Headmaster Philip Waterhouse.

There have been three blockbuster concerts. The original event was "Hastings" (1966) in the school hall, words by Harold Chasey et al with music composed and conducted by Maurice Bailey, then Head of Music. Next came "The Venturers" (1973) and "Bethlehem" (1983) both in the Colston Hall and both with words by Harold Chasey and music composed and conducted by new Head of Music, Stephen Davies.

These blockbusters are dealt with separately later. While they were in-house works involving huge numbers of pupils and staff performing to capacity audiences, regular, often major, concerts were soon expected of Hengrove Music Department. "Bethlehem", for example, was first performed in the school in 1970 and again in 1971 in a packed and appreciative Broadmead Baptist Church, a concert bidding for blockbuster status.

Philip Waterhouse, Oboe.

PERFORMANCES

"Way Out", a youth cantata for chorus, soli and small orchestra, was performed by our school musicians: it was recorded in London and broadcast by BBC TV in 1969. It was composed by Stephen Davies with a libretto by Brian Nash, then Head of English at Torrington County Secondary School. This pair also produced "The Yellow Dragon of Shantung", performed in Hengrove School Hall in 1981. It was a story resembling a Chinese folk tale set as a musical play with solo and choral songs and recitations by all the First Years accompanied by a reduced school orchestra. This was followed by "Alice", a text from the Carroll stories set to music and performed by Stephen Davies and the music department.

Our brass band recorded a TV slot in Cardiff's TWW studios, and we hosted a Bristol Schools' Brass Band Day with celebrity Neil Butterworth as conducting guest of honour. Our brass band held its end up at numerous PTA fund raising summer fairs and the social strength of the Department was manifest at various times in Christmas parties and even in a strawberry tennis tournament!

We have mounted two major concerts annually – some, especially carol services, at Christ Church. We have provided numerous entertainments at old folks' homes, and many woodwind choir performances on visits to our feed primary schools. Despite trophies lying more naturally in the province of a sporting department we once won a fair shelf of silver in the Bristol Eisteddfod.

We combined with St Bernadettes and a contingent of the BBC Training Orchestra to perform the Christmas music from Handel's "Messiah" and later with the South Bristol Choir & Orchestra in a concert which included Vivaldi's "Gloria". We hosted several String Days, when the department was flooded with our own and many younger players from our feed primary schools, gathered to enjoy intensive professional tuition in ensemble playing.

With the nineteen-eighties came a new Head of Drama: Graham Hodson. He inspired and led productions of "O What a Lovely War!" and "The Boy Friend". Our musicians supported these ventures with some direction and instrumental accompaniment.

Concerts were given by various vocal groups and soli, including the following: First Year, Middle School, Senior and Staff Choirs, String and Full Orchestra, Brass Band, Woodwind Choir, miscellaneous Recorder, Guitar and mixed Ensembles, Madrigal Group and numerous vocal soloists. All the foregoing were prepared by classroom staff in extra-mural rehearsal.

THE SCHOOL DAY

An article by Stephen Davies in "The Music Teacher" of December 1972 attracted a visit from Sally Wright, then editor of music books at Oxford University Press. After a critical assessment by Dr Arnold Bentley, a Professor of Music at Reading University and author of a highly respected aural test battery, OUP published our composition course, which became the basis of our classroom composition work.

For their first three years pupils followed these three components: (1) COMPOSITION – theoretical knowledge (2) PERFORMANCE – acquisition of practical skills, and (3) LISTENING – the understanding of aesthetic values. Course work following these logical approaches to learning music was developed but by no means perfected (that might need a lifetime!) but proved a useful preparation for "O" level (later reduced to GCSE) and "A" level work, in the 4th, 5th and 6th forms.

Lessons in timetabled periods were also given by visiting teachers as technical tuition in playing instruments, while classroom music staff provided aural and accompaniment practice in extra-mural sessions. (A debt is owed to the LEAs and Music Advisors of Bristol/Avon for providing access to instruments and their technical instruction for many children). From about 1970 we were a centre for the prestigious examinations of the Associated Board of the Royal Schools of Music*, regularly entering two and sometimes three groups of candidate instrumentalists annually in Grades I to VIII.

Kate Moon

Mr P. Haydon

SATURDAY MORNING MUSIC SCHOOL

During the headship of Pat Bird, when Bill Graves was Avon's Chief Executive, our Music Department was visited by the Duchess of Beaufort. Lady Caroline Thynne, as she was also known, seemed impressed by the education, amused by the eager attentions of the VIPs and entertained by the response of the school orchestra! Anyway, we gained some "extras" (pianos!) and the Duchess agreed to be Patron of our Saturday Morning Music School.

As a suburban centre for youth ensemble playing this was arguably the first of its kind in the country. It was founded about 1970 by Stephen Davies and directed by him for the next eighteen years. He handed over the reins to a past pupil, Trevor Iles, then Head of Music at King Edmunds School, Yate, leaving some 300 young players in Intermediate Orchestra, First Orchestra, Woodwind Choir, Wind Band, Brass Group and Junior Strings plus nine teaching staff and a secretary. Members were drawn from Hengrove School plus many other local schools, and even bussed in from the adjacent North Somerset countryside!

Although most concerts were given in Hengrove School, other venues included St George's, Brandon Hill, St Mary Redcliffe Church, Bristol Cathedral, the Wills' Recreation Hall, Badminton House and the host premises of several residential weekends. Memorable was a performance of our Woodwind Choir under Elizabeth Palmer in Bristol Hippodrome in a concert presented by Sir Geraint Evans as part of the 1984 Festival for Children. Also noteworthy were the reciprocated visits of our Intermediate Orchestra with the county band of

Hildesheim. These events were fully exploited and enjoyed by our active parent/teacher organisation and included performances as far apart as Council House (reception) and Hanover.

Until the late eighties, players from Hengrove formed by far the largest Saturday Morning Music School contingent.

Trevor Iles, Oboe.

THE PROGRAMMES
Introduction

Before "Hastings", the musical excellence of which Hengrove School could be justly proud owed much to grammar school models and practices. The trick was maintaining that excellence while providing for everyone, i.e. going comprehensive. "Hastings", involving so many pupils and staff, showed how large musical productions may turn the trick, and was the first of several blockbuster events.

And so we begin our review with three blockbuster programmes, and follow with five samples of programme content to illustrate our development as a music department in a comprehensive school.

HASTINGS

A Tapestry in Music - libretto by Harold Chasey et al

Music composed and conducted by Maurice Bailey

Chronicler: E Whitnell

Performed in Hengrove School Hall by the Senior and Middle School Choirs and the School Orchestra, Leader: Martin Gould in November 1966

This is the story of one of the great turning points in the history of Britain: the Norman Conquest of 1066. Before this date, the future of Britain was uncertain. Would our links be with Northern Europe and the Danish Empire or would our future be linked to Western Europe?

This work, based on scenes from the Bayeux Tapestry, attempts to capture the spirit of the times as well as recording events. It looks forward to a time when conquerors and conquered live together in peace as one nation.

1066   1966

FRANCIA PVGN

·HASTINGS·

A Tapestry in Music
Hengrove School
Wednesday, Thursday, Friday   16 th. 17 th. 18 th.
November. 7.30 p.m.

admission by programme 2/6 children 1/6

"HASTINGS – A TAPESTRY IN MUSIC"

1 ORCHESTRA – Prelude.

2 CHORUS AND ORCHESTRA – "Visions of a Peaceful Future".

> In these days of Edward's rule, all is peaceful, calm and still.
> Thanes and churls alike pursue their tasks
> To wrest their hard-earned living from the soil.
> Swallows swoop o'er waving corn, and in the forest
> Dappled deer roam undisturbed by hunter's horn.
> Villages in sunshine bask, their calm untroubled,
> And the future years full of hopes yet unfulfilled.

3 CHRONICLER – Seeds of Conflict.

4 CHORUS AND ORCHESTRA – "Children's Song".

> See the children gaily singing, earth is full of bounteous joy.
> Listen to the bells a'ringing, pleasures all for girl and boy.
> Hands are clapping, feet are tapping,
> Summer joys are always with us,
> Happiness, happiness abounds.
>
> Let no terrors now approach us, keep our innocence secure,
> Elders seek not to reproach us, tarnish not our hearts so pure.
> All the song-birds sing, cap and bells to ring,
> And the sun shines always o'er us,
> Happiness, happiness abounds.

5 CHRONICLER – Harold swears loyalty to William of Normandy.

6 CHORUS AND ORCHESTRA – "Requiem for Edward the Confessor".

> Miserere, miserere, now is our sovereign taken.
> Noble Edward, holy Edward,
> Friend of the poor and kind to sinners.
> No man of war, but loving justice.
> Miserere, miserere, lay his frail corpse, a'weeping
> In the Abbey of his building,
> Raised stone by stone to God his maker.
> Miserere, Miserere, can such another like him
> Rule this our land in truth and justice?
> Miserere, Miserere, lay him asleep
> With the Saints as his fellows.

7 CHRONICLER – Harold is crowned in defiance of his oath to William.

8 CHORUS AND ORCHESTRA – "Coronation Anthem".

> Lord Harold be praised your sovereignty endure.
> A champion, a Saxon, a man of great valour
> So fitting an heir to the saintly confessor.
> May he keep our land free from the foreign oppressor.
> To one of our blood restore we our heritage,
> Let England now witness the long years of light.
> Our island, a fortress, shall ere be victorious,
> Our sons and our daughters shall see years of peace.
> All hail to thee Harold, our king now annointed!
> All hail to thee Harold, by God now appointed!

250

9   CHRONICLER – The comet forbodes evil.

10 CHORUS AND ORCHESTRA – "Evil times are at hand".

         See you the comet there on high? It moves again this night
         Cleaving the heavens like some curving sword,
         Making all England shake with terror
         Like the hind when the fell shaft is sent.
         An awesome omen of woe and ill, heralds approaching doom.
         Can the Norse be riding the waves again
         Our plundered land to wound still further with fire and sword?
         Shades of our fathers keep us safe
         From the evils now at hand.

11 CHRONICLER – William orders the invasion – The Building of the Fleet.

12 SEMI-CHORUS AND ORCHESTRA – "How speaks the wind?"

         How speaks the North wind O my father,
         What says the North wind father mine,
         Telling the fate that now hangs o'er thee,
         Filling the void till end of time?
         Guard well the arrow in its swiftness,
         Mark well its course as high it soars,
         List well the bowstring's awesome shudder
         Seeking the nameless face before.
         North wind, North wind I'll not hear thee
         Tell thy message not to me.

         How speaks the East wind O my brother,
         What says the East wind brother mine,
         Telling the fate that now hangs o'er thee,
         Filling the void till end of time?
         Mark well the spear point now a'shining,
         Guard well the shaft that bears its head,
         List to the spearman, arms inclining
         Choosing his foeman target dread.
         East wind, etc. . . . . .

         How speaks the West wind O my husband,
         What says the West wind husband mine,
         Telling the fate that now hangs o'er thee,
         Filling the void till end of time?
         Guard well the sword with shining brightness,
         Mark well its edge with message keen,
         List well the swordsman's flashing lightness
         Seeking the armour's gaps between.
         West wind, etc. . . . . .

         How speaks the South wind O my children,
         What says the South wind children mine?
         Telling the fate that now hangs o'er thee,
         Filling the void till end of time.
         In Harfleur town the ships are gathered,
         Men and beast their working done.
         No more to sleep till tide is weathered
         And Husband, Father, Brother gone.
         South wind, etc. . . . .

13 CHRONICLER – Harold defeats the Norsemen at Stamford Bridge.

14 CHORUS AND ORCHESTRA – "Now Must We Defend Our Soil".

Now has Harold been victorious, his foes be slain on Stamford field,
Long was the battle, fierce and arduous, weary now yet full of joy,
Midst the rejoicing speeds in the horseman, hot with the news from Southern shore
William has landed, landed at Pevensey, greater the danger than ever before !
Gone the weakness, end our rejoicing, ready for action, ready to ride
South the peril, South the Norman. All for country, King and pride !

INTERVAL

15 CHRONICLER – William speaks before the Battle.

16 CHRONICLER, CHORUS AND ORCHESTRA – The Battle.

a) The scene is set.   e) Shoot the arrows high!
b) The scouts go out.   f) The battle of the standard.
c) The Normans attack.   g) The rout.
d) Slaughter in the fosse.

17 CHORUS AND ORCHESTRA – "Hymn of Triumph".

"Now is the victory, ours is the land, triumph attends our cause, our arms
Honour the fallen who this day have made us masters of this soil.
Glory, Glory to our leader. Glory, Glory to William our Prince,
Now shall the sound of Norman ring for ever in our halls.

Now shall our children born and unborn, honour our families,
Both noble and peasant, Lord and man who made us masters of this soil.
Glory, Glory, etc. . . . .

Then let the news abound, let the bells ring, tell it in Normandy that we
Held high the honour of our land, and made us masters of this soil.
Glory, Glory, etc. . . . ."

18 CHRONICLER – "A new nation is born".

19 CHORUS AND ORCHESTRA – "Now has a new day dawned".

"Now has a new day dawned, now is the long night over.
Now has the fighting ceased, now is the battle done.
Learn we now the ways of peace, of happiness and joy.
Tend we now the field and farm, our labour to enjoy.

Now play the ploughman's part, now wield the spade and scythe.
Now let the minstrels sing, and happiness abound.
Craftsmen now shall lend their arts, and things of beauty shine,
And spinning-wheel and weaver's loom shall fill the cottage air.

Now let us brothers be and firmly clasp our hands.
No more of enmity, no more do passions rage.
Man and maid shall sing their praise and pray most fervently
Let there be peace in this our land we love.
Let there be peace."

THE VENTURERS

HENGROVE SCHOOL

HEADMASTER P S WATERHOUSE M A

presents

the venturers

by HAROLD CHASEY and STEPHEN DAVIES

programme

The Great Recorder examines the claims to fame of distinguished men and women of Bristol

PART ONE

Overture	Orchestra
Narrative	
From out of time	Chorus
Robert of Gloucester	Dialogue
Gentle Augustine	Chorus
William Canynges	Dialogue
St. James's Fair	Chorus
John Cabot	Dialogue
Song of The Charter	Chorus
Intermezzo One	Orchestra
Narrative	
Sea Cycle cuttin' sugar	
the Indiaman	
Iberia	Chorus
Muscovy pine	
Bertha of Boston	

PART TWO

Prelude	Orchestra
Judge Jeffreys	Dialogue
Brother against Brother	Chorus
Dorothy Hazard	Dialogue
The Blackbirds	Chorus and Solo
Hannah More	Dialogue
Intermezzo Two	Orchestra
Narrative	
November storm	Chorus
Mr. Everybody	Dialogue
Honour unending	Chorus

600

COLSTON HALL BRISTOL

F K COWLEY FIM ENT
ENTERTAINMENTS MANAGER

MARCH 16 1973

253

BRÍSTOL

The great encampments on the rim of the Avon Gorge, on Mendip, and at Maes Knoll, and the nearby "temple" at Stanton Drew, are witness of the beginning of organised life in this area during the pre-historic period. The Romans left their mark with the great Fosseway, Sea Mills harbour and the many villas around Bristol.

The actual site of what was to become the centre of the old city was, at this time, left alone. We can only guess when the gentle slope between the Avon and the Frome was settled. It was almost certainly during the Saxon period that the first village was established here, safe from seaborn marauders and at a point where the river could be safely forded or bridged. Hence the name Briggestowe—the place of the bridge.

Only a few generations passed after the Norman Conquest before Bristol became more than a mere village. Thanks to the security given by its huge castle, it became the trade funnel for the West Country and soon established trading links with Western Europe. From a few hundreds the population rose to many thousands and the city was second only to London in size and importance. Being confined within the original area, the city at this time was bursting at the seams; by the end of the Middle Ages an urban sprawl led to the creation of the new parishes of Temple and Redcliffe.

The next development coincided with the expansion of world trade during the sixteenth and seventeenth centuries. By 1700 the wealthy merchants were moving into the country areas to the north and north-west of the city: Brandon Hill, Clifton, Kingsdown and S. Michael's Hill saw the rise of elegant suburbs, while the old city rapidly degenerated into an over-crowded slum.

This was only a beginning. The Industrial Revolution heralded another expansion in the nineteenth and early twentieth centuries. The new working-class suburbs of Barton Hill, Easton and Bedminster together with the growth of the coal mining areas to the east, pushed the city limits further into the countryside.

After the first World War, the vast new estates of St. George, Fishponds and Knowle West filled further holes in the complex jigsaw of a continuous urban area.

The rebuilding of the central area has changed the character of the city. New replaces old and the growth process continues ceaselessly. From Warmley to Avonmouth, Henbury to Whitchurch, Bristol has become a great metropolitan area with a population of over half a million. A far cry from the tiny village on the Avon a thousand years ago.

co-ordination:	Geoffrey Thomas, Alison Broderick
costumes & set:	Christopher Drew, Catherine Hooper, David John, Chris Jones
drama:	Howard Mullen, Pamela Brown, Derek Parry, Judith Wood, Gillian Boulton
lighting:	Howard Mullen, Richard Jefferies, Martin Angove, Stephen Avery, Stephen Nash, David Pearce, Mark Tucker
music:	Stephen Davies, Meryl Cook, Hilary Collins, Peter Haydon, Geraldine Atkinson, Gina Martin
finance:	Bob Vince, Eric Veal, Susan Murray, Paul Norris, Kevin Berry, Helen Stock
publicity:	Trevor Crouch, Geoff Hale, David Frost, Tessa Steventon, Stephen Hutton
transport:	William Fletcher
backstage administration:	Ian Merrick

THE PERFORMERS

ADDRESS OF WELCOME: Gina Bryant.

CAST
NARRATOR: Edwin Whitnell, THE GREAT RECORDER: Martin Pearce, ROBERT OF GLOUCESTER: Peter Hellier, WILLIAM CANYNGES: Richard Williams, JOHN CABOT: Brian Colwell, JUDGE JEFFERYS: James Ashley, DOROTHY HAZARD: Deborah Townsend, HANNAH MORE: Cheryl Davis, MR. EVERYBODY: David Rees.

UNDERSTUDIES: Sharon Guest, Mark Boulton, Stuart Wilson.

THE ORCHESTRA
LEADER: Sylvia Meikle
Ann Miller, Mark Mitchell, Susan Phillips, Diane Pountain, Lynn Derrick, Anthony Fernott, Sarah Flanagan, Timothy Pocock, Andrew Rees, Colin Smith, Julie Thomas, Geoffrey King, Anne Wheeler, Paula Williams, Janet Brine, Alison Baggs, Lisa Grant, Andrew Patch, Mary Stock, Christopher Brain, Richard Elliott, Christine Andrews, Anita Hill, Adrian Rowland, Simon Ible, Gary Andrews, Sarah Filer, Martin Jones, David Steer, Tracey Cadman, Elizabeth Broadbent, Paul Carter, Maldwyn Meacham, Gary Morris, Stuart Woodman, Susan Elliston, Dawn Hazell, Nicola Summers, Susan Ludlow, Anne Higgs, Penny Crow, Timothy Martin, Peter Nagel, Sonia Gillard, Susan Johnson, Gina Read, David Tye, Stephen Tye, Julie Cains, Christine Foey, Robert Rogers, John Stinchcombe, Susan Derrick, Graham Cole, Paul Trippet, Julie Ollerenshaw, Glenda Nicholas, Mark Brain, Marvin Evans, Roger Broadbent, Angela Badman, Suzanne Sherwood, Jonathan Dodd, Mathew Wright, Martin Bailey, Janice Batten, Kevin Price, Sandra Trippett, Julie Ollerenshaw, Glenda Nicholas, Mark Brain, Marvin Evans, Bartlett, Penny Smith, Harold Chasey, Ken Hanham, Philip Smith, Susan Angove, Hilary Collins, Meryl Cook, Philip Waterhouse, George Hey, Peter Haydon, Brian Howard, Ruth Camfield, Nicola Chivers, Stephen Rudall, Sarah Jacobs, Linda Richardson, Hazel Poole, Arthur Alexander, Pamela Clapp, Christine Kays, Jane Jacobs, Andrew Tyrrell, Morag Sime, Paul Stephens, Christopher Topley, Richard Lambert, Ruby Coveney, Richard Davies, Stephen Pearce, Judith Ible, Gillian Hazel, Derek Warner.

THE CHOIR

Royston Matchwick, Kevin Mildon, Jackie Pearce, Pauline Reynolds, Julie Miles, Angela Morris, Martin Foster, Julie Dowding, Jane Duckett, Jane Evason, Kimberley Greenslade, Jucith Hall, Karen Duran, Robert Perry, John Shortman, Jane Sampson, Jacqueline Shoreland, Kay Stratford, Julie Talbot, Nocola Silman, Joanna Skeivys, Judith Stephens, Jane Taylor, Jennifer Taylor, Pauline Tavener, Lynn Terry, Timothy Robertson, Judy Hillman, Pauline Holloway, Andrew Kays, Leslie Hallett, Sharon Hutchings, Kerry Jenkinson, Lindsay Jordan, Susan Lees, Susan Jennings, Mark Hardy, Geoffrey Lippiatt, David Stokes, Hugh Wilsdon, Wendy West, Bronwen West, Victoria White, Ann Williams, Tina Thomas, Susan Tomlinson, Amanda Woods, Mark Burton, Mark Cottrell, Dean Cockle, Jane Burns, Tracey Clail, Catherine Crow, Sandra Dando, Deborah Criddle, Stephen Edwards, Martin Clamp, Anita Brunt, Kathryn Davies, Clifford Ayson, David Brassington, Keith Brown, Carol Ashford, Cheralyn Barrett, Karen Booker, Carolyn Beale, Tracey Babbington, Caroline Blake, Julie Barrett, Karen Aslett, Wayne Clail, Pamela Brown, Belinda Hale, Julie Hales, Julie Higgins, Debra Pirett, Jane Parsons, Linda Priddis, Nicholas Capstick, John English, Marion Wilson, Susan Bryant, Julia Mealing, Victoria Ross, Pauline Carr, Jacqueline Elms, Oona Goldsworthy, Caroline Griffee, Sandra Meacham, Karen Miles, Karen Mills, Yvette Sargent, Colin Carfield, Mark Priest, Rachel Morgan, Louise Starke, Adrienne Selwood, Sarah Williams, Julie Abraham, Janet Monk, Amanda Till, Andrew Storrer, Clive Thurtell, Karen Genge, Nicole Harvey, Shelagh Moloney, Gail Thurtell, Heather Gardiner, Ann Baker, Susan Drinkwater, Christine Cains, Stephen Corrick, Kevin Arbon, Andrew Richards, Trudy Nutter, Christopher Stokes, Lynn Burnett, Kim Smart, Jane Tanner, Julie

Horseman, Deborah Paige, Angela Barrett, Gillian Britton, Deborah Smith, Julia Hooper, Leslie Payne, Lynn Southey, Geoffrey Uphill, Mary Church, Kim Court, Jane Mazzie, Pauline Webb, Alison Williams, Caroline Badman, Christine Robertson, Jane Cook, Humphrey Cohen, Greta Maggs, Linda Perham, Theresa Griffin, Shane Cameron, Winston Campbell, David Green, Clive Finlay, Martin Curtis, Andrew Hodson, Paul Doster, Kyle May, Andrew Sheild, Paul Brunt, Glyn Davies, Stephen Beckerley, Stephen Goulder, Gary Doig, Linda Sparks, Katherine Bone, Kim Gardiner, David Thomas, Lynn Clark, Gillian Cockle, Jeanette Lyons, Jane Kibby, Jane Davey, Margaret Nash, Tina Barry, Janet Berry, Brenda Rogers, Marcia Weaver, Carol Crew, Julia Smith, Paul Travill, Josephine Lawrence, Jane Chivers, Susan Alsford, Carolyn Bryant, Angela Carfield, Joy Coleman, Christine Court, Kathryn Turvey, Susan Payne, Tina Robertson, Christine Richards, Fiona Gosling, Jennifer Bradshaw, Elizabeth Selway, Helen Smith, David Howe, Michael Urch, Robert Starr, Malcolm Daw, Geoffrey Morris, Stephen Coleman, Philip Macey, Stephanie Atkinson, Paul Hayman, Adrian Griffey, Helen Stock, James Stirling, Margaret Harrison, Carol MacKenzie, Mary Kybert, Paul Mears, Colston Miller, David Hale, Philip Maguire, Linda Elliston, Sharon Guest, Mark Boulton, Brian Wright, Christine Norris, Sandra Smith, Barbara Winkworth, Pamela Jones, Margaret Moodie, Elvira Chivers, John Jenkins, Edwin Whitnell, David John, Norman Lowdon, William Clarke, Elin Davies, Helen Crooks, Rhiannon Clewer, Rhiwen Davies, Maureen Powell, Caroline Riding, Anne Stephens, Hazel Warren, Hilary Philips, Andrew Spencer, Basil Rogers, Derek Chivers, Theresa Short, Andrew Graves, David Cleverley, Robert Miller, Christine Pennington, Christine Mitchell, Verna Jones, Marie Barton, Eric Huband, Joy Morgan.
SOLOIST: Winston Campbell.

255

FROM OUT OF TIME (Chorus)

Out of the mists of time
Came men of iron and stone,
Came conq'ring hordes of Rome,
Out of the mists of time !

Over the shelt'ring sea
Long boats with dragon heads !
The legions mighty sailed
Over the shelt'ring sea.

Fashioned by nameless hand
Monuments timeless, grand,
Roman homes in alien land,
Fashioned by nameless hand.

Here in the western hills
New laws, new arts, new skills,
Among the Avon's rills
Here in the western hills !

Out of the mists of time
Came men of iron and stone,
Came conq'ring hordes of Rome,
Out of the mists of time !

GENTLE AUGUSTINE (Chorus)

Gentle Augustine, teach us thy way !
Gentle Augustine, show us thy God !
Love we our brother, love we the Lord,
Gentle Augustine, teach us love !

The greying stone solemnly mounts,
And towers, fingers mute, point the sky.
The stones signal our faith
The fruit of a thousand hands
Praises our God.

Tend to the poor and the old, heed the widow's
cry !
Succour the sick and father the orphan !

The house of God eternally reigns ;
We mortal men must come to dust.
The stones echo our faith,
The sound of a thousand tongues
Praises our God.

Gentle Augustine, teach us thy way !
Gentle Augustine, show us thy God !
Love we our brother, Love we the Lord,
Gentle Augustine, teach us to love !

ST. JAMES'S FAIR (Chorus)

Arise ! Arise ! Shake sleep from your eyes !
The fair of St. James has come !
Up and away at the dawning of day,
The fair of St. James has come !

The pedlars cry "Buy ! for your John or your
Jenny !"
Silkens and muslins and fine lace and ribbons and
Ointments and lotions and magical potions—
For this is a market day !
Such a hustling, a bustling, bells ring, maidens
sing,
Such a happy holiday !

The friar calls boldly, so loud in his preaching :
Remember our Saviour, his glorious teaching,
Forget wordly pleasure, your sin without measure,
For this is a holy day !
Such a hustling, a bustling, bells ring, maidens
sing,
Such a happy holiday !

See there the wrestlers with bodies a-swaying,
Hark to the bears where the mastiffs are baying,
Join in the dancing where mummers are prancing
For this is a holiday !
Such a hustling, a bustling, bells ring, maidens
sing,
Such a happy holiday !

. . . the fair of St. James has come !
. . . the fair of St. James has come !

SONG OF THE CHARTER (Chorus)

Remember the men whose courage and honour
The Charter of freedom obtained ;
The journeyman, burgess, apprentice and
craftsman
Whose valour our liberty gained.

Let the church bells ring, let the people sing,
The hour of our freedom is come !
Make happy sound, let joy abound,
The days of oppression are done !

No longer we bow to monarch or baron,
Our own hands will manage our life ;
Our own laws we'll fashion, and misrule abandon,
And justice in peace shall end strife !

So toiling in freedom shall e'er e our custom,
And courage in freedom our aim ;
We'll cherish our freedom for those who come
after
We'll guard it in God's holy name !

256

SEA CYCLE   (Chorus)

Cuttin' Sugar

Chop I Chop ! Daddy's cuttin' sugar I
Chop I Chop I Daddy's cuttin' cane I
O I O I Mammy's in the kitchen,
Cookin' for me Daddy comin' home again.

Play I Play I Playin' in the sunshine I
Buzz I Buzz I Snorin I in the shade.
Scrub I Scrub I Scrubbin' out the washin',
Cleanin' out the shanty—but I ain't bin paid I

Run I Run I Runnin' to the river,
Fish I Fish I Fishin' for me food.
Pull I Pull I Pullin' up the water,
Swillin' out the cabin, make it smell so good.

Down I Down I On the old plantation,
Sweet I Sweet I Is the cane we grow.
Boil I Boil I Boilin' out the sugar
For the lords and ladies we will never know I

The Indiaman

Over the waves with sails a-blowing,
Billowing gently in western wind I
Round and aloft the sea-gulls crying,
Calling us safely home again.

Over the waves with sails a-blowing,
Bringing the playthings of sweet delight;
·Silkens and muslins for my lady,
Pepper and spice and jewels bright.

Over the waves with sails a-blowing,
Bombay and Calicut know us well,
Far off Cathay has oft-times seen us,
To us the Persian merchants sell.

Over the waves, with sails a-blowing,
Billowing gently in western wind,
Filling our holds, the Orient riches,
Calling us back to the East again.

Iberia

Dancers swirling, pipes a-skirling,
Heels a-tapping, fingers clacking,
For Bristol men in Bristol ships, merrily flows the
   wine I

Sultry maiden, senorita,
In Oporto or Malaga,
For Bristol men in Bristol ships, merrily call to dine.

Cease the swirling and the skirling I
Broken-hearted sweethearts sighing . . .
For Bristol men in Bristol ships, merrily sail the
   brine.

Muscovy Pine

I'll sing you a song of the wide rolling plains,
Of the dark forests green on the Muscovy hill;
I'll sing you a song of the white winter snow,
Of the tall icy peaks of the pine trees still.

We carried the wealth of our Cotswold looms;
Mendip's wheels spun the cloth that we bore in
   our hold;
We men of the West, to the men of the North
Carried warmth through the white wintry
   Muscovy cold.

The dark pine trees beckoned from over the sea,
Their dark spears the grey northern sky impaled;
With Muscovy pine did we load up our ships,
And from frosty St. Petersburg port we sailed.

I'll sing you a song of the wide rolling plains,
Of the dark forests green on the Muscovy hill;
I'll sing you a song of the white winter snow,
Of the tall icy peaks of the pine trees still.

Bertha of Boston

O I love a lass in Bristol, she's as fair as fair can be
And I've one lass more in Baltimore and one in
   Tennessee;
There's Polly in Pennsylvania, who's fair and
   fancy-free.
But Bertha down in Boston, she's the girl for me I

There's Susie in Savannah, and Rose in Richmond
   town,
And Mary fair in Delaware, she suits me to the
   ground;
And Harriett in New Hampshire is a pretty sight
   to see,
But Bertha down in Boston, she's the girl for me I

I've Clara up in Cleveland, and Vera in Vermont,
And Kate in Carolina loves me all that I could
   want;
But of all the maids I've ever known, I think you
   must agree,
That Bertha down in Boston she's the girl for me I

There's Olive in Ohio, with dark and flashing
   eyes.
And dear old Flo in Buffalo of quite enormous
   size.
And little Meg in Winnipeg is all a girl could be
But Bertha down in Boston she's the girl for me.

Now Jenny down in Georgia is full of life and
   zest
And Sal in Sacramento has a charm among the
   best.
For Nancy in Nantucket I would go on bended
   knee
But Bertha down in Boston she's the girl for me.

BROTHER AGAINST BROTHER   (Chorus)

The storm gathers, the campfires glow,
The town stirs, the castle lights burn.
People of Temple, look to your arms!
Sharp the sword!
Raise the pike!
Man the ramparts!
Fasten the gate!
For Rupert is about us!

Deadly our work that day. Death wing'd above us!
Cannon on Michael mount,
Swords clashed on Brandon,
And brother fought against brother!

After that clash of arms, make we resolve then:
—O they have died in vain—
Never again
Shall brother fight against brother!

The storm fades, the campfires die,
The town sleeps, the castle lights dim.

THE BLACKBIRDS   (Chorus and Solo)

(i) Chorus

In far-off land there was a child
Born among distant hills;
Warm'd by Afric's sun he lived,
In simple peace he died.

In far-off land there was a child
Born among distant hills;
Bound by Western greed he toiled,
In exiled pain he died.

In Bristol Town there was a child
Born among cobbled ways;
Grown to manhood, on the sea
A cursed trade he plied.

This messenger of living death
In silent bird of prey,
To New Orleans from Afric's shores
With human cargo sailed.

(ii) Solo

I wonder why they treat me so,
The men from o'er the distant sea,
I wonder if they have no heart, no shame, no
    charity?
I wonder why they treat me so, I wonder why?

Helpless, were our weapons, powerful their
    heel!
Why did they then my freedom steal?

Humble was my village, mighty was their town!
Why did they burn my village down?

Simple were our garments, fine was their array!
Why did they take my father away?

I think they must unhappy be—
The men from o'er the distant sea—
To bind a man, to slave his soul,
His freedom sell for gold.
I wonder why they treat me so, I wonder why?

NOVEMBER STORM   (Chorus)

Hush'd in the gathering darkness,
The city for worship prepares.
Save us, O Lord, keep us from war!
Resound the echoing prayers.

Out of the gathering darkness
The sound of the wailing begins.
Save us O Lord, spare us our home!
Echo the worshippers' hymns.

Hard through the gathering darkness
The flash of the man-made stars.
Save us, O Lord, give to us peace!
Ring out the citizens cries!

Loud in the gathering darkness
The crashing of ancient stones.
Save us O Lord! Avon runs blood!
The city's heart is torn!

Grey in the wakening morning
The pallor of dust and death.
Heart barely beating the city rises;
The people draw new breath.

FINALE—Honour Unending   (Chorus)

We honour our fathers of faith and renown,
We honour the founders of o.d Bristol Town,
We honour the lowly who died without fame,
Their toil and their virtue—honour their name!
Their courage has steeled us,
Their skills they have taught us,
Their knowledge inspired us,
Their beauties enthralled us!
Their honour unending!

We look to a future, with vision and youth,
We look to adventure in valour and truth,
We look to an Avon of merciful men,
To honour unending, to glory again!
Our fears we will conquer,
Our hopes we will cherish!
Our learning unceasing,
Our arts be unbounded,
Our honour unending.

GR   And here 'mid the western hills,
      A town is reborn!

We look to a future with vision and youth,
We look to adventure in valour and truth,
We look to an Avon of merciful men,
To honour unending, to glory again!

258

School celebrates Bristol's History

By MAX BARNES

With a nice sense of timing, Hengrove School is mounting a major musical about the history of Bristol to coincide with the next year's celebrations.

The size and scope of their production will be in keeping with the importance of Bristol's red-letter year.

For Hengrove are pulling out all the stops to ensure that their show, "The Venturers", is the biggest and best of all their successful major productions.

Planning began two years ago. They have skimmed the cream off of some of Bristol's richest chapters of history, dramatised it and set it to music.

Last summer they ran a competition to discover the ideal title for their show and the winner of the £10 was Susan Ludlow (13).

So it will be "The Venturers", a musical and dramatic review which will recapture some of the Bristol story at the Colston Hall next March 16 at 7.30 p.m.

When I visited the school to meet some of the people behind the big show, I found that almost everyone had some sort of a hand in the production - more thatn half of the 1300 pupis and half of the large teaching staff.

It will take four coaches to take the cast to the Colston Hall - all 380 of them. For to do Bristol's colourful history justice there will be a choir of more than 300 and an orchestra of 80.

To reduce the history of Bristol into an evening's entertainment strikes me as a daunting challenge. But it is one cheerfully accepted by senior history master, Harold Chasey, who wrote the libretto and senior music master Stephen Davies who wrote the original music score.

The musical mood of "The Venturers" ranges, I was told, from light-hearted shanties and fairground dances to the pathos of the slave trade. A pathos underlined by Winstone Cambell (13) hand-picked from the school singers for the solo role in "The Blackbir ders" seq uence.

.Winstone, who was born in Jamaica, and is one of six brothers, likes dancing and athletics.

Hengrove is the school which produced "Bethlehem" in Broadmead and "Hastings", two successful major productions. Now they want to outdo them both.

"We have an amazing wealth of artistic talent in the school" the Head Mr P S Waterhouse told me.

"There is tremendous confidence that we are going to produce something memorable"

It all finally happened on the evening of March 16th 1973. A beautiful programme had been designed and printed.. It included copies of the Great Seal, some detail from Jacobus Millard's Plan of Bristol dated 1673 and a fine reproduction of a ship seen here on the right.

The Colston Hall was fully booked and the appreciative audience of parents, families and friends and city dignitaries enjoyed a rich feast of music and drama.

Afterwards there were reports of tears in the audience when Winston sang his solo "I wonder why they treat me so". There was also an emotional reception of the chorus 'November Storm' which recounted the events of the Blitz in 1941. Many of the audience were of the age group that remembered it all too well. The audience was stunned by its ending which was a long long note held by the whole choir at the exact pitch of the all clear siren.

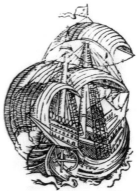

the venturers

"The Venturers" has been noticed by the US Library of Congress and the Australian National Library. Overleaf is a final press report.

Fabulous start to the '600'

Colston Hall, Bristol: Hengrove School in "The Venturers," by Harold Chasey and Stephen Davies.

If the Merchant Venturers who founded the prosperity of this great city could only have been present at the Colston Hall last night they would have been delighted with what they saw.

For in this cavalcade of music and song the combined chorus and orchestra of this talented school — some 300 or more on stage — applauded their achievements in a most impressive way.

To a chronicle of Bristol's illustrious past — narrated by Edwin Whitnell — great names like John Cabot, William Canynges, Dorothy Hazard, and Hannah More (but somehow no Brunel . . .) relate their individual contributions to the Great Recorder.

But it was the city's reliance on slave trafficking that made the most significant impact on the capacity audience with Winston Campbell reflecting all the injustice in his splendid solo "I wonder why."

The excellent chorus and orchestra directed by Stephen Davies was most impressively grouped — almost resembling a miniprom. I enjoyed their lilting "Intermezzo Two" but it was their catchy "Bertha Down in Boston" which caught my fancy.

With effective lighting, particularly in the wartime memories spot, the show concludes by confirming the city's reliance on the ordinary man and placing him with equal prominence in the gallery of the greats.

A fabulous start to the city's charter celebrations and a credit to the school.

DOUGLAS DANIELS.

The Venturers Drama and Narration

The Venturers Organising Staff

The Venturers Participating Teaching Support

The Venturers Orchestra

The Venturers Senior Choir

The Venturers Senior and Middle School Choir

The Venturers First Year Choir

The Venturers: some closing reflections....

> *at the end of the concert the clapping lasted about five minutes ...and as a First Violin, I was proud to be a member of the school orchestra and to be part of "The Venturers"* (Andrew Rees, pupil)

> *the finest success that Hengrove has ever had. At the end of the concert my throat was sore and I could hardly speak, but I was happy to think that all the hard work had been worthwhile.* (Christine Cains, pupil)

> *Although the evening was itself a great success for Mr Chasey and Mr Davies, it was perhaps an even greater success for the publicity team, the finance team, for the people who designed the set and costumes, and for those involved with drama and lighting.* (Susan Murray, pupil)

> *I, for one, feel proud of my school.* (Barbara Winkworth, pupil)

> *After weeks and weeks of effort put in by hundreds of people, be it from the staff or pupils, "The Venturers" is now an historical event in the life of Hengrove School.* (Martin Pearce, pupil)

> *The staff and children have worked and worked to reach the standard of that performance, but, as our daughter said, as a member of the orchestra after the performance: it was worth every minute – to which we say: yes! it was!* (Mrs Smith, Parent)

> *To all those people who saw and heard us on March 16th, their final comment must surely be "here is a school of which we can be proud.* (Harold Chasey)

Note: All the above quotations are from a contemporary edition of To't, the school magazine.

BETHLEHEM

by HAROLD CHASEY and STEPHEN DAVIES

COLSTON HALL
(Director of Entertainment: R.W. MUIR)

SUNDAY
27th NOVEMBER
7.45 p.m.

SOUVENIR PROGRAMME
1983

50p

BETHLEHEM...... PROGRAMME NOTE

"Bethlehem" is basically the traditional Christmas carol service set to music Readings of the lessons are followed by or set within choral arrangements of their texts. Interspersed among these are six orchestral items (all based on Christmas melodies) and six carols for choirs **and** audience.

"Bethlehem" was written in 1970 by Harold Chasey (then Head of History) and Stephen Davies. It was first performed (twice) in the school in December of that year, and again by popular demand in Broadmead Baptist Church the following year. It was scored specifically for the groups then flourishing in the school. For the present performance, the score has been revised and expanded with the assistance of Martin Hogan, Musical Director of the South Bristol Choir and Orchestra.

This evening may be regarded as a school-based community occasion. In addition to the school choirs and orchestra and the S.B.C.O., we add numerous parents, pupils and staff, past and present, and a contingent of players from the South East Bristol (Hengrove) Saturday Morning Music School. In a few cases, whole families are taking part.

HAROLD CHASEY joined the school as Senior History Master, in 1958, and retired as Senior Teacher in 1979. A graduate of Bristol University, he was awarded the degree of Master of Arts in 1953.

His particular interests lay in Economic History and local studies, the latter leading to the publication of his 'History of Bristol' for schools.

He has played violin in the school orchestra, but is best remembered for his part in promoting the large choral and orchestral events which have become an established feature of Hengrove's musical life.

He has produced many scripts (see opposite) including that for the present work, and no doubt others will follow!

A graduate of the University of Wales STEPHEN DAVIES taught first in Torrington, North Devon. Here he founded instrumental work in his school and formed a youth choir of past pupils who toured much both in the area and abroad. He joined Hengrove as Head of Music in 1968, and founded the area music school at Hengrove shortly afterwards.

Since that time the school's instrumental work has expanded, the procession of concerts continues, and a regular string of pupils has entered (and left!) the Royal Schools of Music, Universities and Colleges of Education. Some of these have returned to take part tonight.

His interest in reform of music curriculum has led to the publication of 'Beginning to Compose' and other educational material. He has written and often published music for brass and numerous choral/ orchestral works mainly for young people. In addition to 'The Venturers' and 'Bethlehem', many will remember 'Way Out' (televised in 1969) and the 'Yellow Dragon' of 1981.

Hengrove School has served that area in the south of Bristol between Whitchurch, Knowle, Stockwood and St. Giles for almost thirty years. Originally opened as a 'bilateral' school in 1954, it was recognised as 'Comprehensive' in the early 1960s, and has continued to take children from the ages of 11 to 18 since that time. Currently the school has 1,362 pupils on its roll, and a loyal and hard-working staff, some of whom have served the school for its whole lifetime.

The school enjoys excellent support from the communities its serves. The Hengrove School Parents' Association deserves particular mention for its long and active work in so many facets of school life.

Throughout its existence Hengrove has demonstrated excellence in the wide range of subjects offered in the comprehensive school, the non-academic as well as the academic. The school can be as proud of its achievements in games as it can in English, Mathematics and Science. Music and Drama have always been subjects in which the school has had particular strengths.

Hengrove's musical tradition goes back to its early years, flowering first perhaps in the Chasey/Bailey production of 'Hastings' in 1966. More works by these two followed, to be succeeded by the Chasey/Davies era of 'The Venturers' (1973) and 'Bethlehem'. Works in a lighter vein have not been neglected; these have included 'Alice in Wonderland' and several pantomimes, usually with original music and script.

After several years catering for a small number of local schools, the **South East Bristol (Hengrove) Saturday Morning Music School** was reformed and expanded under the same director in 1978. It now covers nearly forty schools and has more than 150 young players rehearsing for two concerts annually. The main groups (Intermediate and First Orchestras and Concert Wind Band) are coached by ten staff, who also provide instruction in Percussion, Double Reeds, Theory and Junior Strings.

The music school meets on about thirty Saturdays in the school year and is supported by a flourishing Parents' Council. This splendid body not only runs a regular tuck shop and looks after many pastoral matters, but also provides invaluable help in the organisation of concerts and other events. The next will be an annual Christmas celebration from 10.00am – 12.30pm on December 17th next.

BETHLEHEM

text by HAROLD CHASEY   music by STEPHEN DAVIES

edited by Stephen Davies and Martin Hogan

Conducted by STEPHEN DAVIES

Organ: Martin Hogan   Orchestra Leader: Andrea Davey

THE READERS

Lesson I	Christine Alsford *(Senior Choir)*
Lesson II	Rachel Ward *(First Year Choir)*
Lesson III	Mark Madams *(Middle School Choir)*
Lesson IV	Robert Townsend *(Senior Choir)*
Lesson V	David John *(Staff)*
Lesson VI	Caroline Riding *(Staff)*
Lesson VII	Lynda Harris *(S.B.C.O.)*
Lesson VIII	Judy Cole *(Parent/Governor)*
Lesson IX	Harold Chasey *(Staff)*
Understudy	Bernadette Fitzgerald *(Staff)*

265

ORCHESTRA
ORCHESTRA
(* denotes Section Principals)

First Violins

Robert Chadwick
Fiona Cole
Dawn Collins
Andrea Dallimore
Joanne Dallimore
Andrea Davey*
Sarah Dunn
Joanne Fowler
Jane Gregory
Julie Moore
Peter Patch
Deborah Savage
Daren Selway
Claire Stewart

Second Violins

Carol Bullock
Jane Bullock
Helen Coomber
Debbie Fleming
Ann Fowles
Simon Ible
Simon Marriott
Samantha Nash
Alison Paginton*
Lisa Pickford
Kerry Spear

Violas

Elaine Baggs
Nicola Baker
Jacqueline Bishop
Steve Drew*
Sarah Feltham
Christopher Hicks
Georgina Hitchings
Russell Light
James Moriarty
Cathy Smart
Laura Whiteway

Cellos

Gary Andrews
Rachel Coles
Amanda Dorrington
Jennifer Down*
Gordon Hamilton
Jacqueline Hitchings
Julian Light
Ann Moulson
Ruth Polkinghorne
Nigel Powell
Anna Rabbeth
Derek White

Double Basses

Simon Barnes*
Philip Griffith
Bethan Jones
Paul Shearn

Flutes

Wendy Bidgood
Susan Butler
Paula Gabriel
Jean James
Carol Jay
Miriam Michalak*
Helen Richards
Sue Wilkie

Oboes

Linda Boyne*
Joanna Chapman
Catherine Street

Clarinets

Sue Burns
Tracey Cadman
Kerren Davey
Richard Elliott
Jane Gosling
Rebecca Griffith
Lisa Higgins*
Jill Lewis
Elspeth Townend

Bassoons

Sarah Blake
Angela Pitchford*

Horns

Heather Baxter
Brian Howard
Meryl Markall
Jeremy Parsons
Helen Shapter*

Trumpets/Cornets

Patrick Chivers
Philip Mogford
Stephen Palmer
Mike Perkins
Paul Shapter*
Bob Tyley

Trombones

David Bowyer
Christopher Brain*
Ian Coleman
Andrew Foister
Sharon Mogford

Bass Tuba

Paul Stephens

Percussion

Philip Hockley
Simon Jenkins
Brian Wilshere*

FIRST YEAR CHOIR

Sopranos († denotes boy treble group)

Jane Armstrong
Trudi Baker
Amanda Baldock
Jennifer Bradley
Katharine Brookes
Alison Butler
Lisa Butcher
Nochola Carpenter
Steven Catchlove
Heidi Cox
Jacqueline Dallimore
Rachel Fisher
Samantha Fothergill
Anna Gidney
Kate Gillam
Katie Goodman
Suzanne Guy
Vicky Hall
Mark Hannam †
David Haberfield
Stuart Hodge †
Graeme Holland †

Rachel Howell
Beverley Johnson
Mary McArdle
Sarah Nash
Angela Newey
Kerry Pearson
Sarah Penney
Sarah Portingale
Darren Pring †
Kirstie Richards
Tracy Scorey
Mark Sellars
Jane Silman
Paul Smith †
Tracey Steadman
Lisa Templar
Darren Till †
Adrian Williams
Joanne Williams
Justin Wilmott †
Louise Winstone
Rebecca Wright

Altos

Craig Allan
Joanna Barnes
David Birtwistle
Sarah Boucher
Michael Broom
Mark Buck
Matthew Chilcott
Juliet Clark
Maxine Clark
Sara Cleaves
Julie Collins
Neil Davidson
Emma Derrick
Sophia Duxbury
Richard Fletcher
Joanna Glanville
Jamie Griffin
Michael Grist
Nicholas Gwyther
David Hamblyn
Emma Harris
Sarah Hazzard
Stephen Hersly
Philip Higgins
Sarah Hole
Sheralyn Howse
Lisa Jones

Paul Jones
Rachel Jones
Jennifer Kosztan
Paul Lynch
Lisa Manning
Stephanie Morgan
Jonathan Osborne
Stuart Peacey
Claire Pearce
Antony Pollard
Gavin Povey
Jonathan Rees
Joanne Reynolds
Joanne Shipp
Stephen Slocombe
Simon Smallcombe
Andrew Stadden
Andrew Stephens
Stewart Sutherland
Colin Sutton
Melloney Thorne
Sarah Thorne
Stuart Totterdell
Rachel Ward
Christopher Way
James Yandell

MIDDLE SCHOOL CHOIR

Sopranos († denotes boy treble group)

Karen Baker
Alison Bradley
Denise Clack
Julie Clark
Jane Condon
Kim Davey
Tracey Evans
Julia Fearnley
Esther Freke
Bonita Ham
Victoria Hancock
Georgina Hazzard
Stuart Hiles
Rachel Hole
Andrew Jones
Jenny Knowles
Susan Leach
Samantha Lindsay
Alison Nelmes
Hayley Packer
Helen Palmer
Rachel Peacey

Leanne Raine
Susan Ripley
Clare Roberts
Gail Silman
Juliette Smith
Katherine Smith
Simon Thomas
Julie Upson
John Veasey †
Matthew Webb
Jon Weed †
David Williams †

Altos

Catherine Amey
Nicola Anstey
Belinda Bailey
Nicholas Bailey
Nicola Bates
Samantha Bethell
Annette Bird
Rebecca Black

Alison Boulton
Tracy Bryant
Dathryn Bunce
Carole Clark
Nicholas Clark
Sally Coleman
Kristina Collin
Rachael Connolly
Jonathan Davey
Christopher Dimond
Joanne Evans
Shelly Gadsby
Dawn Giles
Alison Green
Sharon Hatcher
Rachael Harris
Michelle Henderson
Allison Higgins
Joanne Hilliar
Sally Hopkins
Wendy Howley
Tracy Humphries

Claire Joyce
Martin Kemp
Karen Lamb
Sally Limb
Mark Madams
Giles Maine
Lisa Mason
Matthew Michalak
Nichola Moore
Natasha Neville
Mark Penny
Angela Popoff
Sarah Pritchard
John Roberts
Emma Rowat
Anthony Ryan
Darren Scorey
Rachel Shore
Sascha Smallcombe
Joanne Smith
Sharon Sutherland
Sheralyn Tippins
Josephine Waller

SENIOR CHOIR AND S.B.C.O. CHOIR MEMBERS

Sopranos	Altos	Tenors	Basses
Roberta Adams	Christine Alsford	Noel Avis	Kieran Argo
Marion Austin	Jean Bartlett	Mark Bethell	Robert Boardman
Anne Broadbent	Hazel Beale	Derek Chivers	Roger Broadbent
Caroline Clark	Lindsay Birtwistle	Brian Dallimore	Martin Burnett
Rhiwen Davies	Maria Brown	Ken Down	Paul Burnett
Joan Down	Sylvia Brunskill	Joyce Forse	Andrew Buxton
Pauline Gammon	Elvira Chivers	Stephen Halls	Mike Compton
Jacqueline Garland	Maureen Cowley	Trevor Iles	Harry Cross
Sally Goodred	Adrienne Dallimore	Richard Long	Matthew Davies
Judy Griffith	Gill Didymus	Robert Miller	David Erskine
Sarah Hamilton	Heather di Nucci	Basil Rogers	Charles James
Lynda Harris	Wendy Froud	Bev Steeds	Andrew Jay
Judith Hobbs	Gillian Hazell	Robert Townend	John Jenkins
Norma Holland	Jean Hogan		David John
Janet Mogford	Christine Jenkins		Brian Lloyd
Janet Monnes	Val Michalak		Philip Moore
Thérèse Plummer	Diane Morris		Gary Panes
Maureen Powell	Brenda Parfitt		Robert Palmer
Wendy Pugh	Katharine Raynes		Andrew Rees
Brenda Purnell	Susan Rees		Glyn Roynon
Caroline Riding	Shirley Thomas		Anthony Warbutton
Ruth Ridler	Jennifer Waller		Edwin Whitnell
Gillian Scott			Dennis Wright
Carole Smith			
Pat Smith			
Jenifer Smyth			
Anne Stephens			
Claire Tutton			
Jocelyn Vaughan			
Rusty Weed			

BETHLEHEM

.....PROGRAMME.....

(PLEASE SEE SEPARATE SHEETS FOR CAROL WORDS)

— THE QUEEN —

No. 1	OVERTURE
No. 2	ONCE IN ROYAL DAVID'S CITY (Gauntlett) — *Choirs & Audience*
No. 3	LESSON I Genesis 3 vv 8-15
No. 4	Chorus: OUT OF EDEN

In the beginning was the word:
I am the Lord, the only true God.

In the cool garden Adam hid,
Adam and Eve they hid from the Lord.

Adam, I call on you, tell me why you fear,
Why taste the fruit forbidden, why hide in the shade.

Woman the temptress him beguiled,
Serpent deceit did lead her astray.

Woe to the cursèd seed, Adam's cursèd seed,
Woe to the people who heed not Godès word.

Nations shall bow their heads in shame,
Bow they their heads in shame to the earth.

Yet shall a Saviour come, come to save us all,
Loving and merciful, Adam's sins to heal.

In the beginning was the word:
I am the Lord, the only true God.

No. 5a   Chorus: THEY SHALL POSSESS THE EARTH

Ref. The Lord said unto Ab'ram: my son, my son,
The Lord said unto Ab'ram: O hear me my son.

1. Your faith it has reached me, it has reached me in heaven,
And I will bless your sons for ever.

2. Like stars they shall shine, and every nation be blessed,
And they the earth possess for ever.

3. My voice you obeyed and you withheld not your son;
Your faith will honoured be for ever.

No. 6   LESSON II   Genesis 22 vv 15-18

No. 5b.   Chorus: THEY SHALL POSSESS THE EARTH

1. The Lord said unto Ab'ram: my son, my son,
The Lord said unto Ab'ram: O hear me my son:
Your faith it has reached me,
Has reached me e'en in Heaven,
Your sons are blessed for ever.

2. Thou hast heard me, thy son gave me,
    Did not deny me, and well pleased me.
    Thy seed great be.

3. Like stars they shall shine, all nations shall be blessed,
    They shall possess the earth for ever.
    My voice you obeyed, and held not back your son,
    Your faith be honoured ever.

4. Thou hast heard me, thy son gave me, did not deny me,
    And well pleased me, thy seed great be,
    They shall my people be.

No. 7   THEME AND VARIATIONS

No. 8   UNTO US IS BORN A SON (Traditional) — *Choirs & Audience*

No. 9   LESSON III: Isaiah 9 vv 2, 6, 7.

No. 10   Chorus: THE PRINCE OF PEACE
Ref: The people who walked in darkness have seen a great light;
          The poor and the low in spirit awake from long night.

1. Great is the joy of the lowly, and their spirit is uplifted,
    For unto us a child is born, for unto us a son is giv'n;
    Wonderful shall be his name, mighty shall his counsel be;
    Great is the joy of the lowly, and their spirit is uplifted;

2. He shall establish God's kingdom, and for ever we shall praise him!
    He shall be called the mighty God, Father eternal, Prince of Peace.
    Wonderful shall be his name, mighty shall his counsel be;
    He shall establish God's kingdom, and for ever we shall praise him!

No. 11.   LESSON IV   Micah 5 vv 2-4

No. 12   Chorus: THE HILLS OF JUDAH

1. Out of the hills of Judah the Prince of Peace shall come;
    Israel the lowly shall glorify his name.
    Bethlehem shall see his birth, and all the world acclaim him king;
    Out of the hills of Judah the Prince of Peace shall come.

2. Out of the hills of Judah shall come our Saviour king,
    Israel the lowly his praises then shall sing;
    Bethlehem shall be renowned and all with grace shall be endowed;
    Out of the hills of Judah shall come our Saviour king.

3. Out of the hills of Judah our joyful song we'll raise,
    Israel the lowly shall mighty be always;
    Bethlehem for evermore shall cry aloud his glorious name;
    Out of the hills of Judah our joyful song we'll raise,

4. Out of the hills of Judah the Prince of Peace shall come,
    Israel the lowly shall glorify his name.
    Bethlehem shall see his birth, and all the world acclaim him king;
    Out of the hills of Judah the Prince of Peace shall come.

No. 13   SUITE

No. 14   HARK THE HERALD ANGELS SING (Mendelssohn) — *Choirs & Audience*

********** INTERVAL **********

269

No. 15   RONDOLETTO

No. 16   O LITTLE TOWN OF BETHLEHEM (Traditional) — *Choirs & Audience*

No. 17   LESSON V   St. Luke 1 vv 26-33

No. 18   Chorus: THE ANGEL AND THE MAID

Blessed be thou Mary mild, maiden meek, maiden mild.
There lived in Galilee a maid, a virgin meek and mild,
Her name was Mary, and on her the angel of God did smile;
A son to you in Galilee, let Jesus be his name,
For great shall be your son, said he, to Mary, maiden mild.
Call him Jesus, thou shalt call his name Jesus.

Blessed be thou Mary mild, maiden meek, maiden mild.
Your son shall reign in Galilee, and great shall be his praise;
Of David's seed, a humble babe, the hope of mankind to raise.
A humble babe in Galilee, let Jesus be his name,
For great shall be your son, said he, to Mary, maiden mild.
Call him Jesus, thou shalt call his name Jesus.

What is the light that shines, where is the voice that speaks?
Why has this come to me, a virgin poor and meek?
Favoured of God are you, blessed above all men,
The son you conceive in your womb shall be mighty ten times ten.
Jesus shall be his name, son of the highest Lord,
O'er the world will he rule, peaceful, without a sword.
In a kingdom without sword.

Whence comes this angel bright, so calm in night so wild?
Why has he come to me, a maid, almost a child?
Favoured of God are you, blessed above all men,
The son you conceive in your womb shall be mighty ten times ten.
Jesus shall be his name, son of the highest Lord,
O'er the world will he rule, peaceful, without a sword,
In a kingdom without sword.   He shall be mighty ten times ten.

No.19   LESSON VI   St. Matthew 1 vv 18-23

No. 20   Chorus: AND THE BABY'S NAME WAS JESUS

1.   Joseph the carpenter had a son, Emmanuel, Emmanuel;
       Joseph the carpenter had a son and he called the baby Jesus.

2.   Mary the maiden mild had a son, Emmanuel, Emmanuel;
       Mary the maiden mild had a son and she called the baby Jesus.

3.   Joseph took Mary to be his wife, Emmanuel, Emmanuel;
       Joseph took Mary to be his wife and they called the baby Jesus.

4.   Laid in a stable in Bethlehem, Emmanuel, Emmanuel;
       Laid in a Stable in Bethlehem for the baby's name was Jesus.

5.   Save us the baby may from our sins, Emmanuel, Emmanuel;
       Save us the baby may from our sins 'cause the baby's name is Jesus.

No. 21   INTERMEZZO

No. 22   WE THREE KINGS (Hopkins) — *Choirs & Audience*

No. 23   LESSON VII   St. Luke 2 vv 8-16

No. 24   Chorus: TELL US O STAR

    Ref: Tell us O star what you see this night in Bethlehem,
              What in the dark'ning shade is passing there below.

    1.   I see the shepherds, poor and humble, keeping vigil, watching,
         Come from the wintry field to see the poor man's Saviour.

    2.   I see three kings, so rich yet humble, homage come to offer;
         Gifts from far lands they bring to give the whole world's Saviour.

    3.   I see tomorrow's lonely children, seeking some salvation;
         This little babe may they know for he's the only Saviour.

No. 25   LESSON VIII   St. Matthew 2 vv 1-11

No. 26   Chorus: SONG OF BETHLEHEM

    1.   Bethlehem, Bethlehem, I went to Bethlehem,
         I saw the child of ev'ry land,
         I heard his cry and I saw his smile,
         And I knew that the world was safe
         In the hands of the child of Bethlehem.

    2.   Bethlehem, Bethlehem, I went to Bethlehem,
         I saw the man of ev'ry land;
         I heard his song, and I saw his toil,
         And I knew that the world was safe
         In the hands of the child of Bethlehem.

    3.   Bethlehem, Bethlehem, I went to Bethlehem,
         I saw the mother of ev'ry land;
         I heard her pain, and I saw her joy,
         And I knew that the world was safe
         In the hands of the child of Bethlehem.

    4.   = No. 27

No. 27   LESSON IX   St. John 1 vv 1-5

    5.   Bethlehem, Bethlehem, I went to Bethlehem,
         I saw the child of ev'ry land;
         I heard his cry and I saw his smile,
         And I knew that the world was safe
         In the hands of the child of Bethlehem.

No. 28   PRELUDE — closes into introduction to No. 29.

No. 29   O COME ALL YE FAITHFUL (Traditional) — *Choirs & Audience*

                               ****

NOTE: *Except for 'We Three Kings', the carols used are from 'Carols for Choirs'*
         Book 1 (O.U.P.) arr. Willcocks.

PRODUCTION TEAM

Co-ordination	Brian Wyatt
Artwork, Display and Decoration	Janet Bovill, Brian Wyatt, Pamela Hawkins, John Newbury, Julie Dando, Angela Brice, Julie Muscat, Sarah Rawlings and the 3Q6 Gardening Group.
Lighting	James Maguire, James Thomas, Tim Thomas.
Sound & Photography	Robert Boardman, Caroline Jordan.
Finance & Front of House	Eric Veal, Val Henson, Graham Hobbs, Amanda Ball, Avril Matthews, Andrea Parsons Catherine Penney, Sarah Cheek, Joanne Herlihy, Alex O'Farrell, Stephen Lippiatt, James Bell, Anthony Friendship, Andrew Parker, Stephen Scally, Douglas McColm, Mark Salisbury, Richard Stephens, Deborah Wring, Helen Gallop, Caroline Eustace, Julia Nelson, Claire Hanham, Pauline Gamblin
Backstage & Registration	Graham Hodson, Lisa Bayliss, Caron Binding, Alison Lee.
Advertising & Publicity	Denis Raymond, Nigel Harrison, Andrew Buxton, Robert Boardman.
Music	Stephen Davies, Martin Hogan, Judith Hobbs, Joyce Forse, Vikki Weed, Sarah Davis.
Readings	Bernadette Fitzgerald
Timetabling	Basil Rogers
Transport	William Fletcher, Graham Hodson
Reception	Ann M. Pert, William Fletcher

ACKNOWLEDGEMENTS

For much generous help in various forms, including finance, resources and professional services, we gratefully thank:—

— DAN BURNS and the South Bristol Camera Club
— The Clerical, Medical & General Life Assurance Society
— PAT DANIELS (Press Officer, Avon County Publicity & Public Relations Dept.)
— The Hengrove School Parents' Association
— The Staff of Express Copy & Printing Centre
— The Music Advisory Service and the Avon Music Centre
— The Parochial Church Council of St. Martin's Church, Knowle.
— DIANE PRESS and EILEEN COBB (School Office)
— DAI REYNOLDS (Sound and Recording)

MEMORIES OF 'BETHLEHEM'

For those who want to recollect in tranquillity, the following items are, or will soon be available at reasonable prices:—
(i) Full Vocal Score : (ii) Photographs, formal and casual : (iii) Cassette Recording of the Performance :
(iv) Christmas Cards.

If you are interested, please enquire at Hengrove School, Petherton Gardens, Bristol BS14 9BU : Tel. 836077

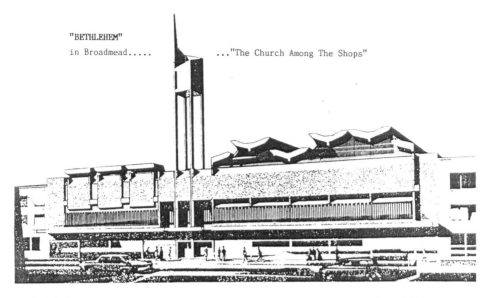

bristol   november 1971

The prequels in School (December 1970) and Broadmead Baptist Church (1971):

*a wonderful presentation of "Bethlehem" by the full orchestra
and chorus of Hengrove School. This was no "Oh! how sweet!"
performance but one of depth and brilliance given by 200 children.
An unforgettable evening …*   (Broadmead Minister)

*The response from the audience must already have told you how very
much the music was appreciated, and I think another factor which
thrilled everyone was the exemplary behaviour of such a large number of
children.*   (from a letter from Gordon Chivers, Broadmead Choirmaster)

BETHLEHEM - In the press:

*"The most impressive aspect of the evening was the large number of
pupils, past and present, who participated …*

It would be difficult to express in words the success of the evening and the
sense of enjoyment felt by both performers and audience. The Evening Post's
critic was full of praise:

*two items in particular stand out as the most memorable. These were
the sweet voices of the lower school singing "Tell Us O Star" and the
exciting sound of the choirs and orchestra combined for the "Song of
Bethlehem".*

I remember that the event's most singular feature was the sight of an enthusiastic senior member of staff attempting to count the number of people in the audience weeping during the climax – the "Song of Bethlehem".

Hengrove School has an enviable reputation for the standard of its musical events, including in recent years a televised performance of another of Mr Davies' works called "Way Out""

PROGRAMME CONTENT OF FIVE CONCERT SAMPLES

School Concert Programme 1967

			Orchestra	"Overture for a Festive Occasion"	Bailey
	National Anthem		Choir	"Pick a Bale of Cotton"	arr. Gardner
Massed Choirs	"Song for a Festival"	Dyson	Orchestra	"March" from "Scipio" "Elizabethan Serenade"	Handel Binge
Junior Choirs	"Old Farmer Buck" "Faithful Johnny"	English Folk Song Scottish Folk Song	From "Hastings"	"Requiem" "Hymn of Triumph"	
Brass Band	"Slaidburn"	Rimmer	Orchestra	"Slow Music for a Ballet" "Breton Fiddle Tune"	Handel
Madrigal Group	"Wenn Einer Tannige" "Guarda Che Passa" "Adieu one last Goodnight"	German Round Italian Folk Song German Folk Song	Choir	"See the Gipsies"	Kodály
Brass Band	"Thanet Seascapes"	Cook	Vocal Duet	"Swansea Town" (Soloists : M. Perrett and W.Plenty)	Ratcliffe
Junior Choirs	"The Locked Door"	Czech. Folk Song	Choir and Orchestra	"Homage to Sul" (See programme note)	Bailey
Recorder Group	"Terzetto" (1st Movement) "Minuet and Trio" "Dance of the Mosquito"	James Hook Mozart Liadov	Orchestra	"Slow Minuet" "Farandole"	Lully Bizet
Junior Choirs	"Leaving Home"	German Folk Song	From "Hastings"	"Now we must Defend our Soil"	
Staff and Orchestra	"Concerto for Staff" (Otherwise known as the "Toy Symphony")	Haydn ?		"Finale"	

*   I N T E R V A L   *

School Concert Programme 1971

1. Full Orchestra ... Suite in D .... Handel

2. String Quartet ... Two Movements
   for Strings .... Parkes

3. Horn Solo .... Third Movement from
   Concerto No. 2 in
   E Flat .... Mozart

4. First Year Choir.. Emmental .... Swiss
   East Virginie ...... American

5. Guitars &   Three Tunes of
   Recorders .... Old England .... Traditional

6. Cello Solo ...... Allegro Appassionata
   .... Saint-Saens

7. Junior Band ..... Minuet .... Handel
   March :"Alceste" .. Gluck
   See the Conq'ring
   Hero .... Handel

8. Bass Tuba Solo .. Andante & Rondo .... Capuzzi

9. Senior Choir .... Summer Carol ...... Traditional
   I Sowed the Seeds of
   Love ...... Traditional
   Quand Tu Venais .... French

10. Cornet Solo ..... Plaisir D'Amour .... Martini
    Alleluia ! .... Mozart

11. Wind Band ...... Gavotte .... Machelbeck
    A Savoy Suite ...... Sullivan

* * *   INTERVAL   * * *

PART TWO

1. Senior Band .... Suite: Cargoes ...... Cook
   Earl of Shaftesbury's
   Pavane .... Byrd
   Full Band .... Belphegor .... Brabsant

2. Recorder Consort ... Fanfare for a Festival .. Hand
   Fugue in C .... Bach

3. Middle School Choir
   ... Irish Lullaby ....Traditional
   Little Spanish Town ..Jenkyns

4. Brass Ensemble ..... Partita for Four Voices ..Posch

5. String Orchestra ... Air from Suite No.3 in D..Bach
   First Movement from
   Concerto for Two Violins..Bach

6. Clarinet Solo ...... Theme & Variations ....Weber

7. Madrigal Group .... David of the White Rock ..Welsh
   Pick a Bale of Cotton ....American
   A Man and a woman ....Lai

8. Middle School &
   First Year Choirs
   ... Donna Donna ....Traditional
   My Tender Musette ......French

9. Finale .... Hammer Song ....American

* * * *

School Concert Programme 1985

PROGRAMME

(1) CHOIR

THE TRAIN ~ Venezuelan
IDLE DAYS ~ Welsh
JAMAICA FAREWELL ~ West Indian

(2) GUITAR GROUP

DANCE ~ Haydn
ENGLISH DANCE ~ Anon.
STREETS OF LAREDO ~ American
YELLOW BIRD ~ American

(3) TROMBONE SOLO   (Ian Coleman)

(4) CELLO SOLO   (Julian Light)

(5) CHOIR

ALL NIGHT, ALL DAY }
ALL MY TRIALS   } Spirituals
SURELY LORD   }

(6) STRING ORCHESTRA

GAVOTTE ~ Gluck
THREE MINIATURES ~ Bridge

(7) VIOLIN SOLO   (Fiona Cole)

(8) BASSOON SOLO   (Angela Pitchford)

(9) CHOIR

WINNSBORO' COTTON MILL BLUES }
EAST VIRGINIE   } American
MINE EYES HAVE SEEN THE GLORY }

School Concert Programme 1986

1986 Programme

1. Full Orchestra

   March from the 'Dramma per Musica' ... ...Bach
   Adagio ... ...Albinoni
   Gigue ... ...Telemann

2. Choir

   Sea Cycle from 'The Venturers' ... ...Davies

3. Full Orchestra

   March, Dance, Fughetto and Allegro ...Handel

4. Guitar Group

   Romance ... ...Anon.
   Allemande ... ...Anon.
   Green Holm Jig ... ...Scottish

5. Cello Solo

   Adagio ... ...Rubino
   Soloist: *Amanda Dorrington*

6. String Orchestra

   Allegro ... ...Marcello
   Adagio ... ...Tartini
   Third Movement from Concerto for Two
   Violins, Op.3 No.5 ... ...Vivaldi

7. Choir

   Three Songs from 'Jonah-Man Jazz' ... ...Hurd

HENGROVE SCHOOL
MUSIC DEPARTMENT

8. Full Orchestra

   Romance in F ... ... Beethoven
   Soloist: *Robert Chadwick*

   Prelude and March from 'Little Suite' No.1 Arnold
   Clog Dance ... ... Herold
   Hoe-Down ... ... Copland
   I want to Hold Your Hand ... ... McCartney
   Caravan ... ... Ellington

9. ALL PERFORMERS   -o-o-o-FINALE-o-o-o-

HENGROVE LOWER SCHOOL CHOIR
and
HENGROVE SCHOOL ORCHESTRA
(Leader: Fiona Cole)

Directed by Judith Hobbs
Robert Chadwick
Monica Sweet
Stephen Davies

THE SOUTH BRISTOL MUSIC CENTRE
(Patron: Her Grace the Duchess of Beaufort)

INTERMEDIATE ORCHESTRA
(Joint Leaders: Jane Gregory & Kevin Eardley)

Conductor: Trevor Iles

SBMC

School Concert Programme 1990

PROGRAMME

1. Full Orchestra

   Allegro.........................Handel
   Ridente di Calma................Mozart
   Ragtime Two-Step................Joplin

2. Lower School Choir

   Come Hasten Ye Shepherds.........Traditional
   See Amid the Winter's Snow.......Goss

   Audience & All Performers

   Once in Royal David's City.......Gauntlet

3. Brass Ensemble

   See the Conqu'ring Hero..........Handel
   Little 18th Century Suite........Traditional

4. Bassoon Solo

   Bucolics.........................Wills

5. Staff Choir

   Shepherds to Bethlehem...........Puerto Rican
   The Boar's Head Carol............Traditional

   Audience & All Performers

   While Shepherd's Watched.........Este's Psalter

6. String Orchestra

   Badinerie........................Bach
   Larghetto........................Handel
   Folk-Song Suite..................Grieg

7. Lower School Choir

   Now the Holly Bears a Berry......Traditional
   Merry Christmas..................Traditional

   Audience & All Performers

   O Little Town of Bethleham.......Traditional

8. Woodwind Choir

   Three Seasonal Spirituals........American
   Dance Suite......................East European
   Pop Three No.2...................Miscellaneous .

9. Violin Solo

   Romance..........................Beriot

10. Staff Choir

    In the Bleak Mid-Winter.........Holst
    Out in a Stable.................Traditional

    Audience & All Performers

    The First Nowell................Traditional

11. String Orchestra

    Allegro, Concerto in A Minor.....Vivaldi

12. Audience & All Performers

    Santa Claus Is Coming to Town....Coot
    Winter Wonderland...............Bernard
    Rudolph the Red-Nosed Reindeer...Marks
    White Christmas.................Berlin

PERFORMERS

THE PEOPLE

Here we acknowledge a universal debt to many singers and players. All but a few of the following listed pupil instrumentalists have performed in public in various school groups.

Second instrument players are not listed, although many have doubled on other band or orchestral instruments, on keyboard, or (especially) guitar. The single reed mouthpiece of the clarinet family has a cousin in that of the saxophones, hence the double choice for clarinettists from Acker Bilk to our three Alto Saxophone and one Tenor Saxophone playing clarinettists.

The following all played for "The Venturers" but their instrument identities have been lost "in the mists of time" … Ann Miller, Mark Mitchell, Susan Phillips, Diane Pountain, Anthony Fernott, Sarah Flanaghan, Colin Smith, Geoffrey King, Lisa Grant, Mary Stock, Christine Andrews, Anita Hill, Adrian Rowland, Martin Jones, David Steer, Susan Ludlow, Anne Higgs, Penny Crow, Julie Cains, Christine Foey, Robert Rogers, Linda Richardson, Richard Lambert and Christopher Topley.

To these and to many recorder players and hundreds of choristers must go our apologies for omitting their names from the following lists. Excuses like lack of space, fading memory and casual archiving must stand in place of compensation.

An asterisk * marks the name of a visiting teacher or a past pupil known to have made a significant contribution of quality and/or quantity to music at Hengrove School. A bold **L** indicates a sometime leader of the school orchestra.

C20 TEACHERS who have contributed to MUSIC at Hengrove School

CLASSROOM MUSIC STAFF	J B Coleshaw
	Maurice Bailey
	Margaret (Kate) Moon
	Stephen Davies
	Meryl Markall née Cook
	Hilary Collins
	Cathy Smart née Moorsom
	Dr Jim Ayres
	Judith Hobbs

OTHER PARTICIPATING SCHOOL STAFF	Peter Haydon (Metalwork) Brass Band Harold Chasey (History) Violin Ken Hanham (Metalwork) Violin Harold Bewley (French) Cello Alan Horwood Trombone Derek Chivers (Chemistry) Keyboard Christine Cowley (Social Studies) Keyboard Roger Grant (English) Clarinet Philip Waterhouse (Headmaster) Oboe
STAFF CHOIR	An inspiring presence which included many Teaching and Ancillary Staff
PERIPATETIC STAFF	i.e. Visiting teachers giving instrumental tuition and support in class and concert Arthur Alexander (Strings) *Monica Sweet née Richards (Guitar) *Richard Pepper (Woodwind) George Hey (Wind) *Bob Chadwick (Upper Strings) *Roger Taylor (Brass) John Wills (Double Bass) Ann Moulson (Cello) Christine Khoo (Cello) Dave Kennard (Double Reeds) *Elizabeth Palmer (Double Reeds) Tim Clark (Guitar) *Tony Warbutton?? (Woodwind) Avril Rump (Lower Strings) Ann Fowles (Upper Strings) *Andrew Foister (Brass) Brian Wilshere (Percussion) Eddie Clayton (Percussion) Glenn Meek (Percussion) John May (Cello) Andrew White (Upper Strings) Brian Howard (Brass)

PUPIL INSTRUMENTALISTS

Jane Allen (Violin), Gary Andrews* (Cello), Susan Angove (Cello), Clifford Ayson (Clarinet)

Daniel Backwell (Guitar), Angela Badman (Flute), Alison Baggs* L (Violin), Elaine Baggs (Viola), Martin Bailey (Cornet), Paul Bailey (Violin), Jeanette Ball (Clarinet), Sasha Banwell (Violin), Sandra Bartlett (Violin), Janice Batten* (Clarinet), Heather Baxter (Horn), Elaine Bethell (Guitar), Caroline Betts (Oboe), Wendy Bidgood (Flute), Anthony Bird (Horn), Helen Bishop (Violin), Jacqueline Bishop (Viola), Jodi Bishop (Violin), Melissa Bishop (Violin), Rebecca Bishop (Bass Tuba), Kim Blake (Clarinet), Carolyne Boseley (Violin), Mark Boyce (Violin), Linda Boyne* (Oboe), Christopher Brain* (Trombone), Mark Brain (Horn), Janice Branfield (Clarinet), Angela Brice (Flute), Janet Brine (Violin), Elizabeth Broadbent (Horn) Roger Broadbent (Trumpet), Sarah Brook (Violin), Michael Broom (Trumpet), Lee Brown (Euphonium), Carol Bullock (Violin), Jane Bullock (Violin), Jane Burns (Clarinet), Susan Burns (Clarinet), Alison Butler (Trumpet), Susan Butler (Flute)

Tracey Cadman (Clarinet), Amanda Carter (Violin), Nicola Carter (Violin), Paul Carter (Horn), Danielle Chapell-King (Violin), Bob Chasey* (Violin), Ruth Chittock (Violin), Nicola Chivers* (Cello), Patrick Chivers (Trumpet), Carol Churchill (Horn), Samantha Churchill (Violin), Pamela Clapp (Violin), Tracey Clark (Clarinet), Tessa Clemenson (Cello), Toby Clemenson (Percussion), Marie-Ann Closius (Violin), Fiona Cole* L (Violin), Graham Cole (Horn), Katherine Cole (Violin), Tyrone Cole (Horn), Zena Cole (Violin), Ian Coleman* (Trombone), Teresa Coles (Violin), Dawn Collins (Violin), Julie Collins (Violin), Kerry Collins (Cello), Helen Coomber (Violin), Paul Coveney* (Trombone), Ruby Coveney* (Horn), Michael Cox (Percussion), Caroline Cridland (Violin), Nicholas Cridland (Cello), Philip Curnock (Guitar)

Christopher Dabbs (Horn), Kirsty Dabbs* (Clarinet), Andrea Davey* L (Violin), Kerren Davey (Clarinet), Matthew Davies (Percussion), Richard Davies* (Cornet), Lyn Derrick (Violin), Susan Derrick (Clarinet), Sarah Dickinson (Clarinet), Lyn Dimond (Guitar), Jonathan Dodd* (Flute), Amanda Dorrington* (Cello), Jenny Down* (Cello), Kelly Duck (Horn), Lucy Ducket (Violin), Sarah Dunn (Violin), Anita Duxbury (Violin), Lucy Duxbury (Violin)

Gayle Eaves (Violin), Kirsty Edwards (Violin), Stephen Edwards (Clarinet), Keith Elliott (Percussion), Richard Elliott* (Bass Tuba), Susan Elliston (Guitar), Judith English (Flute), Marvin Evans* L (Violin), Robert Evans (Percussion)

Jennifer Farr* (Flute), Martin Farrow (Guitar), Sarah Feltham (Viola), Elizabeth Filer (Violin), Sarah Filer (Violin), Claire Fleming (Violin), Debbie Fleming* L (Violin), Jason Ford (Keyboard), Michelle Fossard (Percussion), Joanne Fowler (Violin), Kieran Fox (Cello), Wendy Froud (Guitar)

Paula Gabriel (Flute), Ayshea Gillard (Double Bass), Sonia Gillard (Double Bass), Debbie Goodman* (Clarinet), Katie Goodman* (Flute), Louise Gregory (Violin), Samantha Gribben (Violin), Rebecca Griffith (Clarinet), Catherine Gundry-White (Cello)

Leanne Haberfield * (Clarinet), Maxine Hall* (Clarinet), Stephen Hall* L (Violin), Lesley Hallett (Flute), Martin Hallett (Trumpet), Sandra Hallett (Clarinet), Alison Haydon* (Viola) Dawn Hazell (Clarinet), Paul Hennighan (Trumpet), Jennifer Herbert (Clarinet), Christopher Hicks (Viola), Lisa Higgins* (Clarinet), Paula Hilliar (Guitar), Georgina Hitchings (Viola), Jacqueline Hitchings* (Cello), Lorraine Hitchings (Clarinet), Claire Holland* (Guitar), Christina Hooper (Guitar)

Judith Ible (Violin), Simon Ible* L (Violin), Trevor Iles* (Oboe)

Jane Jacobs* L (Violin), Sarah Jacobs (Cello), Stuart Jackson (Percussion), Carol Jay (Flute), Susan Jay* (Clarinet), Susan Johnson (Clarinet), Andrew Jones* (Clarinet), Kevin Jones* (Cello), Kirstie Jones (Violin), Matthew Jones (Guitar), Melanie Jones (Percussion)

Christine Kays (Violin), Shirley Knowles (Flute), Caron Knowlson (Violin)

Vicky Leese (Violin), Nicola Lewis (Violin), Julian Light* (Cello), Russell Light (Viola) Samantha Lindsay (Guitar), Ruth Lock (Violin), Rachel Lucas (Violin)

Fiona Macey (Oboe), Mark Madams (Oboe), Christopher Marsh (Trumpet), Peter Marsh (Violin), Rachel Marsh (Viola), Claire Marshfield (Guitar), Krissie Martin (Percussion), Julie Martin (Violin), Timothy Martin (Horn), Maldwyn Meacham (Guitar), Sylvia Meikle* (Violin), Linda Merrick* (Clarinet), Miriam Michalak (Flute), Kim Miller (Violin), Cheryl Mock (Cello), Esther Mogford (Cornet), Philip Mogford* (Cornet), Sharon Mogford (Trombone), James Moriarty (Viola), Diane Morris (Flute), Gary Morris (Viola), Zoe Morse (Violin)

Peter Nagel* (Horn), Samantha Nash (Violin), Susan Nash (Flute), Sarah Newman (Violin), Glenda Nicholas (Clarinet), Molly Nicholas (Violin), Stephen Nicholas* (Double Base), Mark Nobbs (Guitar)

Emily O'Hara (Cello), Sara O'Hara (Violin), Julie Ollerenshaw (Viola), Nigel Osborne (Euphonium), Alison Oury (Violin)

Helen Palmer (Clarinet), Kirstie Palmer (Flute), Stephen Palmer (Trumpet), Rebecca Park (Guitar), Jeremy Parsons (Horn), Andrew Patch Violin), Peter Patch (Violin), Aneeta Patel (Viola), Jonathan Pearce (Euphonium), Philip Pearce (Trombone), Rachel Pearce* (Clarinet), Sarah Pearce (Clarinet), Stephen Pearce (Euphonium), Andrew Pearson* (Viola) , Joanne Pearson (Flute), Catherine Penney (Horn), Mark Penney (Percussion), Lisa Pickford (Violin), Sandra Pike (Violin), Angela Pitchford* (Bassoon), Tim Pocock* (Trumpet), Hazel Poole (Violin), Nicola Prewett* L (Violin), Kevin Price* (Trumpet), Joy Purnell (Clarinet)

Cassie Raine (Violin), Sarah Ran (Horn), Susan Rann (Bassoon), Sarah Rawlings (Horn), Gina Read (Clarinet), Andrew Rees* (Violin), Alison Reynolds (Cornet), Helen Richards (Flute), Sheila Rudall (Viola), Stephen Rudall* (Cello), Emma Rush (Flute), Craig Rushforth* (Trombone), Paul Rushforth (Percussion), Donna Russell (Violin)

Shellie Salvage (Guitar), Sarah Sarhandi (Viola), Emma Selway (Guitar), Karen Selway* L (Violin), Helen Shapter* (Horn), Paul Shapter (Trumpet), Susanne Sherwood (Flute), Gillian Smith (Violin), Michael Smith (Percussion), Paula Smith (Flute), Penny Smith (Clarinet), Philip Smith (Cornet), Rebecca Smith (Trumpet), Karen Spear (Violin), Lyn Spodris (Cornet), Paul Stephens* (Bass Tuba), Alison Stevens (Violin), John Stinchcombe (Euphonium), Sarah Stokes* L (Violin), Rachel Strode (Violin), Nicola Summers (Clarinet), Karen Synnuck (Violin)

Alison Thomas* L (Violin), Jacqueline Thomas (Clarinet), Julie Thomas (Clarinet), Ruth Thomas (Clarinet), Roger Thompson* (Euphonium), Sarah Thorne (Violin), Claire Tiley (Viola), Glen Titcomb (Cello), Rebecca Titcomb (Viola), Elspeth Townend (Clarinet), Robert Townend (Cornet), Claire Tutton (Guitar), David Tye (Clarinet), Stephen Tye (Clarinet)

Amanda Vaughan (Violin)

Natalie Ward (Percussion), Nigel Ward (Double Bass), Rachel Ward* (Violin), Gerald Watts (Cello), Rachel Webb (Violin), Lyn Wedmore (Clarinet), Anne Wheeler (Violin), Amanda Whitehouse (Alto Saxophone), Bryony Whitfield (Cello), Lucy Whitfield* (Flute), Hazel Willecome* (Bassoon), Heather Willecome* (Oboe), Paula Williams (Violin), Nicola Winter* L (Violin), Claire Woodcock (Clarinet), Stuart Woodman (Euphonium), Matthew Wright (Euphonium)

Justin Young (Percussion)

DISTINGUISHED ALUMNI & ALUMNAE

Many of the preceding have continued to exploit their musical interests. Here we note a selection of those known to us to have most memorably pursued some musical activity after leaving school, and end by debouching into a rogues' gallery of those who failed to elude Doug Jackman's camera!

We begin in the sixties with **Robert Chasey**, son of Harold and a prodigy, winning a scholarship to the Royal Northern College of Music before sitting his "O" Levels.

 As a virtuoso violinist he has toured in Europe and the USA. He has distinguished himself playing for the Royal Ballet Orchestra and the BBC Northern Orchestra.

Bob has studied conducting under Rudolph Kempe, and is now Artistic Director and Principal Conductor of the Bolton Symphony Orchestra.

Turning to the seventies we find perhaps our most illustrious past pupil: Professor **Linda Merrick**, currently Principal of the Royal Northern College of Music in Manchester. Her alphabet of qualifications ranges from PhD through numerous degrees and diplomas to the ALCM she gained before sitting her "A" Levels, and extends to the highly prized award of ARAM. In addition to her academic duties, Linda has an enviable reputation as a clarinettist and as a recording artist. Despite all the foregoing, she selects as the achievement of which she is most proud, her masterminding of students' coursework development – altruism lives!

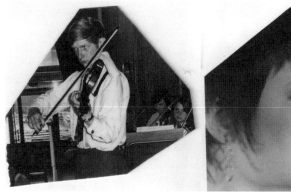

Robert Chasey   *Linda Merrick*

In Scotland, whether in orchestra, band and ensemble, or just brass playing and education generally, one name always stands out: that of trumpeter **Kevin Price**.

A long stint from 1980 followed his appointment (by conductor Sir Alexander Gibson) as Principal Trumpet of the Scottish Opera Orchestra. With the Scottish National Orchestra he has played under the batons of Alexander Lazareff, Walter Weller and Sir Simon Rattle, among others. He has worked as an external examiner and tutor to the Scottish Orchestra. Familiarity with recording studios (e.g. of BBC TV) has followed his work with chamber ensembles. Kevin is currently Artistic Director of Broxburn & Livingstone Brass Band. He played cornet in our school brass band from the late sixties, and became principal cornet of Kingswood Brass Band before the age of sixteen. He then transferred to the trumpet, gaining a distinction at ABRSM Grade VIII. Further study of the trumpet at the Guildhall School of Music culminated in the coveted award of the Brass Prize. Scotland's gain has been our loss!

In the mid-seventies violinist **Simon Ible** was leader of our school orchestra. Now he is Director of Music of Peninsula Arts at Plymouth University, Director of the University Choral Society and Conductor of the Ten Tors Orchestra. His conducting mentors have been Klaus Donath (in Hanover) and Sir Colin Davis (in London). For many years active in and around Bath, he was resident conductor of Bath City Orchestra. Since moving to Plymouth, Simon has continued to expand his freelance conducting activities throughout the West Country.

Kevin Price   *Simon Ible*

For long in the seventies Bristol Youth Orchestra had a brass section heavily reliant on Hengrove pupils. **Richard Elliott** was one of these, in addition to the support of his bass tuba to the school orchestra. He is now Director of Music at Plantsbrook School, Sutton Coldfield, and plays for the Birmingham

Philharmonic Orchestra. He conducts the Sutton Brass ensemble and tutors the lower brass of Birmingham's Youth Band.

A fine trombonist of the eighties, **Ian Coleman** pursued his education at Bath Spa and Exeter Universities before moving to the USA. There he became Doctor of Musical Arts at the University of Kansas, and is now Professor of Music Theory & Composition at William Jewell College in Missouri. He has produced over thirty commissioned compositions, some already performed in Bristol and London. We note especially "Fanfare for All Seas, All Ships" and "A Mass for our Time". Stateside (!) Ian is well known for his dedication to the musical welfare of his students.

Ian Coleman

Also from the late sixties we remember **Trevor Iles**, a pianist and oboist. After leaving college, he taught music at Brislington before becoming Head of Music at King Edmunds School, Yate, and while there he joined the staff of our Saturday Morning Music Centre. While there he proved an organisational deus ex machina, arranging concert venues, residential weekends and the highly successful Hildesheim exchange. He replaced Richard Pepper as Conductor of our Intermediate Orchestra and later took over as Director of the Centre. After some years, Trevor left Bristol to serve Nottingham as an Advisory Teacher.

After a prize-winning period at the Guildhall School of Music, bass tuba player **Paul Stephens** returned to Bristol and for a while was Head of Music at Merrywood Boys' School. Another prize-winning musician, **Sylvia Meikle**, offered in the 6th form a place

Sylvia Meikle

Paul Stephens

at Newton Park College of Education, was last heard of teaching music in a Somerset primary school.

A loss to Bristol's Shaftsbury Crusade no doubt, but **Richard Davies** still plays in a Carmarthen band. Dicky made his cornet sing when leading the school brass band, which included **Roger Thompson** on Euphonium. Roger ("Tubby") after leaving school in the sixties, played for Stanshawe Band, then Bristol's only Category I brass band, now called Sun Life.

Jonathan Dodd was a flautist who left our 6th form in the early seventies and then spent six years in the Band of the Scots Guards. His subsequent repair work must have been excellent – James Galway

Richard Davies

was a customer! Through his flute he has been involved in a variety of music, including some radio and TV work. He now resides on the Atlantic coast of Eire, still repairing and enjoying a diet of both classical and traditional Irish music.

Royal Academy trained, **Stephen Rudall** was a naturally gifted cellist. After joining a cruise ship as a working musician, he spent some time playing with the South African Radio Orchestra. He later returned to Bristol and some peripatetic teaching.

Clarinettist **Lisa Higgins** sought her undergraduate education in Salford with its new university status, while an earlier clarinettist, **Janice Batten**, has provided keyboard accompaniment for Bristol's Unity Singers. Cellist **Kevin Jones** has taught music in St Mary Redcliffe and **Hazel Willecome**

Stephen Rudall

plays her bassoon in the Bristol Concert Orchestra. Viola player **Sarah Sarhandi** chose pop groups (e.g. Rip, Rig & Panic) as an unusual medium for her viola playing.

Sarah Sarhandi

… and finally, below and overleaf a **Rogues' Gallery** of some notorious, some meritorious musicians – you decide!

Clockwise from top right: Roger Broadbent, James Moriarty, Alison Baggs, Anna Wheeler, Andrea Davey, Linda Boyne

Clockwise from top right: Winston Campbell, Chris Brain, Kate Moon and The Madrigal Group, Malcolm Perrett, Jane Jacobs, Sarah Jacobs, Bill Plenty, Tracey Cadman, Angela Badman

Chapter 7
Pupil Destinations

The influence of our schooling does not cease when we leave school. We take with us into 'the world' all that we learned during our school days. This consists of the 'formal education' – knowledge, information, exam passes etc. As important, if not more so, is the 'informal education' learned through extra-curricular activities and the influence of teachers who were our role models and mentors.

The contents of this chapter are extracted mainly from the pupils' replies to the questionnaire. Their replies are preserved in full as part of the archive. We thank all those who responded. In addition we have some official school records. The 1957 School Magazine listed the 1956 leavers and their destinations.

SCHOOL LEAVERS
BOYS
SUMMER, 1956

DENNIS ACKERMAN. Athens House. Drama Group. Swam for School. — Smith's Crisps.

RONALD CURTIS. Sparta House. — Replacement Engines, Ltd.

DAVID DURY. Olympia House. School Prefect. — Leyland Motors.

BRIAN GAINARD. Corinth House. House Drama. — MacFisheries.

DAVID HILL. Corinth House. Prefect. — B.A.C.

TERENCE LIAS. Athens House. — H. T. Warlow.

MICHAEL MILLER. Sparta House. — Ferodo, Ltd.

EDWIN SAINT. Olympia House. 1st XI Soccer. 1st XI Cricket (capt.) House Cricket. Prefect. — Farming.

EUGENE WALTERS. Argos House. House Soccer. School Basketbell. — British Railways.

DONALD WEBB. Thebes House. — Avon Paper Company.

CHRISTMAS, 1956

ALAN FRANCIS. Olympia House. 1st IX Soccer. School basketball. House Drama. — G.P.O.

MICHAEL LEIGH Sparta House. House Athletics. — Messrs. Coles.

MICHAEL MESSENGER. Olympia House. 1st IX Socecr. House Soccer and Cricket. — British Railways.

MICHAEL PARSONS. Thebes House. Capt., 1st XI Cricket, Soccer, Basketball. House Cricket and Soccer. Prefect. — Garaway, Ltd.

ROBIN SALTER. Thebes House. House Soccer. — Balhatchets, Ltd.

BARRY WILTSHIRE. Argos House. 1st XI Soccer. House Soccer and Cricket. — Bristol Co-op.

BRIAN MOCHUM. Olympia House. — Beasley and French.

RONALD EDKINS. Athens House. — Bristol Marble Co.

EASTER, 1957.

MARTIN CHESTER. Athens House.   R.A.F.

MICHAEL CRIDGE. Sparta House. 1st XI Soccer. House Soccer (capt.)
    House Drama.   Jones and Co.

VIVIAN DERRICK. Athens House.   G.P.O.

DENIS GRINHAM. Thebes House.

ROBERT JONES. Thebes. School and House Drama. Reading Team.
    Prefect.   Bristol Hospital Service.

MALCOLM KELLAR. Sparta. House Soccer.   B.A.C.

JOHN MARRIOTT. Olympia House.

JOHN ROBERTS. Corinth House.   Smiths (Ironmongers).

ALAN TILEY. Argos House. House Soccer. Prefect and Cricket.
    House Athletics.   Messrs. Robinsons.

DAVID TURNER. Argos. House Athletics.

DAVID WITHERS. Argos House. House Soccer and Drama. School
    Drama. Prefect.

DEIRDRE BRATCHELL. Athens. School Choir. John Wrights, Printers.

ROSEMARY CHICKEN. Sparta. 1st Netball Team. School Choir.
    Prefect. House Hockey Team.

JOAN COLES. Sparta. House Team Hockey.
                                      " Patricia " (Hairdresser).

PAMELA CRANE. Olympia. House Team Hockey and Netball.
                                       John Hall and Sons, Ltd.

MAVIS OSMOND. Thebes. School Hockey Team. House Netball.
    Prefect.

JENNIFER POWELL. Corinth.   Faimans, Broadmead.

JENNIFER PUGH. Sparta. School Hockey Team.
                              Chappell and Allen and Co., Ltd.

SANDRA ROBINSON. Olympia.   Baker, Baker and Co., Ltd.

PATRICIA SANDERS. Athens House. Hockey and Netball. Prefect.
    School Choir.   College of Technology.

ANN STEPHENS. Thebes. School Hockey and Netball. House Drama
    Group. Prefect.   B.A.C.

JOAN SULLIVAN. Sparta.   Maggs and Co.

GLADYS WALL. Argos. School Netball Team. Budgetts and Co., Ltd.

CHRISTMAS, 1956

BRENDA BABER. Athens.   Bristol Co-operative Society.

JUNE BARNES. Athens.   Bristol Commercial Vehicles.

MARGARET BOSTOCK. Athens. Prefect. House Hockey.
                              Underwood Secretarial College.

VERONICA BRACEY. Athens. Prefect. House Hockey.
                              Bristol Co-operative Society.

DIANE CHICK. Olympia. School Hockey. House Reading Team.
                              Bristol Co-operative Society.

JILL COBLEY. Sparta. Prefect. School and House Hockey and Net-
    ball.   Bell and Nicholson.

DIANE FLOWER. Sparta. Prefect. House Netball.   John Hall, Ltd.

WENDY GAYDON. Argos.   J. S. Fry and Sons, Ltd.

JEAN GRIFFIN. Corinth.   T. C. Marsh and Son, Ltd.

PATRICIA HAWKETTS. Olympia. House Hockey and School Choir.

DOREEN HAYWARD. Olympia. Prefect. House Team Hockey and
    Rounders.   Robert Stotesbury, Ltd.

288

SYLVIA HOPE. Corinth. Prefect. House Hockey. Recorder Group. Senior Choir. Messrs. Woolworth's.

PAULINE JONES. Corinth. School Netball. School of Commerce.

DIANE KING. Corinth. Mardon, Sons and Hall.

JANET MOGFORD. Corinth. Prefect. House Hockey. Morgans, Ltd.

DOREEN SYDENHAM. Thebes. Prefect. House Hockey and Rounders. House Drama Group. Bennett Bros.

BERYL WEEKS. Argos. House Netball and Rounders. Welch and Co., Ltd.

EASTER, 1957

RITA BALL. Athens. Smiths Ironmongers.

DENISE BOWELL. Sparta. Prefect. House and School Netball. Stoke Lodge Nursing.

DIANE BRITTON. Sparta. School Netball. Smiths Ironmongers.

MARY CURTIS. Olympia. Prefect. House Hockey and Swimming. Avery's Scales.

VALERIE DAMSELL. Olympia. Prefect. House Hockey. Eastfield Riding Stables.

MARGARET EDWARDS. Corinth. Jones Store.

ROSEMARY HASKINS. Olympia. Messrs. Gardiners.

VIVIENNE HINTON. Corinth. Grays Gowns.

MARGARET LOWMAN. Corinth. David Grieg.

JANET MARQUICK. Thebes. Prefect. School and House Netball and Rounders. John Hall Ltd.

BERYL MARTIN. Corinth. Prefect. School Netball. Colthurst and Harding.

CHRISTINE PUGH. Thebes. Prefect. School and House Netball and Rounders. Huttons Florists.

JANET WEINLING. Argos. Grays Gowns.

From 1960 until 1985 the destinations of pupils were recorded in a smart leather bound ledger 'On Course'. This will be placed in the archive in the City Records Office. Up until 1965 the names of pupils proceeding to Universities and Colleges were included in the Prizegiving Programmes (see chapters 2 & 3). We reproduce overleaf the 'On Course' entries for 1966-1973.

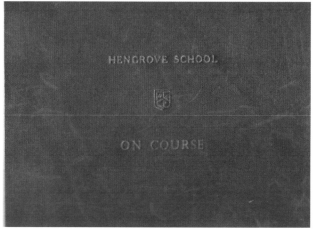

1966 R.Richards - Regent Street Polytechnic, BSc Hons Zoology; C.Topley – Trinity College of Music; L. Harvey – Hereford College of Education; M.Vlaeminke – Dartford College of Education; P.Wait – West of England College of Art, Diploma in Art and Design.

1967 J. Bacon – St Peter's College of Education; D.Bassett – Bath University, BSc Applied Physics; R.Biggs- Bath University, BSc Engineering Metallurgy; G. Batchelor – B.A.C / Bath University; N.Carter – B.A.C /Bath University; R. Dollin – I.A.A.S Course at Bristol Technical College; M. Hamilton – Loughborough University BSc Hons Chemistry; A.Hayward – Cambridge College of Arts and Technology B.A General (Languages); R.Hedges – Leicester College of Technology H.N.D in Mathematics, Statistics and Computing; R.Kays – Leicester College of Technology H.N.D in Mathematics, Statistics and Computing; J. Logan - Rugby College of Technology BSc Applied Physics; P.Vardakis – Rose Burford College of Speech and Drama; J. Blair – Trent Park College of Education; A.Dodge – Salford University, BSc Hons Physics; C.Higgs – Avery Hill College of Education; L.Jordan – NW Polytechnic – Education Department; P.Lowry –Dudley College of Education; M. Southey – Aberystwyth University BSc Hons Botany; R.Sherring – ONC Mechanical Engineering, Bristol Polytechnic; M.Stabb – City and Guilds Heating and Ventilation Course – Bath Technical College.

1968 B.Dawes – Bath University, BSc Mechanical Engineering; A. Forsey – Furzedown College of Education; B. Greenwood – Portsmouth College of Technology BSc Mechanical Engineering; N.Howarth – Bristol Technical College; C.Lee – Westminster College of Education, Oxford; M.Faithful – Hereford College of Education; J.Hellier – Bristol Technical College; S.Vaughan – Hereford College of Education; D.Haskins – Kingston-on-Thames College of Art, BA Architecture; R.Chasey – Royal College of Music Manchester. Awarded the Olive Zorian Prize for Violin playing 1970; A.Greg- St Paul's College, Cheltenham – B.Ed and Geography Hons.

1969 M.Brierley – Somerset College of Art; M. Coombes – Doncaster College of Education; R.Senior – Portsmouth College of Education; C.Tipping – Somerset College of Art; P.Walden – Brighton College of Education; J.Nial – Weymouth College of Education; J.Rorke – Culham College of Education; P.Stokes – Somerset College of Art; H. Arnold – University of Kent, BSc Hons English.

1970 A.Ford – Hartbury Farm Institute, Gloucestershire – OND Agriculture; C.Bacon – Sheffield University, BSc Civil Engineering; P.Cook – Weston Technical College, City and Guilds Cert. 441 and OND Hotel Keeping and Catering – College Award for Outstanding Work (1973); D.Harris - Portsmouth College of Technology, BSc Special Mathmatics; J.Haskins – Southampton University, BSc Physics Hons; T .Iles – Trent Park College of Education; P.Sams – London Imperial College BSc Physics Hons; K.Summers – St Lukes College of Education; C.Thomas – Portsmouth Polytechnic, BSc Hons Maths; B. Eisentrager – Birmingham College of Education; J.Ellis – Exeter University;

F.Griffey – Bedford College of Education; P.Hough – St Katherine's College of Education; S. Hyde – Southampton University, BSc Social Science; A. Plenty – Shenstone College of Education ; L. Rowlands – Kirby Fields College of Education ; C.Slade – Exeter University; D. Holley – Bristol Polytechnic BSc Economics; A.Hedges – Bradford University, BSc Civil Engineering.

1971 N. Avery – Bristol Polytechnic, Vocational Graphics; N.Knowles – HND in Hotel Management, Gloucester Technical College; H.Rowlands – Didsbury College of Education; P.Stephens – Guildhall School of Music; J. Whitehead – Birmingham College of Art, Photography Diploma; K.Connor – J.M. Marsh PE College Liverpool; R.Coveney – Newton Park College; S. Edwards – S.R.N Course in Q.A.R.A.N; S.Gazzard – West Midlands College of Education, Walsall; J.Holley – Westminster School of Nursing; T.Lye – Bristol Polytechnic, Town Planning Diploma; B. Outhwaite – Keele University; S.Pearce – Westminster School of Nursing; J.Smallcombe – Newton Park College of Education; J.Snell – Birmingham College of Education ; R. Taverner – Sarum St Michael College of Education; M. Taylor – Q.A.R.N.N.C Portsmouth.

1972 J.Ballard – Wall Hall College of Education; C.Burlinson – Dartington College of Education; L.Bussell – Portsmouth College of Education; M.Gingell – Portsmouth College of Education; H. Griffey – Madeley College of Education; F.Harper – Rolle College of Education; G.Winn – Birmingham School of Speech; A.Smith – Weston Technical College, Home Economics; D.Brown – Lancaster University; P.Duckett – Bristol Polytechnic; D.Goodman – Coventry College of Education; L.Hughes – Weymouth College of Education; G.Lane – Loughborough University, Chemical Engineering; D.Purnell – Taunton College of Art; A.Robb – Salford University, Electrical Engineering.

1973 S.Angove – Brighton College of Education; J.Batten – Filton Technical College; K.Berry – Chelsea College, London University; R.Campbell – South Bristol Technical College, Engineering; A.Branson – Thames Polytechnic, International Marketing; A.Broderick – Madeley College of Education; D.Crook – Imperial College, Salford; P.Flyng – Birmingham College of Education, French; J.Field – Liverpool University; G.Forster – Weston College of Art; J. Francis – Brunel College, Catering; P.Gast – Bristol Polytechnic, Art and Design; T.Hutton – Liverpool University, Biochemistry; C.Mckenzie – Filton Technical College; P.Mears – Brunel Technical College, Catering; S.Meikle – Newton Park College of Education, Music; I.Massey – NHS Southmead Hospital; S.Morris – Brunel Technical College, Hotel Reception Course; M.Pearce – Chelsea College of Science and Technology, BSc Hons Applied Biology; K.Price – Guildhall School of Music and Drama, A.G.S.M Course; P.Smith – Hockerill College, Geography; R.Walder – Sussex University, Biological Sciences; P.Williams – Brunel College, Bricklaying; J.Wood – Didsbury College, Drama and English. A.Taylor – Bath University, Applied Biology; A. Melrose – Bath Agricultural College.

It is interesting to read of the pupils' destinations after leaving school. Below we have summarised their responses to the questionnaire, listed alphabetically. The dates following the names refer to the duration of their education at Hengrove School.

If you did not receive a questionnaire but would like your details to be included in the school archive you can e-mail your contribution to hengroveschool@ hotmail.co.uk

ROBERT ADAMS: 1957-1962. Nottingham College of Education 1966-1969. Open University degree in History and Education 1976. Primary School Teaching 1976. Became Head of a Primary and Nursery School until 2005. Now studying in retirement for degree in Fine Art at Nottingham University.

DAVID BAGSHAW: 1965-1972. Worked in Department of Environment 1972-1995/1996 when ill health forced him to retire at age 41 years. In 1992 he named one of his hobbies as gliding. He would drive himself to and from the Gliding Club at Nympsfield at weekends. He also travelled the world with the England Football Supporters Club. He died in 1997 aged 43 years – a fulfilled man. He had exceeded everybody's expectations – what an example to us all!

JANET BAKER (nee HOOPER): 1956-1962. Nursery Nurses College, Stoke Lodge, Bristol. Always worked in Nursery Classes and Infant Schools taking a break to raise a family in 1967-1973. Returned to work in an Early Years Centre and Mother and Baby Unit for Teenage Mothers.

GEOFF BANWELL: 1956-1962. Joined the Royal Air Force, then Staffordshire Police. Retired. Worked with people with Learning Disabilities 2001-2011. A referee of Professional Football – on right of picture below.

MARK BRAIN: 1969-1975. First job 1975-1976 Department of Health and Social Security. From 1976-1992 trained to become a skilled print finisher. From 1993-1995 mature student at City of Bristol Further Education College. From 1996-1999 University of the West of England graduated B.A. (Hons) Business Administration. From 1999-2002 various temporary positions – gaining business experience. From 2002-2011 working for the Home Office. Was a Hengrove School Governor, then Chair of Governors resigning in 2003 when elected as Labour Councillor for Hartcliffe Ward. Re-elected 2007 and 2011. Now Chair of Resources Committee.

KAY BULLEN nee BAGSHAW: 1965-1970. Trained to become a Veterinary Nurse 1970-1972. Followed by a practical placement: then Berkshire College of Agriculture 1972-1973. Qualified and worked as Veterinary Nurse 1974-1976. Pitmans Accounting Course 1976. Office work with the Intervention Board 1977-1979. Bristol Department of Environment 1979-1981. Welsh Office now Welsh Assembly from 1981-1993. Founded the Hedgehog Helpline 1988. Running the Hedgehog Rescue Centre 1993. Registered visually impaired 1990's. Published a book "Hedgehog Rehabilitation" 2002.

HEDGEHOG REHABILITATION
by
KAY BULLEN VN

RESCUE REARING and NURSING

CARE DIAGNOSIS and TREATMENTS

WELFARE and RELEASE

Published by the
BRITISH HEDGEHOG PRESERVATION SOCIETY
Hedgehog House, Dhustone, Ludlow, Shropshire SY8 3PL
TO CELEBRATE ITS 20th ANNIVERSARY
© Hedgehog Helpline and British Hedgehog Preservation Society.

Currently a Trustee of the Hedgehog Helpline Charity, The British Hedgehog Preservation Society and the British Wildlife Rehabilitation Council. Also Site Manager for Cardiff Institute for the Blind Gardening Club.

RAY CASHLEY: 1960's. Initially joined Bristol City Football Club, then became Goalkeeper for Bristol Rovers Football Club.

BOB CHASEY: 1970's. Son of teacher Harold Chasey. See Chapter 6 for more details. Was Principal 2nd violin in BBC Philharmonic Orchestra and Artistic Director of Bolton Symphony Orchestra.

RICKY CHANDLER: Served 4 month apprenticeship with Bristol City Football Club June 1978. Made league debut against Watford in January 1979?

BRISTOL CITY FOOTBALL CLUB
Back Row: (L to R) Bill Tovey (Trainer); David Rodgers; Jan Moller; Julian Marshall; John Shaw; Alan Nicholls; Bill Heather (Physiotherapist). Middle Row: Ken Wimshurst (Chief Scout); Alan Hay; Ricky Chandler; Gary Smith; Peter Aitken; Kevin Mabbutt; Tony Fitzpatrick; Howard Pritchard; Russell Musker; Paul Stevens; Gerry Sharpe (Youth Team Coach). Front Row: Jimmy Mann; Trevor Tainton; Gerry Sweeney; Bob Houghton (Manager); Roy Hodgson (Assistant Manager/Coach); Geoff Merrick (Club Captain); Chris Garland; Clive Whitehead.

PAULINE CLAPP nee COOKE: 1957-1963. Became an Office Clerk

VALERIE CLARK nee PRICE: 1955-1960. Prudential Insurance 1960-1962. Raised three children who all went to Hengrove School. 1971 to date Provident Personal Credit (40 years service)

BARRY CLARK: Currently Bristol City Councillor for Hengrove Ward.

PAT CLARK nee MASSEY: 1958-1963. National Provincial Bank 1963-1970. Then joint Licensee with husband of a public house and raising a family. Returned to clerical work with Bristol Water and City of Bristol College 1979 –retired 2010.

CHERRY COLEMAN nee HELPS: 1956-1962. Working in Insurance Office until 1970 when she raised her family. Played in County Netball Team. Her priority became serving the community through activities at her church – Youth

Work, House Group host and leader, Bible study group leader. Started the Mother and Toddler group which still thrives today. Loved by many inside and outside the church circle. Died May 2005 aged 60 years. Greatly missed. Her son Ian Coleman is mentioned in Chapter 6.

PAUL COOK: 1964-1969. Member of Boys' After School Cookery Club run by Miss Griffiths. One of the first boys to take cookery 'O'Level. Proceeded to Weston Super Mare Technical College for 3 years, graduating with the National Diploma in Hotel and Catering Management and 5 City and Guilds Certificates including Advanced Cookery and Advanced Food and Beverage. To gain practical experience he worked in various locations, including Assistant Manager at the Crown Hotel, Lyndhurst whilst building up his own catering business (weddings etc). In 1975 he opened a Fish and Chip shop in Stockwood, continued with his outside catering and also baking bread. In the 1980's he opened the Danish House Restaurant, Blackboy Hill and continued with the outside catering business. In the 1990's whilst catering at the Royal Welsh Show he saw some ostriches on display and was hooked! He decided to rear ostriches and sell the meat. This diversified into his exotic meats business – for more detail see his website osgrow.com. He is indeed an enterprising and versatile entrepreneur.

PAUL COOK: 1954-1959. Entire career at Bristol Aero Engines ONC Mechanical Engineering. Safety Practitioner. Corporate Membership of the Institute of Occupational Safety and Health. Now retired.

STUART COOK: 1957-1964. Graduated 1967 BSc (Hons) Mathematics. Trained for Baptist Ministry Spurgeon's College 1968-1971. Then Baptist Minister in Brixton, Bury St Edmunds and Leicester. Edited "In Good Company" a Book of Readings 1993 ISBN 0551 02245 – 0. Died, Leicester 1998

TONY COOK: 1966 – 1971. Moved his family to Cornwall – bought a fishing boat and worked in the fishing industry. Latterly set up his own building business.

PETER COOK: 1971-1978. Bath College of Higher Education – graduated B. Ed. 1979-1981. British Youth for Christ 1981-1985. Teaching 1985-1989. Regents Park College Oxford. M.A. Theology and Diploma in Pastoral Studies 1992 Baptist Minister in Darlington and Hereford. Since 2003 Hanham Baptist Church, South Gloucestershire.

JACQUELINE COOKE nee ELBROW: 1959 – 1960. Worked for Tobacco Company 1960 – 1964 – then Redcliffe Inks Control Laboratory 1964 – 1966. Career break raising family. From 1978 – 1999 resumed working at Rolls Royce, as a Maths Assistant followed by several promotions. Now retired. She is the cousin of Kathryn Scully nee Mitchell.

TOM DARK 1959-1962. Leicester University 1962-1965 graduating in Physics followed by a PhD. Switched to a career in Business Finance with Ford Motor Company, followed by Xerox and BT, retiring in 1995. In order to give back something to the community he joined the Round Table and the Rotary – also became a Prince's Trust Advisor and served as a voluntary business councellor for the local Enterprise Agency. Now fully retired.

W. DAVIES (Bill): Late 1950s - early 1960s. Very keen on sports (see Chapter 5). Joined Avon and Somerset Police who sponsored him to study for a Law Degree. He retired as a very high ranking Police Officer and is now a Security Consultant for a major Banking Institution.

MARTYN DELLBRIDGE: 1970-1977. Loughborough University 1977-1981; 1979-1983 British Aerospace Bristol; 1983-1985 Cirrus Reynolds, Redditch; 1985-87 System E Controls, Leamington Spa. 1987-2010 Computing Devices Canada, Ottawa, Canada; 2010 to date EMS Aviation, Ottawa, Canada.

BARRIE DUNN: 1955-1960. E S & A Robinson Sales Office 1960 -1963. A J Bingley Ltd. 1963-1987 rising to Managing Director. Since 1987 to date Senior Partner – Orchard Packaging.

MARGARET EAVES nee SMITH: 1957-1961. Office work Baldwin Street 1961-1970 and Night school Typing and Shorthand. 1970 career break – raising family. Voluntary Community service at her church; Boys Brigade, Playgroup, Girl Guides, Catering Team, Copyright recorder for hymns. From 1990 to 2007 full time church cleaner. Now retired.

PETER EYRE: 1957/1962. He served a 5 year Engineering apprenticeship with Masson Scott Thistle, building machines for the tobacco industry and bank note machines for various countries. Left at age 25 years to start his own business EyreVac Plastics. He built his own vacuum forming machines to produce plastic trays mainly for the pharmaceutical industry, also for cosmetics, food and fireworks. During this time he developed machines to recycle waste plastic into spiral rabbit guards, selling in excess of 30 million over a 12 year period. In 2008 he sold the machines and order books to a company in Mansfield.

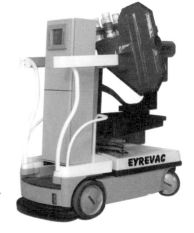

In 1999 he combined his brilliant inventive brain with his passion for tennis. He conceived, designed and developed a robot tennis practice machine. Seven years later, after spending £700,000 of his own money, the EVB4 Tennis Ball Machine

(Boris) was showcased at the David Lloyd Academy and other tennis venues. It was featured on BBC Points West and has been viewed by the Chief Executive of the Lawn Tennis Association. Peter intends to use the forthcoming proceeds of the sale of his factory site to further refine his machine to render it more easily transportable. His wish is to give something back in return for the good fortune he has had in his life. For more information contact peter.eyre5@btopenworld. com

PETER FUDGE: 1965-1972. From 1976-1996 various posts with H.M.S.O including Regional Bookshop Manager Manchester. 1984-1988 General Bookshop Manager, London. In 1997 took voluntary redundancy when H.M.S.O was privatised. From 1997 to date Facilities and Administration Manager at HFT (a charity in Emerson's Green). He very kindly shared his expertise in book selling.

CAROLE GARLAND: 1956-1961. Ledger Clerk T. Walls and Son from 1962-1965. Joined W.R.A.C Lingfield, Yeovil and Bicester, received advanced driving training. From 1965 back to civilian life – many years using driving skills. Various other jobs including Amerind Nursing Home, Veale Wasborough Solicitors and Hungry Bite Café. Now retired.

CAROLYN GILL nee ROBERTS: 1958-1963. Lloyds Bank, then Civil Service until 1974 – raising family. Returned to studying as Mature Student – obtained BA (Hons) degree and PGCE. Then worked in Swansea University Library, and recently retired.

JOHN GILL: 1958-1963. Electrical apprenticeship; work as qualified Electrician then self-employed Electrical and Heating Engineer.

JANET GUILLE–MARRETT nee FREEMAN: 1957-1964 Trained as a teacher at Chichester College of Education. Has taught in various parts of England for 45 years. Still teaching part time in Jersey – the home of her husband.

DAVID HARRISON: 1955-1960? – see newspaper obituary below.

David Harrison: Bristol Evening Post senior feature writer

01 August 2003

David Harrison, the Bristol Evening Post's longest-serving journalist, has died in hospital after a fighting a long battle against heart disease.

The 59-year-old senior feature writer had worked at the paper for more than 36 years. He was a respected authority on the history of the city in which he was born and educated, as well as being a successful author in his own right.

David joined the Evening Post in January 1966 after training with the Wilts and Gloucestershire Standard in Cirencester.

In his early days with the Bristol Evening Post, he covered the Keynsham area, before becoming a regular member of the paper's feature writing team.

His first specialist role on the paper was drama correspondent, during which time he became a wellrespected theatre critic. His last role was editor of the weekly nostalgia supplement, Bristol Times.

David was an authority on many types of music, from opera through to contemporary. He reviewed several famous performers when they visited the city, including the Rolling Stones, the Beatles and, most poignantly, the final performance of rock'n'roll hero Eddie Cochran.

Music was one of David's many interests, which ranged from literature to architecture to steam trains.

He also possessed an encyclopaedic memory for times past in his home city of Bristol.

David published a number of books, some in conjunction with the Evening Post and others in his own right. One of these, The World of Blues, a title on American blues musicians, was a bestseller.

His interest in this particular music went further. David reviewed blues records for Folk Roots magazine for a number of years, where he was respected for his knowledge and forthright views.

Throughout his time on the Evening Post, however, David waged a battle against ill health. He was diagnosed with a form of lymphatic cancer more than 20 years ago.

He triumphed over that, only to succumb in later years to serious heart problems, which required a gruelling heart operation a few years ago. More recently, the heart problems recurred.

David recalled his health problems with typical humour in one of his most recent writings for the paper: "Over the years I've managed to sample the delights of most of the Bristol hospitals and intend to write a book about them unless I receive: a) threats of extra blood tests or b) a large bag of hush money.

"Southmead, Frenchay, the Bristol Royal Infirmary, even the old Ham Green Hospital - been there, done that."

I worked with David for more than 30 years at the Evening Post. He was a phenomenal person with a vast knowledge of a wide variety of subjects. If you wanted to doublecheck what happened where, when, why and to whom, then David was your man.

These past months, although dogged by severe ill health, he continued to amaze us all by showing up for work, retaining his enthusiasm and dedication for the job, yet never complaining about the condition he found himself in. In that respect, he was truly inspirational.

A witty and authoritative writer, David was a friend as well as a workmate and I know I speak for many others when I say I shall miss him greatly.

Evening Post editor Mike Lowe said: "David was a terrific asset to the Evening Post and to the city of Bristol.

His exhaustive local knowledge and enthusiasm for the Bristol Times supplement have left our readers with a great legacy."

David is survived by his mother, daughter Becky, son Corin, and grandchildren.

PETER J HAYDON: 1958-1964 after VI Form he entered the Bristol Fire Service where he remained for his entire career, retiring at 50. At school he had been an active member of the brass band. In retirement he continues to play the cornet with Westerleigh Silver Band, Bristol Veterans Brass Band and Mendip Brass Band.

RUTH HAYNES nee IBBOTSON: 1958-1963. Telephonist/office jobs 1963-1967. Career break raising family 1967-1975. Resumed career - 1975-1990 as a Computer Sales and Computer Systems Analyst and Trainer. Then from 1995-2008 Information Analyst for NHS. Retired 2008.

GILLIAN HAZELL nee VLAEMINKE: 1956-1963. Newton Park College Library 1963-1966. Studley Grange Farm Swindon – Dairy Herd Assistant. 1967 Married John Hazell (Hengrove School 1955-1960). Travelling Farm Secretary 1967-1981. Wills Law Library Bristol University 1982-2006. Retired 2006 to assist husband with family business Great Western Gladiolus in Clutton – see leaflet below.

Our main **Gladiolus** catalogue is published each year at the end of September. It lists our complete range of Dutch and American gladiolus, from large 500 size exhibition corms right down to the popular 200 size for the general gardener. It also includes the 100 size and for the specialist, primulinus and the attractive nanus varieties.

To obtain a copy of this catalogue, please send 4 stamps along with your full name and address.

We also publish a **Specialist Bulbs** catalogue at the end of July. If you are looking for something different, you can choose from a wide variety of both outdoor and indoor bulbs, ranging from giant alliums through autumn crocus, tiny indoor species gladiolus and lachenalia, to specialist tulips and zephyranthes.

This catalogue will be sent on receipt of 2 stamps along with your full name and address.

Great Western Gladiolus
17 Valley View
Clutton
Bristol
BS39 5SN Tel.01761 452036

email: clutton.glads@btinternet.com

www.greatwesterngladiolus.co.uk

Great Western Gladiolus

Suppliers of possibly the widest selection of
Species
Border
and
Exhibition
Gladiolus
and other
Specialist Bulbs

2012

SALLY HEDGES: 1954- 1961. Qualified MBBS London (Royal Free Hospital) 1967. Later became House Physician at King Edward VII Hospital Windsor. No other information.

DIANE HIGGOTT nee FANCY: 1961-1966 Retail – toyshop/shoe shop. Married, raised 3 children. Trained as Playgroup Teacher.

SUE HYDE: 1963-1970 – In 1970 she entered Southampton University – BSc Social Science degree. After some practical experience with Sutton Coldfield Probation Service she took a one year course at Leicester University in Sociology, Law and Criminology. We wonder where she is now? She was featured in a newspaper article in August 1973.

ROY JOLLIFFE: 1957-1964 Nottingham Teacher Training College 1964-1967. Teaching in London area 1967-1980. Returned to Bristol 1980 – worked in Bristol Branch of large Industrial Paint Company. Retired.

CAROL JONES nee EYRE: 1959 – 1964. Ran a business "Chew Valley Canvas" from home while raising 2 children, doing heavy duty sewing repairs. Later started a further business "Cordwainer Crafts" making

Sue joins probation team

Miss Sue Hyde . . . probation work at Sutton Coldfield with a diploma and a career in view. 14 AUG 1973

'I want to meet people'

PEOPLE who need the help of the probation service at Sutton Coldfield may find themselves meeting 21-year-old Sue Hyde — but only for the next year.

Miss Hyde has just joined. She has to complete that and obtain a diploma before she can make probation work a long-term career.

Sue, who lives at Boldmere, has already completed a course in sociology at Southampton University.

She said: "I did not know when I went to Southampton what I would be doing when I left.

"But my landlady there was a probation officer and I found

an interest which developed.

"I would not be satisfied with a 9 to 5 job, but want to get out and meet people and obviously try to help them."

The Sutton team before taking a one-year course at Leicester University in sociology, law and criminology.

period style shoes for historical re-enactment events. She is enjoying playing golf in her retirement!

ROGER JONES: 1960 – 1965. Worked in Retail Management supplying the business trade. Married Carol Eyre in 1977. He is enjoying researching antiques in his retirement.

MIKE LEIGH: 1958 – 1963. Bristol City Council Local Government Officer 1963-1973. Avon County Council 1973-1996. Bristol City Council 1996-2007 – various Departments and promotions - final post was in the City Records Office. His interests in Local History continued from his workplace into his retirement. He joined Knowle and Totterdown Local History Society in 2006 becoming Secretary in 2009. He also joined Avon Local History and Archaeology (ALHA) in 2007 and was soon invited to join the Executive Committee. In September

2008 he was elected as Business Manager for ALHA Books. In June 2011 he was elected Publicity Officer and joined the Local History Study Day Sub-Committee. He is also an Associate Member of the Regional History Centre of the University of the West of England. Thus he is ideally suited to involvement with the Hengrove School History Project and his input has been invaluable.

RUTH LIM nee COWLEY: 1957-1964. Cardiff University Physiology – transferred to Social Science after practical social work experience with Bristol City Council 1964-1966. Diploma in Social Administration – Swansea University 1964-1966. Bristol City Council Childcare Officer 1968-1971. Married and moved overseas. St Andrews Mission School – 1971-1972. Swansea University Degree BSc (Econ) 1972-1974. British High Commission Brunei 1974-1979 Brunei Students Unit London 1979-1981. Career break raising family 1982. Various voluntary Community Projects at church – Mums and Toddlers, Playgroup, Care Team, Bereavement Team. Hengrove School History Project 2011 – date.

ROSEMARY LITTLE nee HASKINS: 1954-1957. Was in first intake of pupils to Hengrove – transferred from Knowle Park Senior Girls School. Various office jobs, nursing for 3 years, married, raised a family.

STEVE MANNING Late 1950's to early 1960's. Became Department of Environment, Food and Rural Affairs (DEFRA) (Formerly MAFF) Senior Animal Inspector in Gloucestershire. Now retired to the Scilly Islands.

ALAN MARSH: 1960-1964. Career in Bristol Fire Service. Twin brother of Derek Marsh below.

COLIN MARSH: 1954-1959? Took UEI exam. As a Mature student became a Baptist Minister. Died 1990's. Brother of Alan, Derek and Malcom.

Colin Marsh Hengrove pupil in the 1950's

DEREK MARSH: 1960-1964 Apprentice Mechanic, Cotham Hill Garage, City Motors then Fry's. Bristol City Council for 23 years as uniformed Parks and Open Spaces Patrolman rising to Deputy Inspector. Life-long learner – obtained 5 'O' Levels by Correspondence Course, then 1 'A' Level. In 1999 BA (Hons) Theology – Cheltenham and Gloucestershire. Later a Certificate in Preaching (URC) and Diploma in Hypnotherapy. Now an accredited Lay Preacher (URC) and Tutor for St Johns College, Nottingham distance learning course in Christian Studies (for Derek's full contribution see the archive material in City Records Office).

MALCOLM MARSH: 1957 – 1961. Worked for the GPO as a Postman and other various. Plays the violin for the Church Music Group.

Hengrove School pupils of the 1960's. From left: Allan, Malcolm and Derek Marsh

LINDA MERRICK: 1974-1981 Royal College of Music London became a clarinettist of international renown. Principal of Royal Northern College of Music. See Chapter 6.

SUE MILLS nee Whitnell: 1958-1963. After passing 'O' Levels she went straight into employment as a Finance Clerk in a Solicitors Office. In 1966 joined Civil Service (War Pensions). Career break 1973-1985 to raise family. 1985 worked with S E Bristol Adult Education Centre – merged with South Bristol College and became City of Bristol College. Retired 2010.

KAREN NICHOLLS nee ASLETT: 1972-1979 Park School of Beauty Therapy Nottinghamshire 1972-1973. Theatrical shop work 1973-1975. Insurance Industry – various jobs 1982-2005.

SALLY OWEN: 1960's Bristol School of Dance Clifton; Rambert School of Ballet London 3 years – accepted into Ballet Rambert 1971 (newspaper article in archive)

LINDA PARKER nee BARRETT: 1961-1965. Lived and worked in Jamaica for one year. Recently returned from living in Spain.

ERIC PAVEY: 1955-1962. In the second intake to the school, to Bath University – graduated BA Architecture 1970; worked as an Architect.

PATRICIA QUANT nee BEECHAM: 1955-1960. Midland Bank then B.R.I. Nursing Training; Southmead Hospital Receptionist, then Civil Service. No dates supplied

KATHRYN REYNOLDS nee KITTLETY: 1957-1963 Office Administration and then part time retail work.

MARGARET ROBINSON nee FRANCIS: 1961-1966. W. D. H. O. Wills Tobacco Co. Typist and Wages Clerk, various other jobs. Raised family – currently a Doctor's Receptionist.

ROGER SALTER: 1957-1961 Apprenticeship – City and Guilds – Electrical Installation (Intermediate and Final Level). ONC Engineering; HNC Electrical Engineering. Certificate in Education for Teaching Further Education level. Development Manager Rotork Controls (Bath) finally Lecturer in Electrical Engineering at South Bristol College (now City of Bristol College).

CHRISTINE SAMPSON nee PURNELL: 1958-1962 Shorthand Typist until 1968 – break to raise a family. By 1975 her children were at school, returned to shorthand / typing at Strachan and Henshaw for 15 years. Early 1990's decided on a career change. To Filton College – Community Care Course, followed by work with Learning Disabled at Hortham and Brentry Hospitals; then Social Services, St George Day Centre. Obtained a Further Education Teaching Certificate and Sociology 'O' Level. Retired 2006.

JEFFREY SAMPSON: 1961-1965 British Rail apprenticeship and beyond.

JANET SAWYER: 1957-1962. Nursery Nurse Training, Stoke Lodge Bristol NNEB Qualification. Novers Hill Nursery - 3 years; Bristol Maternity Hospital for 23 years. Then Bristol University Dept of Child Health Research Project with Premature Babies - 4 years. In 1990's career change – studied for Diploma in Counselling then Student Counsellor at City of Bristol College for 3 years and Staff Counsellor at Southmead Hospital. Now retired.

New year's honour for Kate Scully

The Post-16 Citizenship Support Programme is very proud that Kate Scully of Democratic Action for Bath and North East Somerset Youth (DAFBY) has been awarded an MBE for services to young people. Kate has been involved in post-16 citizenship for many years and is dedicated to giving young people a political voice in their communities. Through her work at DAFBY Kate has supported young people in discussing and taking appropriate action on issues of concern to them through which they have developed citizenship skills, knowledge and understanding. She says: "I have a wonderful job. It is making young people aware of their rights and responsibilities and I am passionate about helping them to make a difference in their community."

KATHERINE SCULLY nee MITCHELL: 1965-1971 A fine gymnast, represented Hengrove School at Regional Level. Imperial Tobacco Co. HNC Maths and Physics. 1987 joined BANES Youth Service promoting the Duke of Edinburgh Award Scheme. Attended many award ceremonies at St James Palace – presented to the Duke in recognition of her work. 2009/2010 awarded MBE for services to Youth Work but unable to attend ceremony as ill with cancer. In 2011 she was presented to Princess Anne at Dorothy House Hospice near Bath and wore her medal. Died February 2011 aged 57.

ANN SELL nee WITHERS: 1959-1965 1st job Imperial Tobacco Co. Laboratory, 1 year – Ryvita Lab, 1 year, then Berger Paints. Child rearing break. Merrywood School Lab, then back to Hengrove School Science Lab – retiring when school demolished – after school gained 5 GCSE's (in addition to 8 CSE's and 3 GCE's passed at Hengrove School), B.T.E.C in Electronics. H.L.T.A, NVQ level 3 and A1 and A2 award – see archive for more memories and details. A valued member of the Hengrove School History Project Team.

RICHARD SEYMOUR: 1954-1958 / 59. Became an Apprentice Chef at Bristol Aircraft Company. Later worked as Chef at Little Thatch Restaurant, Sutcliffe Caterers, on Cruise Ships then ran his own catering company. From 1990 – 2008 he owned and ran the 'Seymour's Family Club' in St Phillips Bristol.

PATRICIA SIMMONS nee BAMBURY: 1954-1961 – Class 1A in the year the school opened. One of the first two pupils to take and pass one 'A' level in Art and Architecture along with J Sherman.

ANN SKUSE nee WEBB: 1955-1960 Imperial Tobacco Co. Research Department for 12 years. From 1972 became a Swimming Instructor for Bristol City Council.

PAUL STEPHENS: 1960's-1970's. Currently Vicar of Winford Parish Church. An accomplished Tuba player – see Chapter 6.

DAVID SUMMERS: 1954-1961 To St Luke's College, Exeter, Teacher Training PE and Music; 1964-1967 Teaching at Cotham Grammar School, Bristol; 1967-1973 Henry Box School, Witney, Head of PE and Year Tutor; 1973-1986 Bradfield Secondary School, Sheffield, Deputy Headmaster; 1978-1980 Sheffield University – MSc in Education Management. 1986-1996 Houghton Regis Upper School (Bedfordshire) Head Teacher; 1996-1998 University of Warwick Business School – Headteachers Into Industry (HTI) Course; 1998-2008 JHP Training (Part Time) NVQ courses for Assistant Teachers. Now retired and living in Oxfordshire.

MICHAEL SUMMERS: Brother of the above, 1955-1962 University of Birmingham 1962-1965 gaining a 1st class Honours Degree in Physics followed by post graduate work at Universities of Essex, Sussex and Bristol. Late 1960's – 1974 Teaching and travelling in Central and South America. Also worked as a Seismologist in Nigeria and the Oman. 1975-1985 teaching in School of Education University of Hong Kong. 1985-2007 Research Lecturer in Educational Studies at Oxford University. Retired, but still travels widely, mainly in Far East.

TREVOR TAINTON: 1950's/1960's. An all-round athlete. Played soccer for England schoolboys. Offered terms by Arsenal but chose to play for Bristol City Football Club. Was an important player in Bristol City's 1970 promotion to Division 1.

ROBIN TOWNSEND: 1954-1961. All round sportsman St Luke's College Exeter – Teacher Training 1961-1964. Teaching Post in Hampshire 1964 onward. Mr Richardson, his games/PE teacher at Hengrove, became a lifelong friend. Died 2009. See copy of article from Knowle Lawn Tennis Club in archive.

PHILIP A WAIT: 1961-1966 Won scholarship to spend one day per week at West of England Academy of Art during final year at school. Gained 7 CSE's – Apprenticeship as a Draughtsman at Modern Engineering Ltd. City and Guilds Certificate 1966-1968. To West of England College of Art and Design Diploma in Art and Design 1968-1971. From 1971-1983 various jobs - mostly managerial in commercial companies. Moved to Wales in 1983 and worked on the land: fencing, shepherding, hedging, Christmas tree felling 1983-1986. Then working for Dyfed Archaeological Trust (D.A. Trust) and Dyfed County Council as a designer of Heritage Interpretation Panels 1986-1988. From 2009 self employed as a Designer of Heritage Interpretation Panels for Phil Wait Designs. See photo below and more in the archive. He very generously gave of his time and expertise to advise on the book cover.

BARRINGTON WALSH: 1958-1964 To BAC for 5 years then CWS for 5 years; W and A Ross for 5 years. Became self-employed at Barrington Stationers for 30 years, then retired. Involved in Bristol Folk Music Scene as a writer and performer – supports 'Marmalade' at the Colston Hall.

JANET WALTERS nee NIAL: 1962-1969 Weymouth Teacher Training College 1969-1971 then Primary School teaching 1971-1981. Joined Civil Service 1981-1990 taking early retirement. Voluntary Charity Work – various. Twenty years with St Peter's Hospice Knowle, Red Cross, Arthritis Research Council, Fundraising Lydbrook Hospital, Society for the Blind – running courses in Bedminster Branch. Still organising social events for ex-volunteers of St Peter's Hospice, Knowle.

Her parents Kath and John Nial made a huge contribution to the Hengrove School Association. Janet sent us a brief resume below.

Kath

Vice-Chairman, Hengrove School Association
John Nial – Secretary
Mr. Waterhouse – permanent Chairman. Other long serving committee members:- Peter Hill, Don Brine, Connie Bassett, Dorothy Sweet.
Organised :- Summer Fetes, Jumble Sales, Dances, with the aim of raising funds for purchase of books and equipment, not covered by school funds.
Kath was involved in child care and first aid classes after school to enable pupils to gain Red Cross certificates, towards Duke of Edinburgh Award
John ran fencing tuition classes in epeé and foil, again after school, as school equipment was not available for this sport.
Kath, John, both involved in checking pupils for Duke of Edinburgh adventure section.

PETER WAYBOURNE: 1950's/1960's – No information but currently Chairman of Knowle Lawn Tennis Club – see also Chapter 5 sports.

JEAN WEBER nee WATTS: 1957-1961. Trained as Shorthand Typist and Switchboard Operator: various Office Work and Retail Shop Work.

PETE WILKINS: 1950's/1960's. A natural footballer. Bristol Boys turned him down – too small! He played Full Back for Bristol Boys Rugby XV. No other information.

MARION WINTER nee COOKE: 1955-1958. Attended Clarks College for Commercial Studies; no other information.

MIRIAM WOODEY: 1958-1963. Bristol Technical College for General Domestic Science Studies. From 1964-1976 Eagle Star Insurance and Evening Classes for shorthand and typing. Childrearing from 1976-1984. Resumed employment at Eagle Star Insurance 1984-2005. From 2005 various part time jobs including Guinness Trust Housing. Retired 2007. Still a musician playing violin, flute and piano in Church Music Group and in local primary school.

MARTIN WOOLAWAY 1954-1962. Graduated in Medicine – worked both in Hospitals and General Practice, then several years in North Africa and Central America with Save the Children. Returned to the NHS specialising in Public Health and became Director of Public Health in Bedfordshire, where he still lives with his family.

PAT YOUD nee EYRE: 1954 –1959 Worked with BT and then the Civil Service/DHSS. In her free time she was able to pursue her musical interests that had been nurtured by Mr Bishop and Mr Coleshaw in Hengrove School. She played the piano/violin in her local church, also founded and led a children's choir. Later she moved to work in a church in south London and joined Crystal Palace Brass Band, playing second Cornet. Now semi retired, living in Kent and is an administrator for a large charity working in prisons.

Chapter 8
Staff Destinations
More about the Teachers

We were delighted that many former teachers responded to our questionnaire. We thank them for taking the time and trouble to respond.

Their responses are summarized below, arranged alphabetically. Some entries are extracted from newspapers or magazines or based on facts generally known to former colleagues and memories of their pupils.

JOHN ATYEO Date uncertain. Mr Waterhouse remembers he did a term's teaching practice at Hengrove under Mr Baggs. He was already famous as the captain of Bristol City football team and played for England. After his death the Football Club named a new spectator stand after him.

JANICE AVERY (née Yates) 1967-1971. Her first teaching post, she taught French and German when Ridley Hollely was Head of Modern Languages. She was later promoted to Joint Head of the Modern Languages Department with Christine Coulson (née Robins). She remembers enjoying her interaction with pupils in a very happy small Modern Languages Department – also the staff camaraderie. She accompanied a Bristol-Hanover exchange visit. She volunteered her time to help with PE and several YHA trips with her form (which she kept from year to year and got to know well) organised by Bob Swift (Swiftie). Went on to teach at Dibden Purlieu School, near Southampton, and ended her teaching career at King Edward's School, Bath.

DEREK BAGGS Dates uncertain. He certainly was teaching 'O' Level in 1962. An excellent Maths Teacher, he became Head of Maths and later left to become Headmaster of Preston School, Yeovil.

KENNETH BAIRD Dates uncertain. Head of Art when Mr Waterhouse was Headmaster. Won a prestigious scholarship awarded by Goldsmith's Society of London. He spent a term in Turkey and Eastern Europe studying Byzantine Art with all expenses paid as well as the cost of a temporary replacement at Hengrove School. He later became Head of Art at a Teacher's Training College in the North West.

FRANK BISHOP 1954-?. Former student David Summers remembers :

"He was the Bristol Cathedral organist and taught me Music up to 'O' Level. He encouraged everyone interested in music. He taught me to play the piano and to translate music into 'tonic-sol-fah'. I made use of this in later life when I composed for school musicals."

This pupil also sat and passed 'A' Level Music.

ALAN BLACKMORE 1957-1967. A graduate of Bristol University – his first teaching post 1955-1957 at Southville Secondary Modern School for Boys. He taught French at Hengrove School from 1957-1967. He was the party leader for The Bristol – Bordeaux Exchange. In addition, he ran the Model Railway Club and was Careers Master. He ran a successful Careers Convention, an afternoon/ evening event attended by parents, pupils and representatives of 40-50 local companies and industries. 1967-1988 Head of French at Weston Grammar School for Girls (became Broadoak Comprehensive School in 1971). 1988, retired and now living in Clevedon.

FRED BUCKLAND 1954-1973. A very tall man, an ex-policeman. In the early years he taught science, and later became Head of the Lower School. One ex-colleague remembers "after he retired, he and his wife made quite a name for themselves as Ballroom Dancers as reported in the Bristol Evening Post from time to time". He served Hengrove School until his retirement in the 1970s.

SUE BULL (née Collins) 1967-1974 Came to Hengrove School from teaching posts in London and Worcestershire. Taught PE to all age groups, 11-18 years – promoted to Head of Girls' PE and Senior Tutor (Head of Year).

Remembers being involved in many extra-curricular activities. Took pupils away for sports tours, mainly netball, plus a few students involved in athletics meetings, all over the country. Weekly matches involving all sports – boys and girls – against other Bristol schools. Remembers beating Millfield at netball. Miss Place volunteered Hengrove School as the venue for the first ever English Schools Netball Association tournament. The whole school – parents, pupils, teachers, school cooks – were involved – see Olga Place for more on this. Staff/ pupil teamwork was also involved in raising money for the new 'Resources for Learning' library, which included a Hengrove Boys football match versus Bristol City. Another big event was the building and opening of the swimming pool.

She writes:-

She left Hengrove School in 1974 to teach in an 11-16 comprehensive school in Solihull, where she was Head of Pastoral Care.

HAROLD CHASEY 1958-1979 Bristol born, Harold Chasey spent his whole life in Bristol. He attended St George Grammar School, and graduated from Bristol University with an MA in History.

He was a dedicated teacher who, according to his son, thought that "teaching was the most important profession on this earth". The majority of his teaching career was spent at Hengrove School until his retirement 1979. He was particularly interested in economic history and local studies.

He made a wonderful contribution to the life of the school. In 1966, alert to the significance of the date in British History, he produced a libretto entitled "Hastings". It told of the Norman Invasion in 1066 and the subsequent changes to life in Britain. The then Head of Music, Maurice Bailey set it to music. It was performed in the Colston Hall and proved a resounding success.

In 1968 he wrote a script entitled "Bethlehem" celebrating the Christmas message. The new Head of Music Stephen Davies put it to music and it was performed three nights in a row in the school hall to a full capacity audience and in November 1983 at the Colston Hall.

In 1973, to celebrate the six hundred year anniversary of the granting of the Charter to Bristol, he and Stephen Davies wrote the "Venturers". It was performed at the Colston Hall and was a great triumph. An L.P Vinyl record was produced which we have placed in the archive. You can read more about "Hastings", "Bethlehem" and "The Venturers" in Chapter 6.

In 1975 Harold Chasey wrote the book "Bristol: An Outline History for Schools". A copy will be placed in the archive should you wish to read the book.

In the words of his son:

He died in 1999. He is remembered for his writing of the lyrics for "Hastings", "Bethlehem" and "The Venturers". Excerpts of "Bethlehem" and "The Venturers" are on the CD which accompanies this book.

DEREK CHIVERS 1958-1986 A Bristolian, he was a pupil at St. George Grammar School where he was taught Chemistry by Mr R Green, who became Deputy Head at Hengrove School. He read Chemistry at Bristol University, 1954-57, and PGCE at Exeter University, 1957-58. He spent his entire teaching career at Hengrove School from 1958 to 1986.

In his first year at Hengrove he taught General Science to years 1 and 2, and Chemistry to Years 3 to Upper Sixth – the latter continued and he became Head of Department in 1960 and Head of Year in 1973.

He was generous with his time and involved in lots of extra-curricular activity – Saturdays with rugby and cricket teams: coached a boys' hockey team one evening per week: involved in lighting for the production of Macbeth in 1958-59, and choir practices.

He sang in all 3 blockbuster musical productions – see chapter 6.

He remembers school dinners were in the dining hall for the pupils in two sittings. Staff were served at tables in the adjacent assembly hall by 5th form girls. Later the dining hall was extended.

After the first few years, when pupil numbers were lower, assemblies could not be for the whole school together. The 1st and 2nd year pupils assembled in the girls' gym. 3rd year pupils upwards assembled in the assembly hall and had a normal non-denominational service.

In the early days the top three classes, A, B & C, were filled with 11+ passes. The theory was that comprehensive schools would help late developers by promoting them to the "grammar school" classes. He remembers one boy who was taking General Science but needed a separate science opportunity. He pushed for him to be promoted – he was, and passed 'O' and 'A' level, went to university and then into chemical research.

Mr Chivers retired in 1986 and set up a business repairing stringed instruments. This kept him in touch with all the schools in Avon and the peripatetic teachers. In 2005 he moved to Devon, where he and his wife work hard on their 'small' smallholding. His detailed contribution and excellent recall of dates has been invaluable.

MARY CLUTTERBUCK 1957-1972/3 She taught Typewriting and Commerce to 14-16 year olds. For the first few years she also worked part-time in the school office. She took students on visits to establishments connected with commerce. She says she enjoyed her time at Hengrove School and didn't want to leave, but needed a full-time teaching post. She went on to teach at St. Bernadette's and then St. George Comprehensive School. Little did she or her pupils know how useful the keyboard skills would be for the computer age.

She has been very encouraging of this history project and very kindly made a donation towards our considerable expenses. See chapter 2 for photo of her teaching.

WILLIAM CORK 1954-1975 Taught English and had responsibility for running the library. Prior to Hengrove, he was Deputy Head at Maxse Road Secondary Boys' School in Knowle. He retired in 1975 and is very fondly remembered by staff and students. Former colleague Graham Hobbs describes him as "a lovely quietly spoken man". Former pupil Christine Sampson (née Purnell) writes:-

"Mr Cork was my English teacher in 4th and 5th years and was brilliant! Not only as a teacher but as a mentor and life teacher, he helped me believe in myself! All through my life I have thought of him as a real inspiration! I always found English quite difficult, I was not a good speller and had to read things a few times to understand them, and reading aloud was a nightmare for me as I always got the words around the wrong way, hence making the rest of the class laugh. Mr Cork believed in me so much that he said I should do 'O' Level English (one of only two I took – the other being Biology). I failed by only one mark which made me realise that I wasn't so bad after all. I received the results card with a message written by Mr Cork saying "Who said 'I can't do English'?"

I remember my friend Pat and I going without school meals to save money to go dancing at weekends and Mr Cork brought us in an apple each and also gave us a bit of a lecture saying we should eat our lunch. Not sure how he knew: we probably told him: we certainly trusted him."

William Cork

TREVOR CROUCH 1969-1974 His first teaching post after University. He taught History to 11-16 year olds, and Politics and Economics to the 14-18 year age group. He gave of his time to help out with football, cricket, and some rugby, and helped run school teams. The Woodcock Shield was won by the under-15 football team in 1973.

He remembers 'The Venturers' performed in the Colston Hall in 1973, written and produced by staff and students.

After Hengrove School he taught at St George School, Bristol

MILLICENT CROWTHER 1954- ? Taught Art. Remembered by many pupils as a gentle person. Valerie Clark (née Price) fondly remembers her for teaching italic handwriting, for which she won prizes. Other pupils speak of a pupil locking Miss Crowther in the cupboard!

She was a sensitive talented artist, and we have a photograph of her work which was exhibited at the Royal West of England Academy, Queens Road, and is now in the possession of an ex-colleague.

She took a sabbatical at Dartington College, Devon, and finished her career at the Diocesan College in Derby.

JOHN STEPHEN DAVIES (also known as J. Stephen Davies or Stephen Davies) 1968-1992 He joined Hengrove School as Head of Music in 1968. Under his leadership the school's instrumental work expanded and produced a procession of concerts. His interest in the reform of music curriculum led to the publication of "Beginning to Compose" and other educational material. He wrote and often published music for brass and numerous choral/orchestral music for young people, including 'The Venturers" and "Bethlehem", "Way Out" televised in 1969 and "Yellow Dragon" in 1981.

He also founded the Saturday Morning Music School as a suburban centre for youth instruction in ensemble playing – probably the first in the country.

He wrote the following article for the Music Teacher Journal in 1972

Music in a comprehensive school

by John Stephen Davies

In Hengrove School one child in ten plays an orchestral or brass band instrument. Except for some children working with glockenspiels, all first and second year pupils play the descant recorder, the vast majority buying their own. The Music Department has two and a half staff, plus a fourth responsible for extramural brass, and three peripatetic teachers (strings, woodwind and brass) for three whole – different – days. Each term we enter between 30 and 40 candidates in the instrumental examinations of the Associated Board of the Royal Schools of Music, held at the school. Extra-mural activities include Wind Band, Senior Brass Band, Junior Brass Band, String Orchestra, Full Orchestra, Recorder Consort four choirs, etc. We run and accommodate an area Saturday Morning Music School for able 9 to 14 year olds. Possibly the first of its kind, it concentrates exclusively on ensemble playing. Four staff rehearse groups of flutes, oboes, orchestral horns, violins and violas, a brass band and a clarinet choir.

In the course which follows in outline, we claim originality for no particular part. In treatment and in organisation perhaps we are different. The seeds of our work were sown in fertile soil: we have modern, almost adequate premises and facilities; we have the active support of the Headmaster, the Staff, and the Music Adviser; the school is well-known for its musical traditions and for its progressive atmosphere. The experiments for this composition course, however, I began in a quite different, more traditional

environment; I found the course flexible, and a marked improvement on the conventional methods of class instruction, even in the formal classroom situation.

If publicity for our work brings not only criticisms which locate our weaknesses, but also makes contact with other work of similar aim, we shall be well pleased.

Thinking Aloud
(1) Music is among the worst-treated subjects in the curriculum. Exciting and successful ideas remain isolated glimmers of light, or become perforce mere steps in a musician's career. In secondary schools there is a dearth of child-centred experiment, of "field experts", of co-ordinated research, of suitable published course-work. Or perhaps (I hope) someone can prove me wrong?
(2) Why learn Music? How?

COMPOSITION: the logical way to approach the learning of theoretical knowledge;

PERFORMANCE: the logical way to approach the acquisition of practical skills;

LISTENING: the logical way to approach the understanding of aesthetic values.

It is not necessary to accomplish the writing or playing of a violin concerto to enjoy Beethoven's masterpiece, but without sufficient experience of composition and performance much is beyond the appreciation of the listener. Accurate and full awareness can only be achieved by a process which involves

Music in the Comprehensive School

(Continued from page 11)

all three elements. There is little more disturb-
ing than the professional double-bass player
who thought Berlioz "great" on the strength
of some interesting bass lines.

(3) The learning process: all children at
some stage need a stimulus for their curiosity
(the wish to learn) and training to sustain it
(the learning habit). Thus, even on a primitive
level: "without opening that drawer, the music
inside cannot be enjoyed". Some children
need the stimulus of teacher-motivation more
deeply and for longer than others, but all
should early be weaned out of such mental
and emotional napkins. Pupils wet-nursed
through "O" and even "A" levels are commonly inadequate in subsequent employment
or education. In our formal little boxes of time
and space does not more teaching mean less
learning? Is self-motivation for the majority
impossible without the miserable social pres-
sures of earlier, harder decades?

Substance

The course is currently working with all
first and second year pupils. Classes are
banded, with two teachers for each double-
class. Projects I (melody writing) and II (two-
part writing) are in use, and Projects III, IV
and V (three-part, four-part and song writing
respectively) are nearing completion. The
main instrument is the descant recorder, but
we use glockenspiels and orchestra and
brass band instruments when available,
preferable or necessary.

The course in practice: write a melody
using the given framework (stave-plan); play
for personal, then for teacher, then for – class
– concert approval. Two additional booklets
provide basic theoretical knowledge (including recorder fingerings) and instructions for
working each section, allowing the child to
progress with minimal explanations from
staff. Thus each child is free to teach itself
not just to compose, but to play and read.
Eventually we hope he will cope musically and
without difficulty with a realistic C.S.E. Mode
III examination plus two-thirds of the usual
G.C.E. "O" level questions.

To write the first tune only three notes
(their position on the stave and their fingerings) and two note-values need be known.
Although obviously the area of personal
choice is here restricted, the course allows
for progressively more compositional free-
doms as skills and knowledge accumulate.
E.g. even when working the first frame:
after three given 2/4 rhythms have been used
to write three melodies, a fourth melody is
required using the pupil's own rhythm.

The course is structured to allow each
child to progress not only at his own pace,
but according to his own peculiar skills.
E.g. a pupil with poor sense of rhythm but
good fingering facility may "skip" the pro-
gression from 3-note to 5-note tunes and
move immediately to using full octaves, while
at the same time working systematically
through all the given rhythms.

In short, the course is an attempt at "pro-
gramming" in which only one new idea may be
met in each new exercise.

12

The music/drama block at Hengrove School.

Complement and Supplement

Man, of course, cannot live by bread alone.
It is important that at least an equal amount of
time be spent in other musical activities,
especially in playing in small groups. A
balanced diet might be:

(A) Ensemble playing: of major importance.
The composition course itself may be
used – three 3/4 tunes may be strung
together in (e.g.) a waltz in rondo pattern, with some percussion added. To
vary the diet, however, much of the ensemble music should be that of *other*
composers.

(B) Recorded Music: the brief but frequent
listening to new and standard works for
reasons topical, illustrative, even emotional. Listen in groups, listen who
wishes.

(C) Singing: short sessions of (i) full
classes, (ii) those who request it and
(iii) selected groups – choristers, problem voices, etc.

(D) General Projects: learning *about* music –
an oblique approach for those deficient
in musical ability and/or motivation who
have failed to benefit from other course
work. Prayer: that these will eventually
return to the fold. Projects may range
from a survey of the work of local brass
bands to the mechanics of sound
production.

We have not got (B) and (D) fully launched
yet, but (A) and (C) are well established. In
some double-classes we can assemble what
is essentially a small orchestra. Training
choirs places less strain during extra-mural
rehearsals, and we are beginning to deal
more effectively with the changing voice.

Logistics

The department is based on three rooms,
one of normal classroom size, one smaller,
and a third, larger, of chamber concert pro-
portions. Music stands, brass and strings
and woodwind have three large storerooms;

these we use along with the cleaners' room
and three conventional practice cells for ensemble groups and course work. A staff
study, a small landing, and a large cloakroom
area complete our accommodation list.

With the drama studio, the department is an
isolated first floor unit, and the cloakroom
area can and does provide useful additional
working space. Here are kept four locker units
for string, brass, woodwind and recorder
music; a cupboard for treble and tenor
recorders and percussion instruments; tables
for marking compositions and for the display
of course – song – and other music books.
Pupils have free access (extra-mural as well as
during lessons) for most of the time to music
lockers and the percussion cupboard and to
most rooms. (For reasons of sanity, the staff
study is out of bounds!)

A visitor to a fairly typical composition
course lesson might well be greeted by the
follwing:

(1) In the large classroom, 20 or so pupils
with some fingering problems are get
supervised recorder practice.

(2) At one end of the cloakroom area three
isolated recorders write their tunes; at
the other end two violins hide in an
alcove while a third plays his tune for
marking;

(3) On the landing, two bass tubas take
"time off" to practise scales for an
imminent Grade III exam.

(4) In the middle classroom and string store,
a flute, cornet, French horn and occa-
sional piano cheerfully compete with a
dozen recorders, all doing course work.

(5) The practice cells conceal recorder ensembles while three clarinets take refuge
in the cleaners' room.

(6) Our woodwind peripatetic teacher in-
structs two oboes in the small classroom
and in the study the phone rings again!

Ten minutes later: all 70 (odd) children assemble in the large classroom for singing.

(To be concluded)

Music Teacher, December, 1972

316

RHIWEN DAVIES 1962-1986 Rhiwen will be best remembered for her work in the Lower School. Here she oversaw the transition of every pupil from Junior School.

She wrote an innovative course for the first year, incorporating History, Geography and Religious Education. Social Studies also included local studies and community involvement. The pupils received a large part of their curriculum through the work of a small group of teachers. This retained the sense of a small, secure unit within a large comprehensive school. It ensured maximum contact with the pupils, and gave opportunity for modules of work, outside speakers and visits to heritage sites.

A close colleague, Mrs Christine Cowley, remembers:-

"I have vivid memories of Rhiwen at the head of an army of schoolchildren walking around the old city walls of Bristol or ascending Maes Knoll."

"Her Christian commitment was seen in the daily acts of worship in morning assemblies and the innovation of Easter services at Christchurch, Hengrove.

Rhiwen was always immaculately dressed. Small in stature, she was fearless and fair-minded, a tough disciplinarian but with a kind heart. Her investigative skills in getting to the bottom of some mischief were legendary. She was an excellent leader and totally supportive of her colleagues.

CHRISTOPHER DREW 1965-1973 First teaching post as part-time assistant in the Art Department, becoming full-time in 1969. Appointed Head of Department in 1970. Taught general art and design – developed a screen printing option for senior students. Involved in making sets for 'Hastings' and 'The Venturers'. One of the founders of the Wednesday evening Open Studio programme.

In 1973 he went to teach at Bristol Polytechnic, later the University of the West of England. Remembers a strict uniform policy, and has many funny and happy memories. In the later 1990's he moved to live in France, where he still paints and also tap dances.

He has very kindly donated a generous contribution towards our expenses and many archive items. We are grateful for his encouragement.

JOY EDMANDS (née Bennett) 1961-1989 After teacher training at Derby College, 1958-1961, Mrs Edmands went straight to teach in Hengrove School from 1961 until 1989. She worked in the PE/Games Department with Miss Place, teaching 11-16's and some boys PE. She also taught swimming, using Jubilee swimming baths in Knowle on alternate weeks. She encouraged pupils to play hockey at club level and remembers inter-school athletics which were held at Greenway North track. She has happy memories of YHA trips with Bob Swift and Mr Richardson. On a trip to Chepstow they temporarily lost a few pupils and one got his foot stuck in a rabbit hole. She also remembers trips to Wareham camp.

She was also involved with the Bristol Central Swimming Club in the evenings. She took early retirement from Hengrove School in 1989 and became Area Examiner for the Royal Life Saving Society. This involved travelling into Dorset, Wiltshire, South Gloucestershire, Somerset and across Bristol examining the Pool Lifeguards. She finally retired in 2004. A former colleague remembers she was recognised nationally as an expert in Life Saving.

JOHN EVANS 1963-1966 Taught English to Middle School and Sixth Form. He was at Hengrove School in the middle of his teaching career, previously at Falmouth Grammar School, Priory School Shrewsbury, and a Bolton school.

He has many happy memories. He co-operated with a "very gifted music man in producing concerts, etc., and programme selling". Remembers some impressive 'A' Level results and University entrants.

His happiest school years were at Hengrove – fond memories of lunch times and sandwiches in the staff room with close friends Bill Cork, Fred Buckland, Rid Hollely and others – staff friendly and helpful. All pupils, from the least academic to the Sixth Form, were pleasant to deal with.

After Hengrove he went on to headships at two inaugural comprehensive schools at Presteigne (John Beddoes), and Hurst School in Hampshire.

WILLIAM (BILL) FLETCHER 1954-1986 Taught Latin and Modern Languages at Hengrove School from 1954 until his retirement in 1986. It was his second teaching post: his first, from 1948-1954 was at Barnsley Holgate Grammar School. He was a graduate of Sheffield University, BA Hons French.

During the 1950's he co-wrote a textbook widely used for teaching French – below is a copy of the cover and first page of the 1970's edition, donated to the archive by his sons.

At Hengrove he was Head of the Language Department and in 1961

became Senior Master. On the retirement of Miss Martin in 1963 he became Deputy Head – then in 1972 the First Deputy Head (there were three).

We have a photograph donated by his sons, taken probably near his retirement in 1986 on the school field.

He was remembered by many pupils as a disciplinarian. One former pupil who was bullied by a group of older boys remembers that Mr Fletcher sorted it all out over a period of months. He says "No-one was sure what went on in Mr Fletcher's office, but the thoughts of it struck terror into most pupils."

He used to sweep along the corridors, his academic gown flying out behind him – sometimes catching it on door handles! One former pupil named him 'Batman Fletcher'. If pupils were seen running he would shout loudly down the length of the corridor.

However, he also had a warm and softer caring side. Derek Marsh sent in a touching tribute:-

> " .... Mr Fletcher used to sweep through the corridors in his black gown, striking fear into everyone who saw him. I remember being on the wrong side of him many times and having to wait outside his office to be punished. Many years later I was waiting for my wife who was working in the school. I saw Mr Fletcher and told him about the exams I had recently taken and passed, and he was so pleased. 'You must have had something we missed' he said. I really was so thrilled that he sent me a letter. I treasure that letter. I never forgot what Mr Fletcher did for me that day, which is why to honour his memory I attended his funeral at St Mary Redcliffe Church, Bristol."

Mr Fletcher retired in summer 1986. Sadly he died soon after in September 1986. There was a family funeral service in St Mary Redcliffe Church and the school held their own Thanksgiving Service for his life at Christ Church, Hengrove, in November 1986.

We hold a copy of the Order of Service in the school archive collection. The cover is reproduced here.

We also have a booklet of the Bible readings, prayers and poems used during the service, including the poem "Ode to Fletch". See below:-

BILL   FLETCHER

Hengrove School

1954 - 1986

Christchurch
28th November 1986, 7.30 p.m.

ODE TO FLETCH

```
They sought him here, they sought him there,
They sought Bill Fletcher everywhere;
They came from near and from afar
To shake the hand of Hengrove's "star":
To teachers old and students green
A father to them all he'd been;
For pupils, parents, and the rest,
He led the way and showed what's best.

For more than thirty years he'd been
A poignant figure on the scene:
His biting wit and dulcet roar
Long echoed down the corridor:
He frowned, he barked commandments brief,
He even smiled through gritted teeth:
In thirty years what had he done
To warrant praise from everyone?

There's 'Fletcher's Road' and 'Fletcher's Gate'
Immortalising "Bill the Great":
"Dogs keep out" or they'd leave here
With Fletcher's boot behind their rear:
But if you smoked he had his say
And smokers suffered every day:
They say there's none so virtuous
As he who "kicked it" without fuss.

"What's your problem, son?" he'd laugh,
"Are you in trouble with the staff?"
"O me miserum!" came the moan
As tales of deadly deeds sank home:
His way with pupils must be seen
As gentle, caring, ever-keen;
He soothed their woes with patience rare;
Some he suspended with a glare.
```

```
We miss this effervescent chap
Who's character still leaves a gap;
For Fletcher was, throughout his rule,
The corner-stone of Hengrove School:
Ad infinitum we'll recall
Our treasured mem'ries of it all:
Though years will pass, there's none will claim,
"Who was that man? - Bill ... what's his name?"
```

He was remembered so fondly by pupils and staff that a commemorative wooden bench was commissioned and placed in the main entrance foyer. This was 'rescued' by Miss Place and the caretaker when the school building was demolished in 2011.

It is now in the safe keeping of his sons – see photos below.

Miss Place with Alistair Fletcher

William Fletcher and the commemorative bench

GEORGE FOOTE 1950's He taught PE with Mr Miller in the early days of the school. He left to do National Service and returned to resume his teaching career. He then left to return home to the island of Guernsey, to a primary school headship and later became Director of Education.

DON FOSTER 1975 Formerly a science teacher, he was appointed by Mr Waterhouse to a National Development Project in 1975, based in Bristol.

Because he had no comprehensive school experience, he was seconded to Hengrove School under the wing of Mr Nussbaum and Mr Swift. From 1981 – 1989 he was an Avon County Council Councillor and served as Chair of the Education Committee. In 1992 he moved into Politics at a national level and was elected Liberal Democrat MP for Bath. He became a spokesman on education from 1992 – 1999. In 2012 he was appointed Parliamentary Under Secretary of State for at the Department for Communities and Local Government.

Despite his heavy parliamentary and constituency duties he made time to write a foreword for this book, for which we are very grateful.

JEAN GITSHAM 1954 – 1989 Jean provided the school meals for the staff and pupils of Hengrove School for 35 years, from the day the school opened. She was highly regarded and Dr Perry attended her retirement party in 1989 – 25 years after his own retirement.

Cook, Jean Gitsham toasting her retirement at Hengrove School. Colin Gitsham standing

KEITH GOLDTHORPE 1967-1972 Head of Biology

"I taught at Hengrove for five years, until early 1972, after being appointed by Mr Waterhouse from Chippenham Grammar School to be Head of Biology within a strong science department. He was very good to me; I was greatly impressed by and grateful for his interest. In my eyes he was an excellent headmaster and I valued his enthusiasm and support in the development of my department. When appointed I was 'green and keen' – he recognised this and helped me enormously. I was made to feel part of an excellent team, which raised the reputation of the school to considerable heights."

BOB GREEN 1954-1960 He was the Head of Science and Deputy Head from 1954 when the school opened until 1960 when he retired. He came to Hengrove from St George Grammar School where he served from 1931 to 1954.

One former pupil remembers going with the school choir to sing at his funeral in Redland Parish Church in the early 1960's.

On his retirement he had been presented with an album of photos of his Hengrove School colleagues taken by Mr Jackman. This was passed to Dr Perry after he died and is now in the possession of his daughter. She has generously donated the album to the Hengrove School History Project team. It will be placed in the school archive at the City Records Office.

Mr Green was featured in the 1956 Evening Post article about the school – see chapter 2.

GEOFFREY HALE 1954-1992. Former colleague, Mr John remembers:

"Geoff was Welsh, and proud of the fact. Born 1926 in Merthyr Vale in the Vale of Glamorgan, he attended a local Primary School from where he gained a place at Mountain Ash Grammar School. He then spent a year gaining further qualifications at Engineering School of Mines in Pontypridd before receiving his call-up papers. This was towards the end of the Second World War and Geoff was to spend the next three and a half years in the army as a member of the Royal Signals Corps.

He gained a place at Loughborough College, which was at the pinnacle of the league table of colleges specialising in the training of teachers of Technical Studies. During his three years there he learned the craft of the classroom teacher and refined his skills as a craftsman in wood and metal.

Geoff's first teaching post was at Sale Grammar School for Boys in Cheshire. During his third year there, he read the advertisement for the post of Head of Technical Studies Department for a soon to be opened Hengrove School. Hengrove and Lockleaze Schools were the fore-runners of a new comprehensive education system and the post offered a new and exciting challenges for a young and ambitious teacher. Geoff was duly appointed and served there until his retirement in 1992.

Geoff's early years at Hengrove were busy ones, establishing his department and increasing his staff there as the school grew. Indeed, in 1958, the second stage of the building programme was completed and the department allotted its own wing.

Geoff was heavily involved with extra-curricular activities of the school.

As a teacher of Technical Studies he was, of course, first on call to help construct scenery for various theatrical productions and house plays, and, as in all things Geoff gave freely of his time. As a student he had become interested in archery He studied the art of bow making, and, using his skills as a fine craftsman, constructed his own laminated bow. He used this to quite some considerable effect and success in both local and county competitions, becoming Gloucester champion. He passed this expertise on to Hengrove School pupils studying for their Duke of Edinburgh Award.

His terpsichorean skills were also put to good use. Bob Swift had formed the Dancing Club and Geoff helped out, teaching ballroom dancing and organising the end of term dances. Colleagues remember what a dashing figure Geoff cut on these occasions sporting a dinner jacket and black bow tie.

Geoff helped too on school trips, travelling to places as diverse as Switzerland and Butlins, Minehead. He was a keen supporter of the Theatre-Goers Club and perhaps more importantly, organised Career Fairs for the leavers, inviting representatives of local commerce and industry to the school.

This was an extension of his work of that of Head of Year, guiding that group of pupils through their stay at the school and helping them in their preparations for employment or Further and Higher Education. In his role as Head of Department, he was as helpful and supportive to the members of staff on his team as he was to the pupils in his charge. In his latter years, as a Senior Teacher, he was given responsibility of maintaining staffing levels on a day to day basis, ensuring there was always cover in the classrooms of absent members of staff. It was a role he thoroughly enjoyed and he brought to it his usual good-humour, enthusiasm and excellent organisational skills, undiminished after over forty years at the 'chalk-face'.

Former colleagues, Mr and Mrs Prowles recall:

"We saw Geoff as one of the bulwarks of the school: Someone you could rely on for sound common sense, who would support you, who had clear ideas and was willing to express them cogently. His ex-pupils will owe him a debt of gratitude for skills taught and examinations passed."

Mr Hale was very interested in the Hengrove School History Project. He and his wife generously spent time recalling many memories and donated photographs. Some have been incorporated in this book and some have been placed in the archive. We are grateful for that encouragement and interest. Sadly he did not live to see the book published. He died in February 2013. His funeral was attended by many ex-pupils and colleagues - he had made a lasting impression on them. Indeed we former pupils owe him a debt of gratitude for all he taught us.

PETER F HAYDON 1962-1980 Taught Woodwork, Metal Work & Technical Drawing with Mr Hale and Mr Hanham.

He went from school to the Royal Air Force until 1951, where he was an instructor. He then took a teacher training course, moved to Bristol in 1953 and taught at Wick Road Boys' Senior School. In 1962 he moved to Hengrove School. He was active outside the classroom – he ran the brass band and was involved in cricket and football. He retired in 1980 but did not put his feet up. He continued to play with the Bristol Victoria (Silver) Brass Band and organised reunions for RAF colleagues. He died in 1996 aged 75 years.

FRANCIS HAYDON (Wife of the above) She taught Needlework & Home Economics at Hartcliffe School, then Hengrove School until 1971/2. She and her husband were very involved in the 'Hastings' production, Mrs Haydon making the costumes.

GRAHAM HOBBS September 1970-1992 Recruited to co-ordinate the courses developed for the ROSLA pupils (Raising of the school leaving age from fifteen to sixteen). This change, scheduled for 1970, did not take effect until 1972, although many pupils were already staying on beyond age 15 years. Mr Hobbs came to Hengrove from Whitecross School in Hereford.

He encouraged his 4th form class to become involved with the local community and made contact with Hengrove Community Association in Fortfield Road, organising parties for pensioners and visiting them at home to help with shopping and gardening. This was so successful, it was extended to the Sturminster Road Community Association area.

He has many positive memories of all his colleagues – too many to recount here but available to read in the school archive in the City Record Office. He writes:

"One important aspect of life at Hengrove School was team work, pulling together to create a 'community school' before that expression was in common parlance. Pupils, teachers, office staff, dinner ladies, laboratory technicians, caretakers, parents and their partners all pulling together.

I was immensely privileged to work at Hengrove School with so many very talented hard working colleagues."

He has been very encouraging of the project and we are very grateful for his donation.

DOUG JACKMAN ? – 1974 Spent the majority of his teaching career at Hengrove School, teaching Geography up to 'A' Level standard. A Yorkshireman who graduated from Birmingham University after the war, he became Head of Geography. He frequently took pupils away on field trips – one particularly wet and windy trip was to Lundy Island. One pupil remembers he was:

"a stimulating teacher with a wicked sense of humour. He drew fantastic geometric maps of the world".

He is remembered by pupils mainly for his motor bikes and his photography.

"He drove to school on a Panther motor cycle combination from Timsbury".

Another former student remembers his collection of old motor cycles. Others remember, in the Sixth form, going to his house in Timsbury for tea and a conducted walk in the local area. Mike Leigh, a member of this History Project team, says that it was Mr Jackman who first interested him in photography – which remains his hobby and passion today.

We have an album of Mr Jackman's photos of his colleagues, donated by Dr Perry's daughter. It is available to view in the school archive collection at the City Record Office. He also produced an album of photos of pupils and the 1968 extensions, which was presented to Mr Waterhouse on his retirement in 1974. Copies are in the archive (see also Chapter 3). Mr Jackman died in 2004 aged 82 years. Opposite is an extract from the Somerset Guardian.

DAVID JOHN 1964-1996 He joined the staff of Hengrove School in September 1964. He was one of the first appointments of Mr Philip Waterhouse.

The Head of the Technical Studies Department was Mr Geoffrey Hale. He became his mentor and a wise counsel in his early years of teaching and a firm friend ever since. The abiding memory of his time at Hengrove is of the warmth, friendliness and helpfulness of the staff.

He taught Woodwork and Technical Drawing. Later he became an assistant to Head of Year, Basil Rogers, and was appointed Head of Year in the early 70s. About that time a new department of Careers and Guidance was formed. He saw the work of the new department as a valuable extension of the pastoral care in which he was involved. He took an extra qualification through the University of Bristol and was subsequently appointed Head of Careers and Guidance, a post which he held until his retirement in 1996.

Life of — Doug Jackman

Village character is lost

CHARACTER: Doug Jackman
Picture submitted

TIMSBURY has lost one of its true characters with the death of retired teacher Doug Jackman.

Up to a year ago Mr Jackman, 82, could be seen riding his bicycle around the village, but he suffered poor health in the last 12 months and spent time at the Laurels Nursing Home, and finally at St Martin's Hospital in Bath, where he died.

Mr Jackman, originally from Yorkshire, attended Birmingham University, where he met his future wife Kate.

The outbreak of the Second World War led to an interruption in his studies, and he volunteered for the RAF.

After training in England and Canada he completed a tour of duty in a Lancaster squadron during the latter part of the war.

At the end of the war he completed his studies and gained a degree, before marrying Kate in 1945.

Mr Jackman spent 25 years of his teaching career at Hengrove Comprehensive School in Bristol.

Teaching was a career for which he was well suited and his ability to get on with school children was a source of great pride to him.

He had a passion for motorbikes and owned more than 50 during his life.

When his sons Robin and Mark were growing up he gave full support to Robin's interest in cycling and Mark's enthusiasm for trials and scrambling.

A true craftsman, he was an expert at woodwork and clockmaking and a proficient photographer.

Mr Jackman is survived by his wife, two sons, five grandchildren and a recently born great-grandson.

Mrs Jackman suffered a severe stroke nine years ago and moved to the Laurels Nursing Home. Until his own illness early this year, her husband visited her there at least twice a day.

Mr Jackman's son Mark said: "Dad was never afraid to speak his mind and did not suffer fools gladly. He was never really at ease with everyday chit-chat and social gatherings.

"Few could argue, however, that he put back into society every bit as much as he had taken out."

The funeral service at Haycombe Crematorium was conducted by the Rev John Potter.

Malcolm Tucker

Extract from Somerset Guardian 25.11.04

We are grateful for his input as a valued member of the Hengrove School History Project Team; also for his donation towards our considerable expenses.

JOAN KELSEY 1974-1979/80 Library assistant, interviewed by Miss Place and Mary Knight, Librarian. Remembers Mr Fletcher well and made many friendships with colleagues.

ALISON MARTIN 1954-1963 A historian who was also Senior Mistress. Students remember she always wore her academic gown; one student describes her as "utterly terrifying". Probably quite a private person – she retired to live in Essex and remained in touch with Miss Place until her death.

BOB MILLER 1955-1966/7 He was in charge of the boys' games and PE and also taught French. We have two versions of his next posting: either he went to Bedminster Down School as Head of Lower School or he went to a school in Nailsea.

GWYN MORGAN 1959-1961 Teaching Geography, English and RE. He also helped with boys' games, Youth Hostel trips, Dance Club, drama and theatre visits. He has very positive memories of his time at Hengrove School. Punishment was not a huge issue, school uniform universal and school assemblies formal and traditional, with Dr Perry begowned. He writes:-

> *"Hengrove School was a happy place to work. There was a real sense of purpose and thrill at being involved in something new and good. The entire staff contributed to the greater life of the school and consequently the children seemed to respond enthusiastically, which made teaching easy and enjoyable. The staff were a happy mix of talent and age, a good proportion under 30 at the start of their careers – but an older element to provide the stable influence that is so essential to any effective school. My short stay was very happy and I made life-long friends with a number of staff and their families."*

Prior to Hengrove, he had taught at Stonehouse County Secondary School in Gloucestershire.

After Hengrove School he taught for five years in the Technical School near Bedminster Bridge. He then became Deputy Head of Whitfield School, then Associate Head of a school in Fishponds. In 1975 he became Head of St George Comprehensive School (formerly St George Grammar School). There he remained until retirement in 1991. He was awarded an OBE in 1984 for his service to education.

ALFRED NUSSBAUM 1950's – 1983 He taught Physics at Hengrove. Several of his former pupils excelled in Physics and went on to study to PhD Level.

We were not aware of his artistic gifts. After retirement he exhibited most years at the Royal West of England Academy. The Wharf Gallery in Tavistock exhibited his collection in September 2011. We reproduce the review opposite.

What a talented man!

MIKE O'CALLAGHAN 1967-1997 His entire teaching career was at Hengrove School. He was a mathematician, and by 1972 had risen to Head of Department. In 1978 he assumed responsibility for the construction of the school timetable – quite a task. In 1981 he became Director of Studies and was Acting Deputy Head from April to December 1988. He was involved in curriculum development from 1989: by the time he retired he had spent some time as Acting Deputy Head (Curriculum). Below is an account of his contribution to the life of the school in his own words:-

THE WHARF GALLERY

ALFRED NUSSBAUM - PAINTINGS - DIASPORA
Monday 26th September to Friday 28th October

Alfred Nussbaum was born into a Jewish family in Poland in 1919 and educated in Austria. Entering the Faculty of Medicine at the University of Vienna in 1937, he spent his free time painting in the studio of a member of the Vienna Kunstakademie.

Forced to leave Austria in 1938, after its annexation by Germany, Alfred lived in Palestine for 10 years. He arrived in the UK as a refugee in 1948. Family members died in Auschwitz and Dachau concentration camps. This had a major impact on his outlook on life, politics and religion, and art work.

Nussbaum qualified as an Art Teacher from the West of England College of Art and taught Art, and later Physics in Bristol.

Retirement from 1983 until his death in 2005 was devoted to painting, exhibiting most years at the West of England Academy and twice at the Royal Academy Summer Exhibition.

Nussbaum's art draws its inspiration from the works of Friedrich Nietzsche, Karl Barth, and Soren Kirkegaard. The tragedy of the Holocaust; the New Testament; Socialism, science and mathematics demonstrate a powerful presence in his work.

This, the first exhibition of his collection, includes work in oils; acrylics; lino and wood cuts; watercolour and line drawings.

"In the early 1970's we ran a 'cultural' evening for Sixth formers every Wednesday evening. Activities relating to Music, Art and Drama were available to those Sixth formers who were interested. I was involved in this, initially running a record session where everyone would bring in their favourite records and play them to the group.

During the 30 years I worked at Hengrove there were a considerable number of changes. I worked under four Head teachers and under (and later with) a number of deputies. Other major changes included the raising of the school leaving age (ROSLA), the introduction of Mixed Ability teaching for the 1st and 2nd years (years 7 and 8 as they are now called). As both these innovations coincided with my promotion to Head of Maths in 1972 they presented enormous challenges. As the school timetabler for 20 years or so, I had to oversee many changes in the structure of the timetable, length of lessons, etc. I also witnessed the change from a Departmental structure to a Faculty structure.

In my early days the use of the cane was still allowed. This could only be administered by senior members of staff and had to be witnessed by another member of staff and recorded in a punishment book. This was soon abolished, however, to be replaced by less draconian punishments such as detention. Later (I cannot remember when) a 'sin bin' (known as 'Time Out') was introduced, whereby disruptive students were sent to a special room with work and were supervised by members of staff on a rota basis.

Also in my early days, the girls were not allowed to wear trousers (indeed, it was frowned upon if female members of staff wore trousers). I remember very lively staff meetings devoted to the issue as there was a cultural clash between the younger members of staff and the more traditional older generation. Eventually the younger generation won the day and the wearing of trousers by girls became commonplace in the 1980's".

BERYL OLIVER Head of Home Economics from mid 1960's – 1972. She married Baron Davies of Llandinem and lives in a stately home in mid-Wales where she is engaged in many good works including being patron of the Welsh National Opera.

REGINALD (RUPERT) PERRY 1954-1964 Headmaster of Hengrove School – his final post before retirement.

We have tracked down Dr Perry's daughter. She has generously donated many archive items and has been very encouraging of the project. She writes:-

"Reginald (Rupert) Perry was born in 1903. His parents had died by the time he was five and he was brought up by his mother's widowed sister. He grew up in Gloucestershire with a deep love of the countryside and the history of the area. He attended a small village school from the age of four, then the local primary school, from where he won a scholarship to Thornbury Grammar School. He won a State Scholarship and, although he gained a place at Fitzwilliam College, Cambridge, he went to Bristol University where he was awarded a First Class Honours degree in History.

After his first degree he trained as a teacher of History in the Department of Education at Bristol University and did his teacher training practice at Monkton Coombe School, near Bath. His first teaching post was at Fleetwood Grammar School, Lancashire, after which he took up a post at Ardingly College in Sussex."

We have a picture opposite of Ardingly College from 'Ardingly 1858-1946 A History of the School' by R Perry, showing handsome buildings set within extensive grounds in a rural setting.

Further research has revealed that Mr Perry became Assistant Master at Ardingly in January 1926 and married in 1930.

In 1932 he was awarded an MA in Education by Bristol University. The topic of his MA dissertation was 'The Life and work of Nathaniel Woodard with special reference to the influence of the Oxford Movement on English education'. The dissertation is stored in the History Archive at Bristol University.

A Statement of Experience as a Teacher was submitted with his dissertation. It

Ardingly College

describes his life as a teacher in a boys' boarding school from 1926 to 1934 and makes very interesting reading.

The Archivist of Ardingly College has extracted a small article from the 1934 school magazine.

"Mr Perry, who has been with us nearly nine years, leaves to take up an important post in a Bristol school, where he will have more opportunity for senior work. He will be missed by those who have enjoyed his teaching of History, and also by the Junior House, to which he was attached and in whose various activities he took a leading part."

Ardingly College still flourishes today, now catering for both boys and girls aged 13 to 18 years, with 50% boarders. Of the 490 pupils, 15% are non-nationals, representing 25 nationalities. The ethos of the school remains the same – being a member of the Woodard Corporation founded to teach the Christian faith, but accepting students of all religions and none.

The Bristol Years 1937-1954

Dr Perry's daughter writes:-

"By 1937 my parents had moved to Downend, near Bristol, and my father became Senior Master at St George Grammar School in east Bristol. A colleague here was Bob Green, a chemist, who became one of the two Deputy Heads at Hengrove when it opened. War broke out in September 1939 and life became increasingly difficult. My father was in charge of the school, as the Headmaster, Dr Baldwin, was away in the army. Father was an officer in the ATC (Air Training Corps) and we

Dr Perry was also busy outside of the school. In 1938 he started teaching Bristol University Extra-Mural classes on Local History, continuing until the 1970's/early 1980's.

In 1945 he published an article, 'The Gloucestershire Woollen Industry 1100-1690', in Volume 66 of the journal 'Transactions of the Bristol and Gloucestershire Archaeological Society'.

It was during this phase of his teaching career, in 1947, that Mr Perry gained a doctorate from London University with a thesis on the Gloucestershire Woollen Industry.

In 1951 the Old Ardinians Society asked Dr Perry to write a history of Ardingly School – 1858-1946. A copy of this book is held in the Special Collections Library of Bristol University and we reproduce the first pages opposite.

In the preface he wrote:

"It has been a privilege to write the story of the school in which I spent some happy years as a young master ... and learned from such men as Thomas Wilson (the Headmaster) and others what a school master should do for his pupils, and the spirit in which he should approach his life's work".

He dedicated the book "to the memory of all those Ardinians who gave their lives in two world wars" He remembered with sadness the many whom he had taught, who died in the Second World War."

ARDINGLY

1858—1946

A History of the School

by

R. PERRY

The Old Ardinians Society
25 Whitehall, London, S.W.1
1951.

The Bristol Years at Hengrove School 1954-1964

Dr Perry took up the headship of Hengrove School in September 1954 – Hengrove was one of the first two comprehensive schools in Bristol. His time at the school is described in detail in Chapter 2.

Throughout this period of his life he continued to lecture weekly on History at Bristol University Extra-Mural classes.

In 1955 he wrote an article entitled 'Hengrove School' in the Bristol Teachers Association Bulletin (see Chapter 2).

In Spring 1956 he contributed an article, 'Christian Education in the Secondary Modern School', to the Student Christian Movement Press Journal entitled 'Religion in Education – a Terminal Review', edited by Dr Basil Yeaxlee CBE, MA, BLitt. A copy is held in the British Library. We reproduce Dr Perry's contribution overleaf.

CHRISTIAN EDUCATION IN THE SECONDARY MODERN SCHOOL

by Dr. R. Perry

Headmaster, Hengrove Comprehensive School, Bristol

THE Secondary Modern School reflects the religious and social attitudes of the district from which its pupils are drawn. Some schools serve old-established suburbs in which religious influences are strong, some stand in housing estates where there is much material prosperity but a general indifference to religion, and yet others in slum areas where children are from an early age exposed to evil. Each district has its own advantages or special problems, and these are so varied that a classification of Modern schools has little value. The work of Christian education may accordingly be comparatively easy or extremely difficult. These widely differing backgrounds affect every aspect of the work of the Modern schools, and, I think, account for the wide divergence of views expressed at any meeting of teachers concerned with them.

In one Secondary Modern School in an urban district in which the Established and Free Churches had long exercised great influence, I found that seventy-five per cent of the children attended services or Sunday schools, though not all attended regularly or continuously throughout childhood. A high proportion belonged to church youth organisations. In this school one rarely encountered complete ignorance of religion, and never contempt or hostility. In another school in the same city, too many children came from homes which were materially and spiritually bad. Here juvenile delinquency was common, and few children had any link with the churches. Some of these boys, though they lived within a mile of the cathedral, did not know it by that name and had no idea of its function.

In such a district the Christian teacher will find his work hard and discouraging. We are not all faced with such great diffi-

45

culties and we need not feel too pessimistic about our task. Of one thousand Secondary Modern children of about fifteen years old who attended schools in West Country towns and cities and who were recently questioned about their religion only sixty-nine said that they disliked religion and 177 expressed disbelief in God. Nearly seven hundred agreed that people needed religion to help them live. Some may be shocked to find that eighteen per cent of a large group of adolescents professed a lack of belief; others will be encouraged by the fact that the proportion was no higher. In many schools in this area, at least, there exist the conditions favourable to success.

The intelligence of the top "stream" of children in Secondary Modern Schools also varies according to the district. It will be in part determined by the social level of the local inhabitants, and partly by the proportion of children placed in Grammar Schools. In some cities this proportion is so high that almost all children in the Modern Schools are below average intelligence; in other places the "A" streams may consist of children capable of preparation for the General Certificate of Education, or who are at any rate not much below that intellectual level.

It is often said that the difference between Modern and Grammar School pupils is one of degree, not of kind. But in many fields the difference of degree is so great that problems of content, method and treatment of the curriculum are as great as if the difference were one of kind. The Christian education of the more intelligent pupils of the Modern School presents only the normal problems, especially as these children are usually drawn from the "good" homes. It is with the remainder, numbering perhaps two-thirds of the pupils of many schools, that we meet with our chief difficulties. These children, whilst most susceptible to emotional appeal, are not capable of abstract thought, nor are they able or willing to follow a long reasoned argument to its conclusion—an important difference between the best "Grammar" and the Modern pupils.

Again, boys and girls leave the Modern School at the age of fifteen, before most of them have begun to think seriously about religion. This is particularly true of boys. Many of them are astonishingly immature at this age, and we have to bear this in mind when planning a course of study for them. Yet, because they are leaving school, we tend to expect a greater mental and social maturity from them than we do from Grammar School pupils of the same age. In fact, however, we can only hope to lay foundations which will be helpful to development in the important years that immediately follow departure from school. This applies to the work of the teacher who tries to foster a love of literature or pride in craftsmanship, just as it applies to the teacher of religion.

Partly because they are young, Secondary Modern boys and girls tend to be inarticulate, shy and reserved, and do not readily discuss with adults their social and moral codes. The teacher has to win their confidence, and must show considerable skill in persuading them to bring their ideas out into the light for examination. In doing this he must be very tactful, for many of his pupils come from homes in which the critical discussion of another person's views is considered to be offensive. But this must be done. If it is not, pupils will passively accept, for the purpose of the lesson, religious and moral ideas put forward by the teacher and will remain completely unaffected by them. Many teachers will say that this attitude is not uncommon in the Grammar School. This is true, but many children in the Modern Schools come from an environment of which their teachers have had no first-hand experience. The kind of family life, the code of the neighbourhood, the rules of the gang, are as unfamiliar to the teacher who has himself passed from Grammar School to University or Training College as are the taboos of a primitive African society. Each Secondary Modern School presents its own problems of this kind, and the teacher's first task is to know and understand the social and religious background of his pupils.

It is the task of all secondary schools to educate children within an active Christian community; this is not an aim restricted to Church of England or other voluntary schools. Since there must be a daily act of worship, and since religious instruction is a part of the school curriculum, the headmaster who does not seek to make his school a Christian society is guilty of inconsistency, and his staff and many of his pupils will come to realise this.

If he tries to do his duty, the headmaster will be faced with the difficulty that some members of his staff do not accept the Christian faith. He is not, however, likely to find himself without support, and if he serves a Local Education Authority which allows its head teachers a voice in the selection and appointment of staff, he will be able to make sure that adequate help is available.

The children of the Modern School especially learn by example. It has often been said that religion is "better caught than taught". Uncritical acceptance of this dictum may lead to the neglect of positive teaching and to an undue reliance upon the ability of children to perceive what is not pointed out to them. It is certainly the duty of a headmaster not merely to administer his school according to Christian principles, but to make it clear to his pupils that he is doing so, and to explain these principles to them.

I once taught under a headmaster whose actions were always firmly based upon the Christian ethic, but he was so reserved about his beliefs that his pupils, and, for that matter, his staff, never realised this, and something of importance was lost. We are rarely diffident or self-conscious about explaining the merits of our own subject, if it happens to be history or science or mathematics, and we must not be more reticent about religion. It is not sufficient that Christian principles should guide us; they must be seen to guide us.

It is in the daily service that the Christian basis of the life of the school can best be made plain to children. The great events of the Christian year, the achievements and the disasters of the modern world, the joys and sorrows of everyday life should all be reflected in this service. It can be a formality, or it can do much to determine the atmosphere of the school. In one district, it will be for the children their only experience of organised worship; in another school, the participants will always be comparing it with the beauty and dignity of the church services they attend. In either instance the need for the highest standards is apparent.

There are still many Modern Schools in which it is almost impossible to rise above the conditions. For several years I conducted morning service in an uninspiring hall which was used every day as a gymnasium and dining-room; this was in a school built during the nineteen-thirties which in other ways was excellent. Five hundred boys were packed into this confined space. Since they could not sit, the service could not well last for more than ten minutes. Communal worship could mean little to them, but I found that many boys enjoyed a simple class-room service, and when on some special occasion we walked a mile and a half to the parish church, their enthusiasm made the service one to be remembered. In many schools the conditions are far worse than those I endured for so long, but there are headmasters who can rise above them.

Good music in a school can do much to make the morning service effective and enjoyable, but in a Modern School one cannot always be sure of getting the right kind of music teacher. But where children have been helped to feel the joy of singing together, where there is a school orchestra and a hall with ample room, it is easy. Fortunately, every year now adds to the number of Modern Schools with facilities of this kind.

One must not exaggerate the effect of a good service upon children. Their capacity for unthinking participation in the routine of the day must always be reckoned with, and the task of keeping the service alive will tax the resources of headmaster and staff. Much will pass over children's heads, but I have often been heartened by the discovery that even on Friday some children remember the lesson read on Monday. It is a good thing to introduce the reading by some explanatory remarks which make it clear why that particular passage was chosen for that day, or what its significance should be to them. Readings can be taken from the authorised version of the Bible, or from one of the many modern translations, and these can be varied by passages from English verse and prose. It is so easy to allow the service to take the same course day after day, but this is fatal to understanding and enjoyment.

The headmaster who is seriously concerned with Christian education will always want to take the service himself. In a large school it is his only means of making contact with all his children, and he should obviously make full use of this opportunity to influence the school and to lead its worship. He must, however, encourage his staff to participate, or children may come to think that he alone is concerned with the daily service.

Dr Perry – the Retirement Years 1964-1992

In his 28 years of retirement Dr Perry could indulge his love of history.

His daughter writes:-

> *"My father retired in April 1964, having completed almost ten years as Headmaster of Hengrove School. He returned to Bristol to a dinner to celebrate the 25th anniversary of the school in 1979. He spent his retirement in Wotton-under-Edge, near his childhood home, where he had lectured for the WEA during the war and had made friends. He travelled extensively in France during the early part of his retirement and had a deep love of French literature, history and art. He continued to lecture on local history and France for the Extra-Mural department of Bristol University at the Folk House until his eightieth year."*

Further research has revealed that he became the President of the Historical Society in Wotton-under-Edge. He became Chair of Governors of Katherine, Lady Berkeley's School, which became a comprehensive school in 1973.

In 1975 he could not resist joining in the debate on the current 'Black Papers' and wrote a letter to The Times, reproduced here.

In 1979 he returned to Bristol to attend the 25th Anniversary celebrations of Hengrove School. We have photographs in the archive.

We come now to the 1980's. In the first half of this decade Dr Perry finally retired from his Extra-Mural lecturing!

In 1983 at the age of 80 years he published a booklet, 'A History of the Church of St Mary the Virgin and the Parish of Wotton-under-Edge'. This was followed in 1986 by a book of 193 pages entitled 'Wotton-under-Edge, Times Past, Times Present'. We have a copy in the school archive for all to see in the City Records Office. In 1988 he published a book of 116 pages, 'Edward the Second – Suddenly at Berkeley'. We have a copy in the archive which was kindly donated by Dr Perry's daughter.

From Dr R. Perry

Sir, The Black Paper suggestion that unwilling learners should be allowed to leave school at 14 to seek "apprenticeships or work" may seem at first sight an easy solution to the problem of discipline in our schools. It is not, however, likely to be successful in practice.

Apprentices nowadays are expected to continue their studies in technical colleges, and even when the leaving age was 15 would-be apprentices were usually told to go back to school for another year and to come back when their CSE or GCE results had demonstrated their ability and powers of application.

Unwilling learners are unlikely to pass any reputable examination at 14, or to get an apprenticeship at that age. As for "work", they are the children who drift into teenage unemployment or at best into dead-end jobs.

The suggestion, in fact, looks like a scheme to transfer the problem pupils of schools to the care of an already overworked probation service. One wonders how much the authors of the Black Paper really know about children, though my letter will not tell Dr Rhodes Boyson anything that he does not know

Yours faithfully,
R. PERRY,
formerly Headmaster,
Warren Orchard,
Wotton-under-Edge,
Gloucestershire.

In 1989 he was invited back to Bristol for the retirement party for Mrs Gitsham, who had served on the catering team of the school since 1954 .

Dr Perry's daughter writes:

"He wrote several books in his eighties, all about Gloucestershire, and was still writing, at the time of his death, a shortened version of his PhD thesis on the history of the Gloucestershire woollen industry. We published it after his death. He died in January 1992, 28 years after he retired, and we were touched that three pupils from Hengrove School attended his funeral in Wotton-under-Edge."

He would have been just short of his ninetieth birthday.

Book completes trilogy at last

A TRILOGY by Reginald Perry has now been completed posthumously.

Mr Perry, known to his friends as Rupert, wrote one of the histories of Wotton-under-Edge most consulted by local people: *Wotton-under-Edge, Times Past – Time Present*.

He followed this with *Suddenly, at Berkeley*, a book about the murder of Edward II at Berkeley Castle.

The third book – *The Woollen Industry in Gloucestershire to 1914* – has just been published.

Reginald Perry was awarded a doctorate for research on this subject and this book is an accessible version of the scholarly work, designed for general readers.

It opens with two sentences that encourage further reading: "Gloucestershire of old was famous for the number of its churches, the taste of its cheese and the quality of its cloth.

"The churches were built in the Middle Ages, Double Gloucester Cheese was an eighteenth century creation, while the cloth has a history that reaches back into the days before the county had been given its name."

Mr Perry died in 1992, having lived in Wotton for nearly 30 years following retirement. During his career he had been headteacher of the first comprehensive school in Bristol. He later lectured extensively on West Country history.

Before his death he had virtually completed the first ten chapters of his latest book, and was still working on chapters 11 and 12.

His close friend, Paul Lester, well

● Nind Mill, near Wotton-under-Edge, a book illustration by Vic Jellings

known in Wotton for his work on the Tolsey Clock, helped him with the typing of the manuscript while he was in Berkeley Hospital.

Mr Perry's daughter, Margaret Thorpe, who lives in Shrewsbury, has written the foreword to the book.

She explains the search to find someone to write the conclusion to the book have not been successful and certain mill families have been unavoidably omitted from chapter 11. Chapter 12 does not appear.

However, it is very satisfying to read about the surviving mills in 1914 and make the link with Cam Mills and Strachan Mills in Stroud, which still exist today, the latter producing cloth for billiard tables and tennis balls.

Mr Lester said: "This would make an ideal Christmas present and at last we have achieved publication,

more than ten years after Rupert's death."

The book, priced £6, is available from Cotswold Book Room, Long Street, with maps, old drawings, photographs and illustrations by Vic Jellings.

It is printed by Manor Printing Services, Kingswood, which printed Mr Perry's earlier books.

A copy of his third book, 'The Woollen Industry in Gloucestershire to 1914', has been donated to the school archive by his daughter. The Stroud Gazette carried an article in December 2003 when it was posthumously published (opposite).

We are most grateful to Dr Perry's daughter, Mrs Margaret Thorpe, for all her help and encouragement, for the donation of two books and an album of photographs of the staff in the 1950's, also placed in the archive. Further, we are grateful for her donation towards the costs of printing the book.

OLGA PLACE 1950's-1980's Taught PE & Games at Hengrove School from the early 1950's until her retirement in the early 1980's. Yorkshire born, she spent her early years in Leeds, attending Cockburn High School. We think that Hengrove was her second teaching post.

She gave freely of her time to supervise after-school and sometimes lunchtime practices with hockey and netball teams. Most Saturday mornings there were matches against other Bristol schools. She also organised the Duke of Edinburgh Award Scheme from its inception in 1957. She was invited several times to Duke of Edinburgh Award Scheme presentations of Gold Awards to her pupils. For more details see chapter 5.

Almost all the pupils, boys and girls who responded to our questionnaire, remember Miss Place – mostly for her help and encouragement. She was indeed inspirational, always enthusiastic – she motivated us. One boy remembers her walking around in her grey pleated sports skirt, a bunch of keys and whistle in her hand – urging all to *"be quick"*.

One of her former pupils wrote to the Duke of Edinburgh praising her hard work for the scheme: we have a copy of the reply.

BUCKINGHAM PALACE

From Lieutenant-Commander W. B. Willett, O.B.E., M.V.O., D.S.C., R.N.   3rd May, 1971.

Dear Miss Place,

The Duke of Edinburgh recently received a letter from one of your former pupils praising your work for the Award Scheme.

Prince Philip is pleased to hear that you are giving entrants so much help and encouragement.

Please forgive my secretary signing this letter in my absence.

Yours sincerely,

Sarah Barfoot.

p.p. Lieutenant-Commander Willett.

Another former pupil wrote to Miss Place in 1974, long after leaving school, to thank her for her encouragement in netball.

11.3.74.

Dear Miss Place

You will be surprised to receive a letter from me after so many years. Infact you possibly will not remember me but I felt that I would very much like to write to you and thank you for all the encouragement you gave me at netball. I have just finished playing for the Independance netball team after many super years. Now that I have two lively children and many other commitments plus a stone or two in weight too much I have had to finish. But the friendships I have made through netball are strong and I know will continue for years to come.

So once again, thank you very much.

yours faithfully

Geraldine Coleman (Helps)

She is also remembered regarding policing of the strict school uniform rules. Ruth Hayes writes that:-

"Miss Place insisted we wear our berets, so we wore them pinned vertically on the back of our beehive hairdos with lots of hair clips – they couldn't be seen from the front. On one occasion she kept all the girls behind after assembly to complain that some girls had been seen sunbathing 'in no uncertain manner' on the school field during break: some of us didn't know exactly what she meant!"

342

Another girl remembers being sent home when in the Sixth form for wearing a white skirt – not an agreed colour. Indeed a former younger member of staff also remembers being asked to go home and change into a skirt – she was wearing a trouser suit – not acceptable attire in the early days!

Another former staff member says that:

> *"Olga had a sixth sense about 'incidents' that were happening or about to happen. She always knew who was responsible and always got a confession."*

Miss Place became Senior Mistress in 1964, when Miss Martin retired, and in 1972 became Second Deputy Head (Mr Fletcher being the First Deputy Head).

Her enthusiasm for netball was so great that it spilled over into the national arena. In the 1970's she became a founder member of the English Schools Netball Association (ESNA). Former colleague Sue Bull remembers Olga volunteering Hengrove School as the venue for the first ever English Schools Netball Assocation tournament.

> *"The whole school was involved. Pupils and parents offered accommodation to participants from all over the country. Staff accommodated visiting staff and took on other responsibilities, and the school cooks provided refreshments. The existing netball courts were resurfaced and new ones laid. A massive effort by the whole school."*

Miss Place retired in the early 1980's. We have a photo below of her retirement party with the former Headmaster Dr Perry, Mr Waterhouse and the then current Headmaster, Mr Bird.

After retirement Miss Place did not put her feet up. We have a cutting from a Keynsham or Bath Evening Newspaper dated probably 1991: "Decade in Bath leaves a mark". Miss Place had initiated the annual ESNA trials in Bath, which continued for ten years – a huge event to organise.

Decade in Bath leaves a mark

Words by David Thorpe
Photos by Will Nicol

NETBALL'S love affair with Bath came reluctantly to an end at the weekend when 128 young hopefuls attempted to prove that they have what it takes to make the quantum leap from the school gym to the international arena.

For the past ten years Bath played host to the English Schools Netball Association trials every December. But from next year the annual fixture will be moved to a new purpose-built arena in Sheffield – a legacy of this year's World Student Games.

"The decision is in no way a criticism of Bath because we have always been made very welcome here," said Pam Telford, one of the selectors faced with the task of reducing 128 candidates to two squads of ten on the strength of a weekend of seemingly ceaseless matches.

"In fact most of the officials are secretly upset because they are very fond of coming to Bath just before Christmas. But the rates and the facilities we have been offered in Sheffield have simply made it too good for us to refuse."

Nobody was sorrier than ESNA founder member Olga Place from Keynsham, who during her reign as the Association's treasurer was responsible for the trials coming to Bath in the first place.

"It is sad in a way," said Olga. "But we've had a good run — and we've seen the game develop into something very different from how it was when the ESNA started in 1976."

Anyone dropping in on the trials would instantly have seen what Olga meant. Though netball has yet to break through in terms of media coverage the very thought that it is to basketball what rounders is to baseball can be instantly dismissed by the briefest peek at the dexterity and speed of even the up-and-coming stars.

"The game is much faster than it was 20 years ago," declared Chris Maylor, a former international who embodies the new direction of the sport in her post as netball's first full-time development officer.

"One of the biggest advances is that the Sports Council now takes more notice and are backing efforts to get better facilities. There have also been more tours to the other side of the world which has provided our players with the opportunity to see a different style of game."

Pam Barham, a former coach of current world champions Australia who is in Britain as a guest of the ESNA, might have been expected to have mixed emotions as she watched the tangible signs of a possible future challenge to the apparently unbreakable Antipodean dynasty.

"I've been impressed," she said. "And I'm certain that England will be a major force by the time the world championships comes to Birmingham in 1995."

■ Friends and rivals: former England player Chris Maylor (left) with former Australia coach Pam Barham (right) and Keynsham's Olga Place, whose initiative took the trials to Bath.

■ In charge: England coach Mary Beardwood keeps a progress check.

■ Now listen carefully: trial organiser Pam Telford issues the next set of team line-ups to 128 would-be internationals.

Miss Place remained active until her death in May 2011 – just one month short of her 90th birthday. Indeed in January 2011 she hosted the inaugural meeting of the Hengrove School History Project in her home, plied us with coffee and cakes and, as always, was helpful and encouraging.

Her funeral was attended by many ex-colleagues and ex-pupils from as far away as Cornwall. One could sense the huge respect we all had for this very special lady.

The nephew of Olive (Olga's life-long friend) described her as energetic, interested in everything, never did anything by halves, loved caravanning in Scotland and the Yorkshire Dales, and loved dogs.

The son of her Yorkshire cousin spoke of her "zest for life".

Mr Waterhouse remembered her as a helpful and supportive colleague from his very first day at Hengrove School. She had high standards, could be strict but had a soft heart underneath. She was an action 'fix-it' lady who had become a good friend.

Two members of the national netball fraternity attended the funeral. Below we reproduce extracts from their eulogies which capture what a special person she was. Kathleen Edwards had travelled from Cheshire to recall:-

"Olga was a bright-eyed and lively lady of impeccable manners, mischievous sense of humour, high professional and personal standards and exemplary qualities of 'doing what is right': truly one of 'the old school' who would now be known as 'a legend'. She was inspirational and the world is poorer for her passing. We who knew Olga Place have been lucky, she enriched our lives."

Jo Clements, representing the Nottingham & East Midlands National Association, had also travelled to be at the funeral. Below is an extract from her eulogy:-

"Olga Place – Honorary Life Member of the English Schools Netball Association.

Olga gave long and valuable service to netball and will be well remembered for the tremendous energy and time she gave to the English Schools Netball Association from its inception to its handover to the All England Netball Association.

Olga will be so fondly remembered by many of the netball fraternity and the teaching staff and their schoolgirls throughout the whole of the country. She will be remembered for her incredible organizational skills at the annual schools finals held at various venues across the land and particularly so at the English Schoolgirls Trials in Bath in early December each year. Olga and her dear friend Olive organized the venue, the accommodation and the feeding of everyone throughout the entire weekend.

To so many of us, she was a wise and great friend and much loved."

Indeed we are all better for having known her and it was a great privilege to be taught by her.

SALLY POPE (née ALLEN) 1967-1971 Taught RE to 11 to 16 year olds and was involved in setting up the first GCSEs. The pupil numbers almost doubled to about 1,200 in her time at the school.

She remembers corporal punishment still existed and some teachers had a cane in their rooms! One teacher was known for his use of the 'dap' (gym shoe).

It was the day of the mini-skirt and then midi length, but skirts were supposed to be knee length for girl pupils. Boys had to wear a tie. She herself was once sent home by the Senior Mistress for wearing a trouser suit!

She recalls that school assemblies were daily for the whole school.

> *"Pupils sat on the floor in class lines, with the teacher at the end of the line seated on a chair. Students walked in silence to and from the hall to the accompaniment of a classical piece played on the piano. Assemblies were always Christian based, as was the RE syllabus. There was always at least one hymn, a prayer, a homily and notices and awards."*

She remembers various concerts and two events for charity (disco type evenings), also 'Hastings', a major pageant to celebrate 900 years since William the Conqueror. Her happiest memories are the help received from other staff members especially when settling in, and seeing pupils begin to enjoy Religious Education and relating it to their lives.

On leaving Hengrove School she raised a family and her husband's job took them abroad for a while. On returning to the UK she did some supply teaching in Redcar, Cleveland, in the late 1980's and early 1990's.

DAVID PROWLES 1967-1972 Head of English and Year Tutor. Mr Prowles came from De Burgh County Secondary School (bi-lateral) at Tadworth in Surrey, where he had taught for seven years.

He has submitted a most interesting and lengthy reply to our questionnaire which will be placed in the City's Records Office. Reproduced below are extracts in his own words.

> *"CONTEXT: Anthony Crossland of the then Labour Government had published Circular 10/65 'requesting' Local Education Authorities to move to a comprehensive style of organisation for their secondary schools. The educational press had stories of how Bristol, a relatively small Authority, had grasped this nettle. Bristol, therefore, was the city to work in, so, when a post was advertised at Hengrove School, I applied.*
>
> *Hengrove was about to start on a major building programme to establish a new library/resources centre, a sixth form centre, and teaching areas*

346

for art, music and drama. The school was also about to increase its annual intake to eight forms of entry, with a view to ending up with a total pupil population of about 1400. Not only could I join another growing school, but the job description also contained this totally unknown (to me) year tutor role.

"Before taking up my appointment I came to the school for a day to meet other staff. My predecessor was going to Shropshire, to be Head of a smallish secondary school on the border of Wales, so the omens for my post-Bristol career looked good. Among others I met was Bill Cork, who had been Deputy Head at Maxse Road Secondary Modern School in Bristol. His main role was to establish and run the new library (not a part of my brief, but obviously one of my interests) and he also taught English. He was a vastly more experienced teacher than I: it was essential that we got on together. We did. He helped me understand how Hengrove worked and my wife and I were friends with him and his wife for the rest of their lives. On that day acquaintance was renewed with Bill Fletcher and Olga Place, but my main interest was in those teaching English: Jenny Stewart, Roger Grant, who was later joined on the staff by his wife Christine, who also taught English, Mr Dyke who had been a good hockey player, but soon retired on grounds of ill-health, Fred Buckland, who was Head of Lower School (Years 7 and 8 in the current chronology) and a number of others.

FLASHBACKS – a list, in no particular order, of memories from my time at the school.

- Maurice Bailey, Head of Music, composed and conducted a work for orchestra and voices. I sang in the chorus and remember that, unlike at my previous school, this orchestra had a tuba, played by Paul Stevens. Also playing were Harold Chasey, Head of History, and his son, Bob Chasey, later of various BBC orchestras, Derek Chivers, Head of Chemistry, who made violins as a hobby, and Philip Waterhouse.

- at a parents' evening a mother whose elder son played football for Bristol City responded to my suggestion that academic achievement was crucial to a good career with – 'Ah, but there's gold in them there boots' – true then perhaps, certainly so today.

- a party for the sixth form held outdoors in the new sixth form centre at the end of the summer term (?1970). A considerable number of uninvited male visitors tried to gatecrash. The event and the fabric of the building were saved by Bill Fletcher talking to the intruders and slowly but surely

ushering them off site. After this, such events were held away from the school.

- the noise in the school dining hall was wholly foreign to me. Generously, I might attribute it to the low ceiling rather than pupils shouting to each other.

- being required to wear academic dress for Speech Day, in 1967, was something I have never had to do before or since. My mother had to quickly parcel up a gown and post it to me.

- Philip Waterhouse introduced a management tool which involved departments being assessed each year against a set of stated objectives. The English Department spent some hours discussing the differences between an aim and an objective and then worked out a list that we thought would be acceptable to the Head and that we would be likely to almost achieve. Luckily it was not payment by results.

- trips to performances at the Bristol Old Vic were routine, with pupils making their own way there and back. Soon after I arrived at the school Maggie (now Dame) Smith and Robert Stephens (later knighted) came to the school to talk and demonstrate.

"AFTER HENGROVE

"In July 1971, I was appointed Deputy Principal designate at Queen Mary's Sixth Form College, Basingstoke, which was to open in September 1972. This was to be the eleventh such college to be established in England and was expected to have about 520, mainly 'A' Level, students. It was in March 1972 that I left Hengrove to help with the final planning and preparation for the new college.

"In due course I became Principal at Hill College, Southampton and was seconded from that post in 1989 to an Education Officer position for Hampshire.

"In theory I retired in August 1992. However, I worked on a part-time consultancy basis for Hampshire, Southampton and Portsmouth LEAs for the next fifteen years, had my arm twisted into serving on the Governing Body of a primary school, and chaired the Governing Body of Itchen College for the first five years after it was removed from Local Authority control to become self-governing.

"My interest in the examining of English Language eventually paid off and annually, for a few years, I went to Malaysia on behalf of Cambridge International Examinations.

> *"Now, wholly retired, I enjoy the '3 gs' of that state: golf, gardening and gossip."*

A little sequel to the above, written by Mr Philip Waterhouse:-

> *"David Prowles won a promotion to Deputy Principal of a Hampshire Sixth Form College. A few weeks before he was due to finish at Hengrove, I sent for him and said 'I want you to tell me how I'm doing'.. During the remaining time he prepared a report on his view of the work of the Senior Management team. It proved to be a refreshing and honest document, and we all studied it assiduously. We called it 'The Prowles Report' and often referred to it during our deliberations.*

SHEILA PROWLES (née Jones) 1964-1970 A graduate of Aberystywyth – University of Wales – her first teaching post was at Hengrove School. She taught Geography, Geology and PE. Geography and PE were taught throughout the school, while Geology was taught to pupils in Lower Sixth as a one year GCE 'O' Level course – shared with Ms. Goldthorpe. As well as teaching she helped with PE matches, ran the Badminton Club, sang in choirs and more.

In 1968 she married fellow teacher David Prowles (Head of English).

Below we reproduce some reflections in her own words:-

> *"My only memories of assemblies are that the Junior School met in the Girls' Gym and was presided over by Mr Buckland and Miss Davies; The Senior School met for assembly in the Main Hall.*
>
> *"I organised and ran a number of Geology field trips and sang in choirs at concerts.*
>
> *"There was much fun and support in PE from Joy Edmands – a great deal of guidance and friendship.*
>
> *"Doug Jackman was Head of Geography, the department I was based in. He came in every day on his motor bike and was brilliant with a camera.*
>
> *"I also took great pleasure in the achievements of the pupils I taught. My tutor group came to Hengrove at the same time as I did. Most continued up the school with me until the 5th year (Year 11 in the current jargon), while some were still in my form in the Lower Sixth – in the new Sixth Form Centre. Sadly, however, one of the form was killed in a motor accident during our first year at the school.*
>
> *"I have many happy memories of my time at Hengrove, especially the companionship and friendship with other members of staff: some of those friendships continue to this day."*

JIM PYLE 1950's-1960's Taught English 'O' and 'A' Level. A former pupil recalls "He taught us to think, encouraging philosphical discussions on set books and life in general. He organised social evenings for 6th formers". Another former pupil remembers learning the art of debating.

DENYS RICHARDSON 1958-1964 Mr Richardson came to Hengrove School from a post in Stratford Grammar School, near Manchester.

He taught PE throughout the school and filled in with Geography, History, English, Maths and Craft to various age groups! He ran the Duke of Edinburgh's Award Scheme for the boys – Bronze Award. Out of school hours he was very generous with his time, being involved with soccer, rugby, cricket, athletics, badminton practices and matches. On Saturday mornings there were five rugby teams playing, each with two members of staff.

Stage II building opened as he started at the school, with a gym for the girls freeing up the original gym for exclusive use by the boys. He remembers the best school assemblies were taken by Mr Whitnell – RE teacher and local Methodist preacher.

He helped Bob Swift with many weekend YHA trips, several summer holiday camps at Wareham and one term time camp at Exmouth.

After Hengrove School he went to Hillview Junior School, then to a Headship at Felton Primary followed by a Headship at Banwell Primary.

He has been a great source of information, memories and photographs for Chapter 5 – thank you, Mr Richardson!

CAROLINE RIDING Taught RE from the 1960's to retirement. She married her former tutor at Newton Park College and served the whole of her career at Hengrove School.

RAY ROBERTS 1959-63 Mr Roberts taught Geography with Mr Jackman as his Head of Department.

He also gave generously of his time outside the classroom. He was involved with boys' sports, the Duke of Edinburgh Award Scheme, choir, regular YHA visits to St Briavels and also Austria, and summer camps in Dorset.

Whilst in Bristol he was on the Lord Mayor's 'Freedom from Hunger' campaign committee. He decided he could better serve by actually going to teach in a developing country. We have a 1964 newspaper cutting (opposite).

Having left Hengrove School he went initially to Dar-es-Salaam in Tanganyika – now Tanzania – the story is best told in his own words below:

"In 1962 I applied to a Government Agency for work abroad and was told I would be sent to Nigeria. When my documents arrived I read that I would be going to a Mission school near Dar-es-Salaam in Tanganyika. This is what the press report was about, probably about May/June 1964.

"I came back after a year when we got married and returned to Dar together. We came on leave in December 1964 intending to return to the school, but I received a telegram to say I had been transferred into Government Service and would be posted to Mkwawa High School, Iringa … 400 miles up country! I then worked at Mkwawa for the next six years teaching Geography and, with a colleague from Cardiff, set up an 'A' Level Geology course, the only school to do so in East Africa. So much happened here that it is difficult to say in a few words. There were great opportunities for travel and our old Morris Traveller went all around Tanganyika and parts of Kenya.

"I returned home in January 1971 and got the job as Head of Geography at Devizes School, newly comprehensive and very much in a state of flux. This is where my experiences of four years at Hengrove really paid off. I taught here for twenty years and in 1991 was offered 'a career change opportunity' along with four other Heads of Department when a new Head arrived. I then re-trained to teach English to foreign students which took me at various times to Norway and Murmansk but mainly to the town of Tornio in Finland. It is Devizes' twin town in south Lapland. Having reached a reasonable age I retired from that three years ago but still am very much involved with twinning, having made lots of friends in Lapland.

Mr. John Roberts

GEOGRAPHY TEACHER GIVES UP JOB TO GO TO AFRICA

A young Bristol geography master is sacrificing two years' teaching time at home and postponing his wedding to teach in an African mission college.

He is Mr. John Roberts, minutes secretary of the Lord Mayor of Bristol's Freedom from Hunger Campaign Committee.

At Hengrove Secondary School today, he said:

"I can help a developing country more by going out there and giving my services than staying here and trying to persuade Bristol people to give their money.

EXAMPLE

"I have always tried in my work for the committee to stress the importance of education to the developing countries.

"Now I hope by personal example and sacrifice to practise what I have been preaching."

Mr. Roberts is engaged to Miss Renate Schaffer, a 22-year-old nurse at Bristol Royal Infirmary.

Miss Schaffer has agreed to put off the wedding indefinitely and may eventually join him in East Africa.

The Rev. Penry Davies, minister at Broadmead Baptist Church, has encouraged Mr. Roberts to undertake the work and is acting as one of his sponsors with the Tanganyika Government's appointments board in London.

Mr Roberts greatly encouraged us in the writing of this book and contributed many photos and memories. Sadly he died in February 2013.

BASIL (BAZ) ROGERS 1960-1965 and 1967-1989. Probably the only teacher who served two separate stints at Hengrove School.

After University he served in the RAEC doing National Service and then started teaching at Hengrove School in 1960. His main subject was Mathematics – 11-18 year olds – but he also taught some 11-13 year old Science classes, and later Careers and Social Studies (combined RE, History and Geography) to 11-12 year olds. In 1962 he became second in the Maths Department. He left Hengrove School in July 1965 to teach mainly 'A' Level GCE Maths at Bath Technical College.

In April 1967 he returned to Hengrove School as Head of Maths and Senior Year Tutor. In January 1972 he was appointed Third Deputy Head (Bill Fletcher being First Deputy Head and Olga Place Second Deputy Head).

Here, in his own words, are some of his extra-curricular activities:

"In the early days I was the treasurer of the school dancing club. I was also a bowling coach for some of the school cricket teams. For most of my time at the school I was heavily involved with the Hengrove School Association (mainly parents). Latterly I was the Vice President of the HSA.

"As a member of the school choir (there were about fifteen members of staff in the choir) I took part in school concerts and on one occasion (which embarrassed my wife) I played the euphonium in the band at a concert."

He remembers examination changes – Summers 1961 & 1962 pupils sat for GCEs and UEI; from summer 1963-1967 they sat for GCE or CSE (these merged in 1988 to become GCSE).

He writes further:

"I have many happy memories of Hengrove School. They include the many staff who supported me when I was a new teacher. The staff met socially and I felt that we were real friends. Many of us have kept in touch long after leaving the school. Since leaving the school I have married some pupils, baptised their children, and taken the funerals

He left Hengrove School in 1989, by then he was First Deputy Head.

Since then he has been the Minister of two churches and the Chaplain at two hospitals for adults with learning difficulties. In May 2011 he conducted Olga Place's funeral, in 2012 Mr Waterhouse's funeral and in 2013 Mr Hale's funeral.

He is remembered fondly by his former pupils. The full account of his questionnaire response is deposited in the school archive – including some amusing anecdotes.

ARTHUR SEYMOUR 1954-1957 At the time of writing he is still alive and alert at 96 years of age!

Hengrove School was his third school – he was the Senior Geography teacher. He brought with him prior experience of a Secondary Boys' School in Cambridge and a Grammar School (co-ed) in Pinner, Middlesex. During his National Service (1942-1949) with the RAF he had been trained as a Meteorological Officer and as a Sports Instructor (PE and drill). He was a graduate of Bristol University and had been a scholarship pupil at Fairfield Grammar School.

He remembers being interviewed by Dr Perry and Alderman St John Reade, the Chairman of the Education Committee and a supporter of the bilateral school system. In 1954 he joined the staff of the newly opened bilateral Hengrove School. In addition to overseeing the teaching of Geography he was greatly involved with the boys' sports. He formed the Rugby Club and helped coach cricket and athletics teams. He was also involved with school plays and has vivid memories of a school trip to Switzerland with Miss Martin and Mr & Mrs

Buckland. He and his colleagues had laid the foundations of the new school.

In 1957 he took the Headship of Sefton Park School and in 1961 became Headmaster of Hatters Lane Secondary School for Boys in High Wycombe. There he found the 11+ exams still in place and a huge distinction between grammar and secondary schools. Nevertheless he encouraged his students to take GCE 'O' and 'A' Levels and pioneered technical education and driving classes. He finally retired altogether from teaching in 1977, and returned to live in Bristol.

We thank him for his encouragement with this project and acknowledge with gratitude his donation towards expenses.

ADRIAN SISMAN 1966-1969 Interviewed by Mr Waterhouse and Bob Miller, he became Assistant to Mr Miller in the boys' PE Department, teaching ages 11 to 18 years. In 1967 Mr Miller left and Mr Sisman became Acting Head, January 1967 – July 1967.

He ran boys' sports team's fixtures throughout the school, which took up a lot of time, during which the Under-15 boys' football team won the Woodcock Shield. He can remember the excitement of the new on-site swimming pool.

His enduring memory of his time at Hengrove School was:

> *"… the enjoyment of pupils in courses in my subject and working with a superb and supportive staff as a newly qualified teacher. I have very happy memories and Hengrove was a wonderful start to my teaching career."*

About ten years ago he attended a reunion of his Hengrove Tutor Group – he loaned his photos and memorabilia and sadly they were not returned. Someone out there still has them – would you care to donate them (or copies) to the Hengrove School archive collection?

He left Hengrove School in 1969 to teach PE at Sidcot School, a Quaker school in Somerset. He was Head of PE and remained until 1999. From 1999 to 2005 he was a supply teacher at Sidcot School and Backwell Secondary School. He was an Examination Invigilator from 2004-2009 and is still a Travel Officer for the foreign students who are boarders at Sidcot School.

BOB SWIFT ('SWIFTIE') 1950's until retirement (date unsure). He taught Science but dedicated a great deal of his time to YHA trips and summer camps at Exmouth and Wareham. The YHA trips were held all through the school year. One former pupil has written:

He was a lover of the outdoor life. He took a year out from Hengrove to teach in Australia and had earlier taught for a year in the USA. He was also a very keen ciné photographer – somewhere there are two 16mm films of Hengrove School from day one. We would very much like to locate these for the archive. Do any readers have any idea where these might be?

He also started the Ballroom Dancing Club on Fridays after school, teaching the waltz, quickstep, Valita and other progressive dances, and Cha Cha. At the end of each term there was a 'proper dance' with a band, and the staff wore evening dress. At least one pupil met their future spouse at the school dance.

We have an Evening Post cutting from the Bristol Times section, 24th June 2003, sent in by the widow of John Hazell – 'Remembering Swiftie' – reproduced below. John was one of many pupils to remember Swiftie with great affection. The photo was probably taken in the late 1950's or early 1960's.

Remembering Swiftie

THIS photo is of Bob (Swiftie) Swift, a teacher an Hengrove School in the 60s. It may have been at Swanage or wherever else we went during a camp at Wareham.

John Hazell
(Whitchurch Primary and Hengrove schools),
Valley View,
Clutton,
Bristol.

TEACHER: Bob "Swiftie" Swift

GEOFF THOMAS Taught English. Married a former pupil and became an adviser to Devon County Council and later a senior executive of the county.

355

BERYL TOWNSEND 1967-1994 Initially appointed to work with Mr Cork, the School Librarian, as Library Assistant. They prepared for the new Library/Resources Centre to be built as part of the Stage III development. There is more detail on the Library in Chapter 3. The Library was a very popular venue – an oasis of peace and quiet in a very busy school of 1400 pupils.

When Mr Cork retired in 1975 Mrs Townsend transferred to clerical duties including administering the school fund, which began with four accounts and grew until there was a turnover of £80,000.

She particularly remembers the rich variety of extra-curricular activities available to pupils – windsurfing in the Greek Islands, skiing in the Alps, canoeing in France, camping at Exmouth, theatre trips and more.

She retired in 1994 after 27 happy and eventful years at Hengrove School which saw many changes, not least the introduction of computer technology.

J. TRIVETT 1954-1960 Maths teacher, Very little information but a former pupil recalls:-

> *"we were taught by some fine teachers, but one in particular stands out for me – Mr Trivett was truly ahead of his time in both his teaching methods and the way he treated us".*

The pupil went on to gain a Degree and PhD in Physics.

PHILIP WATERHOUSE 1964-1973 Headmaster of Hengrove School.

Mr Waterhouse was a northerner, born in a Yorkshire mining area in 1924. After primary schooling in Pontefract Road Junior School he passed the 11+ exam to enter Castleford Grammar School. His undergraduate studies at Bristol University (interrupted by a period of National Service in the Second World War) culminated in a BA in Geography in 1947, followed by an MA in 1952.

His first teaching post was at Cotham Grammar School, followed by a post as Head of Department at Wolverhampton Technical High School. In 1954 he moved to a Deputy Headship in one of Wolverhampton's first comprehensive schools – Highfields School.

He then astonished his colleagues by applying for the headship of Wobaston School, a secondary modern school with a bad reputation, in new buildings on the north side of Wolverhampton. He moved there in 1958 and with able and imaginative staff co-operation they turned the school around. In his own words:

> *"I found myself longing to continue my career in the new comprehensive schools. When I saw that there was a vacancy at one of the Bristol comprehensive schools I couldn't resist it. Hengrove School became my professional home for the next ten years."*

In 2012 Mr Waterhouse wrote more about his time at Hengrove School:-

> *"I spent ten happy years at Hengrove, enjoying the support of some wonderful colleagues and some very good officials at the Bristol Education Department. In a personal sense this period was marked by an increasing awareness of the importance of management style in the running of a large secondary school. I gained a reputation for leading the way in this (although present Heads would regard it as commonplace). I was invited to explain our activities to a conference of Bristol Headmasters, and then invited to deliver the keynote lecture at the very first Government-sponsored course on School Management. More invitations followed and a year after I had left Hengrove I was invited to give the keynote lecture at an international conference at Canberra University. Here I was rubbing shoulders with the Principal of London University, the Professor of Education at Tokyo University, and several others from around the world."*

You can read in detail about Mr Waterhouse's nine years and two terms at Hengrove School in Chapter 3.

After Hengrove School 1974-1981

Mr Waterhouse was seconded to become the Director of the Resources for Learning Development Unit (RLDU). Overleaf we have reproduced two newspaper articles of this exciting and innovative research and development project.

Mr Waterhouse described this phase of his career in his own words:-

> *"I left Hengrove at the end of 1973, invited to run a new Government-funded development project. This was concerned with exploring new ways of encouraging the development of more individual styles of learning in the secondary schools. Up to that time there was an assumption that all teaching in secondary schools would be whole-class teaching. There were two main objectives. First was to create a bank of specially designed learning materials suitable for individual use in the first years of the main academic subjects. Second was to experiment with ways of organising individual and small-group work in the classroom."*

Experiment in learning

AVON County has been chosen by the Department of Education as the testing ground for an educational experiment which could improve teaching.

Called the Resources for Learning Development Unit, it is headed by former Hengrove School Head Mr. Philip Waterhouse.

Although the project is still in its formative stages, it is anticipated that by September it should be in full swing.

Basically the idea is to give secondary schoolchildren of different ability levels the chance to work at their own pace, and get away from learning just from text-books.

Choice

Mr. Waterhouse explained: "Teachers are wanting to create more of a workshop atmosphere where people work individually or in small groups according to the nature of the jobs they are working on.

"It is realised this can only be done with a big collection of the right sort of materials available to the children.

"The standard text book just won't do this job.

"Children have to be able to work at their own

pace — they have got to be able to move on to the next stage when they are ready.

"To a certain extent they have to be given a certain amount of choice in the material they are given."

Teachers were finding they were hampered by a lack of the right materials, many of which had to be purpose made, and the teachers themselves had to become involved in the planning and design of them.

"When an individual teacher tries to do this he just can't cope because of the enormous amount of time that is needed.

"So this organisation has been set up to see

to what extent co-operative action by teachers will be able to bring about the desired results.

"The sort of materials we are likely to produce here are, worksheets, small booklets, audio cassettes, film strips and slides and also educational games."

The exercise was aimed at secondary schools.

Staff

The unit is based in former school building in Redcross Street, St. Philip's, now shared as an annexe for the Florence Brown School and South Bristol Technical College.

It was born after exploratory research on resources by the Nuffield Foundation.

At the unit there will be about a dozen staff, teachers who will act as "editors," graphic dsigners and secretarial staff initially the subjects covered will be restricted to English, maths and social studies.

The elected editorial teachers will be working along guidelines laid down by interested teachers

Mr. Philip Waterhouse.

Philip Waterhouse, director of the unit with other members of the team. From the left are Roger Alston, Sandra Maughan, Mr. Waterhouse, Malcolm Lewis and Mike Jennings.

358

Space age in class

IN SCHOOL with ROGER BURTON

SPACE AGE technology and individually tailored material for schools is what the Resources for Learning Development Unit is all about.

And its director, former Hengrove School head Mr. Philip Waterhouse, believes what it produces is going to help schools to save money on equipment.

The unit was set up in former school buildings in Redcross Street, St. Philip's as an Education Department experiment.

Now they have their first "wave" of full-time staff, comprising an English editor, social studies editor, maths editor, graphic designers, a secretary and an assistant director.

Mr. Waterhouse said they had been working with teachers to try to identify the kind of learning materials needed in schools for maths, English and social studies.

Materials produced are being tested by teachers on pupils. To the individual teacher the new system is a great improvement, because it means that he can illustrate his subject clearly, using pictures, sound recordings, or perhaps a booklet as good as any on the market but dealing specifically with the details he wants to cover.

For example, one of the early projects being produced is designed to show the way people used to live in early Britain, and what homes looked like, and how they were built.

Alive

So at the Resources Unit they reconstructed a model house, step by step, taking photographs at various stages while it was being built to give the children a clear idea of how it was made.

The unit deals with all Avon secondary schools. Children of different ages or ability levels can be helped, and the use of machinery turns what

Graphic designer Jane Newman, busy at the Resources for Learning Development Unit in Redcross Street, Bristol. Picture by Chris Selby.

could just be dull individual study into something alive and immediately clear.

Methods being used by the unit vary, but modern sophisticated machinery means the end product is simple to use.

A tape duplicator can produce three reproduction cassette tapes of high quality, at speed from one tape, and that makes it possible to offer them to schools for around 20p.

Cassettes are the perfect answer to young curious fingers, with no tearing, twisting or breaking of the tape.

Another simple plug-in device means that eight children using headphones can listen to the same tape simultaneously, with earphones cutting out the distraction of noise around them.

Bringing together the teacher and the graphic designer means less wastage in buying books which might only partly cover the subject.

Former Lawrence Weston teacher Sylvia Maughan, who now works as maths editor, visits school to see the kind of material they need, and the reception from teachers has been good.

He had a small staff of outstanding young people, including Dawn Primarolo (Secretary) and Don Foster (Science Editor). They quickly acquired a national and international reputation, and produced seven publications and five classroom management packs with a handbook for each subject. Extracts from the 1978 Final Report are available in the school archive collection.

By 1981 the future of RLDU was uncertain and Mr Waterhouse took early retirement from Avon County Council.

Move into the National Arena 1981-1991

On retirement Mr Waterhouse immediately received an invitation from the National Council for Educational Technology (NCET) to run a project with similar objectives on a national scale – the NCET Self Supported Study Project and Survey. This involved lecturing, writing and running courses. In 1983 two teachers' handbooks were published, followed in 1988 by a report entitled "Encounters in Self Supported Study" and a revised teachers' handbook entitled "Self Supported Study: an Introduction for Teachers 1988".

After eight successful years with the NCET Mr Waterhouse left the project to spend the next six months as a Research Associate at Bristol University. He enjoyed the intellectual stimulus and travelled widely, advising and lecturing.

He then decided to go freelance as an educational consultant to local Education Authorities, Universities, Colleges and Schools. This he enjoyed and the work kept coming. Although tempted to continue, he decided to REALLY retire in 1991 aged 67 years.

Retirement 1991-2012

He much enjoyed retirement, describing it as

"so good, a lovely home life, a garden to maintain, a musical hobby to pursue."

His love of music (oboe) led him to membership and in 1993 Chairmanship of the Keynsham Orchestra. Later he formed a small wind group which grew to become the Saltford Workshop Orchestra. Members speak of his "warmth, enthusiasm and magical organisational ability that inspired all who took part".

His continuing links with former staff and pupils proved very helpful to the Hengrove School History Project team. In December 2010 the demolition of the Hengrove School building commenced. This prompted a few former pupils to recognise the urgent necessity to collect an archive of original material, photos, memories and artefacts in order to preserve the memory of the school. Mr Waterhouse grasped the vision, supplied us with lists of contacts and articles of his own memories. He met with us regularly. As an experienced author he was able to advise and guide us and, more importantly, to encourage us. We had hoped he would live to see the completion of the project in the form of a book. This was not to be.

Mr Waterhouse died on 16th April 2012 aged 88 years. His funeral was attended by many former colleagues, pupils and friends in addition to family. Rev Baz Rogers officiating, spoke movingly of his time at Hengrove School:

"I first met Philip on the first day of the summer term 1964 when he began his headship at Hengrove School. That headship lasted until the last day of autumn term 1973 – a period of 9 years and 2 terms which was known as "A Hengrove" because the first headmaster (Dr Perry) had served for exactly the same length of time.

I think I should say at an early stage that I have many reasons to be grateful to Philip because he appointed me both as Head of Mathematics and later a Deputy Head of the school. But many other teachers will remember him with affection for the way in which he advised them with their professional careers.

Many former pupils also remember him with affection because of the way that he treated them firmly but very fairly. He had a wonderful way of leading from the front but also the ability to be friends with his staff and to gain respect from his pupils.

In those early days he taught some geography lessons. But that was not the only time that he was seen outside his office. He took time to move around the school so that when he made decisions he knew what needed strengthening and what needed to be changed.

He took a lot of care to ensure the non-teaching staff felt that their contribution to the school was valuable. He was courteous and polite to those who came into the school to make a complaint. He was always careful that the image of the school in the local community was a very good one.

One of his many successes was to set up the Hengrove School Association. Even the title was important because he wanted to include anybody who wanted to make a contribution to the wellbeing of the school. Thus it was NOT called the Parents' Association or the Friends of Hengrove School. And many of those who helped the school continued their support long after their children had left the school.

He played regularly in the school orchestra and particularly supported those who played the same instrument as he did. And when the school presented "The Venturers" at the Colston Hall in 1973 he not only played in the orchestra but he made possible all the arrangements necessary – including transporting hundreds of staff and pupils in double-decker buses to the Colston Hall for rehearsals. This whole event was to celebrate the 600th anniversary of Bristol gaining county status.

But his interest in the school continued long after he left the school itself. I saw him at many reunions of pupils, and he also acted as the link between former staff for many years. He has attended many funerals of past staff and some former pupils.

We give thanks for the pleasure of knowing him and working with him."

Members of the Resources for Learning Development Unit remember Mr Waterhouse as follows:

"Vigorous, dynamic . . . all who worked with him developed enormous respect and affection for him." (Don Foster MP)

"I didnt know ex-headmasters could be so nice, always smiling and charming, kind to everyone." (Dawn Primarolo MP)

"An inspiration to many in the world of education . . . an exceptional mentor. " (Ian Gathercole)

"Open minded, measured about judgements . . . uncanny ability to see into the future . . . a great educationalist and a great leader." (Roger Alston - now Director of Education in Cumbria)

Mr Waterhouse's son Michael spoke about "Dad". We have placed his eulogy in the school archive but extracts are paraphrased below:-

"The world of teaching and a love of education ran through Dad's life and family. He started school at the age of three years, following the children into the school next door to his home. The teachers grew tired of taking him back home, so it was agreed he would join the Reception Class early! His own mother had been a pupil teacher, then, as a young widow with two small boys, a teacher's assistant, then an unqualified teacher, and eventually granted qualified status.

After marriage and graduation with an MA, Mr Waterhouse and his wife both became teachers, also their two sons, one in a primary school, the other at the Old Vic Theatre School.

So Mr Waterhouse was a pupil, a sailor, a teacher, a headmaster, a director, an author, a gardener and a musician."

Hengrove School had been privileged to have a man of such calibre as Headmaster from 1964 to the end of 1973.

EDWIN (TED) WHITNELL 1958-1981 Taught mainly Religious Education and was very involved with boys' sports, particularly rugby. Became Head of Lower School after Mr Buckland retired. Fondly remembered by many pupils and former staff. One former teacher remembers he *"took the best assemblies."*

He was born in 1920 in Senghenydd, South Wales – a small mining community still recovering from a major pit disaster in which his mother lost her first husband.

He was a very keen Boy Scout and was awarded the prized King Scout Badge (probably King George VI). His parents moved the family to Bristol, where he met his future wife. With the rumbles of impending war he joined the RNVR and then the Royal Navy when war was declared. He sailed in the Atlantic, and visited Canada, New Zealand and Bermuda. He was in the East Coast Flotilla where a fellow officer was Philip Mountbatten. He rose to the rank of Lieutenant.

After the war he enrolled onto a Teacher Training course at Redland College, Bristol, and proceeded to his first teaching post at Portway School. He moved to Hengrove School in 1958.

He featured prominently in the production of 'The Venturers' at the Colston Hall in 1971, taking the part of narrator. Thus he served his pupils in and out of the classroom, and also the wider community as Scout leader, Sunday School teacher at Totterdown Methodist Church, and Lay Preacher for many years.

He retired from Hengrove School at the age of 61 years in 1981. There followed fifteen years of travelling (his son lived in Denmark, his daughter in Canada), enjoying his other daughter and grandchildren living in Bristol, reading, and watching cricket. He died in 1996 after a short illness. His funeral at Totterdown Methodist Church was attended by many ex-colleagues and pupils as well as family and friends.

LEN WOOD 1950's-19 ? Does anyone remember the dates he taught at the school? He was certainly there in 1957. One ex-colleague writes of the early 1970's:

> *"Len Wood was Head of Remedial Education for many years and these pupils had benefited from his patience and skilled teaching. Out of the classroom he ran the very popular Chess Club – even taking the pupils to play against Russian sailors on a Russian ship docked in Portbury Dock."* (see Chapter 5)

Chapter 9
Conclusion

Has reading this book inspired you to make a contribution to the Hengrove School Archive? We do hope so.

To help you marshall your thoughts and memories we reproduce the original questionnaires in Appendices 9 and 10. If you prefer to write your memories in prose form that is quite acceptable. You may send your contribution to the postal or email address at the foot of the questionnaire or take it direct to the City Records Office to be placed in the Hengrove School file (ref 21131/SC/Heg - contact Julian Warren, Senior Archivist, Tel 922 4222 or the Archive Manager, Richard Burley, Tel 922 4235). You may also upload your material to the digital archive at: www.bristol.gov.uk/knowyourplace.

Although this book only deals with the years 1954-74 we welcome contributions from former pupils / staff / parents between 1954 and 2008 (school closure).

The school no longer exists in name; the building has been demolished, but our memories of Hengrove School will be preserved and accessible for generations to come.

Postscript

Only two days before going to print, the ballad overleaf was donated to the archive! We do not know who wrote it – most likely a staff member in the 1950's.

THE BALLAD OF HENGROVE SCHOOL

All   It was in mid-September, fifty four,
That Hengrove, Bristol first flung wide its door,
It chanced to be the back door, which was steady,
The front door being somehow not quite ready.

Girls   And so, one lovely English morn,
Boys   The usual wind and rain type,
Girls   We picked a path through mud and mire,
Boys   Or balanced on a drain pipe.

All   Before us lay the entrance way,
The kerbstone gleaming white.
Girls   (And that was odd you know, because
No pavement was in sight).

Girls   Surrounded by bricks and by planks and by stones,
+   We did what we could to escape broken bones,
Boys   Avoiding the pot-holes with skill and discretion,
We entered in, and took possession.

Boys   How we extolled in noisy chorus,
The mighty building there before us,
No other building could compare,
Girls   (Although there's something out at Lockleaze
And a little place at Kidbrooke)

Boys   With this building full of space and light and air.
Steel and glass
And stone and glass
Concrete and glass

All   And glass,
A most exciting place to pass
The years we spend inside a class.
Dull would be he of soul and callous,
Who loved not Hengroves' Crystal Palace!

Girls   All within was fresh and new,
With smudge and smear untainted,
No mark at all on any wall,
No wall was even painted!

Boys	The varnished desk lids were so smooth,
	That you could see yourself there,
	And that was fortunate because,
	There were no mirrors elsewhere.

Girls	But sad to say, one eager boy,
	Not meaning to abuse it,
	Carved his initials on his desk,
	So that he should not lose it.
	He did it for the best,
	For the very best,
	For the very, very best,
	There is no doubt, no doubt at all,
	He did it for the best.

| Boys | Shthwack! Shthwack! Shthwack! |
| Girls | Ah me! |

Girls	On every week day morning,
	The assembly hall adorning,
	We looked so neat and charming,
	In uniformed array.
	We looked so neat and nimble O,
	A wearing of our tunics O,

All	Dashing away with (our) satchels O,
	Dashing away with (our) satchels O,
	(We) stole (your) hearts away.

Boys	Our blazers were of green O,
	Our ties of silver-grey,
Girls	Yes very gay and fresh you were,
	Just like the flowers in May.
	Until one day with no warning at all,
	They surfaced a playground and painted a wall.

Boys +	Tar! Ouch! Tar! Ouch!
Girls	Paint, paint, paint, paint,
Boys	Tar.
Girls	Paint.

| All | Over our fingers and over our clothes, |
| | On one person's knee, on another one's nose. |

Boys	Inky blots, pinky spots
Girls	Yellow and green in dinky dots.

Boys	Never was seen such a rainbow array,
Girls	Never was heard such a gasp of dismay.

All	'Till we found out how well we could place our reliance,
	Upon our benevolent Teachers of science,
	Who, frown upon forehead and bottle in hand,
	Rubbed us and dabbed us with every brand
	Of best academical,
	Classroom chemical,
	Till again we were smartest of schools in the land.

All	In classrooms so peaceful, so far from the traffic,
	Our brains were alert, our expressions seraphic.
Boys	We wanted to work
Girls	We hated to shirk.

All	'Till an unexpected orchestra
	Stopped us with a jerk.
Boys	Doyng! Doyng! Doyng! Doyng!

Girls	In the midst of English grammar,
	Came the mallet and the hammer,
	And their rhythmical percussion
	Overwhelmed the class discussion.
	Before it could recover,
	Came the dumper, grab and shover,
	And formed a bass continuo,
	Outside the classroom wind-u-ow

Girls	No pianissimo, always fortissimo,
	Always crescendo, with never a dim,
All	All thoughts of study we had to dismissimo,
	How could we work against noises so grim?

Boys	But intermingled with such moments of disaster,
	Are occasional occasions for a smile,
	The slowest lesson goes a little faster,
	When you watch the clock hands whizzing round the dial.

All	We may have to cope with a few little problems,
	We may not see all we are wishful to see,

Boys	We may not have drawing pins, curtains or footlights,
Girls	A cookery room or a waste paper B.

All	But we wouldn't change places with Kings or with princes,
	Our school is our palace, so please understand,
	Our comments were made by way of a jest,
	For our school is the best in the breadth of the land.

All	We'll take it and shape it and mould its traditions,
	<u>We</u> are the builders, our labour must give,
	Though architects planned it, though workmen erected it,
	<u>We</u> build the spirit that makes the stone live.

The last four lines are particularly poignant. Yes, the architects planned it and the workmen erected it (see chapters 1, 2 and 3).

Yet there is more, as told in the preceeding pages. It was the pupils and staff who "took it, shaped it and moulded its traditions" and who "built the spirit that made the stones live".

The stones no longer remain but the spirit of Hengrove School lives on in our memories and in these pages.

APPENDIX 1

<u>COSTS OF BUILDING HENGROVE SCHOOL 1951-1954</u>

(Sub Contracts approved)

1951   Steelwork – main building
(Power, Deane and Ransome)   £12,715
Woodwork, metalwork and DS Blocks
(United Steel Structural Co)   £1,112
Fabrication of castellated Beams
(United Steel Structural Co)   £2,950

1952   Metal and windows and glazing   £9,178
W/C Cubicles   £350
Metal door frames   £297
Felt Roofing   £2,211
Floor Beams   £5,869
Wall cladding units   £2,005

1953   Sanitary fittings   £916
Lightweight concrete screeds   £1,372
Ironmongery   £764
Addition to estimate for heavier joists   £65
Thermoplastic tile flooring   £1,847
Cork composition floor   £969
Asphalt Flooring   £828
Wood block flooring   £558
Hard wood strip flooring   £741
Gas service mains   £133
Gas installation   £477

1954   Terrazzo floors   £205
Flush doors   £802
Suspended ceilings   £677
Joinery fittings   £1,197
Rolling shutters   £157
Metal screens to gym kit stores   £63
Precast concrete for spiral staircase   £71
Tenders for school furniture   £3,970
Fireproof boasts and acoustic tiles for stage   £60
Portable gym equipment for 3 schools for Olympic gym   £1,040
Blinds for preparation room   £48
Precast concrete windows   £76
Bush playing fields lavatory accommodation   £1,510
Balustrades and handrails   £863
Hygienette incinerator   £27
Servery countertop   £35
Sink units for Domestic Science rooms   £149

Estimated cost of additional science laboratory	£1,650
Precast concrete paving slabs	£389
Cycle racks	£219
Cloakroom fittings	£1,144
Fume cupboard (chemistry lab)	£47
Domestic science cabinets (3 schools)	£919
65 sets of 8 compartment lockers (3 schools)	£838
120 chairs, 60 tables (3 schools)	£258
Thermoplastic tiles for workshop block	£315
3 Weighing machines (3 schools)	£56
8 4ft cupboards	£107

Extracted from the Bristol City Council Education Committee Minutes.

APPENDIX 2

PUPIL NUMBERS HENGROVE SCHOOL 1954-1971

1954	350	216 1st year, remainder 2nd and 3rd year *(no 4th form)*
1955	600	247 1st year
1957	750	
1958	800	Stage II extension opened
1960	1,000	*(estimated)*
(Dr Perry retires: Mr Waterhouse arrives)		
1963/4	60 in 6th form	
1965/6	900-950	
1966/7	900 – 1,000	
1967/8	1,300	8 form entry – Stage III extension under construction *(completed 1969)*
1970/71	1,500	9 form entry

STAFF NUMBERS 1954-1974

1954	?	
1956	15	*(Photograph with Headmaster)*
Late 1950's	42	*(Photograph)*
1963	47	*(Photograph)*
1969	60 +	
1973	86	*(Library Opening Ceremony signatures)*
1974	Mr Waterhouse retires	

APPENDIX 3

TIMELINE - HENGROVE SCHOOL FROM CONCEPTION - 1974

1939	Petherton Road Primary School opens (closed 2006 and demolished)
1939-45	World War II – National and local post-war reconstruction plans
1944	Bush Estate - 45 acres earmarked for Secondary School base
1945	War ends
1947	Bush Estate purchased by Bristol City Council. Census reveals shortage of school places for all ages in the Hengrove area.
1948	Tyning Junior School at planning stage
1949	Tyning Junior School – temporary classrooms erected
1950	New housing and increasing school-age population indicates an urgent need for a secondary school to receive pupils from Tyning School.
1951	Architects' drawings produced for new secondary school, to be named Hengrove Secondary School.
	Tyning Junior School – permanent buildings erected (renamed New Oak Primary in 2006 and now Oasis Academy New Oak)
1952	Building starts at Hengrove Secondary School
1953	Hengrove, and other new Bristol Secondary schools, to provide two grammar streams – there being a deficiency of grammar school places in Bristol.
1954	**Dr Perry appointed** Catchment area fixed to south of Airport Road.
May 1954	New staff appointed. Mr Green – Second Master. Miss G A Martin – Senior Mistress. Mr W Fletcher – French. Mr Seymour – Geography. Mr Trivett – Maths.
July 1954	Governing Body – Alderman Chamberlain, Alderman Reade, Alderman Raymond, plus Mrs Nutt, Mr W Graves and Mr Rogers
Sept 1954	**Hengrove School opens** – One of the first two Bilateral Schools in Bristol (jointly with Lockleaze).
1958	Stage II Extension – New Wing opens
1959	Twelfth Night drama production
1961	Diary of Ann Frank drama production
1962	Mr R Green retired – succeeded by Mr W Fletcher
1963 (Dec.)	Miss Martin retired – succeeded by Miss Place
1964	Dr. Perry retired – succeeded by Mr Waterhouse
	Commencement of the Waterhouse era
1965	Stage III extension at planning stage (Completion in 1968) Certificate of Secondary Education (CSE) exams replace Union of Educational Institutions (UE1) exams.
1966	Hastings musical production

1967	Building of Stage III extension commenced - £200,000 project
1968	Last year of Prefects System
1969 (Jan)	New 6th Form Centre opens
(May)	New Library/Resources Centre opens
1970 (Dec)	Bethlehem (Christmas musical) performed for the first time
1971 (June)	Noye's Fludde – Bristol Schools production
(Dec)	'Bethlehem' performed at Broadmead Baptist Church, Bristol. (Would be performed 12 years later at the Colston Hall)
1973 (Feb)	Alderman Chamberlain (Governor) died
(Mar)	Bristol 600 celebrations: 'The Venturers' performed at the Colston Hall
(Dec)	**Mr Waterhouse leaves**

APPENDIX 4

GROWTH OF COMPREHENSIVE SCHOOLS IN ENGLAND AND WALES 1950-1973

Year	Number of Schools	Percentage of Secondary School Population
1950	10	0.3
1955	16	0.6
1960	130	4.7
1965	262	8.5
1966	387	11.1
1967	507	14.4
1968	748	20.9
1969	960	26
1970	1145	31
1971	1373	38
1972	1591	44 approx.
1973	1825 approx.	48 approx.

Percentages for 1960-1968 given by Minister of State for Education and Science, House of Commons 15th May 1969. Percentages for 1950 & 1955 and number of schools from 1950-1970 derived from DES *Statistics* Vol. 1, p.viii, 1968, and Vol. 1 1970. (From C Benn & B Simon *Half Way There* 2nd edition, 1972, p.102, reproduced by kind permission of MrGraw Hill Book Company and of Penguin Books. Figures for 1971-1963 modified in light of later information.)

APPENDIX 5

SECONDARY EDUCATION PROVISION IN BRISTOL
16th-20th CENTURY

1532	Bristol Grammar School founded by wealthy merchant
1539	St. Augustine's Monastery closes, but school continues as Cathedral School
1586	Queen Elizabeth's Hospital founded – boy's school
1634	Red Maids' Girls School
1700	Colston Boy's School founded by Edward Colston
	The above schools were fee paying, and only accessible to the wealthy, or by scholarship.
18th c.	Churches began to provide elementary education for the poorer population. Anglicans had charity schools attached to every parish church (co-ordinated and controlled by the Society for Promoting Christian Knowledge). Methodists also sponsored charity schools. Robert Raikes and Hannah More pioneered education of the poor. Attendance was voluntary and involved a small payment
19th c.	Clifton College was founded – a public school for boys.
	Badminton Girls School (1858)
	Redland High School for Girls (1882)
	Colston Girls (1891)
	St Brendans / St Ursulas (1896)
	The schools listed above catered mainly for the children of the Upper and Middle Classes.
1870	Education Act: School Board elected for Bristol to build elementary schools all over the city for children 5 – 14 years. Attendance became compulsory in 1893 up to the age of 11 years.
1902	Bristol Corporation established "Higher Grade Schools". (In 1894 St George had become the first Higher Grade School in the West of England, and later Merrywood School). Such education could lead to selection for College or University. Also Central Schools were founded, such as Rose Green, La Retraite, and Colston Girls' School. Vocational training was provided, both technical and commercial, for industry and commerce.
1914-1918 **1939-1945**	Two World Wars brought profound social change. A need arose for an educated population for the 21st century. Socialism was on the rise, with a renewed optimism for the future.
1944	Education Act. Free Secondary Education for all up to age 14 yrs. Introduction of 11+ Exam.
1947	School Leaving age raised to 15 years.

1950's/ 1960's	Purpose-built comprehensive schools were constructed in the new suburbs of Bristol, with excellent facilities and spacious playing fields. These included Hengrove, Lockleaze, Bedminster Down, Ashton Park, Brislington, Monks Park, Withywood, Hartcliffe, Henbury and St Bernadette Roman Catholic (Voluntary Aided).
1950's/ 1960's/ 1970's	Existing secondary schools were converted to comprehensive education, often involving mergers of smaller secondary schools, or joining boys' and girls' schools into mixed schools, e.g. St. George, Fairfield, and Merrywood.

APPENDIX 6

<u>TIMELINE OF SIGNIFICANT NATIONAL EVENTS 1929-1974</u>

Most of us will remember these events, or will have been affected by them.

1929   Idea of a comprehensive or common secondary school introduced by a British educationalist returning to Britain from teaching in the USA. Ramsay MacDonald (Lab) PM

1930's   Discussions between politicians, Trade Unions, educationalists, teachers, sociologists and psychologists regarding secondary education and selection. Stanley Baldwin (Con) PM 1935

1936   Edward VIII abdicates

1938   Coronation of George VI

1939-1945 World War II   Heavy bombing of homes and schools in many cities. In the wake of WWII the idea of comprehensive secondary education was associated with a new democratic settlement and the rise of the welfare state in Britain. The idea of the comprehensive secondary school promised to end early selection and extend educational opportunities. Winston Churchill (Con) PM 1940

1942   Beveridge Plan (Social Security and National Insurance).

1944   Education Act (Butler) Free secondary education for all up to age 14. Introduction of 11 plus exam. White Paper proposes National Health Service.

1945   Clement Attlee (Lab) PM

1948   National Health Service set up. National Assistance Act. XIV Olympic Games in London.

1949/50 Nationalisation of steel and gas industries.

1951   Festival of Britain.   First census since 1931. Dartmoor National Park: BBC radio series "The Archers": TV sets owned by 42,000 people. Winston Churchill (Con) PM

1952   George VI dies: polio immunisation by injection: Joderell Bank – world's largest radio telescope: first British atomic bomb exploded in Australia.

1953   Coronation of Queen Elizabeth II: Queen Mary dies: DNA structure elucidated by Watson & Crick: British atomic weapons tested in Woomera, Australia.

1954   Hengrove School opens.

Kidbrooke, London County Council's first comprehensive school, opens. Increase of West Indian immigrants to Britain: Landlord & Tenant Act (security of tenure): Growth of New Towns: publication of "Lord of the Flies" by W. Golding: "Under Milk Wood" by Dylan Thomas: "Lord of the Rings, part 1, by Tolkien: Musical "Salad Days" composed by Julian Slade: Roger Bannister runs 1 mile in under 4 minutes.

1955   Insulin molecular structure identified at Cambridge University: TB deaths fall by 64%: Heathrow – new terminal buildings open: automation in industry increases: Walt Disney "Lady & the Tramp": "Waiting for Godot" play by Beckett: "Midsummer Marriage" opera by Michael Tippet: "The Quiet American" by Graham Greene. Anthony Eden (Con) PM

1956   Parking meters and vehicle testing introduced: telephone links established with USA: Clean Air Act: Bingo legalised: Suez crisis: new TV transmitter at Crystal Palace: Calder Hall, Cumberland – the world's first large-scale nuclear power station: John Osborne's novel "Look Back in Anger": TV serialises "David Copperfield" by Charles Dickens: Aldermaston marches by Campaign for Nuclear Disarmament.

1957   Harwell – UK Atomic Energy Authority set up: Institute of Computer Science at London University: Homicide Act – death penalty abolished: Wolfenden Report on Homosexuality & Prostitution: school broadcasting on TV: first British hydrogen bomb exploded on Christmas Island in the Pacific: Asian Flu epidemic: Vera Britain publishes autobiography "Testament of Experience"; John Braine writes "Room at the Top"; Llandaff Cathedral, Cardiff – Epstein figure "Christ in Majesty": Henry Moore sculptures; Musical "My Fair Lady" based on Shaw's "Pygmalion". Harold MacMillan (Con) PM

1958   Gatwick Airport completed: Glasgow – Cumbernauld New Town: last steam locomotive made at Crewe: electronic computers in industry and commerce: stereophonic records and radio: TV – new series, "Panorama" presented by Richard Dimbleby: "Your Life in Their Hands" TV series: Manchester United lose seven players in Munich air crash: "Collected Poems" by John Betjeman: "Conscience of the Rich" by C P Snow: play by Peter Shaffer "Five Finger Exercise: Henry Moore "Reclining Figure" at UNESCO building, Paris: "Noyes' Fludde" play to music by Britten (performed by Bristol Schools 1971): Bernstein "West Side Story" (USA): "Dr Zhivago" written by Pasternak.

1959   Driest British summer for 200 years: Hovercraft invented: National Coal Board to close up to 240 mines by 1965: M1 opens – first section of motorway system: first minicar off the production line in Longbridge, Birmingham (ends 2000, and later revived): Huxley writes "Brave New World Revisited": Laurie Lee "Cider with Rosie": I & P Opie "The Love And Language of Schoolchildren": Films "Look Back in Anger" and "Room at the Top".

1960   New £1.00 bank note issued: The farthing coin no longer legal currency: Princess Margaret marries a commoner, Anthony Armstrong-Jones: film version of Lionel Bart's "Fings Ain't Wot they Used to Be".

1961   Berkeley Power Station near Bristol - £2million nuclear power research: Harwell – world's largest and fastest Atlas computer for atomic research and meteorology: Britain applies to join Common Market: Britain census - population 51 million: increase in West Indian and Asian immigration: Universities of Sussex and Essex founded: BBC radio – end of "Children's Hour": BBC TV series "The Age of Kings": Musical

"Oliver" by Lionel Bart: Films – Walt Disney's "101 Dalmations", Hayley Mills in "Whistle Down the Wind", Audrey Hepburn in "Breakfast at Tiffanys": Henry Moore bronze "Standing Figure".

1962   Concorde – world's first supersonic airliner to be developed by Britain and France: Alex Moulton – new bike design: Coventry Cathedral consecrated: Commonwealth Institute opened: fluorine in water to reduce dental decay: Thalidomide drug withdrawn (deformities): British satellite Ariel to study cosmic radiation: Royal College of Physicians produce Report on Smoking and Health: A.Sampson wrote "Anatomy of Britain": Anthony Burgess wrote "Clockwork Orange": Play by Wesker "Chips with Everything".

1963   Application to join Common Market fails: UK with US and USSR signs Nuclear Test Ban Treaty: Beeching Report recommends closing half railway stations and one-third of the tracks: measles vaccine discovered: Channel Tunnel construction recommended – joint British/French project (opens eventually in 1994): University of York founded: University of Newcastle reconstituted: Rachel Carson writes "Silent Spring": Film made of Fielding's "Tom Jones": the Beatles pop group achieve international fame – Beatlemania. Alec Douglas-Hume (Con) PM

1964   Sun newspaper launched: BBC TV Channel 2 launched: Radio Caroline broadcasts from pirate ship: Forth Road Bridge opens: Hire Purchase Act: riots between mods and rockers at seaside resorts: New Universities of East Anglia, Kent, Lancaster and Strathclyde founded: Films – "My Fair Lady", "Zorba the Greek": "Mary Poppins": Cassius Clay world heavyweight boxing champion. Harold Wilson (Lab) PM

1965   LEA's asked to submit plans for comprehensive schools in Britain. Post Office Tower completed – tallest building in London: Winston Churchill dies: North Sea gas discovered: new Universities at Ulster and Warwick Bingo craze in Britain: Films – "Dr Zhivago", "The Spy who came in from the Cold", John le Carré spy thriller "The Looking Glass War": Boot's Circulating Libraries closed in Britain: Beatles awarded MBE's.

1966   Commonwealth Office replaces the Colonial Office (end of Empire): Ministry of Pensions and National Insurance merge and form Ministry of Social Security: first Polaris submarine launched at Barrow: Aberfan disaster kills 116 children and 28 adults: Severn Bridge completed – easy and fast access from Bristol to South Wales: Tay Road Bridge opens – the longest in Britain: the first televised Opening of Parliament: New Universities – Bradford, Brunel, City, Heriot-Watt, and Loughborough University of Technology: Films – "Khartoum", "A Man for All Seasons", "Modesty Blaise", "Who's Afraid of Virginia Woolf?": Paul Scott writes Volume I of his Raj Quartet "The Jewel in the Crown": England wins the FiFA World Cup.

1967   Abortion Act: Decimal Currency Act (effective 1971): Road Safety Act – breath tests: Sexual Offences Act (consenting adults): Defence White Paper proposes drastic reduction in Armed Forces, especially in the Far East: Scientology leader refused re-entry to Britain: Francis Chichester sails solo around world in Gypsy Moth IV: Liverpool Roman

Catholic Cathedral consecrated: Plowden Report (Primary Schools):
first British colour TV broadcast: Donald Campbell killed on Coniston
Water in Bluebird: foot & mouth disease – 422,000 cattle slaughtered:
Queen Elizabeth II, Cunard liner launched: last voyage of Cunard Queen
Mary: Torrey Canyon aground at Land's End: Universities of Salford
and Dundee founded: BBC radio programmes reorganised to Radio
1, 2, 3 and 4 and local stations: BBC TV serial "The Forsyte Saga",
26 episodes: Films "Bonny & Clyde", "Camelot", "The Jungle Book",
"Thoroughly Modern Milly": Desmond Morris writes "The Naked Ape".

1968 Commonwealth Immigration Act to restrict Kenyan Asian immigrants:
Race Relations Act: Labour Government Bill to reform House of Lords
(abandoned 1969): Disturbances in Northern Ireland: Welsh Home Rule
and Welsh Language Society campaigns: end of steam locomotion:
structure of haemoglobin molecule determined – Cambridge University:
Cambridge radio Astronomers discover pulsars: Britain's first heart
transplant patient survives for 46 days: fertility drugs lead to multiple
births: new Euston Station opens: London Bridge sold to US oil
company and re-erected over Colorado River: Alec Rose sails solo
around the world in Lively Lady: Films "Charge of the Light Brigade",
"Chitty Chitty Bang Bang", "Oliver": Musical "Canterbury Tales".

1969 Welsh national extremist bombs: Northern Ireland – IRA activity –
British troops sent: voting age and age of majority reduced to 18 years
(from 21 years): Concorde maiden flight: Oxford University discover
structure of insulin: investiture of the Prince of Wales at Caernarvon
Castle: White Paper "In Place of Strife" proposes reform of Trade
Unions: test-tube babies – Cambridge University: Divorce Reform
Act – breakdown becomes sole ground for divorce: Queen ends live
Christmas broadcasts: Victoria Line opened – the first underground line
for 60 years: Open University founded: halfpenny coin withdrawn from
circulation: first new decimal coin circulated – the 50p piece, 7-sided:
Films – "Battle of Britain", "Funny Girl", "Midnight Cowboy", "Oh What a
Lovely War!", "Women in Love".

1970 Britain still negotiating to enter Common Market: North Sea oil
discovered: Northern Ireland shootings and bombs: Equal Pay Act: site
for London's third airport under discussion: industrial disputes lead
to power cuts – emergency powers declared: Industrial Relations Bill:
charges for National Museums and Galleries: new censorship gradings
by Board of Censors: Films "Anne of the Thousand Days", "Butch
Cassidy and the Sundance Kid", "Cromwell", "Ned Kelly": Musical
"Paint Your Wagon". Edward Heath (Con) PM

1971 UK entry to European Economic Community agreed: decimal
currency introduced (no more pennies, shillings, crowns or guineas):
unemployment highest since 1940: Immigration Bill to end right of
Commonwealth citizens to settle in UK: Daily Sketch, oldest tabloid,
closes: divorce petitions almost 50% increase: end of free school
milk: crash helmets for motor cyclists compulsory: Chay Blyth – first
solo yacht round the world in westerly direction: Rolls-Royce declared
bankrupt: Royal College of Physicians re-affirm link between smoking

and lung cancer – warnings to appear on packets: Ibrox Stadium – 66 spectators killed: Films "The French Connection", "Death in Venice", "Love Story", "The Go-Between", "A Clockwork Orange", "Macbeth": Musical "Godspell" from USA to London: Ballet – "Anastasia (K MacMillan): TV – "Edna the Inebriate Woman": dissolution of the Beatles pop group.

1972   Economic and industrial troubles: miner's strike: national power cuts: industry on 3-day week: State of Emergency declared: pound sinks to a record low: unemployment over 1 million: 24 million days lost through strikes – the highest since 1914: Local Government Act establishes new counties and districts – Avon County Council: first kidney transplant and introduction of kidney donor scheme: birth of children with spina bifida: thalidomide children offered Government financial help: pocket calculators available (micro-chip technology): five Oxford University Colleges admit women: British Museum holds Treasures of Tutankamun exhibition: raising of the school leaving age to 16 (ROSLA): Longford Committee on pornography: Northern Ireland – continuation of troubles – Bloody Sunday 13 killed, direct rule from London imposed – 110th British soldier killed. Films "The Godfather", "Last Tango in Paris", "Young Winston": Musicals "Jesus Christ Superstar (Webber & Rice), "A Little Night Music" (Sondheim): Novels "Watership Down" (Adams), "The Odessa File (Forsythe), "All Creatures Great & Small" and "It Shouldn't Happen to a Vet" (Herriot): John Betjeman becomes Poet Laureate.

1973   Britain joins EEC: State of Emergency continues: strikes, pay and prices freeze and counter-inflation measures: VAT of 10% introduced: new London Bridge opens: Northern Ireland problems continue – car/letter bombs in London and other cities: Capital Radio and LBC open: compensation agreed after 11 years for thalidomide victims: wedding of Princess Anne to commoner Captain Mark Phillips – 500million world-wide TV viewers: Japanese cars now common in UK: TV "The Ascent of Man", "The World at War", "Some Mothers Do Have 'Em" (comedy): Novels "The Honorary Consul (Greene), "Marilyn (Mailer), "The Gulag Archipelago (Solzhenitsyn): Films "Live and Let Die" (Fleming), "The Day of the Jackal (Forsythe), "The Way We Were" (Streisand): Play "Equus" (Shaffer)

1974   Northern Ireland – IRA bombs in various cities in UK and kill 26 people; General Election – Labour win, but no majority – Harold Wilson Prime Minister; end of State of Emergency and 3-day week: Government and TUC agree a social contract: autumn election – Labour increase their majority: serious inflation: NHS free family planning service: BBC TV first Ceefax teletext: Flixborough chemical plant explosion kills 29: the first McDonald's opens in London: Covent Garden market closes: Milton Keyes New Town: first Sunday games of professional football: Films "Murder on the Orient Express", "The Towering Inferno", "Blazing Saddles", "The Great Gatsby", "The Odessa File", "The Godfather Part II": Books – final volume "The Buildings of England" (Pevsner)

APPENDIX 7

<u>TIMELINE OF SIGNIFICANT INTERNATIONAL EVENTS 1952-1974</u>

Most of us will remember these world events – especially the Space Race, the dismantling of the British Empire and various medical advances: we lived through momentous changes.

1952   Apartheid in South Africa

1953   Stalin dies. Mount Everest conquered by Edmund Hillary & Sherpa Tensing.

1954   Concerns about atomic fall-out and radioactive waste polluting air and sea.

1956   Suez crisis

1957   Suez Canal re-opens.   USA face riots and Civil Rights Act: Treaty of Rome between six European countries – not UK: Space Exploration – Russia – Sputnik I and II with dog – earth satellites.

1958   Space Race – USA Earth Satellites Explorer, Vanguard I, Explorer III & IV – Atlas Relay Station, Pioneer I, II and III aimed at moon. Russia launched Sputnik III.

1959   Britain joins European Free Trade Association (EFTA). Cyprus becomes a republic – Britain retains bases: UN condemns Apartheid in South Africa: Dalai Lama escapes turmoil in Tibet to exile in India: Mali becomes Independent: Jamaica – self-government: State of Emergency in Kenya and Nyasaland: Cuba – Castro seizes power: Hawaii becomes 50th state of USA. Space Race – USA and USSR training astronauts: US recovers two monkeys from space unharmed: Moon probes.   Russia launches Lunik I, II and III and photographs of the back of the moon: USA launches Pioneer IV.

1960   President John F Kennedy becomes the first Roman Catholic President of the USA: Cuban crisis: many African countries achieve independence – Ghana, Ivory Coast, Mali, Niger, Nigeria, Senegal, Somalia, Togo. Space Race: Russian Sputnik V: two live dogs orbit earth seventeen times.

1961   Berlin wall erected.   Space Race: Yuri Gagarin – the first man in space, orbits the earth in 1 hr. 48 mins.   USA – Alan Shepard the second man in space – sub-orbital flight, 1,115 miles high.

1962   Cuba crisis ends. General Disarmament Conference (nuclear weapons): US military in South Vietnam.   Independence for Tanganyika, Uganda and West Samoa.   Space Race: USA launches Telstar – a communication Satellite: space flights with astronauts Glenn, Carpenter and Schirra: Ranger Spacecraft hits the moon: Mariner rocket launched to study Venus.

1963   President J F Kennedy assassinated: Martin Luther King leads Civil Rights campaign in Alabama: Independence for Kenya and Zanzibar: creation of Federation of Malaysia: Space Race: USA astronaut orbits the earth 22 times In Mercury capsule: Russia – Valentina Tereshkove, the first woman in space, makes 3-day orbital flight.

1964	Cyprus unrest between Turkish and Greek Communities: UN peacekeeping force sent: Independence for Malta, Nyasaland – becomes Malawi: Tanganyika and Zanzibar become Tanzania: Northern Rhodesia becomes Zambia: Malaysia invaded by Indonesia: XVIII Olympic Games in Tokyo.
1965	Spain renews claim to Gibraltar: Independence for Gambia: Southern Rhodesia proclaims UDI: Vietnam war – USA bombs North Vietnam and increases forces in South Vietnam: Singapore secedes from Malaysia. Space Race: UK – Early Bird, the first commercial communications satellite: USA – Gemini 5 : 2-man spacecraft orbits earth for eight days: Gemini 6 and 7 rendezvous in space. Russia – cosmonaut Alexi Leonov leaves Voskod II to float in space for twenty minutes.
1966	Italy – flooding threatens artworks in Florence: China – the Cultural Revolution: India – Mrs Ghandi becomes Prime Minister: Independence for Bechuanaland (becomes Botswana): Basutoland (becomes Lesotho): Barbados: British Guiana (becomes Guyana). Space Race: USA Buzz Aldrin makes space walk of 5 hrs. 35 mins from Gemini 12: Gemini 10 locates and locks on to Ageria vehicle in space: Surveyor I – unmanned space craft makes soft landing on the moon and transmits photos of lunar surface: Lunar Orbiter I photographs possible landing sites on moon.
1967	Gibraltar – Referendum – result to stay in Britain: Greece – coup d'etat by army – King Constantine II flies to Rome: Israel – Six Day War against Egypt, Jordan and Syria: Nigeria – civil war – Biafra region breaks away: Che Guevara, Latin American revolutionary, killed in Bolivia: Space Race: Russia – spacecraft Venus IV soft lands on planet Venus: unmanned Russian satellites link up in space – basis for future space station building.
1968	Falkland Islands claimed by Argentina – islanders say no: Independence for Mauritius and Swaziland: Treaty on Non-Proliferation of Nuclear Weapons signed by USA, Britain, Russia and 58 other states: Russia invades Czechoslovakia over Dubcek's liberal reforms: France explodes hydrogen bomb: XIX Olympic Games in Mexico City: Senator Bob Kennedy and Martin Luther King both assassinated: Nixon becomes US President: Space Race: USA space craft Apollo 8 carrying three astronauts flies 240,000 miles to moon plus ten lunar orbits and safe return: unmanned satellite is launched to study Xray sources.
1969	Boris Spassky – Russian world chess champion: Prince Juan Carlos to succeed Franco in Spain: Mrs Golda Meir Israel Prime Minister: My Lai – Vietnam – massacre of civilians by US soldiers: UN Scientific Report on Problems of the Human Environment and stresses need for conservation. USA – Boeing produce 747 Jumbo Jet airliner. Space Race: USA – Apollo II carries Neil Armstrong – first man to set foot on moon – TV pictures of landing sent back to earth, and rock samples brought back. Russia – Venus probes surface conditions on Venus – too hot for life: Russian cosmonauts conduct welding experiments in Soyuz 6 while orbiting earth.

1970   Poland – riots against price increases: Czechoslovakia expels Dubcek and other liberal reformers from Communist party: Jordan civil war: Philippines - attempt to assassinate Pope Paul VI in Manila: Egypt – Sadat replaces Nasser as President: Cambodia – communist bases attacked by US forces: China launches first satellite. Space Race: USA – Apollo 13 explodes half-way to moon, crew escape in lunar module Aquarius: Russia – Soynz 9 – 2-man craft orbits earth for eighteen days. Lunokhod I – 8-wheeled robot vehicle lands on moon to explore moon surface from unmanned spacecraft Luna 17.

1971   Strategic Arms Limitation talks (SALT) – anti ballistic missiles. Independence for Sierra Leone, Congo (re-named Zaire), Uganda: Idi Amin takes power in coup: Switzerland – women given the vote: War between India and Pakistan: East Pakistan becomes Bangladesh, an independent state: Ali Bhutto becomes President of Pakistan: Vietnam – US losses 45,000 plus: Laos – incursion by South Vietnam and US troops: Syria, Libya and Egypt form Federation of Arab Republics: Space Race: US and Russia both launch space probes towards Mars. Russia – Soyuz 10 docks with space station Salynt.

1972.   France – Duke of Windsor dies. SALT signed by USA and Russia: International Convention bans dumping at sea: USA and Russia agree to co-operate in science and technology: China appoints first British Ambassador: Pakistan leaves Commonwealth, Bangladesh joins: US President Nixon visits China and Moscow: arrests at Watergate building: West Berliners can enter East Berlin: Uganda – Amin expels all Asians – 25,000 with British passports admitted to UK: Vietnam – last US ground forces withdraw and peace talks: Russia refuses to allow presentation of Nobel Prize to Solzhenitsyn: Space Race: USA – Apollo 16 and 17 continue Exploration of moon – nuclear-powered laboratory placed on moon, Pioneer 10 unmanned space craft launched to observe Jupiter.

1973   European atom smashing research organisation, CERN – unification of electromagnetic and weak forces – important step towards formulating a set of laws to describe structure and behaviour of universe: France – resumes nuclear tests in Pacific: Indochina – US military operations end: Middle East – Yom Kippur War: UN peacekeeping force established: US Watergate Affair – sub poenas served on Nixon: US Pulitzer Prize to Washington Post for exposing Watergate affair. Energy crisis – oil producing states increase oil prices by 20-100% and cut production: Ethiopia – 7-year drought 100,000 died: Flooding in Pakistan and Bangladesh worst on record, and Mississippi River valley worst in 200 years: widespread development of microprocessors: E F Shumacher treatise on alternative technology "Small is Beautiful", a study of economics as if people mattered: Space Race – USA Pioneer 10 sends pictures of Jupiter; Skylab, unmanned space station, in orbit and three manned missions conduct experiments from it. USA and Russia exchange data on Mars: Brussels – European Space Agency set up, joint European space projects.

1974	Argentina – Eva Peron succeeds husband: Uganda – Amin regime causes 250,000 deaths: Greece – monarch deposed, and free elections: Ethiopia – Emperor Haile Selassie deposed: Cambodia – clashes between Government and Communists: Iran/Iraq border clashes: Lebanon – PLO recognised by UN: unrest in Middle East, especially Israel and Suez: USA – Watergate affair – President Nixon resigns: Russia expels Solzhenitsyn – he collects Nobel prize: Bangladesh – half the country is flooded, 10 million homeless: Development of genetic engineering using DNA: World's first test-tube babies born: Concern over chemicals in aerosol cans damaging ozone layer: Space Race: USA astronauts return from Skylab after longest space flight – 84 days: Mariner 10 sends pictures of Venus and Mercury; Pioneer II passes Jupiter en route to Saturn.

APPENDIX 8

TIMELINE OF LEGISLATION – WHITE PAPERS – REPORTS REGARDING SECONDARY EDUCATION 1913-1974

1913	London County Council appointed psychologist Cyril Burt
1914-18	**World War I**
1921	School leaving age extended to 14. Education Act consolidated all previous laws.
1924	**Ramsay MacDonald (Labour) Prime Minister, followed by Stanley Baldwin (Conservative)**
1929	**Ramsay MacDonald (Labour) Prime Minister**
1923-33	Hadow Reports on education for all ages
1935	**Stanley Baldwin (Conservative) Prime Minister**
1938	Spens Report – recommended tripartite system of secondary schools and proposed school leaving age should be raised to 16 (not achieved until 1973)
1939-45	**World War II**
1940	**Winston Churchill (Conservative) Prime Minister**
1941	Green Paper – *Education after the War*
1943	White Paper – *Educational Reconstruction* – formed basis of 1944 Education Act. Norwood Report – *Curriculum and Examinations in Secondary Schools.* Backed tripartite system recommended by Spens.
1944	Education Act 1944 (Butler) – set structure for post-war system of State education. Compulsory free Secondary education for all to 14 years. 11+ exam introduced.
1945	**War in Europe ends. Clement Attlee (Labour) Prime Minister.** *The Nation's Schools* – Government publication explaining tripartite system of secondary schools.

1947	The New Secondary Education – Government publication reiterating its commitment to tripartite system of secondary schools.
1951	General Certificate of Education (GCE) introduced (until 1986)
1951-70	**The Wind of Change**
1951 (Oct)	**Winston Churchill (Conservative) Prime Minister. Florence Horsbrugh – Minister of Education.**
1954	Horsbrugh stopped LCC from closing Eltham Hill Girls' Grammar School and transferring pupils to the new (comprehensive) Kidbrooke School.
1955	**Anthony Eden (Conservative) Prime Minister**
1956	Colleges of Advanced Technology – selected Technical and FE colleges were upgraded to this status. In the mid 1960's most became the "new" universities.
1957	**Harold MacMillan (Conservative) Prime Minister**
1959	*Education Act* – grants and loans to aided schools and special agreement schools. Crowther Report *15-18* – recommended raising school leaving age to 16 (achieved in 1973) and further education provision for 15-18 year olds.
1960	Beloe Report – *Secondary School Examinations other than the GCE:* led to introduction of CSEs in 1965
1962	*Education Act* – LEA's required to provide students with grants for living costs and tuition fees for Higher Education.
1963	Newsom Report – *Half our Future* – on education of 13-16 year olds of average ability and below. **Alec Douglas-Home (Conservative) Prime Minister.** Robbins Report - *Higher Education* – recommended massive expansion of higher education to cater for all who had the necessary ability.
1964	Labour manifesto promised to abolish selection (i.e. end the 11+ exam)
(Oct)	**Harold Wilson (Labour) Prime Minister. Michael Stewart – Minister of Education. Dr Perry retires – Mr Waterhouse appointed new Head Master.**
1965	**Anthony Crosland - Minister of Education.** *Circular 10/65* requested LEAs to submit proposals for comprehensivisation (withdrawn later by Circular 10/70). Certificate of Secondary Education (CSE) introduced in England and Wales
1966	Polytechnics established (would be granted University status in 1991)
1967	**Patrick Gordon-Walker (Labour) – Minister of Education.** Plowdon Report - *Children and their Primary Schools* – promoted child-centred education in primary schools. *Education Act* – grants and loans to aided and special agreement schools, etc.
1968	**Edward Short (Labour) – Minister of Education.** Newsom Report – *The Public Schools Commission: First Report* – made recommendations about integrating private boarding schools into state education. School Meals Agreement – teachers no longer obliged to supervise children at lunch times. Education Act – laid down rules when changing character of a school (e.g. to comprehensive)

1969	Haslegrave Report – promoted technical and business education. *Fight for Education: A Black Paper* – edited by CB Cox & A E Dyson Black *Paper Two: The Crisis in Education* – edited by C B Cox & A E Dyson

1970-74   **Recession and Disenchantment**

1970 (June) Edward Heath (Conservative) Prime Minister. Margaret Thatcher – Minister of Education. *Circular 10/70* – withdraws Labour circular 10/65 – LEAs no longer compelled to go comprehensive (withdrawn later by Circular 4/74): Donnison Report – *The Public Schools Commission: Second Report* – Considered the role independent day schools and direct grant grammar schools might play in a state education system which was in the middle of comprehensive reorganisation. *Black Paper Three: Goodbye Mr Short* – edited by C B Cox & A E Dyson

1971   *Education (Milk) Act* – limited the provision of free milk in schools

1973   *Education (Work Experience) Act* – LEAs could organise work experience for final year school students. *Employment and Training Act* – required LEAs to set up Careers Services. Raising of school leaving age to 16 (first suggested in 1938!) Circular *7/73* – halved the number of places for student teachers.

(Dec)   **Mr Waterhouse retired**

1974 (Feb)   **Harold Wilson (Labour) Prime Minister.**
(Mar)   **Reginald Prentice – Minister of Education.** *Circular 4/74* – reaffirmed the Labour Government's intention to proceed with comprehensivisation.

EX-PUPILS AND PARENTS OF EX-PUPILS QUESTIONNAIRE

HENGROVE SCHOOL 1954–1974
FOR EX-PUPILS AND PARENTS OF EX-PUPILS

Before memories fade we are hoping to produce a DVD, book or a website from material collected from old pupils, parents, teachers and city archives. Some of the old teachers have been contacted and are very keen that old memories should be placed altogether in some form. (This will be a long term project)

- Have you any memorabilia, including photos, reports, letters, newspaper cuttings, school magazines, programmes of plays etc. that you could copy and send to be stored for the future?
- Have you any stories that you would like to share with others?

A questionnaire has been produced to help us with this new venture. If you would like to be part of history, please use the questionnaire and send or post to the address below. **All questions optional.** *(Personal details will not be distributed outside this project)*

1. What is your name, including maiden name if married?
2. What is your current address, postal or email (to get in touch with you if needed)?
3. What is your date of birth?
4. What was your address or postcode when you entered Hengrove School (to indicate who came to the school from outside the area)?
5. What date did you enter Hengrove School?
6. When did you leave Hengrove School?
7. Which school did you attend prior to Hengrove School?
8. On leaving Hengrove School did you go to higher/further education, apprenticeship or similar? Give details.
9. If none of the above applies, what employment did you get? Give details.
10. Will you give a list of careers or life journey with dates since leaving Hengrove School?
11. What qualifications did you gain at Hengrove School?
12. Did you represent the school in sport? Give details
13. Did you learn to play a musical instrument? Give details
14. Did you take part in the Duke of Edinburgh Award?
15. Did you take part in Mr. Swifts Dancing Club or other clubs?
16. Which teachers did you have for what subjects?
17. Have you any memories of punishments/uniform/school dinners/ assemblies?
18. Do you know any ex pupils who have excelled in their career and become rich or famous?

Would you like to help with this project? We are looking for volunteers with a couple of hours spare. Have you any expertise e.g. website wizard, publisher, printing and scanning access?
Do you know anyone that would be willing to fund some of this project or knowledge to get funding?

HENGROVE SCHOOL HISTORY PROJECT
c/o 262 Wells Road
Knowle
Bristol BS4 2PN
email address
hengroveschool@hotmail.co.uk.

387

<u>EX-TEACHERS AND SUPPORT STAFF QUESTIONNAIRE</u>

HENGROVE SCHOOL 1954–1974
FOR EX-TEACHERS AND SUPPORT STAFF

Before memories fade we are hoping to produce a DVD, book or a website from material collected from ex-pupils, parents, teachers and city archives. Some of the ex-teachers have been contacted and are very keen that old memories should be placed altogether in some form. (This will be a long term project)

- Have you any memorabilia, including photos, reports, letters, newspaper cuttings, school magazines, programmes of plays etc. that you could copy and send to be stored for the future?
- Have you any stories that you would like to share with others?

A questionnaire has been produced to help us with this new venture. If you would like to be part of history, please use the questionnaire and send or post to the address below. **All questions optional.** *(Personal details will not be distributed outside the project)*

1. What is your name, including maiden name if married?
2. What is your current address, postal or email (to get in touch with you if needed)?
3. What is your date of birth?
4. When did you commence teaching or working at Hengrove School, and who interviewed you?
5. What subjects did you teach or help with and to what age group?
6. What promotions did you get?
7. Were you involved in teaching or helping with extra-curricular activities?
8. Where did you teach or work before and after Hengrove School?
9. When did you leave Hengrove School?
10. Were there any major changes when you were at Hengrove e.g. change of Head, school name change, change in examinations?
11. Which Heads did you serve under?
12. Who were Deputy Head and Senior Mistress?
13. Have you any special memories of the punishments, school uniform policy, school dinners or assemblies?
14. Were you involved with school trips, plays, concerts?
15. What were the happiest memories?

Would you like to help with this project? Are you still in touch with other members of staff? Can you let them know of this project and pass this questionnaire to them?

We are looking for volunteers with a couple of hours spare. Have you any expertise e.g. website wizard, publisher, printing and scanning access?
Do you know anyone that would be willing to fund some of this project or knowledge to get funding?

HENGROVE SCHOOL HISTORY PROJECT
c/o 262 Wells Road
Knowle
Bristol BS4 2PN

e mail address
hengroveschool@hotmail.co.uk

BIBLIOGRAPHY

Beddow N, Collard R et. al.	*Hengrove's Hidden History* 2001
Benn M	*School Wars: the Battle for Britain's Education* Verso 2011
Ben C & Chitty C	*Thirty Years On: Is Comprehensive Education Alive and Well or Struggling to Survive?* David Fulton 1996
Bettey J H	*Bristol Observed* Redcliffe Press 1989
Bristol City Council	*Education Committee Minutes 1924-58 Secondary Education Committee Minutes Planning and Reconstruction Committee Minutes 1949-53*
Chasey, H	Bristol: *An Outline History for Schools* Georges Booksellers 1975
Chitty C	*Redefining the Comprehensive Experience* 1987
Earlham Sociology Pages	*From Tripartite to Comprehensive Secondary Education*
Elliot A	*State Schools since the 1950's: The Good News* Trentham Books Ltd 2007
Gillard D	*Education in England: a Brief History* 2000 (Revised 2004, 2007, 2011)
Haddrell I	*Lockleaze Schools* The History Press 2008
Hodder & Stoughton: Headway (pub.)	*Encyclopaedia of Dates and Events*
MacInnes C M & Whittard W F	*Bristol and its Adjoining Counties* 1955
Knowledge Magazine	*Knowle Stadium* Dec 1992
McCullock G & Crook D (Ed)	*Routledge International Encyclopedia of Education*
Merchant E M	*A Vanished Age 1850-2000* 2002
Ralph E (Pub)	*Government of Bristol 1373-1973*
Rubinstein D & Simon B	*The Evolution of the Comprehensive School 1926-1972* Routledge & Kegan Paul 1972
Ward S	*Don't Learn my Son no Sums* Yardstick Publishing 2009
Williams C J N BA, FCA	*A Journey from a Higher Grade to an Academy: The Story of St George School, Bristol.* 2011

FURTHER READING

Ball S (Ed)   *Comprehensive Schooling: a Reader*
                                ISBN 0-905273-89-3   Falmer Press 1984

Ball S J   *Beachside Comprehensive: a Case Study of Secondary
                                Schooling* Cambridge University Press   1981

Batley R   *Going Comprehensive: Educational Policy Making in Two
                                County Boroughs* 1970

Burt (Sir) Cyril   *The Examination at Eleven Plus*
                                British Journal of Educational Studies 1959

Boyson R   *Oversubscribed: The Story of Highbury Grove School*
                                Ward Lock 1974

Fenwick P   *The Comprehensive School 1944-1970: the Politics of
                                Secondary School Reorganisation*

Floud J & Helsey A H   *Social Class and Educational Opportunity*
                                Heinemann   1956

Ford B   *The Ford Report*   Bristol Evening Post 22 June 1965

Hargreaves D   *The Challenge of the Comprehensive School: Culture,
                                Curriculum and Community* Routledge & Kegan Paul

Kerckhoff et.al.   *Going Comprehensive in England and Wales* 1996

King H R   *Comprehensive School – a Pattern of Achievement*
                                Forum Vol. 5, No. 1

National Foundation for Educational Research - various

Pedley R   *Comprehensive Education* Penguin 3rd edition 1969

Pedley R & others   *Comprehensive Schools Today*
                                Councils and Education Press 1956

Reynolds D   *The Comprehensive Experiment: a Comparison* 1987

Times Educational Supplement - weekly

Vernon P E (Ed)   *Secondary School Selection*   1957

ACKNOWLEDGEMENTS

Our sincere thanks go to all who responded to our questionnaire. Without their encouragement and help this book would not have been written. Former pupils are listed below: -

R Adams, R Andrews nee Dalling, C Bagshaw, J Baker nee Hooper, L Brine, K Bullen nee Bagshaw, G Banwell, C Barrett, Cllr M Brain, Bob Chasey, C Cherry, P Clarke nee Massey, V Clarke nee Price, P Clapp nee Cooke, I Coleman, P Cook, Rev P Cook, J Cooke nee Elbrow, T Dark, M Delbridge, B Dunn, M Eaves nee Smith, P Eyre, P Fudge, C Garland, C Gill nee Roberts, A Giffey, J Guille-Marrett nee Freeman, P Haydon, R Hayes nee Ibbotson, G Hazell nee Vlaeminke, D Higgott nee Fancy, R Jolliffe, Carol Jones nee Eyre, Roger Jones, M Leigh, R Lim nee Cowley, R Little, D Marsh, Sue Mills nee Whitnell, K Nicholls nee Aslett, S Page nee Wilkins, L Parker nee Barrett, E Pavey, I Quaife, P Quant nee Beacham, K Reynolds nee Kittlety, M Robinson nee Francis, R Salter, C Sampson nee Purnell, J Sawyer, R Scully, J Sampson, A Sell nee Withers, R Seymour, P Simmons nee Bambury, A Skuse nee Webb, D. Summers, M. Summers, J Walters nee Nial, M Winter nee Cooke, P Waite, B Walsh, J Weber nee Watts, M Woodey nee Pavey, M Woolaway and Pat Youd nee Eyre.

The following former staff responded: - J Avery nee Yates, A Blackmore, D Chivers, M Clutterbuck (donation), T Crouch, J Stephen Davies (donation), C Drew (donation), J Edmands nee Bennett, J Evans, A Fletcher for W Fletcher (donation), K Goldthorpe, G Hale, G Hobbs (donation), M Jackman for D Jackman, D John (donation), J Kelsey, G Morgan O.B.E., B Nichols, M O'Callaghan, O Place, S Pope nee Allan, D and S Prowles, D Richardson, R Roberts, Rev B Rogers, A Seymour (donation), A Sisman, M Thorpe, daughter of Dr Perry (donation), B Townsend and P Waterhouse.

Four of the above have sadly passed away and our condolences go to their families.

Our research took us to various Libraries and Archives as follows: Ardingly College Archivist, Brislington Comprehensive School Librarian (Now Brislington Enterprise College), Bristol University Arts and Social Sciences Library, Special Collections – Archivists Michael Richardson and Hannah Lowry, Bristol City Council: City Design Group, Archaeology Officer especially Peter Insole; Planning Office, Property Service Archive, Records Office, especially William Smith and David Emeny, Bristol City Council Libraries, especially Knowle, Stockwood and Central Library Reference Section – Dawn Dyer (Local Studies), Henbury Comprehensive School Librarian, University of West of England Library, Wotton-Under-Edge Heritage Centre (Pat Mansbridge).

Collecting and collating archive material, printing the book and organising the reunion/book launch event incurred considerable expense. We are so very grateful for the following donations and grants. AFC Taxis Ltd, Avon Local History and Archaeology (ALHA) grant towards printing costs, Hengrove and Stockwood Neighbourhood Wellbeing Fund especially Ariaf Hussein, Gemma Dando and April Richmond. Individual former staff members – Mr and Mrs Clutterbuck, J Stephen Davies, C Drew, A Fletcher (son of Mr Fletcher), Mr and Mrs G Hobbs, D John, A Seymour and M Thorpe (daughter of Dr Perry).

Finally we received help, advice and encouragement from numerous individuals and organisations listed below.

A Bantock – Historian, Eugene Byrne, G Brooke – Bristol Times/Bristol Evening Post publicity, E Cammidge – typing 1st draft, R Coles – typing and scanning, Counterslip Baptist Church – production of questionnaires, J Stephen Davies – donation of 'Venturers' LP, 'Bethlehem' CD and compilation of Chapter 6; Trevor Evans, Director ER and B Print - posters; Fiducea Press – K Griffiths, R Gallop and R Tomlinson for their advice; P Fudge – advice; I Haddrell - author, Horfield and Bishopston Local History Group – K Karatzas; D John – comments on initial draft; Knowle West Media Centre – Nicky Williams and Penny Evans; Knowle and Totterdown Local History society – M Leigh and J Reade; Manor Printing Wotton-Under-Edge; C May – typing 1st draft; M O'Callaghan – proof reading; M Pitt – original source CDs duplication; Dr S Poole, Associate Professor of History, UWE; Redcliffe Press and Silverwood Books - advice; P Waite – advice on design of book cover; S Ward - author; M Wilson - scanning.

We apologise if we have omitted to mention any other individuals or organisations. There is still opportunity for former pupils and staff to contact the Hengrove School History Project to contribute memories/photos/archive material either by post to 262 Wells Road, Bristol, BS4 2PP or email hengroveschool@hotmail.co.uk Alternatively you may upload your archive material to 'Know Your Place' which is a combined City Council / Bristol University database for Bristol archive material. See www.bristol.gov.uk/knowyourplace